I WANNA BE LOVED BY YOU

Also by Andrew Wilson

Beautiful Shadow: A Life of Patricia Highsmith

The Lying Tongue

Harold Robbins: The Man Who Invented Sex

Shadow of the Titanic: The Extraordinary Stories of Those Who Survived

Mad Girl's Love Song: Sylvia Plath and Life Before Ted

Alexander McQueen: Blood Beneath the Skin

Agatha Christie series:

A Talent for Murder

A Different Kind of Evil

Death in a Desert Land

I Saw Him Die

As E. V. Adamson

Five Strangers

Murder Grove

I WANNA BE LOVED BY YOU

MARILYN MONROE
A LIFE IN 100 TAKES

ANDREW WILSON

SIMON & SCHUSTER

London · New York · Amsterdam/Antwerp · Sydney/Melbourne · Toronto · New Delhi

First published in Great Britain by Simon & Schuster UK Ltd, 2026

Copyright © Andrew Wilson, 2026

The right of Andrew Wilson to be identified as the author of this work has been asserted in accordance with the Copyright, Designs and Patents Act, 1988.

1 3 5 7 9 10 8 6 4 2

Simon & Schuster UK Ltd
1st Floor
222 Gray's Inn Road
London WC1X 8HB

For more than 100 years, Simon & Schuster has championed authors and the stories they create. By respecting the copyright of an author's intellectual property, you enable Simon & Schuster and the author to continue publishing exceptional books for years to come. We thank you for supporting the author's copyright by purchasing an authorised edition of this book.

No amount of this book may be reproduced or stored in any format, nor may it be uploaded to any website, database, language-learning model, or other repository, retrieval, or artificial intelligence system without express permission. All rights reserved. Enquiries may be directed to Simon & Schuster, 222 Gray's Inn Road, London WC1X 8HB or RightsMailbox@simonandschuster.co.uk

www.simonandschuster.co.uk
www.simonandschuster.com.au
www.simonandschuster.co.in

Simon & Schuster Australia, Sydney
Simon & Schuster India, New Delhi

The authorised representative in the EEA is Simon & Schuster Netherlands BV, Herculesplein 96, 3584 AA Utrecht, Netherlands. info@simonandschuster.nl

The author and publishers have made all reasonable efforts to contact copyright-holders for permission, and apologise for any omissions or errors in the form of credits given. Corrections may be made to future printings.

Simon & Schuster strongly believes in freedom of expression and stands against censorship in all its forms. For more information, visit BooksBelong.com.

A CIP catalogue record for this book is available from the British Library

Hardback ISBN: 978-1-3985-1344-0
Trade Paperback ISBN: 978-1-3985-1345-7
eBook ISBN: 978-1-3985-1346-4

Typeset in Bembo by M Rules

Printed and Bound in the UK using 100% Renewable Electricity
at CPI Group (UK) Ltd

To the many fans of Marilyn

Contents

Introduction: The Marilyn tapes   1

1 Switching on Marilyn   7
2 The many shades of Marilyn   9
3 'She wanted to be wanted'   12
4 Dreaming of Marilyn   15
5 'Bad blood'   16
6 'My heart belongs to Daddy'   20
7 Mother love   27
8 'The only black mark on a white cross'   29
9 Gladys's bid for freedom   31
10 The great imitator   35
11 The original platinum blonde   38
12 My old piano   42
13 'I'm not an orphan'   46
14 The mysterious Mr Kimmel   48
15 The storyteller   54
16 Did Norma Jeane give birth when she was a teenager?   57
17 'A lot of the girls didn't like her because the boys liked her *a lot*'   62
18 'A friendship with privileges'   64
19 The first photographs   68
20 36-24-34   72
21 Mon amour   75

22	'To me, you're a Marilyn'	82
23	'Wolves I Have Known'	85
24	Golden dreams	90
25	'Here's a skull now'	92
26	The men who made Marilyn	93
27	The woman who made Marilyn	98
28	An intimate encounter with Brigitte Bardot	102
29	The 'dumb blonde' and the brain box	107
30	The quest for self-improvement	110
31	All-American hero – or . . . a penis with a man hanging from it	117
32	'She was a damn good survivor'	124
33	The girl with the horizontal walk	128
34	The face of a beautiful ghost	133
35	Joltin' Joe turns jealous	137
36	The 'two-panty shot'	143
37	Letters to 'My Dad'	146
38	The man who nearly died for Marilyn	150
39	The 'wrong door raid'	153
40	Marilyn and her ghostwriter	157
41	The fall-out	163
42	*I Love Lucy* takes on Marilyn	165
43	'The whole inside of her womb was crying'	167
44	A new future	171
45	Pill popping	176
46	'I can make my face do anything'	182
47	Staying in shape	186
48	The most famous dress in the world	191
49	Sex, lies and videotape	196
50	Marilyn and Ella	203
51	'I never heard that she was producing gold when she peed'	206

52	Marilyn and the pink elephant	208
53	A hummingbird in flight	211
54	The Method	215
55	On the couch	222
56	The 'Egghead' and the 'Hourglass'	226
57	Marilyn on a bike	231
58	Love letters	233
59	'You know he never really asked me'	235
60	A fatal chase	237
61	'I want to be a Jew'	241
62	The world goes mad for Marilyn	245
63	Problems on – and off – set	247
64	Miscarriage?	253
65	In therapy with Anna Freud	256
66	Hope for the future	260
67	'It's me, Sugar … It's Sugar, me!'	265
68	A house of dreams	270
69	The joy of cooking	273
70	Enter Dr Greenson	275
71	*Let's Make Love*	280
72	*The Misfits*	286
73	'She had this obsession about being nude'	295
74	The lost footage from *The Misfits*	298
75	Locked up	302
76	Frank	309
77	Looking for a family	316
78	'I am finishing my journey'	321
79	'The greatest lover in the world'?	323
80	*Something's Got to Give*	326
81	The last night	333
82	Saturday night, Sunday morning	341

83	The silent woman	345
84	An alternative timeline	351
85	Digging up dirt on the Kennedys	354
86	Norman Mailer's obsession	359
87	'The Toad'	363
88	The 'missing' diary	368
89	Inside Marilyn	373
90	The rise and fall of a star witness	377
91	Marilyn and JFK	380
92	Marilyn and RFK	385
93	'Listen – talk to Bobby Kennedy'	390
94	The last gentleman caller	396
95	The world wakes up to Marilyn's death	399
96	The funeral	403
97	The battle over Marilyn's memoir	407
98	The mystery of Marilyn's possessions	411
99	Fake or fortune?	416
100	A constant haunting	421

Notes	427
Acknowledgements	477
Index	483

Introduction

THE MARILYN TAPES

I am listening to the voices of the dead whisper their memories of Marilyn Monroe. From an old audio recording comes a hiss, a crackle, the sizzle of white noise, and then Jane Russell begins to reminisce about her *Gentlemen Prefer Blondes* co-star. She remembers being told by a colleague that when the cameras began to roll, Marilyn made a kind of magical transformation. 'It was like a whole electric light went on,' she says.[1]

On another tape I hear the voice of Marion Marshall, who knew Marilyn at the beginning of her career; both actresses had small parts in the 1950 film *A Ticket to Tomahawk*. In her words, Marilyn was 'the most spectacular girl I've ever met as far as having a ... what do you call it? ... a dynamic quality. I remember sitting in the commissary [the Café de Paris at Twentieth Century-Fox] watching Marilyn walk through the room before she'd ever done anything, maybe a bit part in a picture, and everyone in the commissary would stop and watch her. She had that kind of quality.'[2]

William (or Billy) Travilla, who designed costumes for several of Marilyn's films, also remembers the effect she had on other stars. 'Marilyn would walk in, with greasy hair, greasy face, dark glasses, skinny slacks and a big, puffy sweater,' he recalls. 'She wasn't dirty, but she wanted that look. And the whole place would stop. The whole place was silent. Not a movement.'[3]

These ghostly voices from the Golden Age of Hollywood have remained silent for more than forty years. I'm listening to their secrets in an unlikely location: a building on the banks of a river in the south of Ireland. The small cottage sits in the grounds of the home of investigative journalist and biographer Anthony Summers, which he shares with his wife, and frequent co-author of a number of non-fiction books, Robbyn Swan.

During the course of the research for his 1985 biography *Goddess: The Secret Lives of Marilyn Monroe*, Summers interviewed around 650 people, the majority of whom are now dead. He tracked down and spoke to almost everyone who knew Marilyn: friends, lovers, photographers, co-stars, directors, writers, choreographers, journalists, make-up artists, publicists, doctors, secretaries, therapists, maids, wiretappers, including those around her at the time of her death in August 1962. He was given access to unseen documents – letters, notebooks, psychiatric and medical records. He even published a shocking photograph of Marilyn on the mortuary slab, an image that he chose to remove from the most recent edition of the biography. Despite the book's length (*Goddess* runs to over 600 pages), Summers used only a fraction of the contents of these tapes. Although a small selection of his interviews made an appearance in the 2022 Netflix documentary *The Mystery of Marilyn Monroe: The Unheard Tapes*, thousands of hours of interviews with men and women who knew Marilyn remained untapped. For the most part, the extracts from Summers's recordings quoted in this book have never been published before.

After interviewing Anthony Summers for the *Sunday Times* to tie in with the release of the Netflix documentary, I realised that he was sitting on a gold mine of material. His archive comprises not only these unpublished tapes but thousands of documents relating to the life of Marilyn. Summers invited me over to his house in Ireland, where he quizzed me more about my track record (I told him about my biographies of Patricia Highsmith, Sylvia Plath and Alexander McQueen) and my vision for this book.

During the course of my visit, I was given unrestricted access to Summers's vast archive, which covers every aspect of Marilyn's life. The collection of material comprises not only these audio interviews (a set of which has been donated to the Margaret Herrick Library of the Academy of Motion Picture Arts and Sciences in California), but also hundreds of tape logs (detailed breakdowns of every single interview), as well as books, newspaper and magazine cuttings, video recordings and hundreds of paper files. The subject headings are as diverse as astrology, figure, eyesight, poetry, psychiatrists, childhood sex/rape, MM/diary, nude calendar, Joe DiMaggio, Arthur Miller, JFK, RFK, last phone calls/phone records, and autopsy. Summers's alphabetically arranged biographical files range from Rupert Allan (*Look* magazine editor turned publicist) through to Maurice Zolotow (the show business reporter who wrote one of the first biographies of Marilyn). I am the first author to have been granted access to this treasure trove of material and I am grateful for Anthony Summers's and Robbyn Swan's collegiality, kindness and generosity.

Over the years, Summers has attracted a fair share of detractors, particularly for the inclusion in *Goddess* of witnesses who would later be seen as unreliable, such as Robert Slatzer (who claimed to have been briefly married to Marilyn) and actress Jeanne Carmen (who said she was a close friend). One rival biographer, Donald Spoto, even went so far as to claim – falsely – that Summers 'ignored and/or frequently misrepresented those he claims to have interviewed';[4] the allegation resulted in a legal spat between the two rival biographers that was settled in Summers's favour. I can testify that Summers's research was thorough, his reporting accurate. Having said that, the conclusions I reach, particularly regarding Marilyn's death, differ significantly to those drawn by Summers.

Among the Summers archive are the case notes of Dr Ralph Greenson, Marilyn's psychiatrist and psychoanalyst and one of the last people to see her alive. These transcripts – dictated by Summers in the presence of Dr Greenson's widow Hildi – give an unprecedented insight into the star's psychological state during the last two years of her life. I had access to these detailed notes, which include case files and letters to and from Marilyn's other therapists.

The Summers archive – rich as it is – is only one of the sources for this book. I sought out and interviewed those few people still alive who knew or had met Marilyn. I also discovered a wealth of unpublished archival material in a number of special collections: notably in those of the Academy of Motion Picture Arts and Sciences (the Margaret Herrick Library); the Harry Ransom Center (University of Texas at Austin); the Library of Congress; the Newberry Library in Chicago; California State University, Northridge; Ohio State University Libraries; the William H. Hannon Library at Loyola Marymount University; the UCLA Oral History Project; Columbia University Oral History Project; the African American Museum and Library, Oakland; the Jacob Rader Marcus Center of the American Jewish Archives; the British Library in London; and the Wellcome Collection in London. I consulted hundreds of old newspapers and magazines, watched dozens of documentaries, read many brilliant – and not so brilliant – books, and drew on the work of two wonderful podcasts, *All About Marilyn* and *Marilyn: Behind the Icon*.

I hope the resulting portrait – published to coincide with the centenary of her birth – captures the many complexities of Marilyn: her spark, her sizzle, her genius, her sense of fun, her insecurities, her pain, her beauty, her talents, her contradictions, her *power*. Journalist and biographer Maurice Zolotow said that there was something so unique about her, something that he had never experienced with any other movie star, apart from Garbo. 'Monroe was an infinity of character and mystery that it was impossible for me, or anybody else, to explore because it was so vast,' he said. 'There is always more and more and more ... You could never come to the end of her.'[5]

Manchester Guardian journalist W. J. Weatherby met the actress on location while she was filming *The Misfits* (1961) and later at a dingy bar on Eighth Avenue, New York; these conversations were reworked into a book, published in 1976. As Weatherby considered the many faces of Marilyn and tried to penetrate beneath the surface image – 'she was so clever at makeup that one was never sure what she was masking,' he said[6] – he was reminded of Virginia Woolf's observation on life writing. A 'biography is considered complete if it merely accounts for six or seven selves, whereas a person may well have as many thousand,' she said.[7] This is perhaps more true of Marilyn than many of her contemporaries. 'Whichever way she died,' noted Weatherby, 'there were always murderers in her life, trying to kill off 999 of her selves and leave her as a dumb blonde. They do the same today with her memory.'[8]

I hope to do the opposite.

1

SWITCHING ON MARILYN

The woman in the raincoat, wearing sunglasses and no make-up, is blonde and nice-looking, but she doesn't stand out from the crowd of people streaming down Park Avenue. Spotting a group of fans clustered around the entrance to her Manhattan apartment at the Waldorf-Astoria Towers, she turns to her friend and asks, 'Do you want to see me be her?'

A moment later the transformation begins.

'She seemed to make some inner adjustment,' remembered Susan Strasberg, the daughter of Lee Strasberg, artistic director of the Actors Studio. Something '"turned on" inside her, and suddenly – there she was – not the simple girl I'd been strolling with, but "Marilyn Monroe", resplendent, ready for her public. Now heads turned. People crowded around her.'[1]

Sometimes it's easier to go out in disguise. Today, for instance, Marilyn's attending a lecture given by her psychiatrist and therapist Dr Ralph Greenson, at El Rodeo School in Beverly Hills, and doesn't want to be recognised. Free of make-up, she slips on a brown Pucci dress over which she throws a baggy mink coat. She eases a black wig onto her head, manoeuvres it into position and gets into the car driven by Greenson's daughter Joan, an art student, who has become a close friend.

After listening to Greenson talk for an hour, she begins to make her way out of the hall. All heads turn in her direction and although Joan is convinced that no one knows that her friend is famous – that she is Marilyn Monroe – everyone feels drawn to her. 'They didn't know who she was,' said Joan. 'They just watched her. She had that magical something.'

Joan recalls another occasion when Marilyn was off duty, and not wearing the mask of her on-screen persona. She had picked up Marilyn in her decidedly ordinary Hillman Minx and had stopped for gas by a roadside in Los Angeles when all of a sudden the car began to be surrounded by people. 'Marilyn without make-up, wearing a big baggy mink and a scarf over her head, she was just sitting there, you wouldn't think she would attract any attention ... But I would suddenly have five people washing the windows. I don't think for an instant they knew who it was, but there was *something*. It wasn't that she had a provocative dress on or that she was doing anything provocative. There was something not discernible. Whatever it was, it was *there*.'[2]

Whatever that was, the camera loved it. And her. 'When I met her, she did not impress me,' recalled Billy Wilder. 'When I saw what the camera saw, I knew she was special.'[3] Although the director had problems with Marilyn, particularly on *Some Like It Hot* (1959) where she repeatedly turned up late, and reportedly needed as many as forty-seven takes to say a simple line such as 'It's me, Sugar', Wilder regarded her as an 'absolute genius'. There was, he said, 'no way to fathom her – if there was she'd have found it. She tried harder than anybody. She was just as bewildered by herself as we are looking back at her.' When her biographer Anthony Summers interviewed Wilder in 1984, the director told him that he'd been offered ten film projects over the last fifteen years where he thought, '"No, it wouldn't work – it needs Monroe." All else is earthbound.'[4]

2

The many shades of Marilyn

She may have been shy, particularly early in her career, but Marilyn could also be determined, ambitious and, at times, ruthless. 'There was another girl in the band [in *Some Like It Hot*], who had blonde hair,' said Billy Wilder. 'And she [Marilyn] said to me, "No other blonde. I'm the only blonde."'[1]

Marilyn was known as a 'towhead' as a child, having very light blonde hair, but by the time she was a teenager her hair had darkened.[2] In 1945, soon after the nineteen-year-old was taken on the books of the LA-based Blue Book Modeling Agency, she was advised by the agency's head, Emmeline Snively, to dye her brunette hair blonde. Marilyn was initially resistant – 'I wouldn't ever want to be a bleached blonde,' she said.[3] Miss Snively was having none of it. In addition to looking 'a fright' – Emmeline later said that the girl 'knew nothing about carriage, posture, walking, sitting, or posing' – she told her that she would photograph better and would get more modelling work if she became a blonde.[4] The agency sent her off to see Sylvia Barnhart, a stylist at Frank and Joseph's Beauty Salon. Over the course of the next eight months, Sylvia proceeded to straighten and bleach Marilyn's hair until it was golden blonde. 'It was bleached to take it out of the obscurity of dishwater blonde,' noted Emmeline Snively. 'From this treatment, Marilyn emerged a truly golden girl.'[5]

There's a photograph, thought to be taken in 1946, that shows Sylvia at a professional hair show gazing proudly at her creation. Marilyn's hair, noticeably lightened, is piled high on her head.

There's a look in the young model's eyes, as if she knows she's going places. Perhaps it's the new shade that's boosting her confidence, a hunch going blonde might turn some heads and get the attention of casting agents and film producers.

During the early days of her movie career, Marilyn sported many shades of blonde. She was ash blonde in *The Asphalt Jungle* (May 1950); golden blonde in *All About Eve* (October 1950); silver blonde in *As Young as You Feel* (August 1951); smoky blonde in *Love Nest* (October 1951); amber blonde in *Let's Make It Legal* (November 1951); topaz blonde in *We're Not Married* (July 1952); unbleached dark blonde in *Don't Bother to Knock* (July 1952); and finally in *Monkey Business* (September 1952) the famous platinum blonde that came to define her image.

Over the years, Marilyn used a number of different hair stylists. One of them, Gladys Rasmussen, said that keeping the star's hair in good condition was a challenge as it was incredibly fine. 'It gets oily if it isn't shampooed every day,' she said. 'And her hair is so curly naturally that to build a coiffure for her I have to first give her a straight permanent... The way we got her shade of platinum is with my own secret blend of sparkling silver bleach plus twenty volume peroxide and a secret formula of silver platinum to take the yellow out.'[6]

Hairdresser and make-up artist George Masters said that it took him hours to 'get her all pulled together. But eventually, when she was set to go – pow! She exploded!'[7] He created a shade of blonde for her which she described as 'pillow case' white.[8] Towards the end of Marilyn's life, when she was filming her last (and unfinished) movie, *Something's Got to Give*, the star employed the services of 69-year-old Pearl Porterfield, something of a legend in hairdressing circles because she had been the colourist responsible for dyeing Jean Harlow's hair.

As Porterfield painted her roots, Marilyn would quiz her about the original platinum blonde. And as Marilyn studied herself in the mirror – something she could do for hours at a time – she must have asked herself whether the trajectory of her life would have been any different if she had kept her original hair colour. Joshua Logan, who directed her in *Bus Stop* (1956), said that the 'dumb blonde' character that Marilyn created would be remembered – like Charlie Chaplin's Tramp – as one of the great comic creations of the twentieth century.[9]

The blonde bombshell image marked Marilyn out, brought her enormous exposure and success, but would ultimately threaten to define and limit her. As actress and one-time housemate Shelley Winters said, 'If she could have settled to just be sort of a blonde movie star – you know, if she was *dumber* – she might have been *happier*.'[10] Marilyn always possessed much greater potential than her superficial image suggested, as her acting coach Natasha Lytess outlined in a profile of the actress that appeared in *Collier's* magazine in 1951: 'There's more to Marilyn than meets the eye. The trouble is that when people look at her they immediately see her as a typical Hollywood Blonde. It's not their fault, though. Marilyn's soul just doesn't fit her body.'[11]

3

'She wanted to be wanted'

She is standing on a stage, singing, wearing a low-cut 'nude' cocktail dress covered in sequins. The diamonds dangling from her ears illuminate an already luminous face framed by platinum blonde hair. Fragments of reflected light from a glitterball that spins below a cut-glass chandelier caress her voluptuous body. She scans the audience for the object of her affection, but it seems that he's nowhere to be seen. Disappointed, she continues to sing about her desire to make this man her own. These lyrics, sung by Marilyn's character of Sugar Kane in Billy Wilder's movie *Some Like It Hot*, take on an extra resonance in the context of her own life. It's tempting to think that they could almost serve as a potted biography. The words speak to her millions of fans: *Look at me*, she whispers. *Look at me and love me, please!*

'There were times when Marilyn was like this vacuum – insatiable – because she couldn't get enough love, she couldn't get enough attention,' said Susan Strasberg.[1] Before Marilyn was *Marilyn* – pin-up, sex goddess, movie icon – in the days when she was plain old Norma Jeane living in a series of grim foster homes, she used to fantasise that one day she would grow up to be worshipped. 'I dreamed chiefly of beauty,' she said of her childhood. 'I dreamed of myself becoming so beautiful that people would turn to look at me when I passed.'[2] She told one of her early biographers, Maurice Zolotow, that she didn't go into the movies to make money; rather she wanted to become famous so that 'everyone would like me and I would be surrounded by love and affection'. She also told Zolotow, 'I know that I feel stronger if the people around me on the set love me, care for me, and hold good thoughts for me. It creates an aura of love, and I believe I can give a better performance.'[3] Of course, the obverse is also true: that if Marilyn sniffed a whiff of negativity on set – a sensitivity that intensified as her career progressed – then she feared this would be reflected in her acting.

Harry Lipton, Marilyn's first film agent, said that 'She wanted to be wanted – that was the main thing. And I guess she felt that if she were a movie star she'd be loved.'[4] The poet and friend Norman Rosten believed that Marilyn 'needed that proof of being adored; it denied the inner dread of being unwanted, the trauma of the illegitimate and motherless child'.[5] The writer Christopher Isherwood, who only met her three or four times, recalled that 'She was anxious to please people and to fulfil the image which they required of her.' He was charmed by her, but 'she was quite mysterious to me – she was very busy being Marilyn Monroe'.[6]

The lyrics of 'I Wanna Be Loved By You' also express something else: the strength of the public's obsessive need for Marilyn. Each of us wants to be loved by her and her alone. Each of us thinks that, in her presence, she is talking only to us; as if each of us is sitting at a table in the *Some Like It Hot* hotel ballroom, drinking ice-cold champagne and watching Marilyn from afar. The woozy music – the seductive sound of Sweet Sue and her Society Syncopators – transports us back in time. And for a brief moment, we can believe that Marilyn didn't die in 1962, at the age of thirty-six.

One hundred years after her birth in 1926, she is still with us – laughing, whispering, singing, acting, crying, thinking, confessing, *haunting*. She never goes away. It's like she's always on the end of a telephone, a device she loved so much she called it her 'best friend';[7] she was clutching a telephone receiver when her body was discovered lying naked in bed that night in August 1962.

We each have our own Marilyn and she's speaking directly to us.

4

Dreaming of Marilyn

Marilyn's third husband, the playwright Arthur Miller, once had a disturbing dream about his wife. The couple were at a fairground and he noticed the presence of a huge crowd of people waiting for hamburgers to be produced from a gigantic chrome machine. Marilyn got sucked into the engine, but as Miller ran around to the other side of the machine to try to rescue her, he was horrified to see that she had already been turned into a hamburger. The mob went crazy, each of the onlookers desperate to hold and taste the meat, and 'one man pulled it free and ate, blood dripping from his lips'.

Miller was always trying to help Marilyn weave her way through large groups of people, but she was an expert at managing crowds. It was almost as if she came alive in their presence. 'Sometimes it was as though the crowd had given her birth,' he wrote in his autobiography, *Timebends*. 'I never saw her unhappy in a crowd, even some that ripped pieces of her clothes off as souvenirs.'[1]

5

'Bad blood'

Q: What are your earliest childhood memories?
A: [long silence] My earliest memories? ... It's the memory of a struggle for survival. I was still very small – a baby in a little bed, yes, and I was struggling for life. But I'd rather not talk about it, if it's all the same to you. It's a cruel story, and it's no one's business but my own, as I said.[1]

Norma Jeane was a baby, sleeping in a cot in Hawthorne, Los Angeles, at the home of her foster parents, the Bolenders, when she was awakened by the sound of breaking glass. Her 51-year-old maternal grandmother Della had smashed a panel in the front door and was frantically trying to enter the house.

Ida Bolender, Norma Jeane's foster mother, maintained that Della's behaviour was incomprehensible. 'She did come over one day and for no reason that I know of, she just broke the glass in the front door,' she told a documentary film crew in the wake of the star's death. 'And I believe we called the police.' Ida could have said a great deal more to the film-makers, but as a deeply religious woman she kept her counsel.[2]

Marilyn would later tell Arthur Miller that, before this incident, Della had tried to smother her. 'I remember waking up from my nap fighting for my life,' she said. 'Something was pressed against my face. It could have been a pillow. I fought with all my strength.'[3] Although there were those who later questioned the veracity of the incident – Pauline Kael suggested in the *New York Times* that the actress had made up this statement after playing a disturbed babysitter in the 1952 film *Don't Bother to Knock* – one of Marilyn's early biographers, Fred Lawrence Guiles, claimed to have checked with witnesses and found it to be true. It's likely that Marilyn was remembering what was later told to her by the Bolenders. Ida told her daughter Nancy that Della's 'mental stability' was 'bad'. 'She could be in a rage or she could be very sweet and nice,' she said. 'She would come over sometimes and they would have to lock the door because they didn't want any harm to come to Norma Jeane.'[4]

Della was diagnosed as having manic-depressive psychosis and admitted to Norwalk State Hospital, California, where she had a seizure and died of a heart attack on 23 August 1927, when Norma Jeane was just one. Della's first husband Otis Monroe – Norma Jeane's grandfather – also suffered from mental illness: he died in July 1909 in the California State Hospital. Della and Otis's daughter Gladys – Norma Jeane's mother – grew up in the shadow of her parents' mental health problems; she was only seven years old when her father died.

Ida and her husband Wayne, who lived across the street from Gladys, believed that Norma Jeane came from 'bad blood'. 'We have to watch her very carefully,' the Bolenders would say about Norma Jeane. 'It's in the family, you know.'[5] The Bolenders were strict evangelical Christians and as such they were more likely to believe that behaviour such as Della's was a sign of 'evil' rather than a manifestation of a physical or mental illness.

Gladys recognised that she too was vulnerable, which is one of the reasons she gave over her daughter to the Bolenders when she was only twelve days old.

There was another reason too, of course: Norma Jeane was illegitimate and Gladys had no one to provide for her or her newborn child. Her mother was absent during the spring and summer of

1926 when Della travelled to Borneo to seek out her lover Charles Grainger, and on her return in September it was clear to Gladys that her mother was ill. She had no choice but to go back to work as a film cutter. Yet Gladys did not completely abandon her child, as some have reported – she was a regular visitor at the Bolender home and paid the couple $25 a month to look after Norma Jeane. 'Sometimes I would get to see her only early in the morning or at night,' said Marilyn about her mother.[6]

Gladys had found life a struggle even before Norma Jeane's birth. Her childhood was peripatetic: born in 1902 in Mexico, where her father Otis worked as a painter and for the railways, she moved with her parents to Los Angeles when she was one year old. Over the course of the next five years the family lived in at least eleven different apartments or houses. When Gladys was fourteen, she started sleeping with an older man – 30-year-old Jasper Newton Baker, the owner of the boarding house where she lived. Her mother encouraged the relationship because, after Della's short and unhappy second marriage to Lyle Arthur Graves, she had become fixated on Charles Grainger and wanted Gladys off her hands so she could pursue him. When it was discovered that Gladys was pregnant, Della organised a quick marriage for her daughter – on 17 May 1917 – and even went so far as to tell the authorities that her 14-year-old daughter was eighteen. Gladys was fifteen when she became a mother for the first time: she gave birth to Robert (nicknamed Jackie) in January 1918. She gave birth to another child, Berniece, in July 1919.

The household was a chaotic and dangerous environment for young children: Jasper soon turned violent, and it seemed that Gladys was neglectful. 'Jackie seemed destined for disaster,' remembered Berniece later. 'When he was just tiny, he almost lost an eye. Daddy said that my mother had thrown glass from a broken bottle into the bathroom trash can. He said Jackie reached into the can and was playing with the glass and cut himself up.'[7]

Then, in 1921, Gladys and Jasper were driving from California to Baker's home state of Kentucky in an open car when, during a heated argument, Jackie fell out of the back seat and into the road. The accident resulted in a serious hip injury.

The end of the marriage was fractious and would have a significant impact on Gladys's future mental health. This is Marilyn's retelling of the story: 'One day she [Gladys] came home earlier than usual and found her young husband making love to another woman. There was a big row and her husband banged out of the flat.' Gladys divorced Jasper in May 1922, and she was awarded custody of the children. 'While my mother was crying over the collapse of her marriage he sneaked back one day and kidnapped her two babies,' said Marilyn. 'My mother spent all her savings trying to get her children back.' After tracing them to Kentucky, she discovered the children were living with their father, who had remarried, and 'like the mother in the story "Stella Dallas" she went away and left them to enjoy a happier life than she could give them'.[8]

Gladys's hopes were in vain. Jackie lost an eye in a fireworks accident, and then he was diagnosed with tuberculosis of the bone. Against the doctor's order, Jasper took the boy out of hospital and tried to catheterise him at home, which led to kidney failure and his death in 1933.

Berniece – who had only been three years old when Gladys left Kentucky and returned to Los Angeles – grew up not knowing whether her mother was alive or dead. She could remember her father Jasper telling her, 'Your mother was a beautiful woman, but she was also very young, too young to know how to take care of children.'

At church on Mother's Day it was the custom that each child would be asked to wear a rose: red if their mother was alive, white if she was dead. 'I never knew which to wear,' said Berniece. 'On one Mother's Day, when I was about seventeen, I decided she must be dead, so I wore a white rose.'[9]

6

'MY HEART BELONGS TO DADDY'

Marilyn believed that her mother's problems were caused by men – or the lack of them. After the breakdown of her first marriage, Gladys took a job as a film cutter, first at Consolidated Film Industries and then at RKO. It was the very opposite of Hollywood glamour: the job entailed sitting on a high stool, cutting and pasting strips of film in hot humid conditions, the air thick with the smell of glue. But it was here that Gladys met Charles Stanley Gifford, a foreman at Consolidated.

Good-looking – a double for Clark Gable, complete with suave moustache – Gifford had been born in Newport, Rhode Island in 1898. He had been married for four years, with two children, but that relationship broke down in 1923 due to his infidelity and violent behaviour. In the divorce papers of 1925 it was stated that Gifford 'inflicted bodily and physical injury' upon his wife Lillian, 'applied to her and used in her presence vile and opprobrious epithets, profanity, disgusting and vulgar names and references', 'associated with other women of low and dissolute character, has been guilty of habitual intemperance ... has boasted of his conquests of other women', and also exhibited 'marks on his body and declaring that same were caused by a hypodermic injection of narcotic drugs, and boasted that he was addicted'. At 11 p.m. on 20 June 1923, Gifford hit his wife with such force across the left side of her face that she 'was knocked against the bed post'. Her injuries included 'bruises, discolouration ... a blood clot formed in the cheek under the skin'.[1]

Of course, Gladys had no idea of Gifford's true character. To her, he was the consummate handsome charmer. Around the same time Gladys also started to date another man, Martin Edward Mortensen, who read meters for the Southern California Gas Company. On 11 October 1924, Gladys married 27-year-old Mortensen, a devout Christian, whom she regarded as nice but dull. The marriage was short lived, and by May 1925 she had left him.

In the autumn of that year, Gladys discovered she was pregnant.

On Norma Jeane's birth certificate it states that her father was 'Edward Mortenson' – a misspelling of Gladys's second husband's name – and for years there was an air of mystery surrounding her paternity.

'It's true that I was illegitimate,' Marilyn told the French writer Georges Belmont in 1960. 'But everything that's been said about my father – or my fathers – is wrong. My mother's first husband was named Baker. Her second was Mortensen. But she'd been divorced from both of them by the time I was born. Some people say my father was Norwegian, probably because of the name Mortensen, and that he was killed in a motorcycle accident right after my birth. I don't know if that's true, because he wasn't related to me. As far as my real father is concerned, I wish you wouldn't ask ... but there are a couple of things that could clear up the confusion. When I was very young, I was always told that my father was killed in a car crash in New York before I was born. Strangely enough, on my birth certificate under my father's professions there's the word, "baker", which was the name of my mother's first husband. When I was born – illegitimate – my mother had to give me a name. She was just trying to think quickly, I guess, and said, "Baker." Pure coincidence, and then the official's confusion ... At least, I think that's the way it was.'[2]

In 2022, it was proved beyond doubt that Marilyn's biological father was Stanley Gifford. The evidence came from two objects, one of which was a greetings card.

The card was found by Monroe collector Scott Fortner, while working with the Hollywood auction house Julien's on an inventory of Marilyn's filing cabinets. (After the star's death these cabinets passed into the hands of Lee Strasberg and then to his third wife Anna.) The small card – bearing the figure of a little girl in a red dress atop a large musical note on its cover – contained the printed message, 'This cheery little get-well note/Comes specially to say/That lots of thought and wishes, too,/Are with you every day,' along with the handwritten addition, 'Dear Marylyn' [sic] at the top and 'a little prayer too', and signed 'Stanley Gifford, Red Rock Dairy Farm, Hemet, Calif'. When the card later came up for auction, at Julien's in Beverly Hills, in December 2022, it sold for $31,250. 'Oh my God ... this is big, this is going to change history,' said Fortner about his initial reaction when he discovered the card. This was, after all, the first definitive proof linking Marilyn with Gifford.[3]

The card is undated, but it was sent during or after one of Marilyn's hospital admissions. Scott Fortner dates it to November 1954 when Marilyn, aged twenty-eight, was in the Cedars of Lebanon Hospital, Los Angeles, being treated for endometriosis. Marilyn told her half-sister Berniece how one day her father turned up to visit her in person. 'The first time I saw my father I was lying flat on my back in the hospital,' Marilyn said. 'I looked at him and I studied his face and features, and I saw that Mother had told me the truth, that he was my father. I said, "My ears are just like yours." You know how the tops of my ears are thin. They don't curl over; they just sort of stand up. I keep them covered most of the time.' Apparently, father and daughter talked for some time and, according to Berniece, 'he was friendly but not particularly loving or affectionate toward her'.[4]

Marilyn had often day-dreamed about meeting Gifford, whose photograph of him wearing a fedora hat and sporting a slim moustache Gladys displayed on the living room wall. When Norma Jeane had her tonsils removed as a girl she had a vision of her father visiting her in hospital. The little girl was so desperate for his presence that she imagined him fully, manipulating his actions almost as though he were a living doll or a character. 'I kept bending him over my bed and having him kiss my forehead and I gave him dialogue, too,' said Marilyn later. '"You'll be well in a few days, Norma Jean,"' she visualised him saying to her. '"I'm very proud of the way you're behaving, not crying all the time like other girls."'[5]

As Marilyn grew up, tracking down her biological father became something of an obsession. In 1942, the 16-year-old, newly married Norma Jeane wrote to Grace Goddard, asking, 'How can I get in touch with Stanley Gifford? Through Consoladated [sic] films? Or something like that. Which dept?'[6] Her first husband Jim Dougherty remembered how one day Norma Jeane got hold of Gifford's number and called him. As soon as she told him that she was Gladys's daughter he hung up on her.

Marilyn next tried to contact her father in the summer of 1950 when she drove out to Hemet, near Palm Springs, where Gifford had bought a dairy farm. Accompanying her was gossip columnist and friend Sidney Skolsky, who recalled her reaction to yet another rejection. Gifford dismissed her with the words, 'Listen, Marilyn, I'm married, I have children. I don't want you to start trouble for me now, like your mother did years ago.'[7]

A few weeks later, she made the pilgrimage again, this time with drama coach Natasha Lytess. The star took hours to get ready, making an effort to look as beautiful as possible, 'as though she wanted him to love her immediately'.[8] They stopped at a gas station near the farm and Natasha telephoned Gifford, but he refused to see Marilyn. 'He was incredibly rude and horrible,' said

Lytess. 'His voice was common, pinched, with a mid-western nasal quality. He said he was married and had a family and didn't want to know anything about this girl Marilyn Monroe. And when I turned the receiver over to Marilyn he was filthy in his conversation with her.' Marilyn insisted on giving him her contact details in Los Angeles, but during the years that Lytess worked with Marilyn – from 1948 to 1955 – she said he never contacted her. 'She talked about him often afterward and I tried to comfort her, make her feel it was good riddance.'[9]

One afternoon in the autumn of 1961, Ralph Roberts – Marilyn's masseur and close friend – was sitting with her at her apartment on North Doheny Drive when Gifford's daughter called. Marilyn picked up the receiver and a moment later she said in a 'cold, hard' voice, 'Tell him he can contact me through my lawyer, Mickey Rudin,' before hanging up. Marilyn then turned to Roberts and related to him the nature of the call. 'He [Gifford] was in the hospital and wanted to see her, or at least, talk with her,' he recalled. Marilyn was still hurt by one of Gifford's earlier rejections of her and the cruel words he had relayed via his secretary, 'Tell her to contact me through my lawyer.'[10]

Just before Gifford's death on 27 June 1965, the 66-year-old spoke with his local minister, Dr Donald Linden, about his secret connection to the movie star. 'The night he told me, I detected it was a sorrowful thing for him,' said Dr Linden. 'I'm sure, with me being his minister, it could be construed as a confession. We don't reveal confessions, and that's why I didn't tell anyone ... My jaw dropped a little when he talked of his daughter as being Marilyn Monroe, but a minister is never wholly surprised at what he hears. I didn't doubt the truth of it.'[11]

The second piece of evidence linking Marilyn to Gifford is a lock of hair retrieved from the actress's autopsy. After the post-mortem, her body was returned to the care of funeral director

Allan Abbott. It was her misfortune to fall into his hands, as he did her a disservice on two counts.

First, he pocketed a lock of Marilyn's hair and a pair of 'falsies', which she used to slip between her sweater and bra to give her an extra lift; mortuary staff had also used them in a vain attempt at supporting her breasts after the coroner had cut open her chest.

Abbott's second, and later, offence was to write a tasteless tell-all book about his experience as funeral director to the stars. His wife Kathy kept the items in a gift box inside a safe at the couple's house, and would bring them out occasionally to show guests: the breast padding was secured inside a plastic bag, which when opened emitted a ghostly hint of Marilyn's perfume. In 2015, Abbott advertised the padding and the lock of hair for sale via his website for $50,000. 'I waited till now due to the sign from her crypt selling for 224k or so in June,' said Abbott, who died later that year. 'Not in the least creepy – a part of history.'[12]

In the course of making *Marilyn: Her Final Secret*, documentary film-maker François Pomès tested a number of locks of Marilyn's hair, including those snatched out of the mortuary trash can by Allan Abbott. DNA was extracted and this was then compared to DNA samples provided by Stanley Gifford's granddaughter Francine Gifford Deir. The samples were a match, proving once and for all that Stanley was the father of the movie star.

Could Marilyn's life have been any different if Stanley had acknowledged her existence? 'Reflecting on it, I think her life would have been better if my grandfather had done the right thing,' Francine Gifford Deir told a reporter from the *Daily Mirror* in August 2022. 'Her life might have turned out very differently if he had welcomed her in. And who knows, she might still be with us today.'[13]

The absence of a father figure preyed on Marilyn's mind throughout her adult life. She called her first two husbands 'Daddy' or 'Dad', and Joe DiMaggio even signed his letters to her 'Pa'.

Henry Rosenfeld, the wealthy dress manufacturer who became close to Marilyn, remembers a party when the guests started to play a game. 'Everybody said what they'd want most in the world and she said . . . what she wanted was to put on a black wig, pick up her father in a bar, have him make love to her and then she'd say, "But how does it feel now to have your daughter make love to you?"'[14] She may have told the story as a joke, but the anecdote contains rich pickings for anyone schooled in even the basics of Freudian theory.

Indeed, Marilyn's last and most important psychoanalyst, Dr Ralph Greenson, cast himself in the role of a surrogate parent. A few weeks after her death, Greenson wrote to a therapist who had also treated Marilyn, outlining his unconventional treatment: instead of the traditional method of analysis, involving fifty minutes on the couch, he had invited the actress into his house and often spent between three and five hours with her at any one time, especially if she had been suffering an acute mental health episode. 'I realized after the fact that I was trying to create a foster family for her, but a good foster family that would not throw her out like all the others had,' he said. 'In addition, I was her therapist, a good father, who would not disappoint her, and who would bring her insights.'[15]

7

Mother love

When Gladys first told Gifford that she was pregnant, it seemed as though he wanted nothing more to do with her. 'When you love a man and tell him you're going to have his child and he runs out on you, it's something a woman never gets over,' said Marilyn later. 'I don't think my mother did.'

Gifford's abandonment shattered the fragile Gladys. She'd already endured the betrayal of her first husband and the loss of her two children. 'I guess that's what broke her heart,' said Marilyn.[1]

Gladys became moody, depressed and paranoid; occasionally she could be heard muttering to herself; she would forget to change or feed her baby. 'She was a beautiful woman, one of the most beautiful women it was ever my privilege to know,' recalled Leila Fields, one of Gladys's co-workers at RKO. 'She had a good heart and was a good friend and was always happy until she got this sickness. Before that, she was lively and always had a joke to make you laugh.'[2]

Gifford's rejection of Gladys was compounded by the fact that she was also showing symptoms of serious mental illness. There was one incident when, in an attack of paranoia, she accused her best friend Grace McKee of trying to poison her. Gladys picked up a knife and brandished it at Grace, and threatened to stab her. She spent long spells in hospital, but when she was feeling well enough she would sometimes stay over at the Bolender house and take Norma Jeane out on excursions. But because she was an infrequent visitor, the girl regarded Gladys as just a pretty woman with red hair, the one who never smiled. Norma Jeane thought Ida and Wayne were her real parents, until one day, when she was seven years old, she called the spry, wiry woman 'Mama', believing that the word meant 'woman'. 'Don't call me Mama,' snapped Ida. 'You're old enough to know better. I'm not related to you in any way. You just board here. Your Mama's coming to see you tomorrow. You can call her Mama, if you want to.'

When Gladys turned up at the house in Hawthorne the next day, Norma Jeane tentatively said, 'Hello, Mama'. The child interpreted the woman's blank response as bored indifference. 'She stared at me,' she remembered. 'She had never kissed me or held me in her arms or hardly spoken to me.'[3]

It's obvious, however, that Gladys cared deeply for Norma Jeane. As she began to recover from her illness, Gladys started to sketch out plans for her daughter. Each time she visited the Bolenders she would have observed little Norma Jeane at play with Lester Bolender, a boy who looked so similar to her daughter that the children were called 'the twins'. The sight of them giggling, holding hands, playing in the garden with family dog Tippy and walking to the nearby Washington Street School stung her deeply, and no doubt reminded her of the two children – a boy and a girl – she had lost, both now living over 2,000 miles away in Kentucky.

By 1933, Gladys was back at work, dreaming of a future with her daughter. She felt closer to her than ever; in the spring of that year, she'd nursed the little girl through an attack of whooping cough. Soon after, the sight of her daughter weeping over the death of Tippy – who had been killed by a neighbour for the crime of repeatedly rolling in his garden – upset her so much that she made a decision: she was going to take care of Norma Jeane herself.

8

'THE ONLY BLACK MARK ON A WHITE CROSS'

Religion played a central role in Norma Jeane's early life. She was baptised by Aimee Semple McPherson, the founder of the International Church of the Foursquare Gospel, on 6 December 1926. Her strict evangelical foster parents Ida and Wayne encouraged Norma Jeane, along with their other charges, to attend Sunday school and to memorise the solemn oath: 'I promise, God helping me, not to buy, drink or sell, or give alcoholic liquor while I live; from all tobaccos I'll abstain and never take God's name in vain.'[1] The little girl's favourite hymn was 'Jesus Loves Me'. Each night Norma Jeane would kneel by her bed and recite her prayers. She adored going to the Foursquare Gospel Church in Hawthorne – 'the singing and services always excited me,' she said. 'I was sort of in a trance.'[2]

Six-year-old Norma Jeane was thrilled to take part in the Easter celebrations of 1932 as part of an extravagant mass performance at the Hollywood Bowl. The fifty children took the form of a living cross. But all did not go to plan. 'We all had on white tunics under the black robes, and at a given signal we were supposed to throw off the robes, changing the cross from black to white,' she remembered. 'But I got so interested in the people, the orchestra and the hills that I forgot the conductor for the signal. And there I was – the only black mark on a white cross. The family I was living with never forgave me.'[3]

The repressive atmosphere of the Bolender home was something that she could never quite shake off, even as an adult. In a short piece of writing that she scribbled in pencil into a black notebook and dated to around 1955, Marilyn spoke of Ida's continuing negative influence on her life.[4] (She could also be referring to another foster mother, Ida Martin, who was equally as strict.) In another two-page fragment, a stream of consciousness quest for self-identity, she articulated the shame she felt as a child discovering the pleasures of her own sexuality: 'because A.I. [Aunt Ida] punished me/with fear and whipped me —/"the bad part of my body" she said —/must never touch myself/there or let anyone ... and the <u>immediate fear</u>/of any <u>part</u> of my/body there — fear to/ touch my own body.'[5]

9

GLADYS'S BID FOR FREEDOM

'One day my mother came to call,' remembered Marilyn. 'I was in the kitchen washing dishes. I saw there were tears in her eyes. "I'm going to build a house for you and me to live in," she said. "It's going to be painted white and have a backyard."'[1]

The Bolenders were shocked by the news. They tried to persuade Gladys that it would be in the child's best interests for her to stay with them. But Gladys had made up her mind. Norma Jeane was her daughter and she was going to take her away. She was determined that she was better and she should be given a chance to raise her daughter as her own. The Bolenders were bemused and saddened – 'they truly loved her,' said Nancy Bolender, who was also fostered by the couple. 'They had raised her from infancy ... when so much of yourself is put into training, nurturing and loving a child, it is like losing your own flesh and blood.'[2]

Little Norma Jeane was nervous, frightened. When she heard that the woman with the red hair wanted to take her away from her 'aunt' and 'uncle' – terms she had grown to use instead of 'mama' and 'papa' – she ran and hid in the closet before being coaxed out and led downstairs.

Gladys first brought her to a rented house in Hollywood on Afton Place, the home of some English friends, actors Maude and George Atkinson, and their adult daughter Nellie. Then in 1933, she took advantage of the low interest rates under Roosevelt's New Deal and, with a $5,000 mortgage, bought a house in Arbol Street, near the Hollywood Bowl. Marilyn later described the home as 'a pretty little house with quite a few rooms. But there was no furniture in it, except for two cots that we slept on, a small kitchen table, and two kitchen chairs.'³ The atmosphere of the house could not have been more different from that of the Bolenders. Rules and routine went out the window and were replaced by hedonism: the Atkinsons, who continued to live with Gladys and Norma Jeane, were movie extras. 'They drank, they smoked, they swore,' said Marilyn later. 'It used to keep me busy praying for them all.'⁴

On her first day in the house, the hard-drinking adults gave Norma Jeane a whiskey bottle as a toy and soon she was playing card games and hula dancing, 'things that I had been taught were sinful'.⁵ When she'd built up a substantial collection of empty whiskey bottles, Norma Jeane would take them outside and line them up on a plank beside the road. As people would drive by she would ask, '"Wouldn't you like some whisky?" I remember some of the people in the cars driving past my "whisky" store saying, "Imagine! Why, it's terrible!"'⁶

The British-born Atkinsons also gave Norma Jeane informal lessons in diction. Later, Marilyn would say that she picked up traces of their English accents, and in the summer of 1962 she told the photographer George Barris, 'To this day, listen carefully when I speak in my films – you can detect these overtones in my speech.'⁷

Gladys faced renewed pressures at work, according to friend and workmate Grace McKee. 'We were both at Columbia then, but we knew there were going to be strikes and depressions right around the corner. I told her not to buy it. I begged her not to buy [the house]. Gladys said she wanted to have a place so she could have all her children together.' She was referring to Norma Jeane, Berniece and Jackie.

When Gladys heard the news of Jackie's death – on 16 August 1933, at the age of fifteen – she was so sickened and angry, she lost control of herself and screamed at Norma Jeane, 'Why couldn't it have been you?'⁸ The news of her son's death came to her soon after she learned of her grandfather's suicide: 82-year-old Tilford Marion Hogan (Marilyn's great-grandfather) hanged himself in his barn in Laclede, Missouri, while his wife went out shopping. Gladys felt the family 'curse' weighing heavily on her.

Grace McKee was a witness to what happened to Gladys next. 'The first I saw of it, one day she was lying on the couch and she – there were steps in the living room leading upstairs – she started kicking and yelling, staring up at the staircase,' recalled Grace. 'She would lie there on her back and yell, "Somebody's coming down those steps to kill me!" She was having delusions.'

Marilyn remembered that one morning she was having breakfast with the Atkinsons when she heard a commotion coming from the stairway; it was the most frightening noise she'd ever heard. 'Bangs and thuds kept on as if they would never stop,' she said. 'The Englishwoman had me from going to see. Her husband went out and after a time came back into the kitchen. "I've sent for the police and the ambulance," he said. I asked if it was my mother. "Yes," he said. "But you can't see her." I stayed in the kitchen and heard people come and try to take my mother away. Nobody wanted me to see her. But I went out and looked in the hall. My mother was on her feet. She was screaming and laughing.'⁹ Gladys was taken to a rest home in Santa Monica, before being transferred to the LA County General Hospital and then Norwalk State Hospital, California.

Another testimony comes from Harry Charles Wilson, a boat builder and Gladys's suitor from this time who was so serious about the relationship that he wanted to marry her.

At Christmas 1934, before Gladys's final breakdown, Wilson took mother and daughter to watch the festive parade on Hollywood Boulevard, lifting the little girl onto his shoulders so she could see better. That evening they returned to the house on Arbol Street, where Gladys had decorated a Christmas tree.

'Norma Jean [*sic*] stood between the tree and us and sang a pretty song,' he remembered. 'I was entranced by it and about everything else that seemed to have come into my life at the time. After Norma Jean left to go to bed I talked about it to Gladys. I told her I was very much in love with her and her little girl. It was less than a month later when tragedy struck. I almost lost my mind over it.'[10]

10

THE GREAT IMITATOR

What was wrong with Gladys? When she was admitted to hospital, psychiatrists diagnosed her symptoms – hallucinations, delusions of persecution – as classic signs of paranoid schizophrenia. Her belief in Christian Science – that the mind could cure all ills – meant that she was reluctant to take medication. Although there were times when she lived outside the confines of an institution, and between 1953 and 1957 when she lived at Rockhaven Sanitarium and maintained there was nothing wrong with her, it was clear to doctors that she had a very serious mental disorder.

Could the source of her illness lie with the shadowy figure of her father Otis? According to Gladys's mother Della, Otis was as 'neat as a pin, always turned out like a gentleman – or at least a gentleman's gentleman' and something of a romantic figure, dreaming that one day he would travel to Paris to study art, peppering 'his conversation with talk of French painters'. But by 1907, Otis started to exhibit strange behaviour. 'He went nuts and then went to God,' was how Della described his mental decline.[1] After finishing work he would often not return home, forgetting where he'd spent the night; his high standards in his dress and appearance began to slip; he suffered from terrible headaches and terrifying 'fits of rage . . . alternated with fits of weeping', seizures and attacks of paralysis. After being admitted to the Southern California State Hospital in San Bernardino in November 1908, he never left the institution and died there 'completely demented' at the age of forty-three, in July 1909.[2]

There was a certain level of shame attached to his condition – Gladys later told her daughter Berniece that Otis had died from paint poisoning, a reasonable-sounding explanation considering the man's profession. But the family was hiding a secret: Otis was suffering from general paresis, a condition brought about by neurosyphilis or syphilis of the brain.

Syphilis was common at the beginning of the twentieth century. By the early 1930s, it was reported that as many as one in ten Americans suffered from it and around half a million people in the US contracted it each year. The infection was known as 'the great imitator', as it often mimics the symptoms of other diseases and at this time it often went misdiagnosed. It was also one of the main sources of mental illness; many doctors reported that asylums and hospitals were full of patients whose neurological problems could be traced back to syphilis. 'The elimination of these diseases,' stated one contemporary doctor, 'would render one-third, possibly one-half, of our institutions for defectives unnecessary.'[3]

It's possible that Otis passed on the syphilis to Della, who herself started to suffer from delusions and irregular behaviour. Her death certificate states that she died due to myocarditis – inflammation of the heart – with manic-depressive psychosis listed as a contributory factor. And although many have linked Della's heart condition and mental illness to a bout of malaria she contracted in Borneo, it's possible that she died from syphilitic-induced myocarditis. Many doctors – to spare the feelings of the relatives – felt moved not to note the sexually transmitted disease on their patients' death certificates. According to one study at the time, 18 per cent of all deaths from organic heart disease could be attributed to syphilis.

It's also worth remembering that at this time around 60,000 children were born with congenital syphilis in the United States. It's entirely possible that Gladys inherited syphilis from her mother – the infection can be transferred through the placenta or during birth. Sometimes symptoms would not present themselves until years later, and Paul Ehrlich's Salvarsan cure was not discovered until 1909, seven years after Gladys's birth.

It's possible that Della and Otis's son Marion – Gladys's younger brother and Marilyn's uncle – died from the effects of neurosyphilis too. The circumstances surrounding his death are unclear: on 20 November 1929, the 25-year-old mechanic left the family home in Salinas, California – which he shared with his wife Olive and their three children – and was never seen again. According to Marilyn, Marion had committed suicide. After years of legal wrangling, he was declared dead in 1955.

And what about the mental illness Marilyn developed later in life? Her own physician, Dr Hyman Engelberg, believed that she suffered from bipolar disorder, while others have claimed that she had borderline personality disorder. However, inherited syphilis cannot be entirely discounted. 'The symptoms that both Gladys and Marilyn suffered from are consistent with tertiary neurosyphilis, but they are also consistent with inherited mental health diagnoses too,' says Professor Khalil Ghanem, Deputy Director of Education, Department of Medicine, Johns Hopkins Bayview Medical Center and a world expert on syphilis. 'So it is possible that Gladys could have passed on the infection, but there is one important issue to keep in mind: penicillin was introduced in the 1940s and treatment was curative. So one would like to hope that Marilyn, if infected by her mother, would have been tested and treated for syphilis at some point in her life.'[4]

Gladys may never have known the true cause of the mental illness that plagued her and her family, but to her – and to Marilyn – it seemed as though her whole bloodline was cursed. 'For a long time I was scared I'd find out that I was like my mother and end up in the crazy house,' said Marilyn. 'I wonder when I break down if I'm not tough enough – like her.'[5]

11

The original platinum blonde

Before Gladys was institutionalised, she would often take her daughter to one of the nearby picture houses in Hollywood. If she had to go to work, she would leave Norma Jeane alone in the cinema; her babysitters became the giant, projected images of Clark Gable, Greta Garbo, Ginger Rogers and Bette Davis. Later, when her mother was confined to hospital, the darkened movie theatre served as a kind of comfort blanket: here was a special kind of enchantment, a beautiful make-believe world in which little girls lived with and were loved by their parents, a straightforward environment where the good prospered and the wicked were punished. Hollywood produced a seemingly never-ending stream of fantasies for the masses and Norma Jeane took refuge in the excesses of this celluloid heaven.

As a child, Marilyn collected cigarette cards with images of famous actors – Joan Crawford, Clark Gable, Robert Montgomery, Gary Cooper, Charles Laughton – which she pasted into 'An Album of Film Stars', issued by British tobacco company John Player & Sons, next to their potted biographies. She was particularly fascinated to read the entry on Jean Harlow: 'the original "platinum blonde," who was born on March 3rd, 1911 in Kansas City, and educated in Hollywood and Chicago. She gave up the screen when her grandfather threatened to disinherit her, but returned later. Although *Hell's Angels* first made her name, she had already appeared for six months in Hal Roach comedies under her real name of Harlean Carpenter. She has been married three times – to Charles McGrew when she was sixteen, then to Paul Bern, and to Harold Rosson in 1933. Her latest films include *Dinner at Eight* and *Blonde Bombshell*.'[1]

Harlow became a figure of fascination for the young Norma Jeane, partly because she was the idol of both her mother and Gladys's best friend Grace McKee. Grace – who dyed her hair the same shade as Harlow's – told the girl that she looked like Harlow and that one day she could be a famous film star just like her near-namesake if she had 'the right hair colour and a better nose'.[2] Gladys's co-worker Leila Fields observed, 'If it weren't for Grace, there wouldn't be a Marilyn Monroe today. Grace raved about Norma Jean [sic] like she was her own. Grace said Norma Jean was going to be a movie star. She had this feeling about her.'[3]

Was Jean Harlow an appropriate role model? The star hated being what she called a 'sex vulture' but was well aware of the deal she was making with the film studios; once when her agent phoned her with news of a new offer she asked, 'What kind of whore am I now?'[4]

Scandal seemed to follow Jean Harlow around as closely as her infamously bad breath (she suffered from a disorder with which she couldn't process or eliminate waste and she died from kidney failure). In 1932, her second husband Paul Bern, director and MGM producer, was found shot in the head two months after the union. Conspiracy theories raged around Hollywood about who was responsible but the most likely version of events is that Bern had a row with his former common-law wife Dorothy Millette, and then shot himself. A few days later Millette threw herself off the *Delta King* steamboat between San Francisco and Sacramento.

Although Marilyn later self-consciously adopted some of Harlow's quirks – eschewing underwear, choosing to sleep in the nude, adoring champagne – it seems unlikely that she went so far as to model her biography on that of the original platinum blonde. And yet there are some uncanny parallels. Some are seemingly trivial: they both lived at one time on North Palm Drive in Beverly Hills; they both worked on their last films with Clark Gable, who said of Harlow, 'She didn't want to be famous, she wanted to be happy,' a quote that also resonates with Marilyn's life.[5] Others are more poignant: they were both prescribed sedatives by their doctors; they both attended presidential birthday celebrations a few months before they died (Harlow at F. D. Roosevelt's, Marilyn singing 'Happy Birthday, Mr President' to JFK); and they both died at the height of their careers, Marilyn at thirty-six, Harlow at twenty-six.

'She really wanted to *be* Jean Harlow,' said Marilyn's friend Amy Greene, who met the star in 1953. 'That was her goal. She always said she would probably die young, like Harlow; that the men in her life were disasters, like Harlow's; that her relationship with her mother was complicated, like Harlow's. It was as if she based her life on Harlow's – the instant flash, then over.'[6]

When Norma Jeane stepped into the office of casting director Ben Lyon – who it's said discovered Harlow and subsequently went on to act with her in *Hell's Angels* – he took one look at the blonde star and proclaimed, 'It's Jean Harlow all over again!'[7] In 1958, Marilyn posed as Harlow for a *Life* magazine shoot photographed by Richard Avedon. In the accompanying essay, her husband Arthur Miller wrote how Marilyn identified with Harlow – she had a 'deep sympathy for that actress's tragic life'. This particular photograph, said Miller, showed how Marilyn wanted to pay her greatest respects to the actress, 'a star who was dying in the fullest bloom of her beauty while the Hollywood hamburger machine was grinding her up on a picture set, and people were snickering at her and laughing at her behind her back, blind and deaf to her human needs'. In hindsight, these lines from Miller's article take on an extra poignancy; it was obvious he was talking about Marilyn's own experience of fame too. It was as though she was saying, '"I will die, but you will never kill me,"' he wrote. 'I believe that in her heart she was demanding justice for a woman she had never met, as though by her own beauty she were saying to all the brutality in the word, "This is what you destroyed."'[8]

For years, Marilyn wanted to make a film about Harlow's life, starring herself. She worked closely with powerful Hollywood columnist Sidney Skolsky to make this happen, and when the pair journeyed out to the desert near Palm Springs to see Harlow's mother Jean Bello, the older woman was so taken aback by Marilyn that it's said she believed her own daughter had walked into the room. Marilyn talked about the project right at the end of her life and on Sunday 5 August 1962 – the day after her death – she had scheduled a meeting with Skolsky at her house in Brentwood to work on an outline of the script of *The Jean Harlow Story*.

It was important for Marilyn that Harlow's story be presented 'humanly'. She was so appalled by one script sent over by Twentieth Century-Fox – it was too sensationalist – that she told Skolsky, 'I hope they don't do that to me after I'm gone.'[9]

12

MY OLD PIANO

When 7-year-old Norma Jeane was living with her mother at the house in Arbol Street, Gladys bought 'an out of condition' black Franklin baby grand, a piano that supposedly once belonged to the actor Fredric March. 'You'll play the piano over here, by the windows,' her mother told her, 'and here on each side of the fireplace there'll be a love seat. And we can sit listening to you.'[1] The love seat was never built and after Gladys had a breakdown the piano had to be sold.

Marilyn often told the story of how the piano symbolised her lost childhood; to her it was like *Citizen Kane*'s Rosebud, an object onto which she could project a range of deep emotions, a talisman, a repository of memories.

One day when Marilyn was driving through Hollywood with Elyda Nelson, the sister of her first husband Jim Dougherty, she stopped by the Arbol Street house and said, 'I lived there once before Mother was ill. It was beautiful. The most wonderful furniture you can imagine: a baby grand piano and a room of my own. It all seems like a dream.'[2] She never stopped thinking of the piano and everything it stood for and, as she related in her autobiography, as soon as she started to earn money as a model she began tracking it down. 'After about a year I found it in an old auction room and bought it,' she wrote.[3] When she moved into a three-bedroom Manhattan apartment, at 444 East 57th Street, with her third husband Arthur Miller, Marilyn had it painted white to match the rest of the interior.

In 1999, thirty-seven years after her death, the piano came up for sale at Christie's in New York, along with a mass of Marilyn memorabilia. 'As grand pianos go, the one going on the block at Christie's next month is nothing special,' reported the *New York Times*. 'Paderewski did not play it. Neither did Liberace, though he would have swooned over its fondant-white finish and maybe added some stylistic flourishes of his own. And as far as Christie's knows, no one but Marilyn Monroe, its last owner, ever tickled its ivories, though it is possible that Frank Sinatra, a Monroe beau, might have plunked out a tune or two.'[4]

The official auction catalogue detailed the specifics: the piano is 52 inches in length, 57 inches wide and 40.5 inches high; the estimate was between $10,000 and $15,000. 'The white lacquered piano is early-20th century, unknown American manufacturer,' runs the catalogue entry. 'The case with square tapping legs and feet with casters; together with a matching bench. The piano originally belonged to Marilyn Monroe's mother, Gladys. After the star's mother was institutionalized, the piano was sold and it would take years of searching for Marilyn to finally locate the piano and buy it back. Her sentimental attachment to this instrument is well-documented in the 1974 book (published posthumously), *My Story*, by Marilyn Monroe, in Chapter One entitled *How I rescued A White Piano*.'[5]

The bidding for the piano was frenzied and it finally sold for $662,500 – to pop diva Mariah Carey. 'It is a treasure and my most expensive piece of art,' wrote Carey in her autobiography. 'And now, Marilyn Monroe's white baby grand piano is the centerpiece, the pièce de résistance, of my own glamorous Manhattan penthouse.'[6] It was important for her to own Marilyn's piano because, as Carey told a journalist from the *Observer*, 'It was her only piece of the childhood she'd never had. It was very important for her to find something to cling to.'[7]

Carey is a Marilyn super-fan, who identified with the star's struggles even as a child. When she was a girl she caught a clip of Marilyn on television performing 'Diamonds Are a Girl's Best Friend' from *Gentlemen Prefer Blondes*; she thought that the actress had the energy of a fairy, and the looks of a goddess. 'Marilyn was my first vision of a superstar that I could relate to, on an almost spiritual level,' she said. 'We did without a lot of things when I was young, but what my mother couldn't live without was a piano.'[8] Later, in 2001, when Carey was suffering from a period of exhaustion, it's said that she thought Marilyn was trying to communicate with her by leaving a series of garbled messages on her website and even tried to speak to her through the piano.[9]

But was Marilyn's story about the piano true? According to Susan Strasberg, the daughter of Lee and Paula Strasberg, the couple who inherited all of the actress's personal property, Marilyn dreamed up the sentimental scenario of the piano with Sidney Skolsky. Susan observed how the seed of the story was sown by Marilyn, elaborated by Skolsky and then further exaggerated by Marilyn. '"Even when I didn't have enough money to eat, I borrowed money to keep that piano in storage," Marilyn said, improvising on his improvisation,' writes Strasberg. 'It was strange, because her life didn't seem to need embellishment.'[10]

Skolsky's daughter Steffi told Anthony Summers that the story about the white piano had been invented by her father. 'Sure, there was a white piano at Monroe's apartment and later in the S'berg house, but he really had no idea of its history,' noted Summers. 'Steffi pointed out that, earlier in his career, her dad had been a PR man'.[11]

So had Mariah Carey been sold a pup? Like so much that has been written about Marilyn over the years, the story is an intriguing blend of truth and myth, whipped up with a topping of sickly-sweet Hollywood spin. It seems as though Gladys did buy Norma Jeane a piano on or around her seventh birthday. But when Gladys was taken away after her mental breakdown, the piano did not get lost; neither did Marilyn spend years hunting it down. Rather, it was bought at auction by Norma Jeane's foster mother Ana Lower for $235 and kept at her home in West Los Angeles until 1945 when the actress was solvent enough to buy it from her for $10.

Few people ever heard Marilyn at the piano – indeed, she told her half-sister Berniece that she couldn't really play – but one of her early biographers, Maurice Zolotow, claimed that she could perform a couple of 'the lighter classics'.[12]

We do know, however, that Marilyn had at least one piece in her piano repertoire: Chopsticks.

13

'I'M NOT AN ORPHAN'

After Gladys's breakdown in early 1935, it was Grace McKee who took over as the guardian of her friend's estate. An inventory, lodged with the authorities on 25 March 1935, shows that Gladys's assets included a 1933 Plymouth Sedan (she still owed $250 on the car); a radio valued at $25; the Franklin baby grand (on which she still owed $230); and just $60 in cash. She also took on responsibility for the care of Norma Jeane.

Yet Grace felt she could only offer the girl a temporary home in her Lodi Place apartment, near the Hollywood Studio Club, where Marilyn would live in 1946 and again in 1948 in the early days of her career as an aspiring starlet. In August 1935, Grace married Erwin 'Doc' Goddard. A month later, she decided to place Norma Jeane in an orphanage. The 9-year-old girl had already experienced the trauma of separation from her mother and the Bolenders; this subsequent rejection broke her. As she told George Barris in 1962:

> I was living in the home of my mother's best friend [Grace]. Then she remarries. All of a sudden her house became too small, and someone had to go. Guess who that someone had to be?
>
> One day she packed my clothes in my suitcase, and off we went in her car. She drove and drove for a long time without saying where she was taking me. She never said a word when I asked her. She just kept driving, looking straight ahead.
>
> We finally arrived at a three-story red-brick building. She

made me carry my small suitcase as we walked up the stairs to the main entrance of the building. I noticed a sign in huge letters. Emptiness came over me; my heart began beating fast, then faster. I broke out in a cold sweat. I began to panic. I cried. I couldn't catch my breath. The sign said LOS ANGELES ORPHANS' HOME. Please don't let me stay here. I'm not an orphan – my mother's not dead. I'm not an orphan. It's just that she's sick in the hospital and can't take care of me ... I cried and protested as hard as I could; I can still remember, she had to drag me inside ... My heart was broken.[1]

Soon after placing her charge in the orphanage, Grace embarked on a power struggle with the girl's former foster mother Ida Bolender. On 4 December 1935, Grace wrote to the superintendent of the home, Mrs Sula Dewey, outlining who could visit Norma Jeane. 'I especially do not want Mrs. Ida Bollender [sic] to see her again, as her visits seem to upset the child.'[2] Two days later, Mrs Dewey wrote back to Grace: 'When Mrs Bollender was here I told her she should not talk to Norma about her mother. The physicians have said Mrs. Baker would not get well – that means the child must have first consideration ... Norma is not the same since Mrs. B. visited with her. She doesn't look as happy ... I'll do as you request.'[3]

14

THE MYSTERIOUS MR KIMMEL

The upheaval of placing Norma Jeane in an orphanage came after an experience that is one of the most contentious in Marilyn's early life: an incident or incidents of sexual abuse.

In her autobiography, *My Story*, Marilyn describes herself as being eight years old, living with an unnamed foster family, who rented a room to a man called Kimmel, a respectable but 'stern looking man'. One day she was passing his room when he called her in. Thinking that he wanted her to run an errand, she stepped into his room. The man shut the door behind her, smiling as he did so. There was no way she could escape, he said, in a playful tone of voice. But then things turned nasty. Marilyn didn't document exactly what happened, but it's clear from reading the memoir that she knew she was being defiled.

'When he put his arms around me I kicked and fought as hard as I could, but I didn't make any sound,' Marilyn recalled. 'He was stronger than I was and wouldn't let me go. He kept whispering to me to be a good girl.'

When it was over, Norma Jeane ran out to tell her foster mother, but before she could get a word out she was silenced. Mr Kimmel was a 'star boarder' and the matriarch of the house wouldn't hear a word against him.

In her memoir she wrote:

> I started stammering again and couldn't finish. Mr. Kimmel came up to me and handed me a nickel.

'Go buy yourself some ice-cream,' he said.

I threw the nickel in Mr. Kimmel's face and ran out.

I cried in bed that night and wanted to die.[1]

This extract has been pored over, analysed and deconstructed by dozens of biographers, eager to find 'the truth' about what exactly happened to Norma Jeane.

Others have tried to uncover the real 'Mr Kimmel', naming him as George Atkinson, who lived with Gladys and her daughter, or Atkinson's close friend and fellow actor, the British-born Murray Kinnell. According to Donald Wolfe's *The Last Days of Marilyn Monroe*, Gladys rented the upstairs of the house to Kinnell, whom Wolfe names as Marilyn's abuser. 'Clearly the "Aunt" and the "foster mother" was Gladys,' he writes, 'and Mr. Kimmell, the molester, was Murray Kinnell, the British actor who stayed upstairs at the house on Arbol Drive.'[2] Yet I have not seen any proof of this allegation from Wolfe or anyone else. Also, it's worth asking whether an actor with a successful film career – with registered addresses of Beverly Glen Boulevard in 1933 and Glenroy Avenue between 1934 and 1936 – would also want to rent a room in a small, crowded house.

The most literal-minded have gone so far as to dismiss the incident entirely, regarding it as fiction because they could find no evidence that Norma Jeane ever lived in a boarding house with someone named Mr Kimmel; they don't consider the possibility that Marilyn changed certain identifying details to protect herself from the threat of legal action. Others, such as her half-sister Berniece, maintain that the assault could never have happened because Marilyn's first husband Jim Dougherty proudly described her as a virgin when they first married, seemingly discounting the fact that rape can take other forms than vaginal intercourse.

Some go even further. There are those who consider Marilyn's accounts of sexual abuse to be nothing more than the sick manifestation of a disturbed imagination, or even downright lies; a pathetic attempt to gain sympathy. Typical is the response from Lloyd Shearer, who interviewed the actress in 1947. She told him that 'she had been assaulted by one of her guardians, raped by a policeman, and attacked by a sailor'. The journalist – who would later write under the pseudonym Walter Scott – was so sceptical of Marilyn that he didn't run the piece. 'She seemed to me then to live in a fantasy world, to be entangled in the process of invention, and to be completely absorbed in her own sexuality,' he said.[3]

Norman Mailer, in his sloppily researched 1973 book *Marilyn: A Biography*, questioned the existence of the 'wealthy boarder', and concluded that Marilyn had invented the story because she knew its publicity value. His comments are not only incredibly insensitive but deeply offensive. It was more likely, he said, that her rape came 'exactly out of Marilyn's knowledge of the limits to good copy about Ida Bolender's sewing machine, or the English couple who thought to improve her grammar'.[4]

Yet Mailer – whose book is less a biography than a masturbatory wish fulfilment fantasy, an uneasy mix of misogyny and soft porn, with a dash of wild conspiracy theory thrown into the mix – never bothers to do any proper investigation himself. His words summing up Marilyn's appeal make for uncomfortable reading today. 'She was our angel, the sweet angel of sex, and the sugar of sex came up from her like a resonance of sound in the clearest grain of a violin,' he writes. 'Marilyn was deliverance, a very Stradivarius of sex so gorgeous, forgiving, humorous, compliant and tender that even the most mediocre musician would relax his lack of art in the dissolving magic of her violin . . . Marilyn suggested sex might be difficult and dangerous with others, but ice cream with her.'[5]

Although Marilyn did embellish certain aspects of her life, it's clear that this was not one of them. Her mother was absent for most of her childhood; when she did live with her, Gladys was battling mental illness. There were long stretches of time when Norma

Jeane was left alone. She could easily have fallen prey to many of the strangers who passed through and haunted her childhood.

The memory of sexual abuse was still affecting Marilyn even towards the end of her life. In June 1962, she described the assault by the 'star boarder' to photographer George Barris. In this account, she related how the older man made her sit on his lap and how he put his hands under her dress; 'he touched me in places where no one had ever before'.[6] Acting teacher Peggy Feury remembered going to a party in the early part of 1962, and listening to Marilyn talk about what she had endured as a child. 'She seemed concerned about ... childhood memories of being molested as a child, she talked to my husband at great length,' recalled Peggy in 1983. 'She was proud of herself – she knew people who were psychotic from such episodes, and she felt at least she'd survived that.'[7]

There is a further suggestion that Marilyn could have been subject to a serious sexual assault when she was even younger than the incident she described in her memoir. During a series of interviews that lasted ten hours with Brad Darrach for *Time* magazine in 1956, she claimed she had been raped at the age of six by a 'friend of the family'.[8] Darrach recalled the experience years later. 'Out it came for the first time, the whole hideous mess: the foster homes, the religious sadists who threatened her with hellfire, the child molester who raped her when she was six,' he wrote. 'Simply to remember was agony for Marilyn. Sometimes she was racked with sobs; sometimes she choked on anger and disgust. Sometimes tears filled my eyes too.'[9]

Soon after the abuse – and her foster mother's dismissal of her account of it – Norma Jeane started to bathe obsessively; she told her cousin Ida Mae Monroe that she felt 'dirty after the attack'.[10] She also began to stutter. 'I cried all night in my bed,' she told George Barris. 'I just wanted to die.'[11] Later, when she found herself in stressful situations she would begin to stammer once again. The shame of suffering sexual abuse resulted in feelings of guilt that became 'obsessive'. She also 'began to hear a noise in her head at night – and she began to brood about killing herself'.[12]

The culture surrounding sexual abuse – how it's regarded by society, the way we talk about it, the understanding of how it can have a lasting impact on an individual – has changed both since the time Marilyn was a child and since the 1970s when men like Norman Mailer were so dismissive about it. Reading about Marilyn's case today, it's clear to experts in childhood sexual abuse that the actress exhibited many of the classic signs and symptoms.

'To those who have experience with sexually abused children, Marilyn Monroe's story rings only too true,' state Pamala Klein and Zsuzsanna Adler.

Writing in *New Society*, these two experts – a psychologist specialising in child sexual abuse and a research officer in medical sociology – applied the work carried out by the American sociologist David Finkelhor to Marilyn's early life, noting how factors such as growing up in a low-income family, having no or little contact with one's 'natural' mother and living with a surrogate father increase a girl's risk of suffering sexual abuse. 'How does Monroe's background fit this profile?' they ask. 'We know that her family life was almost non-existent. She never knew her father, and her mother was unable to care for her. She was brought up in a series of ten foster homes; spent two years in an orphanage, followed by another foster home; and finally, four years with a guardian after her mother's admission to an asylum.'

The effect of the abuse on the young girl, they concluded, would skew her sexual and emotional responses for the rest of her life. 'It is little wonder that victims of child sexual abuse are often emotionally stunted at an early age,' write Klein and Adler. 'They put much psychic energy into dealing with the abuse, and the natural spiral towards maturity is thwarted. The result is a child in a woman's body, portraying a certain innocence by needing to play the seductress in the long and painful process of trying to come to terms with her abuse, and with her perception of men.'[13]

A few weeks after Marilyn died, her psychoanalyst Dr Greenson wrote to his colleague and friend Anna Freud, daughter of Sigmund Freud, about the matrix of complex emotions that he experienced in the wake of her death. The letter makes clear that, according to his professional opinion, and despite all the therapeutic work she'd done, Marilyn could not escape her past. 'She was so pathetic and she had had such a terrible life,' he wrote. 'I had hopes for her and I thought we were making progress ... God knows I tried and mightily so, but I could not defeat all the destructive forces that had been stirred up in her by the terrible experiences of her past life, and even of her present life.'[14]

15

THE STORYTELLER

Stories – and the lack of them in her early life – played a central role in forming the star's personality. Marilyn's friend Amy Greene remembers how intently the actress would listen when she heard a striking or memorable anecdote. 'Anything to do with a story she was like a child,' she said. 'During her childhood nobody had ever told her stories.'[1] Tony Curtis, who starred with Marilyn in *Some Like It Hot*, would later observe how sad it was that she had never played as a child. 'She never learned how,' he said. 'She had lost her childhood, so she never learned how to be a grown-up. I think a lot of the trouble we had with her was because she was afraid, a little girl lost.'[2]

As a girl, Norma Jeane had no choice but to make up her own stories. Each afternoon when she was supposed to be taking a nap, she would escape into a world of fantasy. One day she would be a beautiful princess in a tower, another a boy walking a dog, or an old grandmother with silver white hair. 'And at night, I would lie and whisper out, ever so softly, the situations that I had heard on the radio before bedtime,' Marilyn later recalled in an article for *Modern Screen*. Near one of her schools – during the course of her childhood she attended at least eight – there was an empty lot, overgrown with weeds. 'But from the moment I stepped onto it, it became a magic and private place where I could be all of the people I had been thinking about all day in the classroom. I didn't need much else to be happy.'[3]

Magazine features such as these gave rise to the accusation that

Marilyn exaggerated her experience at the orphanage, casting herself as a cross between a wretched waif from a Dickens novel and Little Orphan Annie. In interviews, she would often talk about the harsh conditions, the endless chores, the infinite number of dirty dishes that passed through her hands, and the crushing sense of loneliness and desperation. Fellow resident Bill Fredenhall – who arrived before Norma Jeane, in 1934, and was taken under the elder child's wing – recalled his time at the orphanage rather differently, and interpreted Marilyn's tales as 'part of the poor, unhappy child routine ... we were loved, protected, trained and cared for'. One of the more startling details related by Marilyn is that of the wooden cake that would be rolled out for a child's birthday; inside there was only one small slice of real cake for that day's lucky boy or girl; the rest of the orphans would go hungry. 'A wooden cake?' said Fredenhall. 'I doubt it. I never saw it. It sure sounds like one of those "tales".'[4]

Steve Hayes – who as an aspiring actor, Ivan Hayes, supported himself in LA by working as the night manager and maître d' of Googie's, the John Lautner-designed coffee shop next door to Schwab's drugstore on Sunset Boulevard where young actors hung out – also questioned the veracity of some of Marilyn's stories. He was introduced to her at Frascati's restaurant by Sydney Chaplin, who dated Marilyn, together with his brother Charlie Chaplin Jr, in 1947.[5]

Bobby Hall, one of Steve's friends at the time, had a low opinion of Marilyn because he claimed he'd spoken to the people who ran the orphanage, 'and they're really pissed at her for making them look like characters out of *Oliver Twist*'. If Marilyn was dumb, he opined, she was only as dumb as a fox, 'a fox that always eats its chickens'.[6]

Biographer Donald Spoto claimed that Marilyn stole some of her stories of childhood trauma from Eleanor 'Bebe' Goddard, the daughter of Doc Goddard from a previous marriage who came to live with her father and stepmother in 1940. (Norma Jeane had moved back in with the Goddards in February of that year.) Bebe endured a transitory childhood, passed around from one foster home to the next and also suffered from 'near-starvation', whippings and abuse. 'What I told Norma Jeane that winter made a great impression on her,' she said.[7]

There may be a certain amount of truth in this. However, Bebe herself was not beyond a little deception of her own. Towards the end of her life – she died in 2000 – Bebe entered into a scheme to pass off items bought at thrift stores as valuable objects that had once belonged to Marilyn. Working with a New York dealer in memorabilia, Goddard would produce authenticity certificates which stated that the fakes had once been owned by the star. According to a report in the *Los Angeles Times*, 'Goddard advised the dealer to place tissue paper between the folds of a garment and then use a piece of cotton to "very lightly" dab Chanel No. 5 perfume – reportedly Monroe's favourite – on the tissue.'[8]

Marilyn's first husband Jim Dougherty believed that Norma Jeane drew on his family history for experiences she then presented as her own. In his 1976 memoir *The Secret Happiness of Marilyn Monroe*, Dougherty wrote that from his knowledge Norma Jeane had never known grinding poverty; neither had she ever had to forego a meal. 'I began to get the feeling that she desperately wanted some colorful family tale of want and scarcity, something that would clearly put her on the wrong side of the tracks so she could brag about it,' he said.[9]

Marilyn's proclivity to embellish or, in some cases, totally invent certain experiences presents a problem for biographers. This is itself complicated by the fact that her tendency to make up stories could be one of the consequences of suffering sexual abuse as a child, which itself has been interpreted by some as a fantasy.

16

DID NORMA JEANE GIVE BIRTH WHEN SHE WAS A TEENAGER?

It's in this context – and with a dose of healthy scepticism – that one has to approach the question of whether Norma Jeane ever gave birth to a child when she was a young teenager. It's a claim made by a number of people, including her friend Amy Greene, and also Marilyn's New York maid and cook Lena Pepitone, who worked for her from 1957 until her death.

Pepitone's account of what Marilyn supposedly told her is that Norma Jeane was living with one of her foster families when, one day while everyone else was out, the man of the house invited her to have a glass of whiskey. 'Because she had drunk with the English people [the Atkinsons], she didn't get suspicious of this unusual activity,' writes Pepitone in her 1979 ghostwritten memoir *Marilyn Monroe Confidential*. Then the man started kissing her. '"At first it was nice to be held and kissed. No one ever kissed me. But then ... then he wouldn't stop." Still, Norma Jeane kept her composure when she described how the foster parent ordered her to take her clothes off. "I thought I had to do what he said. Whatever he said." She was used to taking orders. Then he forced himself on her. "I didn't scream. I didn't do anything. It hurt a lot at first, then I didn't feel anything. I just lay there. I just cried."'

According to Pepitone, it was when Norma Jeane returned to live with her guardian Grace Goddard and her husband that she discovered that she was pregnant. She concealed the secret until it was too late; her only option was to have the baby.

'I was afraid she'd kill me when I told her,' Marilyn said about Grace. 'But she didn't get mad at all. She just took me to a doctor. Later on, I went to a hospital, where I had the baby . . . my baby. I was so scared but it was wonderful. It was a little boy. I hugged him and kissed him. I just kept touching him. I couldn't believe this was my baby. I had him in the hospital for a few days. But when it was time for me to leave, the doctor and a nurse came in with Grace. They all looked real strange and said they'd be taking the baby. It was like I was being kicked in the head. I begged them, "Don't take my baby." But Grace gave me a dirty look and said it was the best thing. She said I was too young to take care of it, that I had caused enough trouble, and to shut up. So they took my baby from me . . . and I never saw him again.'[1]

What are we to make of this? Pepitone's memoir is often dismissed out of hand by Marilyn Monroe scholars. Some have gone so far as to question whether the maid ever worked for the star and regard the book as a complete fabrication. Yet recent auctions of Marilyn's property, including documents from her filing cabinets, show receipts of payments made out to Pepitone. Lois Banner, a dedicated Monroe historian, states that the maid 'didn't speak English and Marilyn didn't speak Italian' and as a result questions whether the two ever had a meaningful conversation.[2] However, lodged with the Margaret Herrick Library in Beverly Hills is a tape of Lena Pepitone being interviewed by Anthony Summers. Pepitone speaks with a heavy Italian accent, but she can be clearly understood:

Lena Pepitone: Every month she sent money to two old people in California.
Anthony Summers: And the two people were looking after the baby?

Pepitone: [Makes a noise to confirm this.] She was thirteen or
    fourteen years old—
Summers: When she had a baby or an abortion?
Pepitone: A boy.
Summers: And the two people were looking after the boy?
    How did you know about this? She just told you
    about this?
Pepitone: Many times when she was crying she talked about
    the mistakes she had made.
Summers: What – by giving the boy away?
Pepitone: She didn't really give him away – she wasn't per-
    mitted to have an abortion or . . .
Summers: So they were the guardians? You've no idea of their
    identity?
Pepitone: I've no idea.
Summers: Any idea of who the father was?
Pepitone: I don't know.
Summers: What did she say about it?
Pepitone: When she was thirteen or fourteen she was not al-
    lowed to keep it. One old man, in some bedsit, she was
    raped or something like that.
Summers: And you believed her when she told you this
    story?
Pepitone: Yes, she was physically crying.[3]

Although Marilyn also told a couple of friends – including Amy Greene – about giving up a baby for adoption, no written evidence about the birth has been uncovered. It's highly possible that, in the late 1930s and early 1940s, the rape of a teenage girl, who subsequently became pregnant and gave birth to a child, would not have been documented. Grace Goddard may have wanted to hush up the whole messy affair; after all, she knew her friend Gladys and her family had suffered a great deal already. There are other possible scenarios. The star could have been suffering from a delusional episode; at this point in her life, when she told the story to Pepitone, she was desperate to have children of her own. Or there's the prospect that Pepitone could have been making up the whole story about Marilyn's teenage rape and birth of the child to sell more copies of her book.

There's another theory too, one put forward by James Haspiel, who met Marilyn when he was sixteen in September 1954 and who quickly established himself as her number one fan and, later, an unofficial archivist. Haspiel traced the rumour of a teenage pregnancy and forced adoption to Amy Greene, who at the time had one son, Joshua, born in March 1954. Haspiel surmised that Amy became 'potentially jealous' of Marilyn's increasing monopolisation of her husband, the photographer Milton Greene – with whom Marilyn formed her own production company in January 1955 – and in order to get her own back on the childless star boasted about the fact she herself was the mother of a young son. 'I have the distinct feeling that one day the method actress in Marilyn overtook reality and rose to the occasion by giving an Academy Award performance for Amy about "the baby" she had had,' he said. 'Most plausibly this is the real origin of that particular Monroe legend.'[4]

Since Marilyn's death, a number of people have come forward to claim that they are the biological sons or daughters of the star. In 1982, the supermarket tabloid the *National Enquirer* splashed with the news that they had discovered the 'secret daughter of Marilyn Monroe'. Apparently, 28-year-old Janet Raymond was the spitting image of Marilyn, so much so that she had won three Marilyn lookalike contests. Janet claimed that the star had given birth to her during a stay at the Cedars of Lebanon Hospital, where the actress had been admitted for the removal of her appendix. Janet was then adopted by a family in Dallas, before moving to Santa Monica. As a child she said that there was always money to pay for acting and dancing lessons, but this financial aid stopped when Marilyn died in 1962. Janet's account seems almost convincing until you begin to examine the dates: if she was twenty-eight in 1982, it means that she was born in 1954. The problem with the story is that Marilyn underwent an appendectomy two years earlier in 1952. And if she had given birth in 1954 – when she was married to Joe DiMaggio – it's unlikely that she would have given the baby away.

'I was at a party about five or six years ago [in the late 1970s] down in Santa Monica,' said Sheila Stewart Renour, Marilyn's friend between 1953 and 1954, 'and there was this young blonde girl there who was claiming that she was Marilyn Monroe's and Joe DiMaggio's daughter and was introduced as that. I said that's absolutely impossible because it would have been around that time [when I knew her]. And I knew that was the one thing that Marilyn had always wanted – a baby. For a baby to be born without anyone knowing would have been absolutely impossible. And if you look at the publicity pictures you can see that she was never pregnant at that time.'[5]

17

'A LOT OF THE GIRLS DIDN'T LIKE HER BECAUSE THE BOYS LIKED HER *A LOT*'

In contrast to the other girls at Emerson Junior High, Norma Jeane only had a choice of two 'light-blue dress suits' from her days at the orphanage. By 1939, her figure had filled out. She was no longer the girl the other children nicknamed 'String Bean' and although her dear 'Aunt' Ana Lower, the paternal aunt of Grace Goddard, whom Norma Jeane lived with after leaving the orphanage, had done her best to let the dresses out, her clothes still fitted badly. Her choice of footwear was limited – she favoured tennis shoes because they could be bought for ninety-eight cents, while Mexican sandals were even cheaper.

One day a girl made fun of Norma Jeane's appearance and she came back to Aunt Ana in tears. The old woman held her in her arms and rocked her like a baby. 'It doesn't make any difference if other children make fun of you, dear,' she told her. 'It's what you really are that counts. Just keep being yourself, honey. That's all that really matters.'[1]

However, soon after reaching puberty at the age of twelve, Norma Jeane noticed a change in how other people – particularly boys – saw her. A friend lent her a tight blue sweater, which emphasised the shape of her breasts. 'When I walked into the classroom the boys suddenly began screaming and groaning and throwing themselves on the floor,' she recalled. She started to experiment with lipstick and mascara. 'For the first time in my life people paid attention to me. For the first time I had friends.

I prayed that they wouldn't go away.' The neighbours sneered at her, called her 'cheap', but she didn't care; her self-esteem had been given a boost, and her stammer started to disappear. 'I looked back on the whole mess around that time,' she said later. 'And something came up inside me and I said to myself, "Somebody's got to come out of this whole!"'[2]

Kay Little remembered her from this time at Emerson. 'She was very pretty and she was very flirtatious,' she said. 'A lot of the girls didn't like her because the boys liked her *a lot*.'[3] Jim Dougherty recalled that the girls at high school 'snubbed' Norma Jeane 'because she had such big bosoms';[4] the fact that she had been named the school's 'oomph girl' probably didn't help.

For all the novelty that came with this newfound attention, the threat of poverty was always hanging around the periphery of Norma Jeane's life. It was normal for her to stand in line and queue up for day-old stale bread; a quarter would buy enough to last a week.

'I thought to myself, Are we always going to be poor, standing on stale-bread lines? Sensing my sadness, Aunt Ana would squeeze my hand, smile down at me, and say to me, Norma Jeane, when you grow up, you will be a rich, beautiful, and talented lady, a famous model and actress. Only Mom and Aunt Ana knew these were my secret dreams.'

When Marilyn was rich and famous and could afford to eat whatever she wanted, she often found herself at parties nibbling on Melba toast breads, no doubt often topped with caviar. The thin dry slices, a sign of sophistication in 1950s America, reminded her of stale bread.[5]

18

'A FRIENDSHIP WITH PRIVILEGES'

Norma Jeane regarded Jim Dougherty as good-looking, kind and polite, but she said she didn't feel anything for him; he was five years older than her. However, she knew she didn't have a choice: her foster parents Grace and Doc Goddard were moving to West Virginia with their daughter Bebe; and Aunt Ana was too old to look after her. A return to the orphanage beckoned.

Jim – who worked the graveyard shift at Lockheed Aircraft – recalled that when Grace first suggested he take Norma Jeane out on a date, he felt slightly awkward about the arrangement as 'until the evening really got started, I thought I was robbing the cradle', he said.[1] At the time, Norma Jeane was fifteen and in tenth grade at University High School in West Los Angeles.

Over the course of the following few months, Jim said, 'Grace expertly maneuvered' both himself and Norma Jeane, manipulating them so they became closer.[2] In December 1941, the couple went to a Christmas dance at Doc Goddard's firm. Jim remembered dancing with Norma Jeane to 'Everything Happens to Me'; as he held her, the girl 'would lean extra close, eyes shut tight'.[3] Jim would drive her up to Pop's Willow Lake, near the site of what is today the Hansen Dam, in the San Fernando Valley, where they would rent a canoe and make out under the tree branches. They would go hiking in the Hollywood Hills or park Jim's 1940 Ford sport coupe up on Mulholland Drive.

Did Grace realise that her role of matchmaker between an underage girl and an older man mirrored that of Marilyn's grandmother

Della, who had enabled and legitimised the sexual relationship between her 14-year-old daughter Gladys and 30-year-old Jasper Newton Baker? During the early part of 1942, it seems as though Grace was making a conscious decision to distance herself from her charge. In March, she and her husband left for West Virginia. Jim saw the effect this had on Norma Jeane. This 'seemed to her like another rejection, another foster home that hadn't worked out,' he said. 'Of course, she was absolutely right and I was marrying her because they had more or less abandoned her.'[4]

The wedding took place on 19 June 1942, just after Norma Jeane's sixteenth birthday, at 432 South Bentley Avenue, West Los Angeles. The house was owned by Chester Howells, an attorney and a friend of Grace's, but neither Grace nor Gladys attended. The Bolenders did attend; it would be the last time they saw Norma Jeane. It was obvious to Jim that his wife-to-be was nervous. 'Except to go to the bathroom, she never let go of my arm all afternoon,' he said, 'and even then she looked at me as though she was afraid I might disappear while she was out of the room.'[5]

The newly married couple lived in a studio apartment with a pull-down bed at 4524 Vista Del Monte in Sherman Oaks, and then a small, detached house on Bessemer Street in Van Nuys. Jim soon became aware of the young woman's complex personality. There was a part of her that remained resolutely childlike. She propped up her dolls and toys – two ceramic ones from the early years with the Bolenders, a teddy bear with one eye, a stuffed monkey with no tail, two rag dolls – on top of the chest of drawers so they could 'see what's going on'.[6] One stormy night, Norma Jeane became so concerned for a cow that had strayed into the front garden she wanted to bring it inside so that it wouldn't get wet. And she delighted in cooking peas and carrots because she adored the complementary colours of green and orange.

Jim believed that she entered into the marriage knowing 'absolutely nothing' about sex. He was adamant that 'that delicate threshold had never been crossed before'. But, as he writes in his autobiography, after she had experienced 'the first little pain', she came to enjoy sex – 'it was as natural to her as breakfast in the morning'.[7] He said she particularly relished making love outdoors and often when they were out driving through the San Fernando Valley she would squeeze his hand to indicate that she wanted him to pull over so they could have sex. Norma Jeane, he said, was desperate to get pregnant, but he felt that she was 'too young emotionally' to have a child so she used a diaphragm as a form of contraception.[8]

In September 1943, the couple moved to Catalina Island, southwest of Los Angeles, which the government had sequestered as a military training ground. After America entered the Second World War in December 1941, Jim enlisted as a sailor in the Merchant Marines but, according to his recollections, Norma Jeane begged him to make her pregnant so she could 'have a piece' of him in case he died in action. 'She seemed to fear, now that she had me and her life had a direction for the first time, that it would end suddenly,' he wrote, 'that she would be cheated again by life the way she had been so many times before.'[9]

On first reading, Dougherty's account of the relationship seemingly sits at odds with the one provided by Marilyn, who would later describe the marriage as 'like being retired to a zoo' and 'a sort of friendship with privileges'.[10] In her autobiography, she claims that it was Jim who wanted her to fall pregnant; *she* was the one who was resistant to the idea. 'The thought of having a baby stood my hair on end,' she maintained. 'I could see it only as myself... another Norma Jean [sic] in an orphanage.'[11] Marilyn even went so far as to tell one journalist that she was so unhappy in the marriage that she tried to take her own life, but the attempt was 'not a very serious one'.[12]

However, letters that she wrote at the time seem to suggest she was deeply in love with him. 'I love Jimmie just more than anyone (in a different way I suppose than anyone),' she wrote to Grace Goddard on 15 June 1944, 'and I know I shall never be happy with anyone else as long as I live, and I know he feels the same towards me, so you see we are really very happy together that is of course, when we can be together.' But perhaps Norma Jeane was telling Grace exactly what she wanted to hear; after all, it had been Grace who had been partly responsible for the marriage. 'Of course I know that if it hadn't been for you we might not have ever been married,' Norma Jeane wrote in the same letter, 'and I know I owe you a lot for that fact alone, besides countless others.'[13]

While her husband was at sea, Norma Jeane initially lived with Jim's mother on Hermitage Street in North Hollywood. Norma Jeane would write him letters, which he claimed numbered more than two hundred (none of which survive because he destroyed them after the marriage broke down). There were times when he'd return home on leave, but he dreaded the moment when he had to say goodbye; the separation was, he said, 'a destructive thing that hit her extremely hard. She wanted something, *someone* that she could hold onto all the time.'[14]

19

THE FIRST PHOTOGRAPHS

When Norma Jeane turned up for work on a December day in 1944, she had no idea that her life was about to change. She had got a position at Radioplane, a factory at the Metropolitan Airport, Burbank, manufacturing remote-controlled pilotless aircraft – what we now call drones – through her mother-in-law Ethel, who also worked for the company. The job was monotonous: for ten hours each day she inspected, sprayed and packed parachutes, and sometimes worked on the production line fitting together mechanical parts. Neither was it well paid: she started on seventy cents an hour, rising to eighty cents. But she was doing her bit for the war effort, an archetypal 'Rosie the Riveter'.

The factory was owned by British-born Reginald Denny, who after serving as a gunner in the First World War established himself as a successful film actor in Hollywood. Fellow actor and future US president Ronald Reagan, who then ran the First Motion Picture Unit, had contacted his friend Denny and arranged for a small group of photographers and moving picture men to take some publicity shots of female workers at Radioplane. Among the group was army photographer Private David Conover, based at 'Fort Roach', named after the Hal Roach studio in Culver City. Conover, then twenty-five, was a shy, awkward man, with bifocals and a stutter. He walked down the assembly line, taking a few shots with his Speedy Graphic camera, until he spotted one girl wearing a green blouse, a name tag hanging from the waistband of her grey tweed trousers. It took him a while to realise what he'd just seen – her eyes held something that touched him – but he retraced his steps and, fighting his shyness, told her that she should be a model.

He quickly took a photo of Norma Jeane holding a propeller; the colour image, which Conover thought was merely 'a static picture of a pretty girl', is the first professional shot of the woman who would soon become Marilyn Monroe. If he'd left it at this and moved on, perhaps we would have heard no more of her. According to Conover's own written account, he then asked if it was possible for her to change into a sweater. She went to her locker and returned wearing red cashmere. The result was nothing short of sensational. 'Now, singled out and with the attention of camera and cameraman focused deliberately on her,' recalled Conover, 'she came alive with sure and immediate instinct. I was so excited I could hardly hold the camera steady.'[1]

It seems as though the images were not quite as spontaneous as Conover made out, as Norma Jeane wrote to Grace Goddard in a letter dated 4 June 1945:

After they finished with some of the pictures, an army corporal by the name of David Conover told me he would be interested in getting some color still shots of me. He used to have a studio on 'the Strip' on Sunset. He said he would make arrangements with the plant superintendent if I would agree, so I said okay. He told me what to wear and what shade of lipstick, etc., so the next couple of weeks I posed for him at different times ... He said all the pictures came out perfect. Also, he said that I should by all means go into the modeling profession ... that I photographed very well and that he wants to take a lot more.[2]

In 1981, Conover published a memoir, *Finding Marilyn: A Romance*, in which he wrote not only about his discovery of the young woman at Radioplane and the creation of the images they produced together, but also some more intimate matters. He claimed that the two had an affair, initiated by her, while on a photographic shoot in Death Valley during the summer of 1945: 'She dropped the big white beach towel around her breasts and put her arms around me and kissed me and whispered, let's do what comes naturally. We did.' Conover also maintained that the two kept in contact right up until the end of her life; that she told him all about her sexual relationship with President Kennedy while staying at Bing Crosby's house in Palm Springs; her turbulent relationship with Attorney General Robert Kennedy; that she'd fallen pregnant by Robert and that the baby had to be aborted because it was a 'tubular pregnancy'. The book was serialised in the supermarket tabloid the *Star*. 'MARILYN MONROE'S NIGHT OF LOVE IN THE SAND WITH JFK', ran the headline in the 1 September 1981 edition, while the magazine promised yet more revelations next week: 'Marilyn was murdered by someone she knew and trusted.'[3]

When Anthony Summers embarked on research for *Goddess*, he sought out Conover to hear more about these extraordinary revelations. Alarm bells were sounded as soon as Summers started to question him. 'Conover could produce only collated pages, supposedly copied from different years of a journal kept each year throughout his adult life.' Then came the killer detail. 'I noticed that they were partly written in ball-point pen, a miracle that had not been invented in 1945.'

Giving him the benefit of the doubt – for now – Summers asked if he could see the original entries in the original volumes. 'No, they were private,' wrote Summers in a research note. 'What, then, of the letters from Marilyn reproduced in his book? He had destroyed them, said Conover. How then could he reproduce them verbatim? Because, he muttered lamely, "I always copy letters from friends, in full, into my journal." I asked to see one example of this improbable practice, and again was told this would be an invasion of privacy. Finally, Conover could not name a single person able to confirm any contact between him and Monroe after the 1953 visit to the movie set.'

His conclusion? 'I came away convinced that Conover was either a confidence trickster, or mentally ill, or perhaps both.'[4]

Although it's clear that large parts of this memoir cannot be trusted, Conover should be recognised for spotting the young woman's star quality. It was more than the fact that she was photogenic, rather 'there was something special about her,' he said, 'a luminous quality to her face, a fragileness combined with astonishing vibrancy. This girl was going places. I could feel it in my bones.'[5]

20

36-24-34

2 August 1945. Norma Jeane walks through the lobby of the Ambassador, the glamorous Los Angeles hotel set back from Wilshire Boulevard, on her way to her first meeting with a modelling agency. Jean Harlow had filmed parts of *Bombshell* here, and the artificial palms used in Rudolph Valentino's *The Sheik* decorated the Cocoanut Grove inside, one of the West Coast's most fashionable nightclubs. Little did she know when she turned up for the meeting that eight years later she would attend a star-studded party at the venue with husband-to-be Joe DiMaggio or that, six years after her own death in 1962, this would be the site of the assassination of her friend – and rumoured lover – Robert Kennedy.

She's on the cusp of a new future, and she's feeling nervous. As Norma Jeane winds her way down the corridor of the casino floor, by her side is Potter Hueth, a friend of fellow photographer David Conover, who is responsible for organising the introduction to Miss Emmeline Snively, the proprietor of the Blue Book Modeling Agency. Norma Jeane wears a simple white dress which is, according to Miss Snively's notes, 'as clean and white and ironed and shining' as the young woman herself.[1] She's about to sit down in the chair opposite Miss Snively, when the boss of the modelling agency asks her to walk to the door and back. She takes in everything around her: the small bust of Nefertiti on Miss Snively's desk, and the wall plastered with magazine covers featuring some of her girls.

'Do you think I could get my picture on a magazine cover?' asks Norma Jeane.

'Of course,' replies the older woman, who, although born in Ohio, speaks with a fake English accent to make her sound more genteel. 'You're a natural.'

Miss Snively takes her measurements: she's a size twelve; her height is 5 feet 6 inches, with a 36-inch bust, 24-inch waist and 34-inch hips. She notes that the girl has perfect teeth, blue eyes and blonde, curly hair, which she later redescribed as 'dirty blonde, California blonde ... dark in the winter and light in the summer'.

'Do you sing?' asks Miss Snively.

'Just a little, that's all.'

'Dance?'

'A little.'

'Ambitious of becoming an actress?'

'No, not at all,' she replies.[2]

Norma Jeane knows she has to be strategic if she has any chance of succeeding. In addition to hiding her acting ambitions, she also lies about her age to Miss Snively, telling her that she is twenty rather than nineteen. But she doesn't lie about her status as a married woman, even though she knows it might count against her.

Miss Snively then outlines what's going to happen next. If she were to take her on her books, Norma Jeane would have to pay $25 for a photograph in the agency's catalogue, plus an additional $100 for a three-month modelling course. But the agency boss informs her that she could pay this out of any future earnings.

'She was so naive, so sweet and so eager to succeed that my heart went out to her at once,' Miss Snively recalled.[3] She regarded her as an 'All-American girl' who was, she said, 'cute, wholesome and respectable. There was no sultry sexiness about her except that her clothes were a little too tight across her chest.'[4]

On the first day of modelling classes, Miss Snively observed Norma Jeane at close quarters and became acutely aware of the young woman's abundant charms – 'she aroused the good nature in people,' she said. 'She would walk in and in her cute, high voice say

"Hello everybody." Everyone would answer, "Hello!". There was something arresting and sincere about the girl's personality. When I introduced her to a photographer, she would look him straight in the eye and cling to his every word . . . She made everyone she talked to feel as if he were the only guy in the world.'[5]

Actress Marion Marshall – born Marian Tanner, later Marion Wagner – first met Norma Jeane when they both turned up for a call to model a line of bathing suits. Later, in 1946, Marion and Norma Jeane would be signed by Twentieth Century-Fox on the same day, the day that the two young women would also have their names changed. The moment she first saw Norma Jeane is branded on her memory. There were forty or fifty models waiting in line, many of them sporting gloves and smart hats. Norma Jeane turned up late, her hair dishevelled and wearing a modest sundress with a scooped neck. 'And she walked in and it was like the room stopped and everyone knew she was gonna get the job,' Marion recalled. 'And she did. She had that kind of quality. In the days when I knew her, she never stepped on anyone's feet. She was never a bitch. You always felt that Marilyn was like a wounded child, you wanted to protect her in a way, but you could never get close enough to do it.'[6]

21

Mon amour

She is standing – barefoot – in the middle of a Californian highway, seemingly without a care in the world. Her hair is in pigtails, which makes her look younger than her nineteen years. Norma Jeane turns, smiles for the camera, casts her head back and laughs. The photographer, 32-year-old André de Dienes, notices the hundreds of little white stars that cover her red skirt and he tells her that these are a symbol, that she is marked out for fame. 'Sit on the highway,' he says. 'It represents life. You have a long way to go.'[1]

Soon the two will embark on a road trip of their own. But first there are a few more test shots. He drives her down to a beach, where he takes more photographs of her wearing a pair of jeans he's bought for her. She dances in the sunshine, 'laughing, whirring around, prancing, sinking to the ground ... supple as a cat, brimming over with the joy of living'.[2]

She's keen to expand her portfolio, but Norma Jeane would only go on location with him, travelling at close quarters, with the permission of Aunt Ana. And so, over lunch, he charms the old lady, telling her how he's taken photographs of Ingrid Bergman in a field of ripe wheat, captured Dorothy McGuire standing on a clifftop, and shot reels of film with that archetype of American innocence, Shirley Temple. He notices that Norma Jeane is wearing a wedding ring, but he soon learns that the marriage is failing.

And so on that December day in 1945, with the back of his Buick already converted into a sleeping compartment complete with a mattress and blankets, André packs the car with a store of provisions, and sets off from Los Angeles with her on a trip into the American wilderness.

Norma Jeane had first met André de Dienes – born Andor Ikafalvi-Dienes in what is now Braşov in Romania, then Transylvania – at his hotel room at the fashionable Garden of Allah Hotel on Sunset Boulevard. Sent by the Blue Book Modeling Agency, she'd turned up wearing a 'skimpy' pink jumper, a ribbon in her hair. 'She seemed unsure of herself,' he said. 'With her childlike smile and clear gaze, she was absolutely enchanting.'[3] She was to be paid $100 a week – a big increase on her job at Radioplane, which had terminated her contract in March – and de Dienes was to meet all expenses such as accommodation, travel and food. 'We drove through a desolate landscape,' recalled the photographer, 'the sky lowering and stormy at times, although it was December.'[4]

As André drove into the Mojave Desert, Norma Jeane snacked on apples, oranges, slices of tinned pineapple and dollops of cottage cheese; she drank Coca-Cola; she read magazines; and she slept a great deal. He headed first to Darwin Falls where he wanted to recreate Ingres's painting *La Source*. But when they arrived they found that the spring-fed waterfall in Death Valley was nothing more than a trickle. He was desperate to find the perfect backdrop to photograph her in the nude, and so pushed on towards Cathedral Gorge, 'a labyrinth of narrow passes hemmed in between high rock faces, eroded by wind and rain'. There, they encountered a couple of hoodlums who looked at Norma Jeane with undisguised desire. He quickly ushered her back into the car and continued on the epic road trip.

De Dienes had an agenda. Not only did he aspire to take some fabulous photographs – his 'greatest pictures ever' – but he made it his mission to sleep with Norma Jeane too. 'Although I wanted her so badly the last thing I wanted was to hustle her into going to bed with me, even though she would acquiesce,' he said. 'I wanted her to be willing.'[5] Reading his 1985 memoir *Marilyn, mon Amour* today is an uncomfortable experience. It's clear that de Dienes saw his role as Norma Jeane's protector, life guide and sexual educator. By the time they reached Merced County, in Yosemite National Park, he could barely contain his frustration. He wanted to book one room rather than two, but he knew that there was no point in telling the manageress of the motel that they were a married couple; she would ask for proof. 'Norma Jeane now became the object of my suppressed rage,' he writes. 'She let me spoil her, protect her and drive her halfway across the United States, taking it all for granted, "paying" me with a smile here, a thank-you there and the occasional dewy-eyed look to express how moved or pleased she was. I was an idiot not to try anything!'[6]

One night, he wrote her a heartfelt letter outlining his desires, but the next morning he wasn't sure whether she'd read it. Two events seemed to push them closer: an awkward meeting with Norma Jeane's mother Gladys, who had been released from hospital and was now living in a squalid hotel room in Portland, Oregon; and the theft of André's camera equipment and some undeveloped spools of film from his car, which Norma Jeane had forgotten to lock. Guilt shadowed her consciousness: Norma Jeane felt bad after turning down her mother's request to live with her – de Dienes described the older woman as 'emaciated and apathetic ... she had been released from hospital too soon'[7] – and angry with herself about being such a 'scatterbrain'.[8] Did Norma Jeane feel she had no choice but to sleep with him? Did she hope that the union would erase the guilt about the theft? Or was she simply attracted to the handsome older man?

De Dienes described their eventual encounter – which took place in the ski resort of Timberline Lodge, 80 miles north of Portland – as though it were some kind of battle or enforced possession. 'Everything she felt for me, trust, gratitude, even admiration, was fused in her surrender,' he wrote. He chose to draw a veil over the most intimate 'blissful moments' as to share them 'would be a desecration'.⁹ According to de Dienes, both of them wanted to marry, just as soon as Norma Jeane could get a quickie divorce from Dougherty in Las Vegas. But their plans were thrown in the air when the photographer heard the news that his friend who was subletting his New York studio apartment – and looking after his cat – had died in a car accident. He had no choice but to return to Manhattan.

André drove back to Los Angeles, but before he took Norma Jeane to Aunt Ana's, they stopped for a coffee at Schwab's drugstore on Sunset Boulevard. When André turned his back to write out a cheque for Norma Jeane's services as a model, he was alarmed to see her in conversation with another photographer who wanted to book her for a shoot. He had to battle his feelings of jealousy and, after promising her that he would return to LA so they could marry in 1946, he finally steeled himself to leave her behind. Back in New York, André was relieved to find that, apart from a rather messy litter tray, his cat was OK, and he threw himself into work so he could save enough money for the forthcoming marriage. However, later he would confess, in an unpublished letter, 'I was more worried about the cat, starving there, than about my romantic involvement with Norma Jeane.'[10]

Although it would be easy to write off de Dienes as yet another fantasist in the mould of David Conover, evidence shows that the relationship was real. In June 1946, Grace Goddard wrote to Norma Jeane, who was staying in Las Vegas so she could get a speedy divorce from Dougherty, about the young woman's forthcoming plans to reunite with André. 'You deserve more than Jimmy is capable of giving you,' wrote Grace. 'Of course no one but Doc and me know of your future plans. I am so in hopes you will let your heart rule you this time and not let anything keep you from taking the happiness that is being offered you.'[11] Aunt Ana, however, was not so positive. In a letter she wrote to Norma Jeane on 5 July 1946, Ana described the young woman's situation as a 'mess'. Despite the money she had lent her, Norma Jeane was several hundred dollars in debt, 'with nothing really settled'. She apologised for her harsh tone, but she reasoned that Norma Jeane needed to hear some home truths. 'Well, precious, you may feel I am being severe, but it is not so meant,' she wrote. 'I love you dearly and you must not feel hurt because of this letter.'[12]

Finally, after months of separation, André couldn't wait any longer and embarked on another cross-country road trip back to the West Coast. Desperate to tell Norma Jeane that he was on his way, he stopped at a payphone in New Mexico and called her.

The news was not what he wanted to hear: she couldn't marry him after all, as she wanted to get into the movies. Undeterred, André made a date for her to meet him at the corner of Vine and Sunset six days later at 1 p.m. When she didn't turn up, he went to the one-room apartment that she was renting in Santa Monica. As he drew up in his car, he saw a man leaving her building and when he knocked on the door he was startled to see that Norma Jeane was wearing nothing but a lacy black negligee. He later learned the identity of her lover, 'a dear man, who was real good to her, always ... and did his best to make her meet important people ... A well-known Hollywood personality – who died some years ago'.[13]

He tried to make light of the reality – telling his wife-to-be that she was a free agent – but the rejection hit him so hard he took a couple of bottles of whiskey up to the cliffs with the intention of ending it all. The beauty of the sunset – and his subsequent photograph of it – saved him.

In his memoir, de Dienes wrote about how he managed to stay friends with the woman who became Marilyn Monroe – 'no one was allowed to call her by any other name'.[14] He continued to take more photographs of her, including a set of haunting images snapped at night in 1953 on the streets and back alleys of Beverly Hills when Marilyn couldn't sleep and she was 'on the edge of despair',[15] and a startling shot of her wearing a folded dark cloth over her head to symbolise death. 'Death to her was blackness, nothingness,' he said.[16]

As Marilyn's fame grew, so did André's sense of resentment. On 29 March 1960, he wrote to her from his home on Sunset Plaza Drive, criticising her for not mentioning him in the extract of a new biography of her written by Maurice Zolotow that had appeared in the April edition of *McCall's* magazine.

> *I did not find my name somewhere where it should have been mentioned – after all, I was a turning point in your life I always belived* [sic], *and you yourself know it very well.*
>
> *But I am not surprised you never mention me, for years now you did that same thing – got even with me. I shall never forget the incident when one Sunday we were driving along and had a short dispute about something and I told you angrily 'you will never be an actress' and you got out of the car at the next corner. Well, that's what did it, I know, and perhaps other things. I have no hard feelings toward you even if you never think of me, however I think it is a little bit funny that you did not mention all the lovely photos I took of you back in 45, 46, 47, 49, and so on. Some day, when I will have time I will write my memoires also, and will be kinder than you are and will mention you in it.*[17]

In early 1961, when de Dienes learned that Marilyn was experiencing bouts of mental illness, he did his best to cheer her up. He sent her a telegram in February after she was institutionalised at the Payne Whitney Clinic, addressed to 'Turkey Foot', his nickname for her, suggesting that they go on a hike through the redwood forest together. Perhaps he was doing what he thought was best, but his choice of words shows a complete lack of understanding about the nature and seriousness of her illness. 'STOP FEELING SORRY FOR YOURSELF. GET OUT OF THE HOSPITAL.'[18]

The last time André saw Marilyn was on her birthday on 1 June

1961, in Beverly Hills. Again, he was heavy-handed. Although he knew that she was suffering from terrible insomnia and almost unbearable mental strain – 'her whole nervous system was giving way,' he said[19] – he was unsympathetic about her plight. 'What really upset me about her wrecked life was her bitterness: her success was a sham, her hopes thwarted; she had been let down repeatedly, even by the men who had said they loved her,' he wrote. 'Her money had been squandered; fame had become a burden.'

When Marilyn complained to de Dienes that people were exploiting her, he told her to pull herself together. 'For heaven's sake, Marilyn, it's not the end of the world,' he said, before he took her in his arms and tried to kiss her. [20] He still believed that he could rekindle some of the magic of the trip through the desert and the snow of 1945. But he misread the signs. 'Oh please, don't!' she cried out. 'I'm so tired of all that . . . Don't ask anything of me, you of all people.' After leaving the room, André became suspicious, and hung around outside for the appearance of another lover. 'I little guessed that this was our last goodbye,' he wrote.[21]

22

'To me, you're a Marilyn'

In 1972, Ben Lyon, head of casting at Twentieth Century-Fox, recalled his memories of July 1946, when he met Norma Jeane for the first time:

> My secretary rang and said, 'Mr Lyon, there's a very beautiful young girl here to see you, but she doesn't have an appointment.' I said, 'Mary, you don't have to have an appointment to see me – send her in.' So a moment later, in walked the most gorgeous young girl you've ever seen in your life, with this golden hair and beautiful little print dress ... I said, 'Sit down.' So she sat by the desk and I began by asking various questions, what she'd done and she told me a little extra work, a bit here and there. I said, 'What's your ambition?' and she said to be a film star. And I looked at her and I said, 'Well, honey, you're in pictures and I think you will be a film star.'
>
> I said, 'I don't think you can use the name Norma Jeane Dougherty if you're going to be a star – we've got to change your name. And by the contract we've got a right to change your name.' So she agreed and we looked in the book and thought of all kinds of combinations of names and nothing suited us and finally I remembered a girl I knew in New York, a stage star by the name of Marilyn Miller. I said, 'To me, you're a Marilyn,' and she said, 'That's a lovely name.' I said, alright, that's your first name. We couldn't find a second name, but she suddenly turned to me and said, 'Mr Lyon, could I use my grandmother's name?' I said, 'What was that?' 'Monroe.' Marilyn Monroe.

She would take dramatic lessons for three hours, she'd have lunch, after lunch she would take dancing lessons for an hour, singing lessons for an hour, fencing lessons for an hour and then go on the back lot and ride horseback. I said to her one day, 'Why do you work so hard? The other kids on contract I call sometimes at eleven o'clock, twelve o'clock, they're still in bed sleeping from being out the night before.' She said, 'Mr Lyon, I work hard because one day maybe opportunity will knock and I want to be prepared.'[1]

Speaking to a BBC documentary film crew twenty-six years after the event, it's understandable that Ben Lyon melded together a number of different encounters into one meeting. However, there's something more than the passing of time at work here, something else that may help explain the conflation of Lyon's memories. The young woman had such an effect on those she met that often quotidian details such as dates, places and times seem to have been erased by the overwhelming experience. It's impossible to define, but she drew on all the techniques she'd learned as a model and then applied something else – a sixth sense particular to those who become stars – so she was able to become pure image. Marilyn had the seemingly contradictory presence and absence of a projection, a hologram; at once everything and nothing. Perhaps that's one of the reasons why she continues to maintain her iconic status: she's a symbol of the modern, visual age.

Aesthetic chance – the *mise en scène* against which Lyon encountered Norma Jeane – may have played its part during that first meeting, as Fox's casting director later recalled in another interview. 'That office was, without a doubt, one of the most beautiful rooms I have ever been in,' he said. 'The walls were dark leaf green, the settee was Chinese red, the lamps chartreuse, and the curtains Scots plaid ... The girl who walked through that door took my breath away ... That dark green wall, the striving colors of that office of mine, made the perfect setting for her golden hair, peaches-and-cream complexion and the simple little flowered cotton dress she was wearing – an inexpensive dress but nicely cut and very nicely filled out. The girl's entrance to my office was a picture I shall never forget. Maybe if my office had been in any other color or if Marilyn had worn black, the effect would have been different and the whole story never would have happened.'[2]

When she stepped in front of a movie camera, something magical happened. Leon Shamroy, the distinguished cinematographer who is said to have shot Marilyn's first screen test, initially regarded the young woman as distinctly average. 'When you analyze Marilyn, she is not good-looking,' said Shamroy, who had won Oscars for *The Black Swan*, *Wilson*, *Leave Her to Heaven* and would win another for *Cleopatra* in 1963. 'She had a bad nose, bad posture and her figure is too obvious.'

But when Shamroy started to shoot that screen test, first in black and white and then in colour film, on the empty set of a Betty Grable film, he noticed a rare alchemy between camera and subject. 'Marilyn has the kind of glamour that explodes right into the camera lens,' he said. 'She's so pyrotechnical she practically curls the edges of the film. You name the angle – she does the most with it, and for it.'[3] There was something else too. The combination of her beauty with her 'natural inferiority complex' gave her a 'look of mystery'. She reminded him of the great film goddesses of the silent era. 'She had a kind of fantastic beauty like Gloria Swanson ... and she got sex on a piece of film like Jean Harlow,' said Shamroy, who would work with Marilyn on *There's No Business Like Show Business* (1954). 'Every frame of the test radiated sex. She didn't need a sound track – she was creating effects visually. She was showing us she could sell emotions in pictures.'[4]

There was only one problem: all new talent had to be approved by studio head Darryl F. Zanuck.

23

'Wolves I Have Known'

In the 2022 film *Blonde* – an adaptation of Joyce Carol Oates's novel, published in 2000 – we see a young Marilyn (played by Ana de Armas) reading from a script in the office of a studio boss, Mr Z. He walks over to her, manoeuvres himself behind her, easing her to the ground, positioning her on all fours, before he anally rapes her.

Darryl Zanuck had a reputation for being, to use the film slang of the time, a 'wolf'; what we today would call a sexual predator. 'They all said you couldn't get a contract unless you went to bed with Zanuck,' said gossip columnist Sheila Graham.[1] There is a legion of tales about his reprehensible behaviour; it's said that each day at 4 p.m. a different young woman would make her way through the subterranean tunnel that led to his green-panelled office for sex. According to Zanuck's biographer, Marlys Harris, 'everyone at the studio knew of the afternoon trysts . . . He was not serious about any of the women. To him they were merely pleasurable breaks in the day – like polo, lunch, and practical jokes.'[2]

One of the central myths surrounding Marilyn's rise to stardom is that she slept her way to the top. Although the names of the powerful men have varied (lists have included playboys such as Howard Hughes and Porfirio Rubirosa), the narrative remains the same: Marilyn was just a combination of a pretty face and a sexy body, and she would never have succeeded by virtue of her meagre acting talent had it not been for the fact that she 'put out'. Certainly, there are quotes from her friends that seem to support this. Marilyn supposedly told Amy Greene, 'I spent a great deal of time on my knees.'³ Young, aspiring actresses often found themselves vulnerable to abuse by powerful studio executives. Tony Curtis, speaking on a CNN special in 2001, claimed that 'the only way a young woman in those days could make it – maybe today, too – was to make themselves accessible to men's passions and lust'. The injustice was something that bothered Marilyn until the end of her life, he said.⁴

In 1961, W. J. Weatherby asked Marilyn about the realities of the 'casting couch' – a polite euphemism for what could be seen as institutionalised rape – and she replied that although it did exist, 'You can't sleep your way into being a star, though. It takes much, much more. But it helps. A lot of actresses got their first chance that way. Most of the men are such horrors, they deserve all they can get out of them!'⁵

Actress Joan Collins remembers the time when, soon after arriving in Hollywood at the age of twenty-one, she was groped by the cigar-chomping studio boss. As Zanuck lunged towards her, he told her that she hadn't had anyone until she'd had him. 'I'm the biggest and the best and I can go all night,' he said. She heard the story of another young starlet who was subject to the same 'seduction' technique, but on hearing his boast about his so-called sexual prowess she quipped, 'You better be, honey, 'cause you're only five foot-two!' Zanuck promptly fired her.⁶

There was always a certain animosity between Zanuck and Marilyn, right from the beginning of their time together at Fox. He wasn't that impressed by her 1946 screen test and had to be persuaded of her merits by Ben Lyon and Leon Shamroy. She told Maurice Zolotow that Zanuck never saw her as a true actress. Rather, he regarded her as 'some kind of freak', and typecast her in a series of trivial, light-hearted roles in sex comedies.⁷ 'She's a dumb tomato and half-crazy to boot,' he said about her performance as a delusional babysitter in *Don't Bother to Knock*. 'She's a sex pot who wiggles and walks and breathes sex, and each picture she's in she'll earn her keep, but *no more dramatic roles*.'[8] According to Amy Greene, the studio boss 'never understood Marilyn, never for a million years gave her credit for anything, and as his way of putting her down he would call her strawhead'.[9] One of Marilyn's lovers, the actor Nico Minardos, said that 'Zanuck hated her guts'.[10]

Could there have been something else behind their mutual animosity? Had Marilyn had the nerve to turn down the all-powerful Zanuck?

When Marilyn met Joan Collins at a party at Gene Kelly's house in 1954, she told the younger actress, 'There's nothing like the power of the studio bosses here, honey. If they don't get what they want, they'll drop you. It's happened to lots of gals.' Then she added, 'Specially watch out for Zanuck. If he doesn't get what he wants, honey, he'll drop your contract.'[11]

Marilyn was clearly speaking from personal experience. In July 1947, after only a year with Fox, her initial $125 a week contract — which increased to $150 a week — was not renewed, and although she tried to schedule an appointment with Zanuck, apparently she couldn't get past his secretaries. 'They always told me he was in Sun Valley,' she said. 'I'd come back a week later and they'd say, "He's in Sun Valley, we're very sorry, he's very busy." After a while you just give up.'[12]

Zanuck, when prompted by his biographer, spoke of his feelings towards Marilyn in starker terms: 'I wouldn't have slept with her if she paid me.'[13] The statement hisses with the sting of rejection.

Learning to negotiate this dangerous territory of Hollywood sexual snakes and ladders was far from easy. In 1953, Marilyn described her many toxic encounters with men in an article for *Motion Picture and Television* magazine entitled 'Wolves I Have Known'. One day, before she'd broken into the industry, she was walking down a street in Los Angeles when a man in a car stopped and told her she should go into the movies. He told her that he could arrange a screen test at the Goldwyn Studios, but when she turned up there one Saturday afternoon she discovered that he had borrowed a friend's office with the intention of seducing her. 'He was fat and jovial and of course drove a Cadillac,' she recalled. 'He gave me a script to read and told me how to pose while reading it. All the poses had to be reclining, although the words I was reading didn't seem to call for that position. Even as naïve as I was then, I soon figured out that this wasn't the way to get a job in movies. He was getting sillier by the minute and I maneuvered towards the door and made a hasty exit.'

Hollywood parties were particularly tricky affairs to manage. One night, Marilyn was hit on by a famous director who wouldn't take no for an answer. When she went upstairs to retrieve her wrap, he followed her and tried to trap her before she ran into another room. 'Shut out, he pounded on the door and pleaded that he just wanted to talk with me,' she recalled. 'I found a magazine and sat quietly reading while he roared. After a while, he left. Later when I went back downstairs, I saw another fellow bop him on the nose for flirting with his wife. And you know, it's a funny thing, I've met the fellow several times since and he told me he respected me for not letting him get fresh.'[14]

In 1948, Marilyn had a particularly toxic encounter with Harry Cohn, the boss of Columbia. The man was not popular – 'You had to stand in line to hate him,' quipped gossip columnist Hedda Hopper. After completing *Ladies of the Chorus*, Marilyn was called into his office, where Cohn asked her whether she would like to accompany him on his yacht at the weekend.

In a spirit of faux-innocence, perhaps, Marilyn told him she'd never attended a yachting party before, forcing Cohn to confess that it wouldn't be a group affair, that it would be just the two of them. 'I'd love to join you and your wife on the yacht, Mr Cohn,' she said, a comment which made the Columbia co-founder furious. 'Leave my wife out of this!' he shouted. As she left his office, it's reported Cohn barked, 'This is your last chance, baby'; another version has him calling her a 'goddamn cunt'.[15]

John Huston recalled how, while he was making *We Were Strangers* (1949), Marilyn was brought to the set by the film's producer Sam Spiegel on the pretext of making a screen test. 'She was a very pretty girl, a very attractive girl – rather timid, shy,' said Huston. 'She'd been promised a test – other girls had been promised tests that led to the casting couch rather than to the floor of a stage. So I said, by all means, if you're given a test, I'll be glad to make it. I didn't know who was trying to get Marilyn into the hay, but I had a suspicion that that was the plot rather than the furtherance of her career. The test never happened, and she was not allowed to come to the set again.'[16] She also turned down the advances of veteran actor and producer George Jessel, who met her early in her career. He told the columnist Earl Wilson that she was 'no pushover, no nymphomaniac . . . she wouldn't sleep with him [Jessel] when she could have used the favors he could have tossed her way.'[17]

It seems clear that if Marilyn had solely relied on the 'rewards' of the casting couch, it's likely that she would have become a star a lot quicker. In fact, it took her six years – between 1946 when Zanuck first signed her at Twentieth Century-Fox, and 1952, when she featured on her first cover of *Life* and starred in *Don't Bother to Knock* – to establish herself as a household name. 'I can't imagine Marilyn going to bed with someone just to get a part or anything like that,' said Jane Russell.[18]

24

GOLDEN DREAMS

Marilyn begins to undress. She takes off her low-cut blouse, kicks off her red high heels and pushes down her blue jeans. She slips on a loosely fitting robe and prepares herself for the shoot. The photographer Tom Kelley and his wife Natalie put her at ease. She lets the robe slip off her shoulders, and lies down on the expanse of soft red velvet. Kelley, standing 10 feet above her on a ladder, begins to snap away as Marilyn strikes pose after pose. In the background, the woozy melody of Art Shaw's 'Begin the Beguine' helps her relax.

The 1949 nude shoot takes two hours and at the end of it she signs the release form as 'Mona Monroe' and is given a much-needed $50. Marilyn thinks nothing more of the quick modelling job, but the resulting colour images that feature in two calendars – 'Golden Dreams' and 'A New Wrinkle' – would resurface three years later in a scandal that threatened her career.

In 1953, Hugh Hefner bought the rights to these photographs for $500 and ran them inside the launch issue of *Playboy*, while Marilyn was paid nothing for the centrefold. 'I was looking for something special for that first issue: because I had no money I needed something to promote it,' said Hefner. 'For someone of already some fame to be nude in a magazine was unprecedented.'[1]

The magazine was an instant success – its initial print run of 50,000 sold out – and Hefner went on to build an entire empire of soft porn on Marilyn, without her consent. 'I never even received a thank-you from all those who made millions off a nude

Marilyn photograph,' she said later. 'I even had to buy a copy of the magazine to see myself in it.'[2]

Although the founder of *Playboy* never met Monroe, she became the ultimate fantasy for him — even if it was not to be fulfilled until after his death in 2017 at the age of ninety-one. In 1992, Hefner bought the crypt next to Marilyn's at Westwood Village Memorial Park Cemetery for a reported $75,000. 'I'm a sucker for blondes, and she is the ultimate blonde,' he said. 'I will be laid to rest in a vault next to hers. It has a completion notion to it. I will be spending the rest of my eternity with Marilyn.'[3]

25

'Here's a skull now'

Imagine Marilyn playing the 'Alas, poor Yorick!' scene from *Hamlet*. The idea is not as far-fetched as it might seem. In fact, it's something she acted out in real life when she learned Aunt Ana Lower had died on 14 March 1948 from a heart problem. She was so devastated by the loss that, on the following day, she lay down on the deceased woman's bed for a few hours. Later, she drove out to a cemetery where she came across a couple of gravediggers who were in the process of excavating a fresh plot, complete with a ladder leading down into the earth. 'I asked if I could get down there and they said sure, and I went down and lay on the ground and looked up at the sky from there,' she said. 'It's quite a view, and the ground is cold under your back.'[1]

After Marilyn's death in August 1962, that same cemetery – Westwood Memorial Park – would serve as the star's final resting place.

26

THE MEN WHO MADE MARILYN

In the early days of her acting career Marilyn aligned herself with a trio of powerful, older men: 69-year-old Joseph M. Schenck, co-founder of Twentieth Century-Fox, whom she met in 1947; 32-year-old Fred Karger, her vocal coach at Columbia, who captured her heart in 1948; and 53-year-old agent Johnny Hyde, whom she dated between 1949 and 1950.

Marilyn was one of Schenck's 'gin-rummy girls', whom he invited to his Holmby Hills mansion. 'I was invited as an ornament,' she said, 'just someone to brighten the party.'[1] She always denied she was Schenck's lover, a view echoed by fellow actress Marion Marshall, who attended the same parties. 'As far as Joe goes, I think he was like a father to her,' she recalled. 'And I think that's all it was. He was a very wise, lovely old man.'[2] James Bond film producer Albert 'Cubby' Broccoli, a frequent guest at Schenck's, also supported this view. 'He just wanted to have this sweet and giving creature as a friend,' he said.[3]

Schenck gave Marilyn a chihuahua, which she called Josefa, a feminised version of his name. Marilyn by turn spoiled the dog, feeding it calves' liver and letting it sleep on a little satin pillow, and also neglected it: sometimes she would be too busy or lazy to take the dog out for walks; it limped for lack of exercise and occasionally the room in which it slept would become, in the words of Natasha Lytess, 'unbearable because of the dog's filth'.[4]

In contrast to Schenck, Marilyn fell desperately in love with Karger, who looked a little like the photograph of her father

Stanley Gifford that Gladys had once shown the young Norma Jeane. Marilyn regarded the handsome vocal coach as her first real love, discounting the feelings she'd had for Jim Dougherty, and she was desperate to marry him. But Karger, divorced with a young daughter, didn't think that the starlet was marriage material. He was also dismissive of what he regarded as Marilyn's inferior mind. 'You cry too easily,' he told her. 'That's because your mind isn't developed. Compared to your breasts, it's embryonic.'[5] However, after the breakdown of their relationship, Marilyn remained close friends with Karger's mother Anne and his sister Mary; both women attended Marilyn's funeral.

The affair was short-lived, but the loss of Karger made Marilyn so unhappy that she ran straight into the arms of another man. The transfer of her affections was so rapid that Natasha Lytess commented, '*On chasse un clou avec un autre*,' which translates as 'One nail drives out another.'[6]

The nail that drove Karger from Marilyn's mind was Johnny Hyde, the man who was responsible more than any other for making her a star. 'He had faith in her when she was a starlet and a damn unimportant starlet,' said film producer Arthur Hornblow Jr. 'When you had Johnny in your corner, you had a pipeline to the guys who really count in Hollywood. He made this town Marilyn Monroe conscious.'[7]

Hyde was a diminutive but dynamic presence in Hollywood. Born Iván Haidabura in 1895, the son of Russian-Jewish vaudeville performers, he arrived in America with his family as a three-year-old boy; drive, determination and a zeal for hustle led him to be rewarded with the position of vice president at the William Morris Agency's West Coast office, managing the careers of stars such as Lana Turner and Rita Hayworth. Soon after meeting Marilyn, at the end of 1948, he became obsessed with the young actress. The age difference between them was thirty-one years – he was fifty-three and she was twenty-two. In the spring of 1949, he left his wife and family for Marilyn. 'It's happened and I can't do anything about it,' Hyde told his wife Mozelle. He set up home on North Palm Drive in Beverly Hills, while Marilyn took an apartment at the Beverly Carlton Hotel (now the Avalon).

'He said I would be a very big star,' Marilyn said later. 'I remember laughing and saying it didn't look like it, because I couldn't make enough to eat three squares. He explained something to me that I had not realized before – that if you are a star it is hard to find little roles. They either have to give you a star part, even if it isn't big, or nothing.'[8]

Hyde began to transform his younger lover and new client, booking her for regular sessions at the beauty salon – her hair needed straightening and regular colouring to keep its platinum sheen – and a consultation with Beverly Hills cosmetic surgeons Dr John Pangman and Dr Michael Gurdin. In 2018, Dr Gurdin's medical notes about his famous patient, together with facial X-rays, came up for auction at Julien's in Hollywood; the documents sold for $25,600. The file revealed that Marilyn had undergone a chin implant in 1950, but despite the rumours, there was no evidence to show that she had a bump from the tip of her nose removed.

One day at a party, Marilyn had overheard someone describe her as a 'chinless wonder'. After examining her the doctors thought she had a 'mild flatness of the chin' and could benefit from a small chin implant, which at that time was made out of cow cartilage. It is claimed that Marilyn – who was due to take a screen test for a forthcoming film – postponed the test by saying she'd fallen and hurt her chin. When she turned up on set the director is reported to have said, 'Honey, you should have cut your chin two years ago.'[9]

Now her agent, Hyde had grand plans for Marilyn and he began to tout her around Hollywood. 'Johnny was a little fellow, but he had an eye for beauty, and he was trying to get anybody to hire her,' recalled screenwriter and producer Nunnally Johnson. 'I daresay I might have hired her if I'd had any picture with a part small enough to justify a girl who had no experience.'[10] Hyde refused to accept defeat; he managed to persuade John Huston to let her read for a small part in *The Asphalt Jungle* and helped secure her a role in Joseph L. Mankiewicz's smash hit *All About Eve*.

In both films, she plays a blonde on the make. In *The Asphalt Jungle* she is Angela Phinlay; in *All About Eve* she is Miss Casswell, who, in the words of cynical theatre critic Addison DeWitt (played by George Sanders), is 'a graduate of the Copacabana school of the dramatic arts'. There were many who thought the same about Marilyn. Hyde, who negotiated a $500 a week contract for Marilyn at Twentieth Century-Fox, wanted to marry her. He repeatedly told her that if she became his wife he would make sure that she would inherit a sizeable chunk of his fortune. Sickly since a child, and plagued by a heart condition, he guessed he didn't have that much time left. But Marilyn refused. 'There were two words that she feared more than anything else in the world – and that was home wrecker,' said Amy Greene. 'And the reason she didn't marry Johnny Hyde was because he was married – she didn't want to hurt the woman; she didn't want to hurt the children.'[11]

Of course, there were others who saw it differently, interpreting Marilyn's behaviour as manipulative. 'I tried to take it for a long time, but in the end, it was impossible,' said Hyde's wife Mozelle.[12] In December 1950, Natasha Lytess remembered taking a phone call from Hyde, who was ill with heart failure. He was desperate to see Marilyn but he couldn't get hold of her. 'I've been waiting, waiting,' he told her. 'Natasha, never in all my life have I known such cruelty, such selfishness.'[13] He died in Palm Springs on 18 December 1950, aged fifty-five. Hyde 'died like a hero', joked Nunnally Johnson, 'because Johnny had a heart attack, and the doctor told Johnny by leading a quieter life that he had a life probability of a good many years, but leading a proper life meant not sleeping with Marilyn Monroe. Johnny died like a man.'[14]

Marilyn's reaction to Hyde's death was extreme. Some reports claim that at his funeral at Forest Lawn, she screamed Johnny's name over and over again. 'It shook everyone,' recalled Hyde's son Jimmy.[15] Soon after, Marilyn took an overdose. In her unpublished memoir, Natasha Lytess – who was sharing a home with Marilyn on North Harper Avenue, West Hollywood – recalled the moment she returned to the house and found Marilyn in bed.

I ran to my room and found a note on my pillow. 'I leave my car and my fur stole to Natasha.' On the door of Marilyn's room another note read 'Don't let Barbara [Natasha's small daughter] come in.' The door was shut, perhaps locked, I don't remember. I hit it with all my weight. The room looked like hell on earth. Marilyn was in bed, undressed, her cheeks puffed out like an adder ... I jammed her mouth open and reached in and took out a handful of wet, greenish stuff she hadn't yet swallowed. On the night table was an empty bottle that had contained the sleeping pills.[16]

27

THE WOMAN WHO MADE MARILYN

Can Lytess's account be trusted? According to Milton Greene, who between 1955 and 1957 served as vice president of Marilyn Monroe Productions and became a close friend of the star, this particular detail in Lytess's unpublished manuscript is an embellishment of the truth. If we believe Greene, Marilyn told him that the 'wet, greenish stuff' that Lytess wrenched from her mouth was nothing more than the remnants of a sleeping pill. The suggestion is that Lytess exaggerated the incident so as to cast herself as a heroine, Marilyn's saviour.

There's another possible interpretation. Could Lytess have projected onto Marilyn something of her own personal history? In February 1943, when she was working as an actress and living at 1306 1/2 North Harper Avenue, Natasha took an overdose of sleeping pills herself. She was discovered lying unconscious in bed by friends and taken to West Hollywood Hospital. According to a police source quoted in the *Los Angeles Times*, 'Miss Lytess was upset due to personal reasons and had mistakenly taken too many tablets in order to get some rest.'[1]

No doubt the sting of rejection coloured Lytess's recollections: when she sat down with ghostwriter Jane Wilkie at the end of the 1950s to compile her short memoir of her eight years working with the actress, she was speaking as yet another person cast into the dark outer reaches of the Marilyn universe. (In 1956, the relationship between the two reached crisis point when Marilyn employed another acting coach – Paula Strasberg – and delegated the news of Natasha's dismissal to a lawyer.)

Certainly, reading Lytess's *My Years With Marilyn* one gets the feeling that she wrote from the perspective of someone who had once been infatuated with her subject but who now suffered from the frequent miseries of banishment.

Lytess regarded herself as an essential part of Marilyn's success. And it's true that over the course of the years that they worked together – from *Ladies of the Chorus* in 1948 to *The Seven Year Itch* in 1955 – Marilyn's acting skills improved dramatically. It's also true that Marilyn felt so attached to Lytess that she demanded her presence on set and looked to her – rather than the director – for guidance.

When the acting coach first met Marilyn in early 1948, she was distinctly unimpressed. 'She was more than inhibited, more than cramped,' she recalled. 'She couldn't say a word freely. Her habit of speaking without using her lips was unnatural, obviously superimposed. Her voice, a piping sort of whimper, got so on my nerves that I asked her not to speak unnecessarily until we had progressed.'[2] Lytess worked hard with Marilyn on technique, telling her that she had to regard her body and voice as instruments controlled by the rigours of the mind. Control was essential, she said. But soon after she began teaching her, Lytess realised that the young woman had little strength of purpose, a problem that she believed stemmed from her psychological insecurities. 'You are too negative about yourself,' Lytess told her. 'You must throw out this insecurity, this guilt complex. You must learn to love instead of hate yourself. You must grow up.'[3] Marilyn was also bad at learning lines, she claimed, because she was lazy.

Lytess saw Marilyn as a cross between a siren and a chameleon, who used a heightened sense of intuition to reflect back to any person exactly what they wanted to hear or see. She said Marilyn would absorb other people's views and opinions, often without quite understanding their meaning. Lytess began to style her, encouraging her to dress in a less sexual manner. She also began to educate her in the Russian novelists Tolstoy and Dostoevsky, and classical music such as that of Brahms and Schubert.

It soon became obvious to the coach that her protégé kept many aspects of herself secret. She came to think of Marilyn as a 'veiled woman',[4] and noticed that when she was being particularly guarded she would weave her right hand back and forth like a serpent dancing in the air, 'a gesture of evasiveness and of survival through expediency'.[5] Yet Marilyn could be extraordinarily generous. Once, when the two were shopping for antiques, Natasha commented on how much she liked an old cameo brooch, which Marilyn subsequently bought for her. When Lytess needed a quick cash injection of $1,000 to pay some debts, Marilyn sold the fur coat given to her by Johnny Hyde and gave her the money.

According to Jane Russell, who witnessed the acting coach at work on the set of *Gentlemen Prefer Blondes* (1953), Lytess 'was utterly dedicated to Marilyn – she ate, slept and breathed Marilyn'.[6] And it was this – Natasha's dedication to and obsession with the star – that resulted in her downfall, as she herself realised. 'My work had not been that of a mere coach,' she wrote. 'I had carried her step by step on a thorny road. I had been her private director for long eras, working with her day and night. What I had given her, no money could buy, and by this time she was the only thing that protected me.'[7] Their relationship deteriorated after Marilyn met and then married Joe DiMaggio in 1954, and Natasha went through 'hell' when the star didn't contact her for five long months. When Marilyn returned to Hollywood to make *There's No Business Like Show Business*, Natasha realised that something had changed between them; she felt as though Marilyn had become a 'stranger'. One night, Marilyn turned up at Natasha's house in her Cadillac and the two women had a heart to heart.

'I want to love you, but you make it difficult,' Natasha said.

Marilyn's reply was professional and to the point. 'You don't have to love me, Natasha,' she said, 'as long as you will work with me.'[8]

There are some who believe that this 'love' was more than just maternal or professional and that it tipped over into the sexual. According to Marilyn's New York maid Lena Pepitone, the star told her that she'd slept with Lytess. '"I was so confused back then, I'd let any guy, or girl, do what they wanted if I thought they were my friend,"' Pepitone claims she said. But over time, Lytess became increasingly jealous of Marilyn's relationships with men. '"She [Natasha] thought she was my husband,"' Marilyn supposedly told Pepitone. '"She was a great teacher, but that part of it ruined things for us. I got scared of her, had to get away."'[9]

According to Marilyn's friend Henry Rosenfeld, Lytess would say about her famous protégé, 'If I had a cock, I'd never lose her,' a reference to the fact that Marilyn was not attracted to her own sex. 'Marilyn liked men,' Rosenfeld maintained.[10]

James Haspiel, the fan who has built up an enormous archive of Marilyn material, is sceptical about such rumours. 'I'm not saying that it couldn't happen, I'm saying that I don't believe that it happened,' he says. 'I believe Natasha Lytess became so vindictive when that relationship, the professional relationship, ended. I have in my archive a twenty-minute interview with Lytess on film and one of the things she says repeatedly – something like twenty times during those twenty minutes – is Marilyn Monroe was not beautiful. That's [a sign of] meanness. Marilyn was so incredibly discreet about so many things it is possible that the lesbian factor – because she [Lytess] herself was apparently lesbian – contributed to Marilyn ending the relationship. Maybe Natasha was approaching her, and maybe that was not welcome.'[11]

28

AN INTIMATE ENCOUNTER WITH BRIGITTE BARDOT

Since Marilyn's death, her name has been linked romantically with a number of famous leading ladies. Biographer Lois Banner recounts an anecdote from Sidney Skolsky's 1975 memoir *Don't Get Me Wrong – I Love Hollywood*, in which Marilyn was often visited on set by 'noted actresses ... really lesbians on the make'. She was even sent flowers by a 'well-known actress, noted for her stylish, masculine wardrobe'; Banner surmises that the mystery woman was Marlene Dietrich.[1] But what Banner fails to account for is what Skolsky writes next: 'Marilyn read the card that accompanied the flowers, refused to put them in a vase to keep, and tossed the flowers in the nearest wastebasket. She was not at all ready for Gay Liberation. In fact, romantic overtures from gay women frightened her.'[2]

Cultural wish fulfilment also plays its part in these kinds of stories, a desire to imagine an erotic goddess of Marilyn's stature engaging in the clichéd heterosexual male fantasy: two women having sex with one another. Perhaps the most eye-opening rumour is of a thirty-second clinch between Marilyn and Brigitte Bardot in the ladies' toilets of the Empire Leicester Square during a reception for Her Majesty Queen Elizabeth on 29 October 1956. Marilyn, in England with her third husband Arthur Miller for the filming of *The Prince and the Showgirl* (1957), had been invited to the Royal Command Performance of *The Battle of the River Plate*, along with a host of celebrities, including the 22-year-old Bardot. That night Marilyn was wearing a gold lamé dress, complete with topaz straps and a gold cape, and a pair of long white gloves; in short, not the kind of ensemble that would lend itself easily to a quick fumble in the ladies' before being presented to royalty.

So how did such an absurd rumour begin? Bardot, writing in her 1996 autobiography, confesses her rapture on meeting Marilyn. The encounter did indeed take place in the toilets of the Empire Leicester Square, and Brigitte was breathy in her description of her fellow blonde, noting her ravishing gold dress and her beautiful skin. '*C'était la première et la dernière fois de ma vie que je la voyais, mais elle m'a séduite en trente secondes,*' she writes, which translates as, 'This was the first and the last time that I saw her, but she seduced me in thirty seconds.'[3] It's clear from reading this that the 'seduction' that took place was on a purely aesthetic level, and that the rumour-mongers misconstrued what happened due to a case of extreme literal-mindedness, an inability to read French, or perhaps an unfortunate combination of the two.

Joan Crawford is another star who is often rumoured to have slept with Marilyn. The origin of the supposed liaison can be traced back to Fred Lawrence Guiles's 1984 biography *Legend: The Life and Death of Marilyn Monroe*, in which he writes, 'No sooner had she extricated herself from her entanglement with Natasha than she became involved in a serious friendship with Joan Crawford.'[4] In her ghostwritten memoir *My Story*, Marilyn tells of their initial meeting at a dinner party thrown by Joe Schenck where Crawford, wearing a 'beautiful evening gown', offered to give the young starlet advice on how to present herself: she told her that the white knitted dress she wore that night was 'utterly incorrect for a dinner of this kind'.[5] After observing Marilyn at church – Joan was also a devotee of Christian Science – Crawford criticised her grey suit with its black trimming and her flat heels. 'The main thing about dressing well,' Crawford informed her when she invited Marilyn out to her elegant house in Brentwood Park, 'is to see that everything you wear is just right – that your shoes, stockings, gloves and bag all fit the suit you're wearing.'[6] The star of *Mildred Pierce* told Marilyn to make a list of all the things in her wardrobe, but the younger woman couldn't bring herself to tell Crawford that she had already seen all the clothes in her possession.

In his biography, Guiles claims a 'slightly drunk' Crawford made a 'sexual pass at Marilyn and the friendship abruptly ended. Marilyn, who saw nothing wrong with lesbianism, recoiled more from shock than offense.'[7] Crawford's biographer David Bret is sceptical about the possibility of this seduction, but his dismissal of Crawford's interest in the younger Marilyn – there were seventeen years between them – is based on nothing more than the two women's differing attitudes towards their personal hygiene. 'Joan's extreme fastidiousness – showering several times daily – and Marilyn's already legendary propensity towards dreadful manners and *lack* of cleanliness – never wearing underwear, even during her monthly cycle,' he writes.[8]

If one believes these rumours, it was Marilyn's rejection of Joan that prompted Crawford's vicious remarks following Marilyn's appearance at the *Photoplay* awards held at the Beverly Hills Hotel on 9 February 1953. That night, the young star had to be sewn into a spectacularly tight and spectacularly low-cut gold lamé dress. Its designer, Billy Travilla, pleaded with Marilyn not to wear it, but she insisted, and proceeded to drop a couple of dress sizes by an excessive regime of colonic irrigation. As Marilyn walked to the stage of the Crystal Room to pick up her award for Fastest Rising Star of 1952, the audience went wild; the men wolf-whistled their appreciation and Jerry Lewis, one of the masters of ceremonies, threw himself onto a table in imitation of an overexcitable chimpanzee. 'Marilyn Monroe stole the show last night at the *Photoplay* awards banquet ... and she did it with one little twist of her derriere,' said Florabel Muir.[9] But Joan – who felt her star was now fading – was left seething.

'It was like a burlesque show,' said Crawford in a widely syndicated article. She claimed that Marilyn's recently released film *Niagara* (1953) was doing disappointing business at the box office, 'and I'll tell you why. Sex plays a tremendously important part in every person's life,' she said. 'People are ... intrigued with it. But they don't like to see it flaunted in their faces.' Without evidence, Crawford said that the 'kids' didn't like Marilyn because they didn't like to see sex exploited, and neither did she appeal to women. 'The publicity has gone too far. And apparently Miss Monroe is making the mistake of believing her publicity ... She should be told that the public likes provocative feminine personalities, but it also likes to know that underneath it all, the actresses are ladies.'[10]

It's said that Joan put it even more bluntly when she told one reporter, 'There is nothing wrong with my tits, but I don't go around throwing them in people's faces.'[11]

In 2005, the story of Marilyn and Joan's alleged sexual relationship resurfaced again with the release of the 'Marilyn tapes', transcripts of audio recordings that the star was supposed to have made for her psychiatrist Dr Greenson, in the days leading up to her death. 'We went to her house from a cocktail party,' Marilyn is supposed to have said. 'We went to the bedroom and went down on each other. Credit Natasha. She could teach more than acting. Next time I saw Crawford she wanted another round. I told her straight out I didn't much enjoy doing it with a woman. After I turned her down, she became spiteful.'[12]

This conversation is meant to provide the definite proof that Marilyn engaged in sexual activity with both Natasha Lytess and Joan Crawford. Only there's a problem. The tapes don't exist. The so-called transcripts were released by John W. Miner, the deputy district attorney who was present at Marilyn's autopsy. In 2003,

Miner made the sensational claim that, on condition he never reveal the contents, Greenson had played him this secret tape of Marilyn free associating on various topics. He said he then went home and – from memory – wrote down its contents.

In 1995, Miner tried to sell the transcript of the 'tapes' to *Vanity Fair* magazine, claiming that he possessed between seventy and eighty pages of handwritten notes he had made 'in a sort of shorthand' back in 1962. Marilyn biographer and *Vanity Fair* contributor Anthony Summers was brought in to help verify the story. But after Summers flew from his home in Ireland to the East Coast of America, Miner produced only thirty-five pages of 'cursive narrative' on a yellow legal pad. 'Original notes containing "exact quotes," Miner said, were in storage,' stated Summers. 'He would look for them. He never produced the notes, conceded that he had put the 35 pages together only recently, and accounted for their astonishing detail by saying he was gifted with a remarkable memory – and had virtually total recall of audiotapes he had heard more than 30 years earlier! Neither I nor the editors at *Vanity Fair* thought such vaporous stuff merited publication.'[13]

Yet this did not stop Miner from selling the rights to the 'transcribed tapes' to author Matthew Smith, who used them in his 2003 book *Victim: The Secret Tapes of Marilyn Monroe*, in which he argued that the star had been murdered and that her death was brought about by the administration of a poisonous enema. 'I believe he is a man of integrity,' said Smith of Miner. 'I've looked at the contents of the tapes, of course, and, frankly, I would think it entirely impossible for John Miner to have invented what he put forward – absolutely impossible.'[14] However, when Summers did a background check he discovered that Miner 'had been the subject of a bankruptcy case in 1996, just months after he had come to me with the purported Monroe material. The following year, John W. Miner was suspended from the practice of law for a period by California's state bar, and placed on probation for two years.'[15]

29

THE 'DUMB BLONDE' AND THE BRAIN BOX

In 1951, after moving out of Natasha Lytess's home, Marilyn was sharing a two-bedroom apartment on Holloway Drive, Hollywood, with fellow actress Shelley Winters. One Sunday morning, while listening to classical music on Shelley's Capehart record player and flicking through a copy of the *Academy Players' Directory* – a résumé of actors' careers accompanied by their photographs – Winters turned to her flatmate and said, 'I wonder why we put ourselves through this agony called love.' Marilyn, who had just broken up from an unhappy affair with an unnamed lover, replied, 'Wouldn't it be nice to be like men and just get notches in your belt and sleep with the most attractive men and not get emotionally involved?' Shelley hated the double standards that applied to women and agreed that they should be able to be free to have sex with anyone they found attractive, just like men. 'What a wonderful idea,' Marilyn said, taking up the copy of the actors' directory. 'Let's get pencil and paper and go through the *Directory* and make lists.'

After an hour, the two young women had compiled their lists of ideal lovers. On Shelley's roll call were Clark Gable, Peter Finch, James Mason, Cary Grant and Laurence Olivier, mostly 'handsome actors I had fantasized about when I was an adolescent'. On Marilyn's list there was a different calibre of men, more known for their intellect than for being beefcake: Zero Mostel, Eli Wallach, Lee Strasberg, Nick Ray, John Huston, Yves Montand, Ernest Hemingway, Charles Laughton, Clifford Odets, Arthur Miller and Albert Einstein.

'Marilyn, there's no way you can sleep with Albert Einstein,' said Shelley. 'He's the most famous scientist of this century, and besides, he's an old man.' (In 1951, he was seventy-two.)

'That has nothing to do with it,' Marilyn replied. 'I hear he's very healthy.'

In Winters's autobiography, published in 1980, the actress remembers visiting the apartment of Lee Strasberg, Marilyn's acting coach who inherited many of the star's possessions. There, sitting on top of Marilyn's mother's white piano, was a photograph of Einstein which bore the inscription: 'To Marilyn, with respect and love and thanks, Albert Einstein.'[1] It seems as though Winters believed that it was certainly possible that Marilyn and Einstein were lovers. 'She respected intellect,' she said later. 'She was attracted [to] father figures, older men who are very smart.'[2] In 1989, Winters told the chat show host David Letterman that Marilyn didn't really like any man under fifty years old, adding, 'I would guess given his [Einstein's] white hair and everything, it happened.'[3] In 1993, Winters told Ruby Wax, 'How did he think of the theory of relativity? – she inspired him.'[4]

Despite the delightful absurdity of the idea, the truth is that Marilyn and Albert never enjoyed a secret tryst. The handwriting on the signed photograph does not belong to Einstein; instead, the inscription was scribbled by Marilyn's friend and *The Misfits* co-star Eli Wallach, who sent it to her as a joke after the actress had given him a volume of the physicist's letters. Even so, there's something so alluring about the encounter of these two archetypes – one the embodiment of physical beauty, the other a symbol of the intellect – that it gave rise to a 1982 play by Terry Johnson, *Insignificance*, which was made into a film, directed by Nicolas Roeg, three years later. In the film, Marilyn – using a series of model trains, a magazine with the image of a car on the front, a flashlight and a toy figure of Charlie Chaplin as props – explains the theory of relativity to Einstein, who looks on admiringly.

The speech goes on for a page and a half of dialogue before she concludes:

Actress: However, the main point I have demonstrated is that all measurements of time and space are necessarily made relative to the observer, and are not necessarily the same for two independent observers. That is the Specific Theory of Relativity! Isn't it?

Professor: Yes it is.

[She sighs a huge sigh of relief and falls back on the bed.]

Actress: Now you have to show me your legs.[5]

A meeting between the 'blonde' and the 'boffin' also mutated into an urban myth that goes like this: Marilyn and Einstein are seated next to one another at a dinner party. After a couple of glasses of champagne, Marilyn leans over to Albert and whispers into his ear, 'I would love to have your child. With my looks and your brains, it will be a perfect child.'

Einstein replies, 'But what if it has my looks and your brains?'

30

THE QUEST FOR SELF-IMPROVEMENT

Marilyn – a high school drop-out – wasn't stupid, but she felt her lack of education keenly. One day in April 1950, with her friend Shelley Winters, she met the Welsh poet Dylan Thomas, who was visiting America on a reading tour. Although it was obvious that Thomas was attracted to Marilyn, he did not make a pass at her. He 'seemed aware that behind the eyelashes and platinum hair and terrific body, there was a fragile and sensitive girl,' said Winters. Thomas sensed that 'she very badly needed not to be thought of as just a tits-and-ass cutie'. That night, after dinner, they had arranged to drive Thomas up to Charlie Chaplin's house – the poet was keen to meet the star and director of *Modern Times* and *The Great Dictator* – on Summit Ridge Drive, but Marilyn decided not to go. 'It was a long time before Marilyn ever felt intelligent enough to mix socially with important intelligent people, if she ever did,' said Winters.[1]

Realising that she often found herself out of her depth in conversations, Marilyn became determined to educate herself. When Winters first met her at the Studio Club in the late 1940s, she noticed that the softly spoken Norma Jeane (as she still was then) carried about with her a large library book such as an encyclopaedia or dictionary. There were others who noticed that she was on an accelerated quest for self-improvement. 'I think what she wanted from me was my education,' said Scottish-born photographer Bill Burnside, who met Marilyn in 1946. 'She was into Shelley and Keats, as well as some lighter stuff. She knew that she needed knowledge.'² Jane Russell, who starred with Marilyn in *Gentlemen Prefer Blondes* – which features the knock-out number 'Diamonds Are a Girl's Best Friend' – stated, 'Diamonds were never of interest to Marilyn. She would rather collect and read a library of good books.'³

During Marilyn's 1949 publicity tour for *Love Happy* – which took her to eight cities including New York, Chicago, Cleveland and Detroit – it was reported that in her spare time she was reading the novels of Thomas Wolfe and Proust, as well as Freud's work on dreams and their interpretation. She had a seemingly insatiable desire for culture and a curiosity that took others by surprise. 'Every now and then I go into the Pickwick [the bookshop in Beverly Hills] and just look around,' she told Joseph L. Mankiewicz, the director of *All About Eve*. He had been taken aback while, one day on set, he caught her reading Rilke's *Letters to a Young Poet*. The next day, Marilyn sent Mankiewicz a copy, a gesture that is said to have prompted him to say that he would have been 'less taken aback to come across Herr Rilke studying a Marilyn Monroe nude calendar'.⁴

Marilyn's quest to educate herself took another turn in January 1951 when, during the filming of *As Young as You Feel*, she began an affair with the actor and director Elia Kazan, or Gadge as his friends called him. He'd first met her the year before with Johnny Hyde, and at a house party of agent and producer Charlie Feldman he learned that she was now single. 'The men around Charlie considered Marilyn Monroe a kid to pass around and someone now available,' he said. 'But apparently she'd been true to Johnny and was now completely broken up by his death. The tribal report had been confirmed: No one had scored there yet. She hadn't even gone out with anyone, which puzzled these men.'⁵ Kazan, together with Arthur Miller, turned up on the set of *As Young as You Feel*, where they observed her crying in a corner, grieving for Hyde who had died three weeks previously. Kazan introduced himself as a friend and former client of Johnny's and finally persuaded her to accept his offer of dinner. The more he got to know her, the more he realised that she had a depth to her that he found surprising. 'When I met her, she was a simple young woman who rode a bike to the classes she was taking, a decent-hearted kid whom Hollywood brought down, legs parted,' he said. 'She had a thin skin and a soul that hungered for acceptance by people she might look up to.'[6] They often spent nights together at Feldman's house – in a bedroom that had its own entrance to the street – and Marilyn would weep as she told him stories about her past. 'I gave her comfort,' said Kazan. 'She had a bomb inside her. Ignite her and she exploded. Her lover was her saviour.'[7]

In 1955, Kazan confessed his feelings for Marilyn in a letter to his long-suffering wife Molly, who regarded the actress as nothing more than a 'little dizzy character' and a 'freak'.[8] 'She was talented, funny, vulnerable, helpless in awful pain, with no hope, and some worth and not a liar, not vicious, not catty, and with a history of orphanism that was killing to hear,' wrote Kazan. 'She was like all Charlie Chaplin's heroines in one. I'm not ashamed at all, not a damn bit of having been attracted to her. She is nothing like what she appears to be now, or even appears to have turned out . . . She was a little stray cat when I knew her, total possessions a few clothes, and one piano.'[9]

Soon after the affair began, Kazan wrote a lengthy letter to the young actress. It covered her previous relationships with her first husband Jim Dougherty – who 'had no real use for you except to make him fall asleep fast' – lover Fred Karger, who 'said you were only good for one thing', and 'the best of the three' Johnny Hyde, who Kazan later described as having a small penis. Kazan went on to give Marilyn advice. He urged her to do the necessary work to become a professional actress; she needed to get her own place and improve herself. 'You piss away too much time on the telephone with idiots, being photographed by idiots, etc., riding around, christ knows doing what ... keep at least six hours of EVERY FUCKING SINGLE GODDAMN day for yourself. Doing what you want to do, not what other people want you to do,' he said. He told her to rid herself of her acting coach Natasha Lytess and steer clear of people like the louche actor and producer Pat DiCicco. It was important that she should be proud of herself and he urged her to read Emerson's essay on self-reliance. She shouldn't dye her hair too much and neither should she let people dress her in 'floozie' outfits. It was imperative to speak up, and have confidence in herself. 'Don't take any shit from anyone. But listen to everyone's point of view.'[10]

Marilyn took Kazan's letter seriously and, in April 1951, she enrolled on a course at UCLA entitled Backgrounds of Literature. Each Thursday she would travel downtown and between seven and nine in the evening she would listen to her lecturer, Claire Soule, talk about classic novels, plays and poetry. Although she tried to keep a low profile, it was difficult – just before the course started, on 29 March, she had presented an Oscar at the Pantages Theatre – and her fellow students began to stare at her. When Miss Soule enquired about why her pupils seemed to be fixated on the young woman, she was amazed to find out that Marilyn was famous. 'Why, I thought you were a young girl straight out of the convent,' it is claimed she said.[11]

In early 1952, when Philippe Halsman went to photograph Marilyn for a *Life* magazine cover, he was surprised to find her cheap one-bedroom apartment alive with culture. There was an image of the Italian actress Eleonora Duse, famous for her roles in the plays of Ibsen and Gabriele d'Annunzio. 'Thinking it was just an affectation, I asked her about Duse and learned to my surprise that she knew everything about her,' said Halsman later. He also noticed that her shelves contained works about the history of Fabian socialism, 'the Negro in American literature', some of the classics and books by intellectual heavyweights. 'I realised that here was a girl not satisfied with what nature or education had given her and who worked all the time trying to improve herself,' he said.[12]

There were many who sneered and mocked Marilyn for her interest in highbrow culture – symptomatic, of course, of the failure to understand that a woman could be both sexy *and* intelligent. 'She *reads*, doesn't she?' the playwright Clifford Odets asked Arthur Miller, 'as though she were a prize gazelle or a genius chimp.'[13] One interviewer even subjected Marilyn to a fake 'intelligence' test, the journalist firing off a number of questions which hoped 'to prove that she has an I.Q. along with the S.A.'. Could she define heat? What was the principle of the atom bomb? How many stomachs has a cow? How long does a whale stay under water? And what were the twelve labours of Hercules? These were just a few of the questions put to her. Marilyn knew, of course, that the accumulation of knowledge was different to natural intelligence. 'Because I have had so little education, I know my limitations,' she said. 'While I want to be neither a quiz kid nor a pseudo-intellectual, I would like to know what makes things tick.'[14]

Arthur Miller – introduced to Marilyn by his friend Elia Kazan in early 1951 on the set of *As Young as You Feel* – remembered accompanying her to a bookshop years before they married, where she bought the works of poets E. E. Cummings, Robert Frost and Walt Whitman. He understood that her image – constructed by herself, the studios and the press – was so powerful that it resulted in a fundamental dissonance between the reality of her personality and the range of elaborate fantasies projected onto her. 'She was a poet on a street corner trying to recite to a crowd pulling at her clothes,' he said.[15] Even when she was browsing in the bookshop that day, and wearing nothing at all provocative, she attracted the unpleasant attention of a fellow shopper who was staring at her and masturbating in his trousers. Miller led her away so she didn't see the voyeur and instead tried to engage her with a reading of Cummings's poetry.

At some point in the early 1950s, Marilyn started to write poetry herself. Her friend Norman Rosten – whose work would appear in the *New Yorker* and who would write the libretto for the 1993 opera *Marilyn* by Ezra Laderman – described her as having the instinct and reflexes of a poet, but that she lacked control. 'She knew the interior floating world of the poem with its secrets, phantoms and surprises,' he said.[16] The quality of her verse varies, but the opening of one of her better poems is reminiscent of something written by a young Sylvia Plath:

Life –
I am both of your directions.[17]

When Marilyn's collection of over four hundred books was auctioned at Christie's in 1999, it was discovered that she owned collections of poetry by A. E. Houseman, Shelley, Blake, Shakespeare's sonnets, Lorca, Browning, Burns and Edna St Vincent Millay. Despite many believing that Marilyn's interest in literature was nothing but a superficial pose, many of the books contained pencil annotations, inserted bookmarks and notations, evidence that she engaged deeply with their contents. The other volumes in her library included classics by Aristophanes, Plato and Plutarch; Russians including Chekhov, Turgenev and Pushkin; American authors such as Twain, Steinbeck, Hemingway and Whitman; the lives of Adolf Eichmann, Colette and Carl Sandburg's twelve-volume biography of Abraham Lincoln (one of her heroes); and twentieth-century works by Proust, Camus, Thomas Mann, D. H. Lawrence and James Joyce.

There's a famous 1955 photograph taken by Eve Arnold of Marilyn sitting in a children's playground, wearing a striped bathing suit, reading a battered copy of *Ulysses* given to her by Eli Wallach. From where the book is open, it seems likely Marilyn is reading Molly Bloom's stream of consciousness soliloquy at the end of Joyce's 1922 novel. 'I asked her what she was reading when I went to pick her up (I was trying to get an idea of how she spent her time),' recalled Arnold. 'She said she kept *Ulysses* in her car and had been reading it for a long time. She said she loved the sound of the sentences and would read it aloud to herself to try to make sense of it – but she found it hard going. She couldn't read it consecutively. When we stopped at a local playground to photograph she got out the book and started to read while I loaded the film.'[18]

Another of her favourite books was Antoine de Saint-Exupéry's *The Little Prince*. On his birthday, Marilyn gave her second husband Joe DiMaggio a gold medal for his watch chain, inscribed with the following quotation from Saint-Exupéry's strange, philosophical masterpiece: 'True love is visible not to the eyes, but to the heart, for eyes may be deceived.' When presented with the love token, DiMaggio turned to Marilyn and said, 'What the hell does that mean?'[19]

31

ALL-AMERICAN HERO – OR ... A PENIS WITH A MAN HANGING FROM IT

So why did Marilyn – clever, curious, culture-loving Marilyn – fall for and then marry the baseball star Joe DiMaggio, whose idea of a good time was a night slumped in front of the TV? There are some who say it was because of the size of his manhood. 'The best way to describe Joe DiMaggio is [that] he was a penis with a man hanging from it,' said fellow baseball star Pete Rose, who entertained the troops with DiMaggio in Vietnam.[1] Another friend said he was so 'well hung' that apparently prostitutes 'retreated' when they caught sight of him naked.[2] 'She always said there was no one in her life who was as good in bed as Joe was,' said Marilyn's friend Amy Greene.[3] And according to one of DiMaggio's closest friends, the New York foot surgeon Dr Rock G. Positano, Joe said that 'Marilyn told me that no man ever satisfied her like I did'.[4]

There are others who describe Marilyn's attraction to the sportsman – whom she called her 'slugger' – as being based on a shared understanding of what it was like to endure a difficult childhood. She herself stated that she was drawn to him because of his 'sensitive nature'; the baseball player had endured 'a very difficult time when he was young,' she said. 'So he understood something about me, and I understood something about him, and we based our marriage on this.'[5]

When Marilyn first met Joe, in early 1952, she was surprised that her assumptions about him – that he would be brash, loud and uncouth – proved to be unfounded. Born in 1914 into a poor family who had emigrated from Sicily, and raised in San Francisco, Joe had been a shy boy. During a meal at a Hollywood restaurant, Marilyn thought him 'reserved', the kind of man who on first impression was more likely to be a congressman or a steel magnate than a baseball star. 'His silence wasn't an act,' she said. 'It was his way of being himself.'[6]

Both these attributes – his status as a well-endowed man, his reserved demeanour – may be true, but something else was happening in Marilyn's life in the early 1950s that made it advantageous for her to align herself with an all-American hero like Joe DiMaggio. She realised that the baseball player, who was regarded as something of a god for his records on the field, could help her win a public relations battle. If she played her cards right, she could use him to establish herself as a star at Twentieth Century-Fox, and secure her place in the hearts of the movie-going public.

Marilyn had developed a talent for image manipulation, befriending photographers, the studio's PR men and charming newspaper columnists such as Sidney Skolsky and Earl Wilson. But she knew that wasn't enough. After a dozen or so small or supporting roles in films, if she wanted to be a star – a real star – she knew that she needed a greater degree of public recognition. What she did was high risk, but if she pulled it off it could guarantee her top billing and the attention of the masses. As she was filming *Clash by Night* in September 1951, Marilyn contacted Tom Kelley – the man who had shot her risqué nude calendar back in 1949 – and dropped by to have another look at the photographs. Tom's wife Natalie, who had been present at the shoot, showed Marilyn the 1952 calendar and remembered later that the actress was not at all shocked. Rather, she regarded the photographs with the dispassionate eye of a true professional. 'Just looked at it as though she were looking at a stranger,' said Natalie. 'She was proud of it.' Marilyn put in an order for twenty-five calendars and began to distribute them on the set of *Clash by Night*, gifting some to her coterie of reporters and photographers. 'How do you like my new hairdo?' she scrawled across the calendar she presented to Earl Wilson. 'Dumb? I should say not,' said Natalie Kelley. 'That girl knew her stuff.'[7]

By early 1952, Marilyn realised that the story of the nude calendar – which had been released without her name attached in 1949 but which now had the potential to damage her career – was about to break. The studio was furious with her – they feared that the exposure would not only kill her career but reflect badly on them – and the publicity men were keen to kill the story. But Marilyn was determined to be in charge of her own narrative. During a lunch with United Press International reporter Aline Mosby, whose syndicated column appeared across hundreds of news outlets, Marilyn accompanied the journalist to the ladies' room where she confessed that she had posed in the nude because she desperately needed the money. 'Oh the calendar's hanging in garages all over town,' said Marilyn in Mosby's scoop that splashed across the country on 13 March. 'Why deny it? ... Besides, I'm not ashamed of it. I've done nothing wrong ... I was told to deny I'd posed ... but I'd rather be honest about it.' She told Mosby's readers that there was nothing seedy about the shoot – after all, Tom Kelley's wife had been there watching it all. Indeed, according to Marilyn's version of events, there was something innocent about the resulting images, almost as if she had thrown her clothes off with the blameless abandonment of a small child. 'I'd never have done it if I'd known things in Hollywood would happen so fast for me,' she added.[8] This is Marilyn at her most disarming, and on the surface the quote is truthful: back in 1949, as a model and bit-part actress, she could never have realised that she would actually make it in Hollywood. Yet there's also something disingenuous about this statement of surprise, as she herself must have realised. Her desire – her desperation – for success, as expressed in the pages of her autobiography, is so intense that its sweet, heady smell infuses every page. 'I used to think as I looked out on the Hollywood night, "There must be thousands of girls sitting alone like me dreaming of becoming a movie star,"' she said. '"But I'm not going to worry about them. I'm dreaming the hardest."'[9]

Marilyn realised early on in her career that publicity was essential, a necessary catalyst in the creation and maintenance of the glitter that surrounded a star's halo. And celebrity, she observed, was often bestowed on a person from outside the arena of the studios. 'In Hollywood a star isn't only an actor or actress or movie executive,' she wrote in her autobiography. 'It can also be somebody who has recently been arrested for something, or beaten up or exposed in a love triangle. If it was played up in the newspapers then this person is treated as a social star as long as his or her publicity continues.'[10] By feeding into the public's fantasies, the Kelley images helped go some way to create the Marilyn icon. As Richard B. Woodward writes, 'to gaze at a Hollywood star without a stitch on, even if she looked too young in 1949 to correspond to the platinum-haired fleshpot who had wowed you in the theater and in *Life* magazine, was to have a dream threesome: sex and fame and you.'[11]

Marilyn milked the nude calendar story for all it was worth, and the coverage was extensive. 'When you come right down to it that calendar is not repulsive,' said director Billy Wilder. 'It's quite lovely ... when it became known that she had posed for it, I think that, if anything, it helped her popularity ... Here was a girl who needed dough, and she made it by honest toil.'[12] Marilyn employed her natural comic gifts to bat away criticism: when one huffy female reporter stood up at a press conference and asked, 'Do you mean to tell us you didn't have *anything* on when you posed for that nude picture?' Marilyn replied, 'Oh no, I had the radio on.'[13] This both shocked and titillated in equal measure. 'This flip attitude in the very conservative 1950s added immeasurably to her appeal,' said Hugh Hefner. 'It is an early sign that attitudes towards sexuality were starting to change and Marilyn Monroe was very much part of that and a pioneer in those changing values.'¹⁴

Marilyn also realised if she aligned herself with Joe DiMaggio – a Catholic who was a symbol of everything good about America (an immigrant success story, a man who had reinvented his fortunes through natural talent and hard work) – she could seize the opportunity not only to guarantee thousands of column inches but that the public could be persuaded to view her through a different prism. Yes, she was sexy, but she could be wholesome too. 'Our little Marilyn Monroe, the town's newest glamour girl, is being seen more and more often with Joe DiMaggio, former centerfield star with the Yankees,' purred gossip columnist Louella Parsons in March 1952. 'Marilyn snagged more magazine space last month than any other actress. Her face and her figure are more money in the bank, and Joe seems fascinated with her. Joe is strong on the looks, too, and his popularity, both as a person and as a baseball idol, is great.'¹⁵

With DiMaggio by her side, Marilyn survived another scandal that had the potential to take the shine off her blossoming stardom. Up until this point, studio bios had claimed that Marilyn was an orphan: in a Twentieth Century-Fox publicity mail-out dated 7 February 1951 it was stated that 'her mother was a helpless invalid and her father was killed in an automobile accident shortly after her birth. Marilyn has never known either.'¹⁶ However, on 3 May 1952, gossip columnist Erskine Johnson broke the story in the *Los Angeles Daily News* that Marilyn was not an orphan and that her mother was still alive. 'Marilyn Monroe – Hollywood's confessin' glamour doll who made recent headlines with the admission that she was a nude calendar cutie – confessed again today,' begins the story. The interview was far from being an entirely true confession. 'Unbeknown to me as a child, my mother spent many years as an invalid in a state hospital,' she told Johnson. 'I haven't known my mother intimately, but since I have become grown and able to help her I have contacted her. I am helping her and want to continue to help her when she needs me.'[17]

With immaculate timing, Marilyn made the confession from her hospital bed; she had been admitted to the Cedars of Lebanon Hospital at the end of April for the removal of her appendix. Conscious of her public image even in the most challenging of circumstances, she arranged to have a series of syndicated photographs taken in her hospital bed, employing her trusty make-up man Allan 'Whitey' Snyder to make sure she looked her best. She also had other concerns, as the gynaecologist Dr Leon Krohn recalled. On 28 April, he was on duty at the hospital when he was paged and asked to hurry to surgery. When he arrived, he found Marilyn on a trolley; she refused to go into the theatre until she'd spoken to him. She knew of his reputation and wanted to ensure that her reproductive organs were not damaged during the procedure. She also took the trouble to write a note to the surgeon, Dr Marcus Rabwin, which she pinned to her gown:

> *Dr Rabwin – <u>most important</u> to read before <u>operation</u>! <u>Cut as little as possible</u>. I know it seems vain but that doesn't really enter into it. The fact that I'm a <u>woman</u> is important and means much to me. Save please (I can't ask you enough) what you can – I'm in your hands. You have children and you must know what it means – <u>please Dr Rabwin</u> – I know somehow <u>you</u> <u>will</u>! Thank you – thank you – thank you. For God's sake Dear Doctor, <u>No ovaries removed</u> – please again do whatever you can to prevent large <u>scars</u>. Thanking you with my all heart. <u>Marilyn Monroe</u>.*[18]

Joe DiMaggio sent two dozen red roses to the hospital and by 16 May, while she was living in a bungalow at the Bel Air Hotel, it was reported that Marilyn was seeing the baseball star each day. She'd already told Elia Kazan that she intended to marry DiMaggio. 'He comes all the way down from San Francisco just to have dinner with me,' she said. She also confessed to Kazan that she and Joe did not rush into having sex with one another. 'He wants to marry me, and I really like him,' she told Kazan. 'He's not like these movie people. He's dignified.'[19]

Yet from the beginning the couple had their problems. In July 1952, they had a row that prompted Joe to write Marilyn a letter full of remorse. He told her of his feelings of guilt which haunted him since he left for New York. He worried that he had 'bit' her feelings and reiterated how she was the last person in the world he wanted to hurt. He regarded her, he said, as a 'real, solid, human soul' with a great capacity for feeling emotion and concluded that the ball was in her court now: all he asked for was forgiveness.[20]

Perhaps Joe had an inkling that Marilyn was seeing other men; one of these was costume designer William Travilla, who worked with her on eight films between *Don't Bother to Knock* and *Bus Stop*. 'We became close at a time while my wife was away in Florida and she had just met DiMaggio and he was away,' he said. 'So we dated for a couple of weeks. She tore me apart inside, it was crazy. She was the only woman that I've ever known that makes a man feel tall, handsome, fascinating, because she only looks dead in your eyes, doesn't even blink. The best looking guy with a cock this long could walk by bare-assed and she wouldn't turn. You – *you* – are the king of the evening. She enjoyed teasing – if there ever was a prick teaser, it would be Marilyn.'[21]

Over the years men had tried to use her; now it was time for her to turn the tables.

32

'SHE WAS A DAMN GOOD SURVIVOR'

'Sometimes Marilyn would use people as stepping stones ... she was a damn good survivor,' said Nico Minardos, a young extra Marilyn met on the set of *Monkey Business*; he is listed in the credits as nothing more than 'handsome guy at pool'. 'I was a young buck, and she was pretty,' he said. 'She was – I think – an unbelievably bright girl, an unbelievably sensitive girl, but she had tremendous psychological problems.' Born in Athens, in 1930, Minardos arrived in America in 1950 with only $80 in his pocket; he took jobs as a dishwasher and busboy to pay his way through UCLA. His dark good looks secured him a contract with Twentieth Century-Fox. 'He loved the limelight, he loved people admiring him,' said one of his friends, while another observed that 'he had the pick of beautiful women'.[1]

According to Minardos, in the spring of 1952 he and Marilyn embarked on a seven-month relationship. In his version of events, the couple lived together and she begged him to marry her, but he refused because he didn't want to play the role of 'Mr Monroe'. Instead, he wanted to be a star – and a director – in his own right. One night, the couple were in her hotel room when she asked him if he wouldn't mind leaving and returning in about an hour, as she had a 'business appointment'. But before the twenty-two-year-old could leave there was a knock at the door, accompanied by a cry of 'It's me, darling'. The visitor turned out to be Spyros Skouras, the president of Twentieth Century-Fox, who was nearly sixty. The sight of the 'young buck' standing only in his trousers infuriated Skouras and, according to Minardos, 'he barred me from the studio then. And later, when I knew him, he never called me by my name – he would always call me "Marilyn's boyfriend".' Minardos believed that Marilyn used men like Skouras and Johnny Hyde to get ahead. 'She succeeded through what I considered a dishonourable way by using people.'

But there were consequences. Minardos told Marilyn as much in 1962 when, during the filming of her last, uncompleted film, *Something's Got to Give*, the couple had lunch.

> I think I was very nasty to her. I called her a slut. I don't think she was seeking power at all. She was seeking acceptance – and the more important the man, the more accepted she was. I also told her that one day you will kill yourself, because that's the only solution for you. She gave everything she had to reap what she thought would be the greatest happiness and when she [achieved] that, she realised that what she had given was sometimes more precious than what she got. She had given too much of herself to obtain this so-called happiness, by becoming a star.[2]

Although Nico's career spanned the 1950s to the 1970s, he never reached the same level of fame as Marilyn. His roles were minor ones, and often he was confined to playing Mexicans in second-rate television dramas.

Always attracted by the trappings of materialism, Minardos went to work for the Saudi arms dealer Adnan Khashoggi – he loved being able to fly around the world on the billionaire's private jet, complete with its enormous double bed – but his downfall came when he fell foul of an undercover sting operation in December 1985. Minardos found himself – together with a number of other businessmen – labelled one of the 'brokers of death' for allegedly helping to supply $2.5 billion of arms to Iran. He was locked up in jail for three months, had to raise $2 million in bail and, as a result of the stress, his marriage suffered. It took three years before prosecutors dropped charges of conspiracy – all this occurred during the so-called Iran-Contra scandal under the Reagan administration – and Minardos lost not only whatever wealth he may have enjoyed but also, to some extent, his reputation too. Towards the end of his life, he entertained various film crews at his Fort Lauderdale condo, where he talked about his golden days in Hollywood.

Of course, people really only wanted to know about one thing: his relationship with Marilyn. 'She wanted to get married, and I said "no",' he told one interviewer a year before his death in 2011, at the age of eighty-one.[3] But did Marilyn really ask to marry him? He told Anthony Summers that although Marilyn was beautiful, bright and sensitive, she was 'a lousy lay' – 'She never had a climax, I had to work for like ten hours.'[4] Was this because he felt used by Marilyn? There was nothing he could do to boost her career – after all, he was a student, a mere extra at the time – but could she have been using him for her own sexual pleasure? In a documentary made about his life in 2010, Minardos categorised himself at this time as a man with a permanent erection. 'You're a young man in your twenties – you walk with a hard-on, always, right?'[5]

There's also something suspect about the way he described his decision to turn down Marilyn's proposal. 'Sure enough when she married one of the best writers that America produced, he was called Mr Monroe. The headline in the newspaper in LA at the time was "Marilyn's Mate – Arthur Miller." Come on!'[6] Minardos once again used this expression – a choice of words that betrays a certain level of masculine insecurity – in his interview with Summers back in 1983 to describe Marilyn's second husband Joe DiMaggio, a man he called 'weak'.

The affair between Nico and Marilyn ended in November 1952, around the time it was being reported that the Monroe-DiMaggio relationship was undergoing a period of intense crisis. On Thanksgiving Day, Marilyn kept Joe waiting for two hours at the Brown Derby restaurant, and although it was said this was because the actress had work commitments, that night she'd also had a date with Nico. Did DiMaggio force her to dump Minardos? Was it a question of asking her to choose? After all, Minardos was aware that Joe was 'extremely jealous'.[7] The other guest at that Thanksgiving Dinner – DiMaggio's friend, the press agent Bernie Kamber – was forced to watch as Joe and Marilyn gave one another the silent treatment. Rumours started to whisper their way around town that the relationship was on the rocks. 'It's time for a change on the love-front in Hollywood,' wrote gossip columnist Sheila Graham on 22 November. 'Marilyn Monroe has given the old heave-ho to Joe DiMaggio.'[8] The rift did not last long, but soon Marilyn would witness Joe's jealousy begin to spiral out of control.

33

THE GIRL WITH THE HORIZONTAL WALK

She walks down the steps to the waiting car. To the outside world – and to the kind couple who have offered to drive her back to the motel overlooking Niagara Falls – Rose Loomis, played by Marilyn, looks like a woman grieving: she's just discovered that her husband George has thrown himself into the torrent of water below. But then as the clock tower in the distance begins to play the haunting melody of 'Kiss', she realises that the bells are playing a song that she chose with her lover Patrick as a sign that their plan has worked: that Patrick has succeeded in killing her husband. Dressed in a red bolero jacket, white blouse and a black skirt, she turns from the couple and tells them that although they've been kind, she'd rather walk.

And what a walk.

As she begins to stride away, her hips begin to sway, and an expression of joy breaks out over her face. The camera focuses on her hips, her buttocks, accentuating the fluidity of her form. It's like watching water move.

Indeed, the sequence taps into the essence of the highly sexualised nature of *Niagara*, which Marilyn shot on location in Canada in June 1952. A publicity poster for the film shows a buxom Marilyn lying across the top of the falls, water gushing from her low-cut blue dress as if she is the source of both the violent cascade and an ensuing flood of destructive desire. 'Marilyn Monroe and "Niagara" a raging torrent of emotion that even nature can't control!' runs the caption underneath. Marilyn's leisurely paced stroll from the car towards the bell tower was said to be the longest walk in cinematic history, taking up 116 feet of film. The camera – resolutely focused on her back, her hips, her buttocks – forced the viewer into the role of a voyeur and whipped the (male) critics into a frenzy.

On release of the film in January 1953, Marilyn was immediately dubbed 'the girl with the horizontal walk'.[1] The implication was clear: in 1950s America this was the nearest a movie-goer could get to watching a woman have sex on screen. Marilyn pretended to be naive about the effect the swaying of her hips and the movement of her buttocks had on viewers. 'I don't get what they mean by "horizontal walk",' she said. 'Naturally I know what walking means – anybody knows that – and horizontal means not vertical. So what?'[2] But in the 1950s – an era when sex before marriage was frowned upon and heavy petting or 'parking' was elevated to a stylised ritual in which desire had to be balanced against self-control – the Marilyn walk was the equivalent of a cinematic orgasm. 'She can squeeze more meaning out of a few steps than most actresses can get out of six pages of dialogue,' said Harmon Jones, who directed her in *As Young as You Feel*.[3] The photographer Philippe Halsman later said that 'everything she did, every motion, was a mixture of conscious and unconscious appeal and challenge to the desire of men. The way she giggled, the way she stood in the corner flirting with the camera, and especially the way she walked, for with every step her derrière seemed to wink at the onlooker.'[4] Gavin Lambert, the novelist, screenwriter and biographer, commented that 'she walks ... as if the whole earth were a tightrope on which she has to balance'.[5]

One male gossip columnist claimed that the secret of Marilyn's walk was down to the fact that she'd cut quarter of an inch off one heel, so that when she moved 'that little fanny would wiggle'.[6] It wasn't true – later, when her possessions were auctioned, none of her shoes had been doctored in this way.

In public, Marilyn would insist that she had never done anything to change her walk. 'People say I walk all wiggly and wobbly, but I don't know what they mean.'[7] A physiognomical quirk could help explain her style: Emmeline Snively attributed her charge's signature shimmy to the fact that she had double-jointed knees and the model agency boss did everything in her power to change 'that horrible walk'.[8]

Even so, Marilyn was highly conscious of the purpose and effect of every muscle movement, no matter how minute. From 1951, she worked with Michael Chekhov, the nephew of the famous playwright, and a student of the Russian theatre practitioner Konstantin Stanislavski. Chekhov introduced her to the work of Mabel Elsworth Todd, whose 1937 book *The Thinking Body* Marilyn bought second-hand and soon came to treasure. 'Walking, then, is a perpetual falling with a perpetual self-recovery,' wrote Elsworth Todd. 'It is a most complex, violent, and perilous operation, which we divest of its extreme danger only by continual practice from a very early period of life ... Man is a *wheel*, with two spokes, his legs, and two fragments of a tire, his feet. He *rolls* successively on each of these fragments from the heel to the toe.'[9]

Marilyn practised Todd's exercises repeatedly, particularly 'walking on the sitting bones', out of which her famous walk emerged. Arthur Miller observed that if Marilyn were to stroll along a beach the footprints she left in the sand would be marked out in a straight line, 'the heel descending exactly before the last toeprint, throwing her pelvis into motion'.[10] One day, she demonstrated her new technique to fellow actor, and one-time lover, Charlie Chaplin Jr. 'His jaw fell to the floor,' she remembered. '"Marilyn, what on earth! That's wonderful! So titillating."'[11]

From Elsworth Todd's book, Marilyn learned the importance of the psoas muscle, which joins the upper and lower parts of the body together. Later, Marilyn told her close friend and masseur

Ralph Roberts of her passion for learning about how the psoas muscle controlled the pelvic girdle and about how the thigh bone connected with the hip bone towards the centre of the body, making a kind of bridge. 'Learning the truth [about this] gave me a wonderful sense of mastery on several levels,' she said. First of all, there was the matter of creating – and controlling – her signature walk. 'Then a childish delight knowing something that wasn't common knowledge, outside medical people.'[12]

At the end of March 1962, Marilyn called Ralph from Bing Crosby's home in Palm Springs, where she was staying with President John F. Kennedy. JFK was surprised that she didn't walk as she did in the movies and Marilyn told him that she developed the technique after reading *The Thinking Body*. However, she couldn't remember the name of the muscle and rang Roberts. 'She called and said, "I'm with a friend and would you tell him the name of the muscle that I use for the walking,"' he recalled. 'And I said, "Yes, it's the psoas muscle – p-s-o-a-s." And she put him on the phone for me to tell him [the president] and then he said, "Well, thank you." I recognized the voice after hearing it those several years.'[13]

Marilyn also went on to study the intricacies of the human body by reading about the work of sixteenth-century anatomist Andreas Vesalius. One of the books in her collection that went to auction after her death was Vesalius's *De Humani Corporis Fabrica Libri Septem* (*On the Fabric of the Human Body*) and images from the text by Jan Steven van Calcar decorated the walls of her apartments since the days when she was a struggling starlet. 'What makes the difference between her and Jayne Mansfield?' said Joan Greenson, who was an art student when she first met Marilyn. 'It's easy to look at her, say it's the way she moves her fanny, or the way her butt moves. To my way of thinking it's much more complicated. It's the way that she moved that was extremely unique. She was fascinated by [the images of] Vesalius's bones, how the skeleton would react. She felt that is how you had to act, from the bones out — that's how she moved.'[14]

Marilyn wore her learning lightly and instead of explaining the complicated theory behind what she had read about the intricacies of the human body, she told Sheila Graham, 'Let everything go limp except for the coccyx, and you can move in any direction without too much trouble.'[15] She incorporated the detailed teachings of Vesalius, together with the techniques she had learned from Chekhov and Todd, into both her acting style and her everyday life. But the effect was subtle, almost hypnotic.

'Whereas people normally move their arms and head in conversation, these gestures in Marilyn Monroe were reflected throughout her body, producing a delicately undulating effect like the movement of an almost calm sea,' said prima ballerina Margot Fonteyn, who met her in July 1956 at playwright Terence Rattigan's house in Sunningdale, England. 'It seemed clear to me that it was something of which she was not conscious; it was as natural as breathing, and in no way an affected "wriggle," as some writers have suggested.'[16]

34

THE FACE OF A BEAUTIFUL GHOST

They were brought together so they could hate one another – Marilyn, the American pop cultural icon, and Edith Sitwell, the poet and high priestess of English avant-garde experimentalism. It was early 1953, and unlikely as it may seem, Sitwell – who was sixty-five at the time – was in Los Angeles to try to turn her 1946 Tudor-set novel *Fanfare for Elizabeth* into a Hollywood movie. *Life* commissioned a feature about Sitwell's impressions of LA, and organised a meeting with Marilyn since 'it was obvious that we were born to hate each other, would do so at first sight, and that our subsequent insults to each other would cause a commotion when reported,' said the poet. 'They never made a greater mistake.'[1]

Writing in her notebook, in a section that has never been published, Sitwell praised Marilyn for her strength of character and extraordinary willpower.[2]

The poet was immediately struck by the gap between the star's public image and the intelligent, sensitive young woman who arrived at her rented apartment in Sunset Towers. 'In private life she was not in the least what her calumniators would have wished her to be,' said Sitwell. 'She was very quiet, had great natural dignity (I cannot imagine anyone who knew her trying to take a liberty with her), and was extremely intelligent. She was also exceedingly sensitive.'[3] The two women talked about the philosophy of Rudolph Steiner and posed for a photograph taken by George Silk. 'In repose her face was at moments strangely, prophetically tragic, like the face of a beautiful ghost – a little spring-ghost, an innocent fertility-daemon, the vegetation spirit that was Ophelia,' Sitwell wrote in her autobiography.[4] The curious relationship was later dramatised by Simon Berry in his 2021 audio play *The Dame and the Showgirl*, starring Emma Thompson as Sitwell and Sinead Matthews as Marilyn.

Although Edith was born into the English aristocracy, she shared with Marilyn a sense that she had grown up feeling unloved. As a result, according to her biographer Victoria Glendinning, Sitwell 'came to identify herself with the sad, the lonely, the scared, the outsider, the mistreated, whether human or animal'.[5] She sensed Marilyn's vulnerability. 'I thought that she had been disgracefully treated, most unchivalrously treated,' Sitwell said later. 'If people have never been poor perhaps they don't know what it is like to be hungry. That girl allowed a calendar to be made of her – well, there have been nude models before now, it means nothing against the person's moral character at all. This poor girl was absolutely persecuted by people. She has, or had, an unfortunate attraction for an extremely unpleasant kind of man who she avoided assiduously – I have seen her do that. She behaved like a lady.'[6]

And what did Marilyn make of Edith? 'I expected her to be a real English snob, but she wasn't,' she said.[7]

After the press sniffed out news of the encounter between what they saw as a highbrow poet and a lowbrow actress, they could not get enough of this improbable friendship. Sitwell was constantly besieged by reporters and wrote that one 'moron' in particular took it upon himself to telephone her repeatedly. 'Is Miss Monroe going on the same boat as you, to England?' asked one of these 'lower-grade mental defectives'. And it wasn't only in England – it seemed as though the feeding frenzy had stretched across the world. 'A Calcutta paper says I live only "to be a mother to Miss Monroe",' Sitwell wrote in a letter. 'An Egyptian paper says I am going to "teach her philosophy" (sic). The behaviour of these people is intolerable. I understand from a mutual friend that poor Miss Monroe is allowed no friends by the Press, and that she hardly dares go out for fear of being mobbed. The whole lot of these people ought to be ashamed of themselves.'[8]

Edith and Marilyn met again in October 1956 when the actress came over to England to film *The Prince and the Showgirl*. 'When she and her husband . . . came to London they were asked who they wanted to see and I was one of the first people who they wanted to see. And they came but of course we couldn't talk because every kind of person was just hanging about outside and interfering and all the rest of it, you know, going about telling lies.'[9] One afternoon in London, over beakers of gin and grapefruit juice, Edith and Marilyn discussed the poems of Dylan Thomas and Gerard Manley Hopkins, whose 'I wake and feel the fell of dark, not day' particularly spoke to the star's experiences of insomnia:

> *What hours, O what black hours we have spent*
> *This night!*

Friends of Sitwell's were keen for an introduction. In the summer of 1956, the composer Benjamin Britten wrote to the poet asking whether she could persuade Marilyn to open the fundraising bazaar and garden party at the Aldeburgh Festival; unfortunately Marilyn was too busy to grace Suffolk with her presence. There were many others from the world of high culture – such as the Russian-American writer Vladimir Nabokov – who expressed an interest in, and enthusiasm for, the actress. Novelist Saul Bellow said of her, 'Surrounded by thousands, she conducts herself like a philosopher.'[10] When the Danish author Karen Blixen met her, with the American novelist Carson McCullers, in 1959, she observed:

> It is not that she is pretty, although of course she is almost incredibly pretty – but that she radiates at the same time unbounded

vitality and a kind of unbelievable innocence. I have met the same in a lion cub that my native servants in Africa brought me. I would not keep her, since I felt that it would in some way be wrong ... I shall never forget the almost overpowering feeling of unconquerable strength and sweetness which she conveyed. I had all the wild nature of Africa amicably gazing at me with mighty playfulness.[11]

35

JOLTIN' JOE TURNS JEALOUS

It's morning. The couple have just made love. She is naked in bed, laughing. He pours her some orange juice, but on returning to the sitting room he finds her getting dressed. His eyes darken with suspicion. She tells him that she's going to the bus station to buy tickets for their journey home, but he doesn't believe her.

George: Where're you going?

Rose: Here we go again. All right, I'm not going to the bus station. Does that make you feel any better?

George: You smell like a dime store. I know what that means.

Rose: Sure, I'm meeting somebody – just anybody handy, as long as he's a man.

This scene from *Niagara* between Rose (played by Marilyn) and George Loomis (Joseph Cotten) anticipated the highly charged – and at times toxic – relationship between Marilyn and Joe DiMaggio. The couple, who had been dating since March 1952, could be warm and tender to one another. Marilyn appreciated Joe's gestures of kindness; on Christmas Eve 1952 he turned up at her hotel with a Christmas tree. Marilyn comforted him in May 1953 when his brother Mike drowned at sea during a fishing accident, while he did the same for her when she learned of the death of Grace Goddard, her stand-in mother, in September the same year. In an unpublished extract from her ghostwritten memoir, Marilyn told how one night she visited Grace's body in the mortuary in Los Angeles. Although she was reluctant, she forced herself to look – inside a casket she saw her guardian, her skin deathly white. Marilyn believed that Grace had died from uterine cancer – it wasn't until years later that it was revealed that she had killed herself by an overdose of barbiturates – and she wanted to make sure that the fifty-nine-year-old appeared dignified in death. She instructed the assistant at the morgue to frame the woman's hair just so around her face and to tie a little scarf around her neck.[1]

Joe was also there for Marilyn when she hurt her ankle while filming *River of No Return* in Canada earlier that summer. As Marilyn told Sidney Skolsky: 'I know how Joe hates publicity and movie sets . . . But when he phoned and asked if he should come on, I said yes.' Skolsky then explained how 'she said that after Joe's arrival everything straightened out.'[2]

Yet underlying the outwardly happy relationship was a dark undercurrent. According to Natasha Lytess – who described Joe as having a 'closed, vapid look' – during 1952 and 1953 the actress would phone her at all hours, sometimes in tears, and complain about how DiMaggio 'misused' her.[3] And although Lytess can be an unreliable witness at times, her testimony is backed up by others close to Marilyn. At the heart of the issue lay Marilyn and Joe's differing outlooks on what it meant to be a woman. 'He came from a poor Italian background where the women are mothers, sisters, wives,' said Amy Greene. '[Women] are either family and [you] protect them, or you're whores.'[4]

Soon after the couple's marriage – on 14 January 1954 in San Francisco, with Marilyn promising to 'love, honour, and cherish' but not obey her new husband – DiMaggio's sister Marie was interviewed for *Parade* magazine. In the article, Marie outlined why she thought her brother had found the perfect match. 'They're both the same kind,' she said. 'They like the same things. Joe's idea of a good time is to have a home cooked meal, then lie down on the sofa and watch television. Marilyn's the same way.'[5]

Nothing could have been further from the truth. During 1953, Marilyn had starred in three films: *Niagara* in January, *Gentlemen Prefer Blondes* in July and *How to Marry a Millionaire* in November. The trio of movies were 'box-office blockbusters' and at the end of that year, according to *Time* magazine, Marilyn 'had made more money for her studio than any other actress in Hollywood'.[6] Marilyn's star was shining at its brightest and she wasn't about to snuff out its brilliance now. On 22 January 1954, while they were on honeymoon in Japan, Marilyn won the Henrietta Award for World Film Favorite at the Golden Globes. It was clear her fame had spread outside America and its effect could be frightening.

On 29 January, while on a stopover in Honolulu – DiMaggio was combining the honeymoon with a baseball tour with his former manager and friend Lefty O'Doul, together with Lefty's wife Jean – the famous couple was greeted by a crowd of 2,000, some of whom tried to grab Marilyn's hair. There was a near-riot when the honeymooners arrived in Tokyo and, to avoid the mob, they were forced to exit through a baggage handling hatch. The escape plan did not work: as they pulled away in their limousine, a clutch of fans threw themselves on top of the car, 'threatening to collapse the roof'.[7] There was more chaos at the Imperial Hotel when a crowd surged forwards with such force that windows broke, people got stuck in the revolving doors and a couple of overeager onlookers even fell into the ornamental Koi carp pond. 'These people, they're mad,' said Marilyn, but that didn't stop her from giving them what they wanted: her attention.[8] She was quick to answer with wit and grace the questions fired at her by reporters.

Q: Do you wear underwear?
A: I'm buying a kimono.

Q: How long have you been walking that way?
A: I started when I was six months old and haven't stopped yet.
Q: What kind of fur are you wearing?
A: Fox. And not the 20th Century kind.[9]

She appeared on the hotel balcony waving and blowing kisses to the throng of fans below, an experience she said was like being a 'dictator'. DiMaggio was sidelined, and although he assured reporters, 'I don't mind playing second fiddle to Marilyn,' it was clear that the scale of his wife's fame dented his ego.[10]

Early on in the trip Marilyn hurt her hand – photographs show one of her thumbs in a splint – which she said had been caused by an accident. 'I just bumped it,' she said.[11] According to Amy Greene, there was more to it than that: 'She went to put her arms around him, but she annoyed him – he had hands like hams – and [although] all he did was fling [her] away', the action resulted in an injury. 'She was physically afraid of him.'[12]

When, in February 1954, Marilyn travelled without Joe to entertain American troops on active service in Korea, she encountered adulation on a scale she had never experienced before. Over the course of four days, she performed in front of 100,000 troops and, although it was freezing, Marilyn insisted on wearing nothing but skintight dresses with spaghetti straps. When her pianist Al Guastafeste suggested she slip on her fur coat, she replied, 'Oh no! This is how they want to see me.'[13]

Over the course of the tour, Marilyn slept in a tent in sub-zero temperatures – she returned with pneumonia – and gave away the army rations she didn't finish to local children. She signed autographs and posed for so many photographs that it was said that Korea ran out of film. 'I never felt like a star before in my heart,' she told Amy Greene. She regaled her new husband with descriptions of what it was like to witness a seemingly endless sea of soldiers stretched out before her. 'It was so wonderful, Joe,' she said, perhaps forgetting that DiMaggio had enjoyed decades in the public eye. 'You've never heard such cheering.' Joe didn't miss a beat and responded, 'Yes, I have. Don't let it go to your head. Just miss the ball once. You'll see they can boo as loud as they can cheer.'[14]

Joe's jealousy began to manifest itself during their trip to the Far East. 'He started to accuse her of going to bed with everybody' during the first few months of their marriage, according to Henry Rosenfeld. On Marilyn's return home from Korea – first to a house at 2150 Beach Street, San Francisco, and then the newly married couple's rented home at 508 North Palm Drive, Beverly Hills – she found herself being forced to play the role of a subservient wife. 'He used to have his friends over and talk baseball or watch baseball and play poker and she'd be upstairs in her bedroom,' said Rosenfeld. Joe would call out, '"Make me spaghetti!" – Marilyn was not a good cook – or "Make me a steak!" She was very unhappy.'[15] To the outside world, however, the star presented herself as a happily married woman, telling Sidney Skolsky that 'marriage makes a woman less neurotic. Well, anyway, it does when I'm the woman.'[16]

On 11 June, Marilyn wrote a syndicated newspaper column in which she answered some of her fans' enquiries, many of which focused on the issue of how to find – and keep – a man:

> I am certainly no authority on the subject, but when someone asks me how to hold a husband, I tell them this: Be yourself... If a man marries a happy girl and one who keeps herself well groomed and desirable, he's entitled to live with that same person and not a frowsy grouch...
>
> The husband should be the head man and the wife should always remember she's a woman. The girl who gets her man by virtue of her femininity, and then suddenly turns into a domineering female in the home, is due for trouble...

> I approached marriage thoughtfully as well as happily. I intend to make mine work by being honest, by being as attractive as I can at all times, and by making a real home when I'm not in front of the cameras.[17]

If her legion of fans read this piece – which appeared in a wide range of newspapers all across America – they would have assumed that Marilyn was enjoying a happy and fulfilled marriage. The reality was much more disturbing.

36

The 'two-panty shot'

It's a hot and sticky night in New York, so hot in fact that the girl has taken to leaving her underwear in the ice box. The couple – Richard (played by Tom Ewell), a middle-aged married man in a light suit, bow tie and hat, and 'The Girl' (played by Marilyn) in a white, pleated halterneck dress – walk out of the Trans-Lux cinema on 52nd Street and discuss the movie they've just seen: *The Creature from the Black Lagoon*.

> **The Girl:** [Noticing the grille below her feet, her face lights in childish delight.] Do you feel the breeze from the subway? [Her skirts fly up.] Isn't it delicious? [The man strains his neck to see the girl's exposed legs.] It sort of cools the ankles, doesn't it?
>
> **Richard:** Well, what do you think would be fun to do now? [We know what's on his mind.]
>
> **The Girl:** I don't know, it's getting pretty late.
>
> **Richard:** It's not that late . . .
>
> **The Girl:** [Hearing another subway train below . . .] Oh, here comes another one. [The breeze from below lifts her skirt higher and the camera focuses on her exposed legs.][1]

This scene from *The Seven Year Itch* is one of the most famous in movie history and perhaps the one most often associated with Marilyn Monroe. Although the final sequence was shot in a studio, its director Billy Wilder initially chose to film it on location in Manhattan. The shoot began at 1 a.m. on 15 September 1954 and once word got out that Marilyn was shooting a scene in which her skirt blew up over her head – and that they might be able to catch a glimpse of her legs, perhaps even her thighs – thousands of spectators, mostly men, descended on Lexington Avenue to watch.

Before she stepped out for the cameras, Marilyn checked her underwear, worried that it might be possible to see through it. She was advised to slip on an extra layer as protection; Wilder called this the 'two-panty shot'.[2] However, when the bright arc lights hit Marilyn's midriff the beam shone straight through them, exposing the star's pubic hair.

With each shot, the crowd went wild, with the mob shouting, applauding and whistling. The noise was so deafening that at times Wilder would try to calm things down. 'I asked the crowds to be quiet,' he said. 'Nothing. Just the same noise. Then, Marilyn Monroe put a finger to her lips. Absolute silence.'[3] Wilder also had to deal with the voyeuristic desires of his own crew, who wanted to snatch a private view of the star from below. 'I had guys fighting as to who was going to put the ventilator on, in the shaft there, below the grille.'[4]

In the crowd that night stood a fierce-looking Joe DiMaggio, who had been dragged along to the shoot by wily reporter Walter Winchell, perhaps hoping to get a rise out of the baseball star. With each gust of wind, each rise of the skirts, each flash of Marilyn's famous curves, DiMaggio's mood darkened until he could bear it no longer. 'Just what the hell is going on here?' he said. Amy Greene was standing next to him and witnessed his anger, before he stormed off in a foul mood. 'The man physically flushed,' she recalled. 'That was his woman showing her fanny off.'[5] Later that night the couple fought so loudly their argument could be heard through the walls. The next day Marilyn's hairdresser Gladys Whitten covered up the bruises she saw on the actress's shoulders.

Amy remembered visiting Marilyn's hotel suite, where Marilyn confessed to her friend that DiMaggio was a wife beater. 'He was knocking her about at the St. Regis,' said Amy, who recalled the moment with the clarity of a movie playing inside her head. She was trying on Marilyn's mink coat – an item of clothing she coveted – and as she sat on the bed she watched Marilyn get undressed so she could change for dinner.

She had never known a girl or a woman like me, who was so open about everything. If I saw black and blue marks I would say, 'Hey!' – I wouldn't take the time to think should I [speak]. She didn't know what to say, and she wasn't a liar so she said, 'Yeah'. You must understand how 'Miss Bigmouth' feels [herself] when she's got to spend another four hours with the son of a bitch. Sometimes she was a smart ass to him and if she was drinking champagne she would goad him. They weren't intellectuals – Virginia Woolf it wasn't – so they wouldn't sit around and discuss their pain. They lashed out at one another. He was a very silent man who held it all in.[6]

37

LETTERS TO 'MY DAD'

For years, the relationship between Marilyn and Joe was shrouded in a level of secrecy. Although Marilyn talked about the short-lived marriage – it lasted only nine months – DiMaggio remained tight-lipped, and as a result biographers had to make do with a one-sided perspective, wild surmises and second-hand gossip. However, since the baseball star's death in 1999, a number of private letters between the couple have surfaced, documents that can be used to help understand the shifting dynamics between them.

At 11:38 p.m., on the night of 28 February 1954, Marilyn, alone in the Beach Street house in San Francisco, wrote a two-page letter to Joe who was working in New York. She told him how much she missed him and how she wanted to spend the rest of her life with him. She apologised for being so late, and promised to try harder. She wanted him to be proud of her, both as a person and as the mother of his children; she declared she wanted at least two. She couldn't wait until they were reconciled and she begged him not to leave her alone again.[1]

The letter – which sold at auction in 2006 for $45,000 – is significant for a number of reasons, not least the way she addressed her new husband, one with whom she enjoyed a highly active sex life, as 'My Dad'. The letter reeks of desperation, but there's also something a little phoney about it too, as we now know that, soon after writing this letter, Marilyn would embark on a relationship with her vocal coach Hal Schaefer.

The newly married couple may have been dynamite in the

bedroom – Joe told his friend Rock G. Positano that when they got together 'it was like the gods were fighting; there were thunderclouds and lightning above us'[2] – but during 1954 their arguments became more frequent. Another Marilyn letter – undated, but written while they were still married – shows that while she was able to recognise that she had made mistakes, surely DiMaggio couldn't blame her for her silly words because she didn't know any better. She told him that she acted the way she did because she was hurt and pleaded with him not to be angry with her. She signed the letter not Marilyn, but Mrs J. P. DiMaggio.[3]

Joe kept this letter – written on the back of a dry-cleaning receipt – in his wallet until the end of his life; repeated handling resulted in the document splitting into four equal segments. Yet DiMaggio was unwise to take the letter at face value, as it shows the ease with which the actress could slip into a role, using the personae she had fashioned to excuse her behaviour. Yet Marilyn was not so innocent. Some cynical observers even accused her of playing the victim, such as the time when, on 6 October 1954, she wept in front of a pack of reporters and cameramen outside the rented marital home on North Palm Drive. (The swarm of pressmen did so much damage to the lawn and rosebushes that the woman who owned the house sent a hefty invoice to the couple for urgent gardening services.) Marilyn didn't say a word that day as her high-profile lawyer Jerry Giesler announced that the actress was divorcing DiMaggio because of mental cruelty; she said nothing about the beating that she had suffered at the St. Regis hotel in New York. One reporter who witnessed the scene called it 'Marilyn's greatest performance ... she sobbed almost to the point of collapse.'[4]

Joe left the house with his bags packed and, on leaving in his Cadillac, snapped at reporters, 'San Francisco always has been my home.' Joe wrote a letter to Marilyn three days later. Addressing her as 'Baby', he said he felt concerned by reports of her illness, which was no doubt exacerbated by the demands from the studio and the intrusive questioning of the press. He reiterated that he loved her, and wanted to be with her. He told her that his home at 2150 Beach Street would be open to her and that the decisions about remodelling the house would be put on hold until her arrival. He reiterated his feelings for her and told her that he loved her 'irregardless of anything'.[5]

The letter doesn't read as though it's written by a man who has just heard the news his wife is divorcing him. In Joe's eyes, there was every hope of reconciliation. It's clear that Marilyn had lost confidence in him, and that she was ill – but it seems as though he bore no responsibility for any of her problems. And instead of looking into his own failings – particularly his violent temper and the way he used his fists to inflict physical and emotional pain on his wife – Joe laid the blame squarely with Marilyn and what he saw as her range of strange symptoms and unknowable issues. He believed that all it would take for her to feel better would be to take charge of the makeover on the house on Beach Street – he would even let her choose the paint colours.

Despite Joe's best efforts to persuade Marilyn to change her mind, she was determined to press on with the legal separation, and at the hearing at Santa Monica Courthouse on the morning of 27 October, Judge Orlando H. Rhodes granted her an interlocutory divorce. 'My husband would get in moods and he wouldn't speak to me for five to seven days, sometimes even longer,' she said during her brief appearance in the courtroom. 'When I would ask him, "What's the matter?" he'd say, "Stop nagging me!"' He also didn't like Marilyn inviting friends over to the house. 'I don't believe I asked to have visitors more than three times during the nine months of our marriage,' she added. 'Once when I was sick he allowed a friend to visit me, but it was under considerable strain. I volunteered to give up my work in hopes it would solve our problem, but it didn't.'[6]

In an interview she gave to Maurice Zolotow, Marilyn expanded on the problem. 'He didn't talk to me,' she said about Joe. 'He was cold. He was indifferent to me as a human being and an artist. He didn't want me to have friends of my own. He didn't want me to do my work. He really watched television instead of talking to me.'[7]

38

THE MAN WHO NEARLY DIED FOR MARILYN

'I was not the cause of the break-up – she was already broken up with him,' said Hal Schaefer. 'It was not to do with anyone else, but DiMaggio couldn't believe it.'

Schaefer, Marilyn's vocal coach, met the star in 1952 and first worked with her on *Gentlemen Prefer Blondes*, shaping her singing performance for 'Diamonds Are a Girl's Best Friend'. He was a year older than Marilyn and something of a musical prodigy: he started to study piano at the age of six and as a teenager played in bands, soon becoming a protégé of Duke Ellington. 'I first saw her in the rehearsal hall at Twentieth Century-Fox,' he recalled. 'She struck me as she was not wholly here, not in the world.'

By the early summer of 1954, while working on *There's No Business Like Show Business*, the friendship between Marilyn and Schaefer had turned into a sexual relationship that lasted three or four months. 'Marilyn's true feeling was that I was the kindest man she'd ever been with, that I was a generous, sensitive soul. I was very supportive, I cared about her, I didn't use her. My style was not married ladies – I was young, and I had a lot going for me. Marilyn and I thought that perhaps we could build something for the future.'

Yet the figure of Joe DiMaggio – and his retinue of shady friends – stood in their way. Soon, Hal began to get the feeling that he and Marilyn were being followed. 'I guess I figured they must have bugged Marilyn's car, this big, black convertible Cadillac.'

Hal didn't take too kindly to this attempt at intimidation. 'She was terrified, and also furious because she felt she couldn't live her life. I threatened to go to his [Joe's] house in Beverly Hills. He thought he was gonna scare me, but he didn't. He said, "Come in about an hour," and I said, "I'll be there." Somehow or another Marilyn heard about it and she called me up and said don't do that.'

Yet the pressure of the situation – the stress of finding himself between Marilyn and Joe, together with a severe drinking problem – brought about a psychological crisis for Hal. On the night of 27 July 1954, at his bungalow on the Fox lot, he took one hundred or so pills, washed down with a quart of brandy and the cleaning fluid carbon tetrachloride.

'It was desperation. I didn't want to go on anymore. A great deal of the focus was Marilyn, but it was also just the way I was in my life – I was highly depressed. I was miserable.' Hal was discovered by friends and rushed to hospital. Although doctors managed to save his life, for months he was incapacitated. 'I would have a relapse because of the damage done to my liver and kidneys,' he said, 'and often I couldn't lift my head off the bed.' He rented an isolated house in Ventura County and employed a team of male nurses to look after him. But when Marilyn drove out to visit him, the harassment by heavies employed by DiMaggio began again. 'On one of these occasions they followed her – they were saying they were going to cut the phone lines,' he said. 'They sat out there all night – they said they would come in, get her and leave me alone.' Both Hal and Marilyn were terrified and she managed to sneak away without either of them coming to any harm. 'I don't think Marilyn and I had any sex at that point or if we did, it certainly wasn't very often because I had just come back from the dead.'

However, when Hal was fit enough to return to Los Angeles the couple began to meet in secret again. By this point, Marilyn knew there was no way to save her marriage. Yet DiMaggio could not accept that it was over and he was determined to do everything in his power to get his wife back. Instead of talking to Marilyn about how best to fix their relationship, he decided to embark on a mad-cap scheme to try to catch her and Hal in bed. Joe employed the services of notorious private detective Barney Ruditsky and his team to follow them. 'If he ever caught her in the act, that would nullify their separation in California,' said Schaefer.[1]

39

THE 'WRONG DOOR RAID'

On the night of 5 November 1954, Joe DiMaggio was drinking with his friend Frank Sinatra in the Villa Capri in Hollywood. During the evening, a call came through to the bar from Barney Ruditsky to say one of his men, Philip Irvin, had tracked Marilyn to an apartment building on the corner of Kilkea Drive and Waring Avenue. Joe had employed the sleuth to find out if Marilyn was having an affair and now this was the opportunity he had been waiting for: DiMaggio and Sinatra sped to the scene, where they were joined by their posse.

Inside the two-storey Hollywood apartment building, a middle-aged secretary, Florence Kotz, was fast asleep when, at around 11 p.m., five or six men battered down her door, 'tearing it from its hinges and leaving glass on the floor'.[1] According to a report in *Confidential* magazine, which in 1955 detailed what happened in what became known as the 'wrong door raid': 'The human battering ram backed up and struck again – four or five times in all – before the hinges gave, the door toppled with a terrible crash, and his momentum carried him sailing inside. The rest of the amateur raiders tumbled right after him. A faint light coming from the window told the private eye they were in a bedroom. Any further confirmation he needed was coming from the bed in the form of shrill screams. The investigator had a camera slung around his neck and – without waiting for the lights to be turned on – he blasted away with his flash bulbs.'[2] Kotz woke up to find a bright light shining in her eyes, and the men standing over her bed, holding what she thought was some kind of weapon, perhaps an axe.

Hal Schaefer and Marilyn, in a different apartment upstairs, heard the commotion. 'The whole house shook,' he remembered. 'It was as if somebody had set off a bomb – I mean it was like a bad movie.' The couple managed to sneak out of the block without anyone seeing them. 'If they had found us in bed I think they would have gone for her, I think they would have done something terrible. But they kicked the wrong door in.'[3]

At the time, the police regarded the break-in as an unsuccessful burglary and no one was charged. However, in light of the *Confidential* revelations, the State Senate launched an investigation into the unethical methods of private detectives and their links to scandal sheets. At 4 a.m. on 16 February 1957, Frank Sinatra was in bed at his Palm Springs house when he was served with a subpoena ordering him to appear before a State Legislative Committee. When the hearing opened on 27 February, Sinatra denied that he had ever set foot inside the apartment, insisting that he had remained in his Cadillac throughout the whole debacle.

Sinatra's testimony, however, was called a 'lie' by one of those present that night: private detective Philip Irvin, who had been armed with a camera ready to snap images of Marilyn *in flagrante* with Hal Schaefer. 'Irvin, who had heard Sinatra's testimony, coolly told the committee that Sinatra not only was among the raiders all the time,' reported the *Los Angeles Times*, 'but probably was the man who brought about a panicked scramble for the doorway when he switched on the light and showed the raiders the error of their ways.'[4]

Another witness called before the committee was actress Sheila Stewart Renour, who first met Marilyn in 1953. 'Marilyn had come up to my place for dinner,' she said. 'She was sitting in the living room and I was washing dishes when it all happened. I heard all of this running. It sounded like a whole army. I walked out on the back steps to see what was going on. My first thought was, "Is Florence having a party?" I thought someone was running out to get something. I hadn't even heard the door crashing because I had the water running.'

Sheila maintained that she and Marilyn had been alone in the apartment and it was only years later she finally revealed the truth that Hal had been there that night. 'This particular evening the three of us were there [Sheila, Marilyn and Hal] and I made dinner,' she said. 'She was going over her script for the next day. They were sitting in the dining room and I had taken the dishes from the table into the kitchen and was washing them when I heard the crash outside ... There were so many rumours surrounding the whole thing. I even heard in one report that it was purported that I was a lesbian. I don't know where that came from. I had been married for a number of years at that time – my husband was in Texas at the time this happened. Marilyn was a little fearful and disturbed about that night. We walked out together and she went home and he went home and I cleaned up the mess upstairs, grateful that my door had not been broken into. When Marilyn was going with someone in particular she was one hundred per cent in love with that person – how or why she would lose interest, I don't know.'[5]

Soon after the 'wrong door raid', the relationship between Marilyn and Hal Schaefer cooled. One day towards the end of 1954 he received a call from her to say goodbye, with the hope that they would meet again. It never happened.

'Marilyn once told me that she loved me but I don't think she really knew what that meant,' said Schaefer. 'Marilyn Monroe had slept with eighty million different guys. I wouldn't use the word promiscuous, but I think that she regarded her role – her function – being an attractive female that she was supposed to have sex with somebody, because that's something she could do, that was something she could give, that was what she was *supposed* to do.

But nobody ever had to pay such dues for it like I did. Nobody went after Freddy Karger or Johnny Hyde, or this guy or that guy. That little involvement just about destroyed my career. I paid for this thing over ten thousand times. In this business it's all connections and the number one influence was Frank Sinatra. I've had a circle around my name since that time. I mean, the whole thing with Marilyn was a nightmare.'[6]

40

MARILYN AND HER GHOSTWRITER

The Monroe–DiMaggio marriage was subject to multiple pressures, some internal, others external. One of the most imperceptible, but at the same time insidious sources of stress, was Marilyn's book deal. According to Maurice Zolotow, 'after these stories [about Marilyn's life] were shown to Joe DiMaggio he hit the roof. He was vehemently opposed to the publication of this material.'[1]

The idea for a Marilyn Monroe memoir originated in 1953, when Joe Schenck – with Marilyn's permission – contacted the New York-based literary agent Jacques Chambrun (who had represented H. G. Wells, Zora Neale Hurston, Somerset Maugham, and for a time in the mid-1940s the suspense writer Patricia Highsmith), to ask whether one of his clients, the screenwriter, novelist and journalist Ben Hecht, would be interested in ghostwriting the autobiography. Marilyn knew Hecht from his screenwriting work on *Monkey Business*; he was one of the most highly paid writers in the business, sometimes earning as much as $100,000 for one month's work in Hollywood.

In January 1954, Ben Hecht travelled to San Francisco, where he spent four days interviewing Marilyn about every aspect of her life: her childhood, her early ambitions, her dreams of stardom and her difficult journey to the top. Hecht was accompanied by his secretary Nanette Herbuveaux, who transcribed everything accurately, while he also scribbled down key quotes and facts in a yellow legal pad. He found the actress '100% clinging and cooperative'.[2]

In San Francisco the two agreed terms: as Hecht was doing all of the writing, Marilyn was happy to give him 50 per cent from the book deal, together with 85 per cent of fees from a magazine serialisation. She informed Hecht that she would telephone her lawyer Loyd Wright Jr and ask him to draw up a contract. On his return to Hollywood, Hecht heard from Wright, who agreed to this split of profits and, in turn, drew up a legal document. 'He checked the terms with me that Monroe had told him,' said Hecht. 'They were exactly what Monroe and I had agreed upon, in San Francisco. I was, as always, very pleased by this evidence of female integrity.'[3]

On 16 March, Marilyn wrote to Hecht via her lawyer, stipulating that he was 'to write the story of my life to date, using material concerning my life which I have heretofore given you'. She outlined how all the copy had to be presented to her prior to publication, adding 'neither you nor any other firm or corporation shall publish the whole or any part of said material without having first received my approval to do so'.[4]

Hecht worked quickly, writing thousands of words over the course of four or five days, 'literally without stopping'. In light of the deal, Jacques Chambrun had negotiated an advance of $5,000 from the publisher Doubleday for Hecht, but in March the writer heard that Marilyn had changed her mind, and that she only wanted the interviews to be used as the basis for a magazine piece, not to exceed three instalments. 'I thought this a little crooked on someone's part but in wanting no trouble agreed to go along with just the mags,' wrote Hecht to his lawyer Gregson Bautzer, and duly returned the $5,000 advance.[5]

Hecht was optimistic about the overall direction of the project, but he realised that he would need some more time with Marilyn. Yet he noticed a certain reluctance in her after she returned from honeymoon. 'She got married and the picture changed ... My next session with her may have to be in a ball park,' he said.[6] Hecht rented, at his own expense, a bungalow at the Beverly Hills Hotel, where, in April, he interviewed the actress over the course of two full days. 'I read her the 70 pages in the presence of two witnesses, my secretary and [the director and screenwriter] Charles Lederer,' he said. 'She laughed, cried and told both of them as well as me that she was delighted with the copy. She said to them and me she had never expected it to turn out half as good and that it was the best stuff about herself that she had ever read, and that her whole life seemed finally to have been put down in a dignified and exciting manner.' Marilyn wanted to make a few minor changes here and there, she told him, and two weeks later she met with Hecht again to go over her corrections. 'She had made a dozen minor changes – a phrase removed here, a word stuck in there,' he said. 'There was no indication from her two weeks' work that she had run into anything she didn't approve.' Hecht read aloud an additional seventy pages of material, of which she approved 'as heartily as she had of the first 70 pages'.[7]

By mid-May – by which point the memoir had been sold to *Collier's* magazine – Hecht was waiting for Marilyn's edits. He had seen some of her corrections already, amendments he described as 'intelligent and helpful to the script – and of a minor nature'. He wrote to Loyd Wright, asking whether he might be sent the rest of Marilyn's edits and also outlining his case for a reassessment of the Doubleday deal. 'The book under her name would receive serious literary attention from the entire press and magazine world,' he said. 'It would bring her a high and widespread type of publicity superior to any she has received.' In the same letter, he addressed the fact that Wright had 'admonished' him for shopping the material around in its unedited state, prior to Marilyn's final sign-off. 'It would be rather impossible to sell it without showing it and since you agreed on my selling it and having it published (after Mailyn's [sic] editing) I had it submitted under those conditions,' he said.[8]

On the other side of the Atlantic, a downmarket, Manchester-based newspaper readied itself for one of the scoops of the decade:

the sensational story of Marilyn's life, told in her own words. On 2 May, the *Empire News* splashed with:

No star has ever before dared to write so frankly
MARILYN MONROE confesses The TRUTH about

- My foster mother
- My first love affair
- The men in my life
- Hollywood wolves

Starting next Sunday, the *Empire News* will publish the life story of Marilyn Monroe – BY MARILYN HERSELF.

It's a story that even shock-proof Hollywood is awaiting nervously. Because no star has ever before dared to lay bare so frankly the intrigues behind the glittering front that Hollywood presents to the world.

Marilyn of the honey-blonde hair, pouting lips and hour-glass figure is the top pin-up girl in every country ... And now, she has written her story. FOR THE FIRST TIME she will confess in her own words –

- How I posed nude for a calendar portrait that intrigued America.
- How film agents promised me jobs – on their own unsavoury terms.
- How I starved from studio to studio in search of a job.
- How I suddenly leaped to fame in a city where beauties are a dime a dozen.

But Marilyn will tell more than that – a lot more. This is a personal story – very personal indeed. It starts with a childhood that other stars would be only too glad to forget and publicity agents keen to cover up.

Marilyn, the girl once described as Hollywood's answer to TV, will tell you about her life as a drab little orphanage girl who –

- WAS FARMED OUT AS A SLAVE;
- NEVER SAW HER OWN FATHER;
- CROUCHED IN TERROR WHILE HER MOTHER WAS TAKEN AWAY TO A MADHOUSE;
- MARRIED AT 16 TO ESCAPE THE DRUDGERY OF THE ORPHANAGE.
- FOUND HERSELF IN LOVE FOR THE FIRST TIME – WITH A MAN WHO DIDN'T LOVE HER.

Fiction? Ask the Hollywood gossips. They've been trying to dig up the facts for years. ONLY MARILYN COULD SUPPLY THEM – AND NOW SHE'S DONE IT.

The truth won't, however, appear in the gossip columns but in a book by Marilyn – 'This is My Story' – to be published in America soon.[9]

Although the *Empire News* claimed it had secured the British rights to Marilyn's story, there was a certain mystery surrounding this, as neither Hecht nor Marilyn knew about the deal. It took a while for news of the publication – which was spread over thirteen instalments – to make its way to her, and when her lawyers heard, they were furious. They suspected Hecht or one of his associates of underhand tactics. On 1 June, Loyd Wright dashed off an angry letter to Ben Hecht and Jacques Chambrun asking for the immediate return of all documents and manuscripts relating to Marilyn's life story. 'Without prejudicing the right which Miss Monroe has for damages against you and each of you due to the unauthorised publication of the story in certain British newspapers or newspaper,' wrote Wright, 'this is to demand that you immediately notify said British newspapers . . . that they have no right to publish any further material concerning Miss Monroe written by Mr. Hecht or supplied by Mr. Chambrun.' He also required assurance that no further extracts be printed in Britain, otherwise he would have to take action in the British courts. Wright demanded that Hecht and Chambrun cease negotiations with book publishers regarding the possible sale of the memoir, adding in a censorious tone that it was 'shocking that men will break their word as well as their written contract in a manner such as has been evidenced by the written publication of this material'.[10]

The next day, Rose Hecht – Ben's wife, and under the name Rose Caylor, a journalist, playwright and screenwriter in her own right – wrote a spiky missive back to Wright, defending Hecht's own position and outlining what she saw as Marilyn's shabby behaviour. Answering Wright's accusation that Hecht had profited from the sale of the series, Rose stated that they hadn't made a cent out of the deal; if anything, the project had cost them a fortune. She recounted the history of the deal, and how Marilyn had told everyone present how happy she had been with the material presented to her. Rather than damaging the star's reputation, Ben Hecht had taken her story, often told and retold in the popular press, and had raised it to a higher level. In addition, he had cut out about 30 per cent of material which he thought might have the potential to harm her reputation.

Rose also accused Marilyn of lying to Louella Parsons when she told the gossip columnist that she had never seen or approved any of the material. Her conclusion was brutal and to the point and accused Marilyn of a series of 'lies, fantasies and broken promises'. She and her husband had no choice but to wash their hands of the star, 'with all the perfumes of Arabia'.[11]

41

THE FALL-OUT

But how did Marilyn's memoir – once destined for the highly respected New York-based publisher Doubleday and serialisation in either *Ladies' Home Journal* or *Collier's* – end up running in a rather grubby Sunday newspaper based in the north of England?

The fault, it was soon discovered, lay with Hecht's agent Jacques Chambrun, who had not only sold the rights to the autobiography (for £1,000) without his client's knowledge, but had forged his signature too. As soon as Hecht learned of the extract in *Empire News*, he sent Chambrun a telegram demanding that he stop the serialisation and return any fees paid by the British newspaper. 'I am making all these statements because your action has put me personally into the sort of hole I have never been in before,' said Hecht. 'That of breaking my word. The only redress I can imagine in the matter is to destroy the entire Monroe copy, which I ask you to do on the receipt of this telegram.'[1]

Chambrun refused and the extracts continued to be published. Each of the thirteen instalments boasted headlines such as 'At sixteen I was a frightened bride' (16 May); 'MARRY ME! SAID A DYING MILLIONAIRE' (27 June); and 'JOE puts me well in the shade!' (18 July). Hecht never received a cent for all his troubles because the crooked Chambrun pocketed all the proceeds from the deal himself.

It soon came to light that the agent – who dyed his hair raven black, dressed in smart pinstripe suits, employed a chauffeur and maintained a smart office opposite the Plaza Hotel in New

York — was in the business of filching money from his clients' accounts. Writers who fell victim to Chambrun's highly creative accounting included Somerset Maugham, who was left out of pocket to the tune of $30,000, and Mavis Gallant, who was unaware that the agent had sold two of her stories to the *New Yorker*. When his authors discovered Chambrun's 'literary pyramid scheme' — siphoning off the money from one writer's account to pay off the debt he owed to another — he would tell his clients that it would be best not to bring a legal case against him. 'If you put me in jail, I can't earn any money, and I can't pay you back,' he would tell them. 'If you don't sue me, I'll pay you back.'[2]

The fall-out over the publication of the memoir rumbled on all through the summer and into the autumn, adding discord to Marilyn's already troubled marriage. 'DiMaggio . . . belted her good when he read some of it,' said Robert Slatzer.[3] His statement is backed up by Rose Hecht, who in 1974 told a journalist from the *New York Post* that publication of the extracts infuriated DiMaggio. 'When he heard about the series he was irate,' she said. 'He told Marilyn he would not allow the autobiography to be published [as a book]. So she then backed out of the deal.'[4] In an attempt to save face, and further distance herself from the material, Marilyn issued statements to say that she was considering legal action. Yet she chose not to do so, possibly because, as one Hollywood insider commented at the time, the 'sexsational' extracts only added to her appeal. 'Even this bad publicity didn't seem to hurt her. It's almost as if Marilyn has gotten too big for anything to touch her.'[5]

42

I Love Lucy takes on Marilyn

We glimpse an ankle, a leg, and the rest of the figure oozes its way through the door. A blonde woman in a low-cut, tight-fitting, strapless dress, a diamond necklace encircling her throat – she sways as she walks, a cigarette in her right hand. As the audience whoops with delight, she opens her mouth, pouts, simpers, batting her eyelashes at the camera in a familiar ritual of cinematic seduction. As the laughter and applause reverberate around the studio, Lucille Ball camps up her performance, but then her act is interrupted by two incongruous figures sitting on the sofa:

> **Ethel (dressed as a Spanish dancer):** Hey, who are you supposed to be?
>
> **Lucy:** Guess!
>
> **Fred (dressed as a toreador):** Humphrey Bogart in a wig.

By the time this episode, 'Ricky's Movie Offer', of the TV sitcom *I Love Lucy*, aired on 8 November 1954, the visual symbols of Marilyn – the lips, the hair, the pose, the exaggerated mix of smouldering sexuality and faux innocence – had seeped into the popular consciousness to such an extent that the lead character played by Lucille Ball had no need to name the subject of her impersonation. *I Love Lucy*'s audience was vast – seven out of ten households with televisions watched the show – and everyone got the joke. Marilyn had become that rare thing: a star made up of a small number of simple but instantly recognisable signifiers. The reproduction of her image was everywhere.

She had become an icon. Or a cartoon.

43

'THE WHOLE INSIDE OF HER WOMB WAS CRYING'

As Lucille Ball was playing Marilyn for laughs at the Desilu Studios on Cahuenga Boulevard in Los Angeles, the actress was lying in a hospital bed just a few minutes away. Earlier that day – Monday 8 November 1954 – she had undergone surgery at the Cedars of Lebanon Hospital on Fountains Avenue in Hollywood. She was admitted under the name Mrs Marilyn DiMaggio, and although it was only three days after the trauma of the 'wrong door raid', she was accompanied by Joe, who slept at the hospital that first night so he could see her before she was wheeled into the operating room.

The procedure was described by gossip columnist Louella Parsons as 'an operation of a corrective nature' carried out by Beverly Hills gynaecologist Dr Leon Krohn.[1] When asked by reporters to elaborate on the nature of the surgery, Dr Krohn stressed that it was a 'minor' one and that it would entail no longer than four nights in hospital.[2]

But Marilyn's condition was anything but minor. She suffered from endometriosis, a serious and debilitating condition in which tissue similar to the lining of the uterus grows outside the womb. She had endured intensely painful periods ever since she began to menstruate at the age of twelve, but endometriosis manifests itself in a range of chronic symptoms: fatigue, heavy or irregular periods, pain when having sex, urinating or defecating, constipation and/or diarrhoea. 'The whole inside of her womb was crying,' said Amy Greene. Amy was so distressed by watching her friend suffer that she had booked Marilyn an appointment with a gynaecologist in New York. 'The whole time that he was examining her she would not let me leave the room.' The doctor prescribed Marilyn medication to suppress her period, 'which in retrospect was very dangerous because what you're doing is turning off the faucet and all that stuff is backing up and sooner or later you're gonna have to open that box,' said Amy. The New York doctor suggested a hysterectomy, an idea Marilyn rejected; as she told Amy: 'I have to go through all this pain because I want to have children – I want to have a child, I want to have a son.'[3]

At that time treatment for the condition was limited and, apart from the removal of the ovaries, confined to the excision of endometrial growths. Krohn – Marilyn's gynaecologist since his presence at the removal of her appendix in 1952 – monitored her progress, and was often called to the set during filming. He performed repeated operations to help relieve the symptoms over the next few years.

Doctors who examined Marilyn's records for a paper in the *International Medical Journal* published in 2022 suggested that Marilyn could have been suffering from a prostaglandin imbalance in her brain and reproductive system. 'Dysmenorrhea [period pain] is thought to be caused by the release of prostaglandins in the menstrual fluid, causing uterine contractions and pain,' they write. 'Unfortunately for Marilyn, endogenous prostanoid studies in clinical research blossomed only since the 1970s. Drug therapies using prostaglandin inhibitors for premenstrual syndrome, dysmenorrhea and endometriosis came to be promoted since the 1980s.'[4] In other words, if Marilyn had lived another decade or two she might have benefited from medical advances that could have given her some relief.

Recent academic research has also discovered a link between childhood physical and sexual abuse and endometriosis. In a study in the scientific journal *Human Reproduction*, epidemiologist Dr

Holly Harris said that women who reported severe to chronic physical or sexual abuse had a 79 per cent higher risk of developing the condition. 'It's a strong association,' she writes. 'There's also a dose-response, meaning the risk increases with increasing severity and type of abuse.'[5]

It was highly likely Marilyn would never be able to carry a child to full term. Each time she got pregnant she either suffered a miscarriage, or had to have the foetus surgically removed because the fertilised egg lay outside the womb. At the end of June 1961, in preparation for an operation to remove Marilyn's gall bladder, New York doctor Richard Cottrell carried out a thorough investigation. Before surgery, an air test was conducted to rule out any other factors that might be contributing to her internal discomfort. 'The air entered her tubes very slowly, verifying what her gynaecologist had previously observed: her tubes were blocked by residue,' said Cottrell.[6]

Over the years there's been a great deal of speculation about whether Marilyn had abortions – and, if so, how many. Amy Greene maintained that the actress told her that she had undergone as many as twelve terminations, but Marilyn could have said this either to shock her friend or as a result of her emotional and psychological state. Certainly, this anecdotal evidence is called into question by the testimonies of both Dr Krohn – who said that Marilyn had never had any abortions – and also Dr Lee Siegel, the physician employed by Twentieth Century-Fox. 'If she had that condition [endometriosis], she wouldn't need an abortion – she would have aborted,' said Siegel. 'It's very difficult to get pregnant with endometriosis.'[7]

Such is the public's continuing fascination with Marilyn that when X-rays of her pelvis and chest cavity – taken during her November 1954 hospital stay – came up for auction in 2017 they sold for $3,840 and $5,120. Later, a radiologist at the Cedars of Lebanon Hospital used the X-rays as a teaching aid; apparently, the fact that the patient was Marilyn Monroe was enough to guarantee that the trainee medics paid attention.

On 12 November 1954, after the gynaecological procedure, Marilyn was discharged from hospital. She knew there was a crowd of reporters waiting for her outside, so she tried to leave via a basement. But the pack of photographers and journalists was waiting for her, keen to learn whether there was any truth in a rumour that there might be a reconciliation between her and Joe DiMaggio.

Footage shows a tired, make-up free Marilyn being led through a hospital corridor by a nurse. When she realises she is being filmed, she turns up the collar of her fur coat, in a half-hearted attempt to protect herself. Undeterred, the cameraman continues to film her. As she approaches the elevator she realises she is cornered; with downcast eyes, she turns her back on the camera, looking like a trapped animal.

44

A NEW FUTURE

It was no wonder she wanted to escape. And photographer Milton Greene offered her a way out. One night, towards the end of December 1954, Marilyn, disguised in a black wig and travelling under the name Zelda Zonk, boarded the red-eye with Milton from Los Angeles to New York. There, in early 1955, the 28-year-old film star and the 33-year-old photographer – regarded by Richard Avedon as 'the greatest photographer of women'[1] he'd ever encountered would launch Marilyn Monroe Productions, a joint venture that would give the actress a greater degree of control over future projects.

Most biographies relate how the two met in the late summer of 1953: according to this well-worn version of the story, the baby-faced Greene had been commissioned by *Look* magazine to take photographs of the actress. And as Marilyn was flicking through his portfolio, she commented, 'Why, you're nothing but a boy!' Without missing a beat, Greene replied, 'Well, you're nothing but a girl!' However, it seems now that the pair first met back in 1949, at the LA house of *Look* magazine editor Rupert Allan; according to Donald Spoto, the two embarked on a brief affair. After that relationship cooled, Marilyn and Milton remained close, and she became friends with his new wife.

On Milton's wedding day to the Cuban-born model Amy Franco in September 1953, Marilyn sent the new bride five dozen long-stemmed American Beauty roses. 'We actually met on our honeymoon when we went back to California,' recalled Amy later. This meeting was at a party at Gene Kelly's house, where everyone was playing charades, except for Milton and Marilyn, who was still so fresh from a recent bath that Amy described her as looking less like a sex siren and more like a wet chicken. 'At this point, Marilyn was such a recluse that no one within the industry really knew her. Really all she did was eat, sleep and work. She never had any clothes – whenever she needed something to go out, she'd go to her friend at the wardrobe department at Twentieth and she'd borrow something and the next morning she'd bring it back. She was vital, a very pretty young woman who was a sponge absorbing life.' Amy repeatedly rejected the idea that her husband and her good friend were lovers. 'I was secure in my marriage, I was secure with her,' she said. 'Also, I trusted her. There was no way in the world she would shaft me to bang Milton.'[2]

During an interview in the early 1980s, Anthony Summers asked Amy about the nature of the Milton–Marilyn relationship. Occasionally, she said she felt annoyed if Milton failed to turn up to a social engagement or when he missed the first half of a play due to his obligations with Marilyn, but she never doubted the fidelity either of her husband or her friend. 'I never felt threatened as a woman,' she said. Maybe Amy never felt threatened in the sense that whether Marilyn went to bed with Milton or not, she wasn't about to take him away from her? 'She knew I would have killed her,' she replies, laughing. 'But she was not a home wrecker. That was one of the problems [later] with Arthur [Miller].'[3]

Marilyn had turned to Milton because she hoped that the professional image-maker would help kick-start her career. During 1953 and 1954, Marilyn had felt increasingly dissatisfied with the studio and her relatively small salary – her Fox contract meant that her pay was capped at between $500 and $3,500 a week, while her co-star in *Gentlemen Prefer Blondes* Jane Russell earned $100,000 for the film – and the superficial nature of roles that she was offered. Marilyn was keen to play the part of the Babylonian prostitute

Nefer in Michael Curtiz's *The Egyptian* (1954), but lost out to the Polish actress Bella Darvi.

Instead of *The Egyptian*, Fox insisted Marilyn star in *The Girl in Pink Tights*, a new version of Betty Grable's musical comedy from 1943, *Coney Island*. Marilyn wanted to read the script before agreeing to the role, but Zanuck refused. The battle came to a head at the end of 1953 and beginning of 1954. After failing to persuade her to start work on the film, Zanuck then tried to lure her back into the studio for retakes on *River of No Return*. When she refused, Zanuck was so furious he said he would 'destroy an asset' – namely Marilyn – and leak the story to the press. 'It will be all over the whole damn industry,' he said.[4] Marilyn, although nervous about the consequences, stood her ground and refused to comply with Fox's demands. The title of the next film chosen for her – *The Girl in the Red Swing* (a role that eventually was taken by Joan Collins) – can hardly have persuaded her that things might improve.

When Marilyn didn't turn up to the set of *Pink Tights* twice in January 1954, Fox suspended her and threatened her with legal action. But the studio hadn't reckoned on Marilyn's tenacity. Throughout 1954 she raged a war of attrition with Fox. They cast her in Nunnally Johnson's *How to Be Very, Very Popular* – a film about a couple of showgirls who witness a murder and disguise themselves as boys at a college (a plot that Billy Wilder would riff on for *Some Like It Hot*) – but Marilyn turned it down. 'She sent the script back,' said Johnson later. 'I have no idea whether she read it or not. They just said she returned it and said she's not going to do anything until her contract was rewritten.'[5]

It wasn't just about money: Marilyn wanted greater control of her films – particularly of their scripts, directors and cameramen – but Charles Feldman, her agent at Famous Artists, persuaded her that most of her demands were unrealistic. A new draft contract, sent to Marilyn in May 1954, gave her control only over her choice of choreographer and dramatic coach. A scathing review of *River of No Return* in the *Hollywood Reporter* did not help her cause: 'If *River* proves anything at all, it is that Marilyn Monroe should stick to musicals and the type of entertainment that made her such a box-office lure. If the film fails to bring in smash returns, Twentieth Century-Fox can attribute it to Marilyn's inability to handle a heavy acting role.'[6] There are some reports that claim she screamed when she read the review.

It was at this point, with Marilyn at a low ebb, that Milton Greene flew back to LA for another photographic assignment for *Look* magazine. During the day the couple worked on images shot on location in Laurel Canyon, and on the backlot of Fox's *What Price Glory*, where Marilyn dressed as a peasant girl in Jennifer Jones's costume from *The Song of Bernadette*. 'It was the ultimate in-joke to put the world's leading sex symbol in Saint Bernadette's clothes,' said Amy Greene.[7]

One night, over dinner, Milton, after listening to the actress's ongoing troubles with the studio, suggested something radical and daring: what if Marilyn formed her own production company, which would give her the creative control she longed for? The idea thrilled her: 'Who's she gonna trust – not Zanuck, not Charlie Feldman, not DiMaggio,' said Greene. 'She had no one she could trust except me. Because I'm gonna give her a straight answer.'[8] She agreed that Milton could send her Fox contract to his lawyer, Frank Delaney, for review. He pronounced it nothing better than a 'slave labor agreement'.[9] Greene also discovered that 'one [contract had] lapsed and the other had not been signed – that's how the fight started'. The outcome of this process was the creation of a new production company, with Marilyn owning 51 per cent, and Milton 49 per cent. Soon Milton's work for the company became all-consuming and he had no choice but to resign his $100,000 a year job with *Look*. 'When I got involved with Marilyn there was no time for anything else but Marilyn.'[10]

After Milton and Marilyn landed in New York that cold December morning in 1954, Amy picked up her husband and his new business partner and drove them to the Greene family home in Weston, Connecticut, with its sixteen rooms and 11 acres of garden. There, Marilyn was installed in the guest room, which the couple had decorated just for her, with its lavender wallpaper, pink quilted bedspread and dark purple velvet throw pillows. 'She felt protected, we cocooned her, whereas no one else had done that before,' said Amy.[11]

Interviewed in 1955, Amy was described by the journalist from *Photoplay* magazine as 'Slender, tiny – not quite five feet tall – she looks about fifteen years old. A sprinkle of freckles dusts her gold-tanned face. She wears no make-up, not even lipstick ... While she looks like a child, her quick actions, crisp speech and well-formulated observations have the sureness of an intelligent woman who has thought things through, knows who she is, what she wants out of life, and is extremely happy with the situation in which she finds herself.'[12] Amy was never intimidated by Marilyn's presence; if anything, the actress was more often than not overawed by her. Marilyn was impressed by Amy's strong character, her outspoken nature and her education. The two talked about inspirational, strong women who had made their mark: Emma Hamilton, Marie Antoinette, Joséphine Bonaparte, Isadora Duncan and Juliette Récamier. 'She was fascinated by women who had made it,' said Amy.[13]

Marilyn helped Amy around the house, and with the Greenes' young son Joshua, who had been born in March 1954. The actress also adored being so close to nature in Connecticut. As an LA native, she'd never really been conscious of the changing seasons; she'd never seen snow before. Amy recalled how her new friend pointed out the bare skeletal limbs of the trees, which came into bud with the onset of the spring. 'To her, it seemed like a miracle,' said Amy.[14]

45

Pill popping

Despite taking decisive steps to reshape her career, other things were slipping out of control behind the scenes. Fixed in popular consciousness is the image of Marilyn the pill addict, dependent on a toxic mix of uppers and downers, amphetamines and barbiturates. It seems unlikely that she began to take drugs recreationally; what's more probable is that she turned to pills as a way of relieving the agonies of her endometriosis. 'She knew that every month when she menstruated, she would have this terrible pain that only drugs could ease,' said Susan Strasberg.[1]

Maurice Zolotow recalled that when he visited Marilyn's dressing room at the Fox studios he saw as many as fourteen different boxes of pills. These included Ergotrate, which helped relieve the symptoms of endometriosis, and Empirin with codeine, which she took when she suffered menstrual cramps. Friends remembered how she would be driving in her car when suddenly she would be so overcome by pain that she would have to brake, stagger out of the car and fall to the ground in agony.

But how did the addiction to medication begin and what was its particular allure for her? According to Amy Greene, Marilyn told her that she was 'only a baby, eighteen or nineteen' when she started taking pills.[2] In *My Story*, Marilyn related how in the summer or autumn of 1947, soon after losing her initial short-term contract with Fox, she turned to sleeping pills while suffering the symptoms of a bad cold. She hadn't slept for several nights and felt she needed something to knock her out. 'I don't usually recommend sleeping pills,' a doctor told her, 'but you've been having hysterics too long. A good sleep will not only be good for your cold but cheer you up.'[3] In October the same year, it's been reported that Marilyn turned to barbiturates when she was shooting a bit part in the musical comedy *You Were Meant for Me* (her small role ended up on the cutting room floor).

It's not difficult to imagine why sedatives and tranquillisers appealed to Marilyn. Her talent, as she saw it, was to be beautiful: in her modelling days and early Hollywood career, she was required to be all surface. The pills smoothed away the sharp edges of anxiety that threatened to claw their way into her interior world. They helped her smile when she wanted to scream. They brought sleep in a terrifying world. They functioned as a salve to the stab wound of her psyche, a lesion that had been left red-raw and exposed since the days of her sexual abuse all those years ago. In an unpublished letter, Marilyn's psychiatrist Dr Greenson wrote that her habit of taking sleeping pills 'was her way of escaping the miseries of life'. In the same letter – which Greenson wrote to Norman Rosten shortly after her death – he said, 'Marilyn was a bottomless well, one could not fill her, with all the deep, deep holes her lack of family had left her with.'[4]

Marilyn often needed to take pills before public events. For instance, on the evening of the premiere of *How to Marry a Millionaire*, on 4 November 1953, Marilyn was travelling in a car to the house of Nunnally Johnson – the screenwriter and producer of the film – for a pre-screening dinner party with fellow guests Lauren Bacall and her husband Humphrey Bogart, when she was asked by Maurice Zolotow how she felt. 'I guess this is just about the happiest night of my life,' she said. 'Somehow it's like when I was a little girl and pretended wonderful things were happening to me. Now they are.'[5]

However, what Marilyn didn't reveal was the trauma she'd had to endure to prepare herself for the night. That morning, she had woken up feeling so nervous she felt sick. 'She swallowed a painkiller,' said Zolotow. 'She retched and threw it up. She squeezed a glass of orange juice for herself and stirred a packet of gelatine powder into it. She couldn't keep solid food down. She prayed the juice would stay down. It did. Then she took two more painkilling capsules.' After having a bath and dressing she took two more pills, before she drove in her Cadillac convertible – a gift for appearing on the Jack Benny television show a couple of months earlier – to the Fox studio. There, she transformed herself into a star worthy of the public's expectations. She had her hair freshly dyed, her nails were painted with platinum polish. She stepped into the high-waisted white lace dress lined with crêpe de chine the colour of flesh and covered with thousands of sequins and slipped on a pair of long gloves that stretched to the tops of her arms. A fur stole around her shoulders, a muff for her hands, and the addition of a pair of diamond earrings completed the picture. 'It had taken six hours and twenty minutes to get her into a disguise for the festivities,' said Zolotow.[6]

The frenzy that greeted Marilyn at the premiere would have unsettled the strongest of constitutions. When the crowd caught sight of her there was an enormous roar, 'like an approaching earthquake,' said director Jean Negulesco. Four policemen had to carry her over the heads of her fans – all crying out 'Marilyn! Marilyn!' – and when she made it safely inside the theatre, the guests stood on their chairs to get a better view of the star. 'I witnessed beyond any expectation the luxury of her fame,' said Negulesco.[7]

It was easy for Marilyn to get hold of pills. They were everywhere in Hollywood. Anthony Summers identifies two men as being responsible for introducing her to prescription drugs. The first was the actor Edward G. Robinson Jr, her one-time lover, who was known around town as a 'pill freak'.[8] The second was Sidney Skolsky, who based himself at Schwab's drugstore and had an 'unlimited supply'; Joe DiMaggio reportedly referred to Skolsky and Marilyn as 'pill-pals'.[9] Skolsky was also a hypochondriac who 'knew every pill manufactured', according to his daughter Steffi. 'Marilyn would call him up for recommendations of doctors.' Sometimes, the drugstore's owner Jack Schwab would ring up Skolsky because Marilyn had come in with yet another prescription. 'What should I do, Sidney? . . . she's taking too many,' he said. 'What can we do?' replied Sidney. 'If you don't fill it, someone else will.'[10]

Those in the showbiz world regarded the prescription of uppers and downers as normal. 'In those days, pills were seen as another tool to keep stars working,' said Dr Lee Siegel, one of the medics at Twentieth Century-Fox. 'The doctors were caught in the middle. If one doctor would not prescribe, there was always another who would.'[11] Another of Siegel's famous patients was Judy Garland, who would die from an accidental overdose of Seconal in London in 1969. Garland told *McCall's* magazine that as a seventeen-year-old the studio 'had us working days and nights on end. They'd give us pep pills to keep us on our feet long after we were exhausted. Then they'd take us to the studio hospital and knock us out cold with sleeping pills – Mickey [Rooney] sprawled out on one bed and me on another. Then after four hours they'd wake us up and give us the pep-pills again so we could work 72 hours in a row. Half of the time we were hanging from the ceiling, but it was a way of life for us.'[12]

Slowly, it became a way of life for Marilyn too. During the shooting of *There's No Business Like Show Business*, in the summer of 1954, she turned up for work feeling, and looking, the worse for wear, 'groggy, moody, weepy . . . confused, shaky and unprepared'. Marilyn was experiencing marital difficulties – and enduring bouts of domestic violence – with Joe DiMaggio. The pills represented an escape route for her. Yet she also knew that they were dangerous. According to Donald Spoto, one day in 1955 Marilyn thrust a bottle of sleeping pills into Amy Greene's hands, informing her to keep them from her. 'If she asked for them, I was to give her an argument,' said Amy. 'I told her she'd come to the right person. But soon she cajoled and begged me, and Milton insisted I give her the pills.'[13] Milton also supplied Marilyn with Dexamyl – a potent mix of sodium amobarbital and dextroamphetamine sulfate – 'pills to pick you up, they were triangles,' recalled Milton. 'They came in different colours. In New York they used to be blue and in London [in 1956, when filming *The Prince and the Showgirl*] I got them in pink.'[14]

It has to be remembered that the use of such stimulants was so widespread and commonplace that even establishment figures such as British Prime Minister Anthony Eden were being prescribed Drinamyl (the British name for Dexamyl) for severe abdominal pain brought on by botched gall bladder surgery.

Drugs such as Dexamyl may have made users like Marilyn feel immediately energised, but she soon fell victim to the inevitable downward spiral of the 'crash' or 'come down', which manifested itself in symptoms such as inability to sleep, anxiety and irritability. The only answer was then to take barbiturates like Seconal or Nembutal, which in turn made her feel sluggish and lethargic. And so the vicious circle, which eventually led towards addiction, was complete.

By the mid-1950s, Marilyn had become something of an expert in pill-taking, as her friend Susan Strasberg recalled. Strasberg was seventeen at the time and starring in *The Diary of Anne Frank* on Broadway. She first met Marilyn during the filming of *There's No Business Like Show Business*, and got to know her well a year later when Marilyn began to study in New York with her father, the acting coach Lee Strasberg. 'I was given sleeping pills because I couldn't sleep and Marilyn as a matter of fact said to me if you puncture them, they work faster,' recalled Susan. 'So I started puncturing them to work faster, but we didn't know the damage . . . you weren't as aware in those days.'[15]

Marilyn's mother, Gladys Pearl Baker. 'For a long time I was scared I'd find out that I was like my mother and end up in the crazy house,' said Marilyn.

Marilyn's father, Charles Stanley Gifford. Tracking him down became something of an obsession for Marilyn, who was born illegitimate.

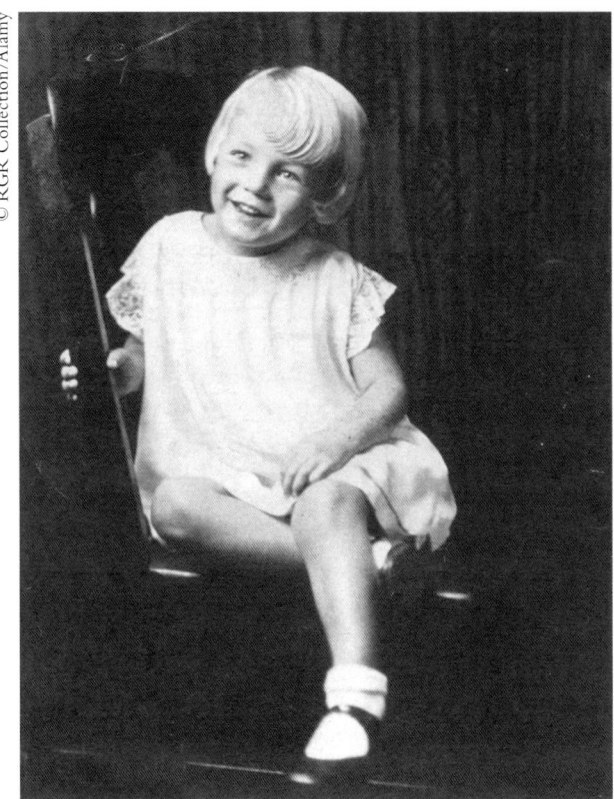

'I dreamed chiefly of beauty,' Marilyn said of her troubled childhood. 'I dreamed of myself becoming so beautiful that people would turn to look at me when I passed.'

Marilyn, then known as Norma Jeane, with her beloved 'Aunt' Ana Lower. One day a girl made fun of Norma Jeane's appearance and she came back to Ana in tears. 'It doesn't make any difference if other children make fun of you, dear,' she told her. 'It's what you really are that counts.'

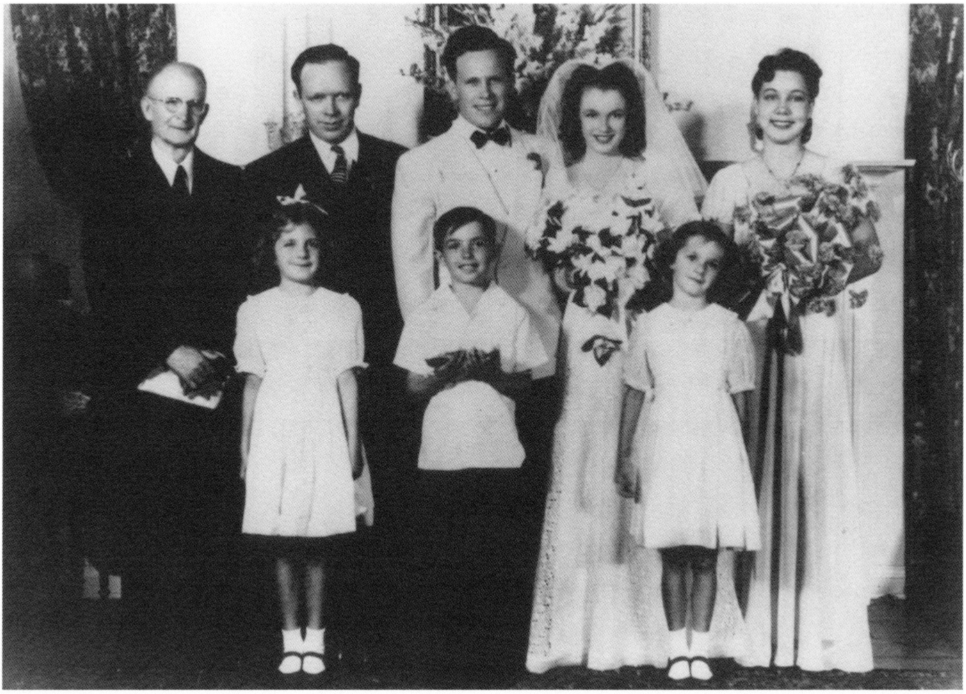

© Kobal/Shutterstock

Norma Jeane on her wedding day to first husband Jim Dougherty in June 1942. She was just sixteen years old. 'She wanted something, *someone* that she could hold onto all the time,' he said.

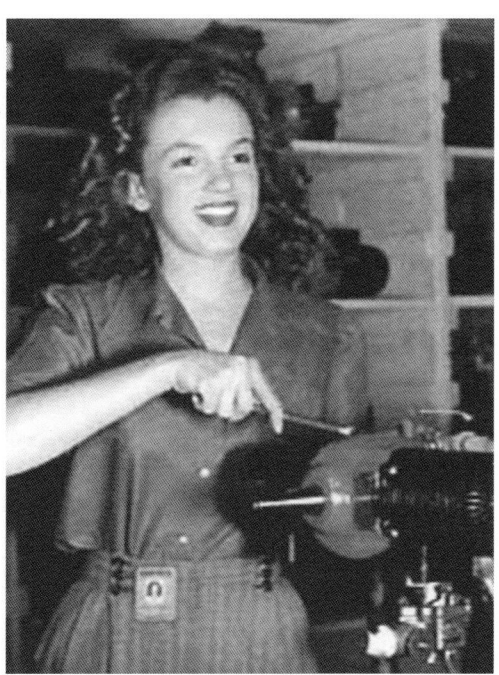

One of the first professional photos of Norma Jeane, taken in December 1944 at the Radioplane factory in Burbank, California.

© Album / Alamy

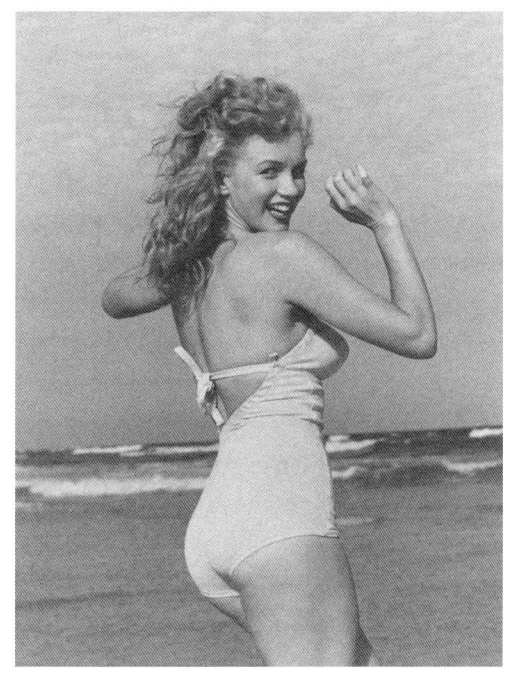

An early modelling shot taken by André de Dienes. 'With her childlike smile and clear gaze, she was absolutely enchanting,' he said.

Marilyn with acting coach Natasha Lytess, early 1949. 'The trouble is that when people look at her, they immediately see her as a typical Hollywood Blonde,' said Lytess. 'Marilyn's soul just doesn't fit her body.'

Marilyn with agent and lover Johnny Hyde. 'He made this town Marilyn Monroe conscious,' said one film producer.

In 1953, Marilyn starred in three breakthrough films: *How to Marry a Millionaire*, *Gentlemen Prefer Blondes* and *Niagara*.

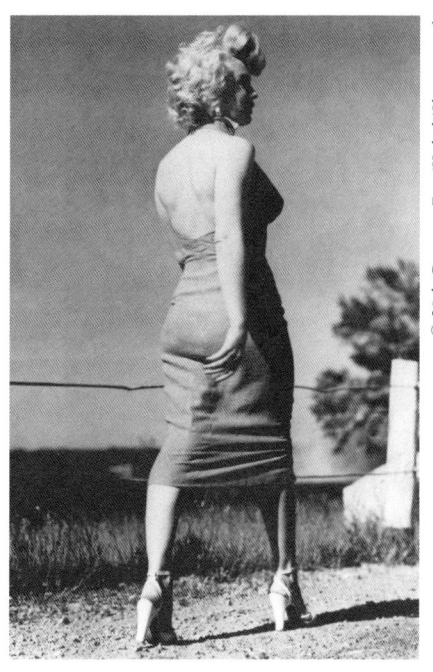

On release of *Niagara*, Marilyn was immediately dubbed 'the girl with the horizontal walk'.

© Kobal/Shutterstock

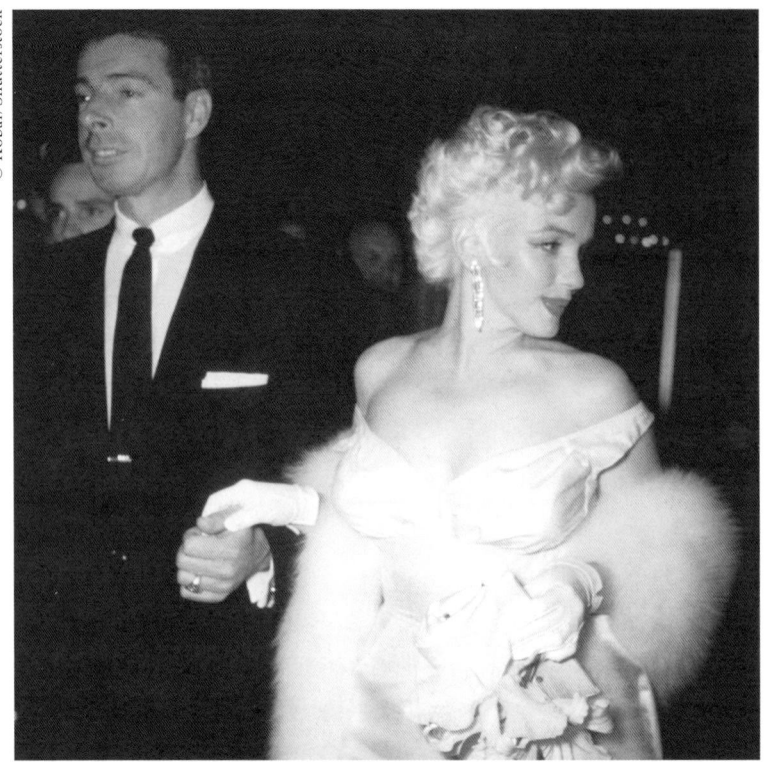

Marilyn with second husband, baseball star Joe DiMaggio, whom she married in 1954. 'The best way to describe Joe DiMaggio is [that] he was a penis with a man hanging from it,' said one of his friends.

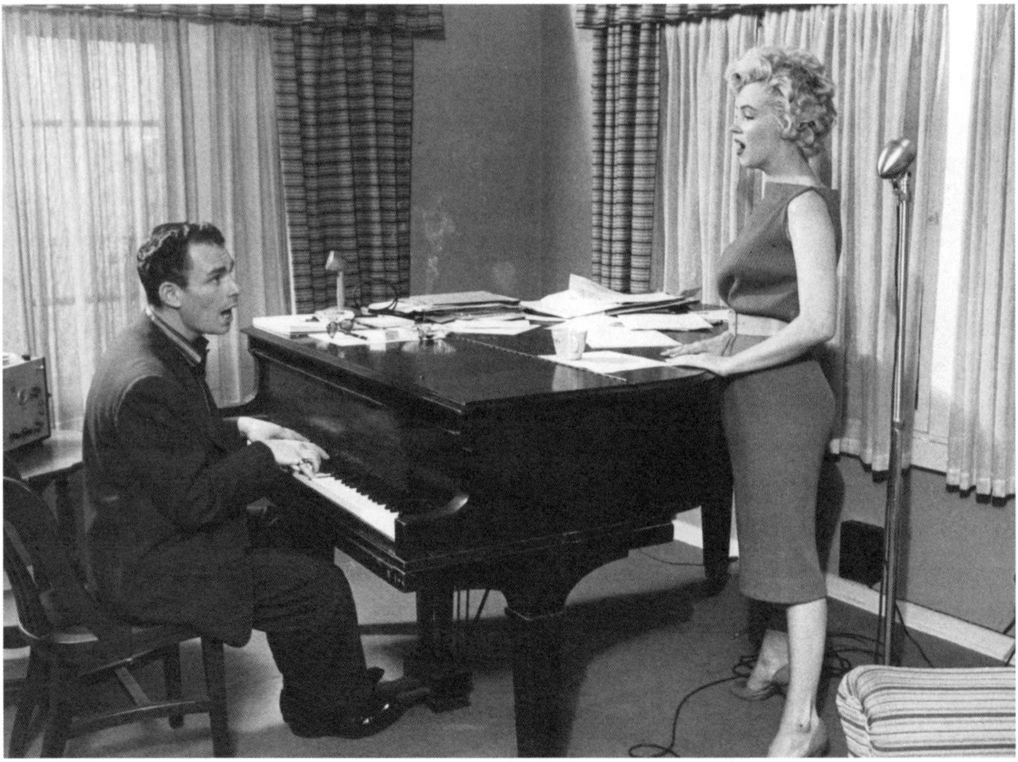

Marilyn with vocal coach and lover Hal Schaefer. 'She struck me as she was not wholly here, not in the world,' he said.

Marilyn, a high school drop-out, felt her lack of education keenly. 'She very badly needed not to be thought of as just a tits-and-ass cutie,' said poet Dylan Thomas, who met her in 1950.

With Danish author Karen Blixen. 'I shall never forget the almost overpowering feeling of unconquerable strength and sweetness which she conveyed,' said the *Out of Africa* author.

Dame Edith Sitwell with Marilyn: 'She was very quiet, had great natural dignity (I cannot imagine anyone who knew her trying to take a liberty with her), and was extremely intelligent. She was also exceedingly sensitive,' wrote the poet after their meeting in 1953.

© Associated Press

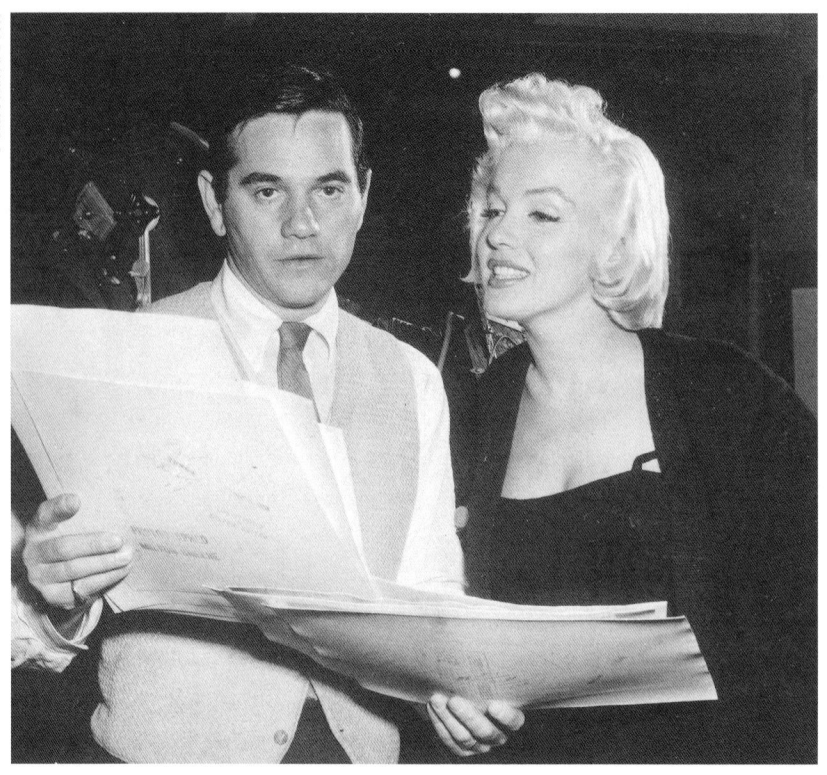

In early 1955, the star formed Marilyn Monroe Productions with Milton Greene in an effort to maintain greater control over her film projects.

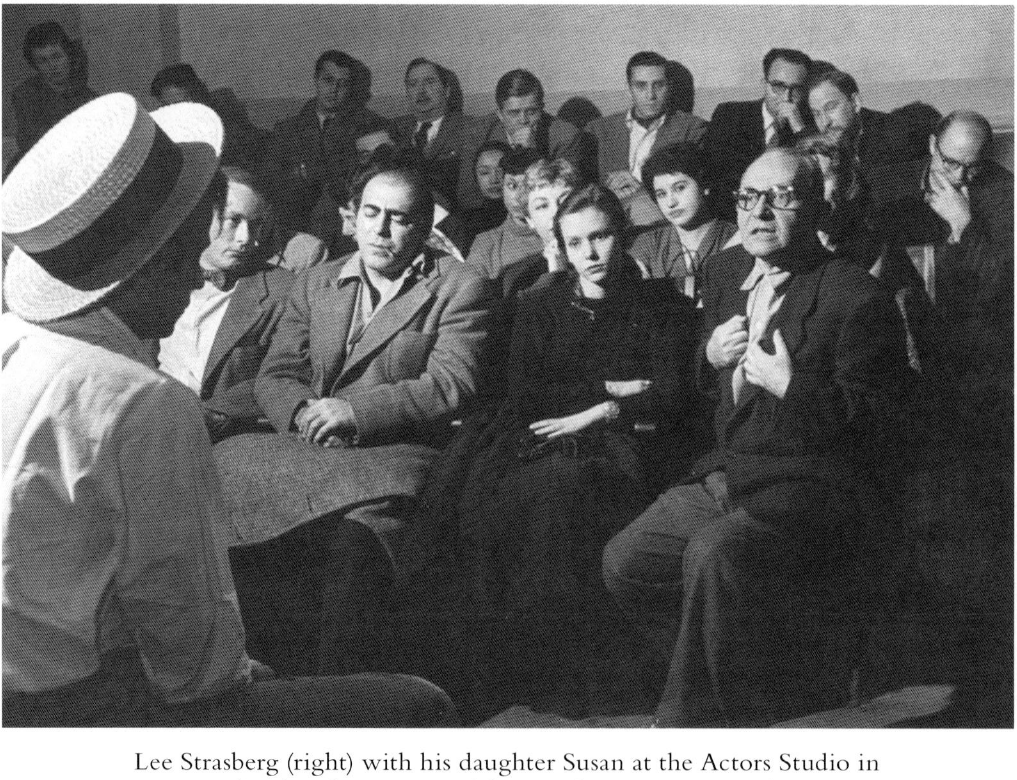

Lee Strasberg (right) with his daughter Susan at the Actors Studio in New York. 'I've always wanted for people to see *me*, not the actress, the real person,' Marilyn told Susan. 'Your daddy does.'

Marilyn described herself to her new, younger friend as a 'war veteran of the night. If I haven't tried it, it doesn't exist.'[16]

Even though she had her own place in New York, Marilyn would often go over to the Strasbergs' large, ten-room apartment on Central Park West when she couldn't sleep. She would arrive, sometimes in the middle of the night, with no make-up, her hair all messed up, her clothes dishevelled. Susan would watch as her father rocked Marilyn to sleep, singing a lullaby to her as she dozed. 'She just wants to be held, she wasn't held as a child,' Lee told her. 'If I hold her, she can go to sleep without pills. I won't give them to her, she's got to stop the pills.'[17]

One night, after Susan had returned late from a performance of *The Diary of Anne Frank*, she was in the kitchen when she heard a sound coming from the corridor. As she peeked around the door, she tried to make sense of what she saw: a figure dressed in a white robe crawling on hands and knees along the red carpet. 'It was Marilyn,' she remembered. 'A loose robe fell open over her nude body; luminous, she seemed to glow in the dark ... she was moving slowly, sluggishly, on all fours. Her progress was interminable ... "Lee ... Lee," she whimpered.' Just as Susan was about to go and help Marilyn, her father came and carried the actress back to her bedroom. 'She'd taken too many pills again,' recalled Susan. 'She would forget and take more and then remember, too late.'[18]

46

'I CAN MAKE MY FACE DO ANYTHING'

In the October 1953 issue of *Photoplay* magazine, Marilyn revealed her beauty secrets:

> I get letters asking me how I keep my skin so clear, and I'm sure many of the girls who write me expect I'll come up with some name of a miracle cream or lotion. Well, let me tell you that while cream and lotion can keep your complexion soft and smooth, they can't hide the dullness that overeating and over-drinking, particularly of alcoholic drinks, will give your skin. And there's nothing like your face scrubbed clean with good soap and water, the glow you can only get from plenty of rest, an easy-to-digest diet, and cleanliness, cleanliness about your face, figure, hair and clothes. I honestly know what I'm talking about.
>
> When a man looks into your eyes, he doesn't like looking into an over-heavy mess of mascara and eyeshadow. On screen, I do have to make up my eyes considerably, but offscreen I use eye make-up so that it looks completely natural. Following the same principle, I use natural-colored fingernail polish, but I do use bright red toenail polish. And I use toilet water, lavishly ...
>
> I try to find a shampoo that is mild – because of my bleaching – and I dry my hair by hand, but never directly in the sun for the same reason. I dry it partly with a big Turkish towel, partly by brushing. Before it is quite dry, I

rub a touch of toilet water into it. Then I set my pin curls in big loose waves.

One thing practically every actress in Hollywood possesses, and which I think is the best possible beauty possession, is a professional, standing hair dryer. I got mine second-hand from a beauty parlour, and so can you, from one in your home town. This way they cost about $65. I know that's an awful lot of money – but it is the investment of years ... Then all you have to do is take the pins out of your curls, give your hair a fast two minutes of brushing, and the man of your dreams will think your hair is that-a-way just naturally ... I carry a very tiny, but stiff-bristled hairbrush with me wherever I go ... when no man is looking, I brush my hair during the day. I honestly think beauty 'secrets' should be 'secret'. I no more think you should use a lipstick, powder, deodorant, or hairbrush in public than you would take a bath in public.[1]

Marilyn had another beauty secret too. 'Marilyn never closed her mouth,' said the photographer Richard Avedon. 'A lot of girls had great laughs, but she took it to the furthest point, so that it became iconic – the gasping mouth, the laughing mouth, the open mouth, which represented the possibility of pleasure.'[2] Joyce Carol Oates, in her novel *Blonde*, went one step further: 'Mouth like a cunt. That's her secret.'[3] If Marilyn was about to shoot a scene in which she wanted to appear more sexual, she would smear a mix of Vaseline and wax over her lips to give them an extra sheen. On top of this she would apply a blend of three different shades of lipstick to make her mouth look even more open. Recently, Monroe's lipsticks have come up for auction: in December 2022 a tube of Max Factor Ruby Red sold for $15,625, while back in 1999 Marilyn's make-up case fetched $266,500. The black case with five metal drawers contained the following, as listed in the Christie's auction catalogue:

- Three lipsticks by Max Factor, labeled LS/7-22/N.I [Ruby Red]
- One highlighter and two Elizabeth Arden cream eyeshadows in gold tone tubes named 'Autumn Smoke' and 'Pearly Blue'
- Two Elizabeth Arden 'Eye Stopper' eyeliners, one brown and one black
- One cream 'Light Green' eyeshadow in a pot by Leichner of London
- Two bottles of nail polish by Revlon, one 'Cherries a la Mode', the other 'Hot Coral', and a bottle of cuticle oil
- An eyeliner and a box containing flash eyelashes by Glorene of Hollywood
- A bottle of black liquid eyeliner
- A box of 'Hollywood Wings'
- Two bottles of perfumed lotion from the 'Quintess' line by Shisheido, in their box
- Anita d'Foged 'Day Dew' cream make-up and cover-up
- Two pots of Erno Lazlo make-up
- A box of tissue
- A selection of matchbooks, including one printed MMM and others from restaurants including Sardi's
- Two paper fans
- Three satin purses
- Two pocket mirrors
- A bottle of smelling salts[4]

Some accused Marilyn of extreme narcissism, constantly obsessing over the maintenance of the mask she'd created for herself. According to her last psychiatrist Dr Greenson, the star 'gloried and revelled in her personal appearance, feeling that she was perhaps the most beautiful woman in the world';[5] her many fans would not disagree with the assessment.

The film critic Pauline Kael believed that Marilyn only came truly alive in front of an audience. 'She was a little knocked out; her face looked as if, when nobody was paying attention to her, it would go utterly slack – as if she died between wolf calls,' she said.[6] Yet, there was something else at work here, a steely professionalism that often went unnoticed. 'She adored her face,' said William Travilla, 'constantly wanted to make it better and different. She once told me, "I can make my face do anything, same as you can take a white board and do a painting. I paint it [her face] all white and paint the shadows how I'd want, the highlights, shape the mouth, and so forth."'[7]

Marilyn had a fear of ageing. Once, after a class at the Actors Studio in New York, she accompanied Jane Fonda to the Russian Tea Room, where they discussed the parts they could both play as they got older. Fonda said she would embrace it, but Monroe threw her hands up to her face and said, 'No, no, it can't happen to me!'[8]

The writer Truman Capote – who had first met Marilyn when she was filming *The Asphalt Jungle* – recalled how one day in New York, in April 1955, after he followed her into the dimly lit ladies' room of a bar, he observed her applying ruby red lipstick and studying her reflection in the mirror.

'What are you doing?' asked Truman.

'Looking at her,' she replied.[9]

47

STAYING IN SHAPE

In a 1996 interview with the *New Yorker*, the comedian Roseanne Barr claimed that Marilyn Monroe had been a size sixteen.[1] Four years later, the actress and model Elizabeth Hurley observed, 'I've always thought Marilyn Monroe looked fabulous, but I'd kill myself if I was that fat. I went to see her clothes in the exhibition [the Christie's auction held in New York in 1999], and I wanted to take a tape measure and measure what her hips were. She was very big.'[2]

It's true that Marilyn's weight varied over the years. Early studio biographies list her as weighing 118 pounds. It's estimated that at the end of the 1950s she reached 140 pounds, while at the end of her life (according to the LA coroner's report) she was 117 pounds. However, Marilyn was never overweight.

Norma Jeane's record card from the Blue Book Modeling Agency, dated 2 August 1945, lists her dimensions: she was 5 feet 6 inches tall, weighed 120 pounds, with a bust of 36 inches, waist 24 and hips 34 – in other words she possessed a classic hourglass figure. She watched her weight – there's a photograph of her taken in 1951 jogging (in jeans and bikini top) through a Los Angeles back alley – while a year later she had devised a fitness plan that she claimed suited her body.

Each morning after cleaning her teeth and washing her face, she worked out on the floor by her bed. 'I have evolved my own exercises, for the muscles I wish to keep firm, and I know they are right for me because I can feel them putting the proper muscles into play as I exercise,' she told *Pageant* magazine. 'It is a simple bust-firming routine which consists of lifting five-pound weights from a spread-eagle arm position to a point directly above my head. I do this fifteen times, slowly. Then, with my arms at a 45-degree angle from the floor, I move my weights in circles until I'm tired. I don't count rhythmically like the exercise people on the radio; I couldn't stand exercise if I had to feel regimented about it.'

She went on to tell the magazine that she liked to sleep between five and ten hours a night – this was before she became hooked on pills – and that she slept in the nude. Accompanying the article a double-page photograph showed the actress in bed – naked – with just a white sheet pulled over her to cover her body and breasts. Marilyn is also shown about to crack an egg into a glass of milk, an illustration of her typical breakfast. 'I've been told that my eating habits are absolutely bizarre, but I don't think so,' she said. 'Before I take my morning shower, I start warming a cup of milk on the hot plate I keep in my hotel room. When it's hot, I break two raw eggs into the milk, whip them up with a fork, and drink them while I'm dressing. I supplement this with a multi-vitamin pill, and I doubt if any doctor could recommend a more nourishing breakfast for a working girl in a hurry.'

For dinner, she ate either broiled steak, lamb chops or liver, with a side of raw carrot, sometimes as many as four or five. 'I must be part rabbit; I never get bored with raw carrots,' she joked.[3]

Marilyn sometimes suffered from anaemia; endometriosis brings on heavy bleeds, resulting in lower levels of red blood cells. To counter this, her doctor, Elliot Corday, prescribed her iron and vitamin shots as well as a special diet, which included a lunch of a glass of tomato juice mixed with two tablespoons of raw ground liver; a snack of a hard-boiled egg and gelatin at five o'clock and a dinner of rare steak and spinach. According to Twentieth Century-Fox studio doctor Lee Siegel, if Marilyn wanted to lose weight quickly she would opt for an enema, while she also followed a 1,000 calories a day diet plan drawn up for her by Dr Leon Krohn.

Breakfast would be half a grapefruit, two rye crisps and a poached egg (254 calories); lunch would comprise half a cup of cottage cheese, one cup of boiled summer squash, and celery hearts, with a portion of canned peaches (270 calories); and dinner could be one-third of a pound of either meat, fish or fowl, half a cup of vegetables, a large salad and one serving of fruit (513 calories). Marilyn was also allowed one pint of skimmed milk a day, which she could add to coffee or tea. 'All foods contain calories but cooking without fat, oil, cream, flour ... sugar, honey and wine reduce the total daily intake,' he advised. 'Eat your meals at a specific time each day and don't skip meals.'[4]

Marilyn didn't wear a girdle. She said she didn't like the extreme 'slim look' that it produced, even though she could see that it made clothes look better. 'Girdle or no, there's always the weight problem,' she said. 'It's grim, I know, as a girl who really likes to eat – but with all the chatter about special diets and special exercises, there is still only one way to get slim and stay slim – and that's by eating less. When you begin to see that bulge under your belt, the only exercise for you, baby, is that old, old one of shaking your head from left to right at the dinner table.'[5]

Records from the Blue Book Modeling Agency show that Marilyn – then 19-year-old Norma Jean Dougherty – was a size twelve. But this is a size twelve according to 1940s and 1950s standards, not those of today. Vanity sizing – the relabelling of larger sizes with smaller numbers, introduced by manufacturers who believed that women didn't want to know, or reveal, their true size – partly explains the difference. So for instance, in 1958 a woman who took a size eight would have a bust of 31 inches, a waist of 23.5 and a hip measurement of 32.5. By 2008, a size eight had increased by 5 or 6 inches in each of these three areas to become the equivalent of a size fourteen or sixteen fifty years later.

If Liz Hurley had studied closely the dimensions of Marilyn's clothes on display, she would have been surprised to learn that the star was far from 'fat'. A soft leather brown belt that was sold at the Christie's auction in 1999 – and which Marilyn wore in 1951 – measured 27 inches when fastened over clothes. And items of clothing that Marilyn wore when she was at her heaviest, such as a black silk cocktail dress from 1959, show that her waist was still only 28.5 inches.

Even with these measurements there was a popular perception that Marilyn sported a fuller figure, so much so that her name came up in a debate held in the British Parliament about Scotland's high rate of tuberculosis. On 24 July 1957, Arthur Woodburn, a Scottish Labour MP, stated that there was a direct correlation between body size and tuberculosis in young women – it seems the thinner you were, the more likely you were to contract the disease. 'Some people blame Christian Dior fashions for making girls slim,' he said. 'Now, Marilyn Monroe is getting the credit for improvement in the tuberculosis figures by reversing the process and getting the girls to concentrate on their figures. When their figure improves our figures improve, in relation to tuberculosis.'[6]

So what size was Marilyn in today's terms? A clue lies inside the collar of the lime green Pucci blouse that she bought from Saks Fifth Avenue and which she wore during rehearsals for the Madison Square Garden 'Happy Birthday, Mr President' gala in May 1962, and during a weekend at the Cal-Neva Lodge two months later. Next to the Emilio Pucci logo is another, smaller label bearing the number fourteen. Scott Fortner – Marilyn collector and owner of the blouse – discovered that the Pucci number fits perfectly on a size six to eight dress form today.

According to William Travilla, Marilyn's waist measured only 22 inches when he was creating costumes for her at Twentieth Century-Fox in the early to mid-1950s. A woman with that size waist today is classified as being size double zero in the US and a size two in the UK. 'Marilyn was shockingly and unimaginably slender,' writes Simon Doonan, who designed the installation for the Christie's auction of her possessions in 1999. 'She was sort of like Kate Moss but fleshier on top. When it came to finding mannequins to fit her dresses, I simply couldn't. M.M.'s drag was too small for the average window dummy.'[7]

48

THE MOST FAMOUS DRESS IN THE WORLD

It's 2 May 2022. A blonde Kim Kardashian – reality TV star turned billionaire businesswoman – is standing on the red carpet outside the Metropolitan Museum in New York. As a bank of photographers call her name, flash bulbs light up hundreds of small, round crystals hand sewn into her flesh-coloured dress, a dress so tight that her walk is confined to a shuffle.

Kim's appearance at the Met Gala caused a sensation, not so much for her presence but for the fact that she was wearing one of the most iconic dresses of all time. 'This is Marilyn Monroe's dress and it's sixty years old and she wore this when she sang "Happy Birthday" to President John F. Kennedy in 1962,' Kardashian told the television personality La La Anthony. 'I had this idea to put it on ... and then they came with like armed guards and gloves. I tried it on and it didn't fit me. And so I looked at them and said, "Give me, like, three weeks." And I had to lose sixteen pounds down today to be able to fit this. But it was such a challenge. It was like a *role*. I was determined to fit it ... I don't think they believed me. I don't think they believed that I was going to do it.'[1]

When this Jean Louis-designed dress belonging to Marilyn was sold at Christie's in 1999 it fetched $1,267,500; the winning bidder was Bob Schagrin, owner of Gotta Have It Collectibles in New York, before it passed into the hands of financier Martin Zweig, who displayed it in a climate-controlled zone in his penthouse at the top of the Pierre hotel. In 2016 the dress came up for auction again – this time at Julien's in LA – and sold for

$4,800,000 to Ripley's Believe It or Not!, the global chain of 'odditoriums'.

The high price – Ripley's promoted it as the most expensive dress in the world – reflects the global fascination with an event that is fixed in the popular consciousness: the Democratic Party fundraiser and celebration of John F. Kennedy's forty-fifth birthday at Madison Square Garden, New York, on 19 May 1962, when Marilyn shimmered onto the stage and caused a sensation. The audience gasped as she slipped off her white fur coat to reveal the 'nude' creation underneath. Her erotically charged performance took all her familiar tropes (sexiness, breathiness, unpunctuality – 'Mr President, the *late* Marilyn Monroe!' proclaimed Peter Lawford in a joke that still stings today) and intensified them to such a degree that she appeared to be approaching a parody of herself.

The dress, although gossamer thin, carries the heavy weight of symbolism, redolent of the souring of the American dream. Three months later Marilyn would be found dead; eighteen months more and JFK would be assassinated; six years later, his brother Robert would also be shot dead. There's an added allure surrounding the dress because of the rumoured affairs Marilyn was supposed to have had with both the president and Robert; she was photographed wearing the gown with the brothers at a party later that night, an image that has helped feed a rash of conspiracy theories.

Ripley's Believe It or Not! kept the dress in a darkened vault at its museum in Orlando, Florida – where it was protected in a controlled environment of 40–50 per cent humidity and an optimum temperature of 68 degrees Fahrenheit – until Kim Kardashian contacted them to ask whether she could borrow it for the Metropolitan Museum's American fashion-themed event. 'What's the most American thing you can think of?' mused Kim, as she talked through the concept of her costume with a reporter from *Vogue*. 'And that's Marilyn Monroe. Nowadays everyone wears sheer dresses, but back then that was not the case. In a sense, it's the original naked dress. That's why it was so shocking.'

Before she was given the go-ahead to borrow the dress, Kim had to try on an exact replica, which she said fitted perfectly. But when the original dress, created from a sketch by designer Bob Mackie, arrived at Kardashian's house in Calabasas, there was a problem. 'I always thought she [Marilyn] was extremely curvy,' said Kim. 'I imagined I might be smaller in some places where she was bigger, and bigger in places where she was smaller. So when it didn't fit me I wanted to cry because it can't be altered at all.'

Kardashian was so determined to fit into the dress that she wore a sauna suit twice a day, restricted her diet to vegetables and proteins (no sugar or carbs allowed) and ran for hours on a treadmill. Apparently, after a month of this kind of self-punishment the dress 'fit like a glove' – 'I wanted to cry tears of joy when it went up,' she said. Barricades were set up outside her hotel room so when Kardashian left wearing a dressing gown the paparazzi wouldn't be able to take snaps of her. When she arrived at the Met, she was led to a fitting room near the steps where a conservationist wearing white gloves helped her into the dress. 'I'm extremely respectful to the dress and what it means to American history,' she said. 'I would never want to sit in it or eat in it or have any risk of any damage to it.'[2]

Although Kardashian only wore the dress for photographers for a few minutes – once she had walked up the steps of the museum she changed into a replica – fashion historians and commentators questioned whether it was appropriate. 'I thought it was a big mistake,' Bob Mackie told *Entertainment Weekly*. '[Marilyn] was a goddess. A crazy goddess, but a goddess. She was just fabulous. Nobody photographs like that. And it was done for her. It was designed for her. Nobody else should be seen in that dress.'[3] Dr Justine De Young, professor of fashion history at New York's Fashion Institute of Technology, told *People* magazine, 'Such an iconic piece of American history should not be put at risk of damage just for an ego-boost and photo-op.'4

Keen-eyed fashion observers noted how, on the night of the gala, Kardashian screened the back of the dress with a white fur stole; later it came to light that instead of being zipped up, the gown had been fastened using a length of white string. Soon allegations started to swirl around social media claiming that the dress could have been damaged. 'Marilyn stood nude as the fabric for the dress was literally sculpted to her body to precisely match every curve,' said Scott Fortner. 'The fabric, which is a flesh-colored soufflé gauze imported from France, was layered strategically so she wouldn't need to wear undergarments ... The gown worn by anyone else will not be a precise fit. In this case, Kim Kardashian's measurements are somewhat different than Marilyn's. It's logically assumed the fabric and seams were stressed.'5

In a press release, Ripley's Believe It or Not! maintained that 'Great care was taken to preserve this piece of history. With input from garment conservationists, appraisers, archivists, and insurance, the garment's condition was top priority. No alterations were made to the dress, and Kim Kardashian even changed into a replica before entering the Gala.'6

Yet when Scott Fortner compared photographs taken of the dress before and after the Met Gala – images that he says show a number of missing crystals on the back, a tear to the right shoulder and a frayed kick pleat – he came to the conclusion that the garment had been 'permanently damaged'. 'A gown of that age and those fragile materials will inevitably be damaged if it is worn,' observed fashion historian Kimberly Chrisman-Campbell. 'Sequins fall off historic gowns if you so much as breathe on them.'7

On Fortner's Marilyn Monroe Collection web page – which details the world's largest privately held collection of the star's personal property – he questions whether the people who run Ripley's Believe It or Not! regret paying $4.8 million for 'an iconic piece of film, political and American cultural history' that he suggests has been ruined. Everybody wants to know, 'Was it worth it?'[8] However, Ripley's think the publicity surrounding the Kim Kardashian Met Gala stunt has only increased the value of the JFK–Marilyn Monroe 'Happy Birthday' dress.

The new price tag? An estimated $10 million.

49

Sex, lies and videotape

Kim Kardashian first entered public consciousness on the back of a sex tape. Similarly, for years there have been rumours that her heroine Marilyn made a porn film, supposedly shot in the lean years before she became a star.

The quest to uncover an erotic film starring Marilyn has turned into something of a mini-industry. In October 1980, *Penthouse* splashed with the cover line 'EXCLUSIVE: MARILYN MONROE'S SECRET STAG FILM'. Inside, under the headline 'THE BLUEST MARILYN MONROE', readers could peruse a series of images taken from a 16mm black and white film unearthed by a Swedish photographer who first sold the stills to the men's magazine *FIB aktuellt*.

The pictures show a blonde woman in a variety of sexual positions with a dark-haired moustachioed man, together with a selection of images of Marilyn herself. The accompanying text stinks of the kind of rancid misogyny employed by (usually bad) male writers of the time who only saw her as a sex symbol. Marilyn was, in the *Penthouse* universe, 'A queen of a castrator who was ready to weep for a dying minnow, a lover of books who did not read, and a proud inviolate artist who could haunch over to publicity when the heat was upon her faster than a whore could lust over a hot buck ... a dank hunched-up crab at her worst, a sexual oven whose fire may have rarely been lit.'[1]

Despite the desperate wish fulfilment of *Penthouse* and protestations that the stills suggest that 'the legendary star may have been a lady with a past', even a brief perusal of the two sets of images illustrates the fact that they show two different women. The star of the erotic film had blonde hair, while we know that when this short movie was supposed to have been shot – in the 1940s – Norma Jeane was a brunette. In addition, the scantily clad woman looked as though she had a fuller figure than Marilyn. Soon after the magazine hit the shelves, a man who gave his name as 'Carlos' contacted a reporter from the *Hollywood Star Newspaper*. He said that he was the stud of the 'stag film' – shot in Florida – and revealed that the female in question was not Marilyn but a thirty-six-year-old called Maria Warren. 'Notice the double chin on the girl in the film,' said Carlos. 'Marilyn was thin at the beginning of her career. She didn't even have a double chin when she was older!' The most likely scenario is that a pornographer, hoping to cash in on the Marilyn Monroe craze, spotted what he thought was a resemblance between Maria Warren and Marilyn. What he failed to take into account was that Maria looked like a mature Marilyn, not Marilyn in her Norma Jeane years. As the *Hollywood Star Newspaper* concluded, 'Sorry, PENTHOUSE. You guys will have to do better than that.'[2]

There was no shortage of porn merchants keen to pick up the baton. Shortly after breakfast, on a hot summer's morning in August 1984, Anthony Summers and a friend walked through the rugged landscape on the Greek island of Symi, and climbed the steep steps up to a villa where a man – whom Summers described as 'lechery personified' – was waiting for them. The three of them enjoyed a stiff brandy before settling down in a living room, 'cluttered' with a variety of objects from the owner's travels: ecclesiastical manuscripts, statuettes pilfered from ancient temples and a connoisseur's collection of imported pornographic films. They had been assured that the one they were going to watch that day was 'the only genuine blue movie of Marilyn Monroe'. Soon after the informal screening, Summers typed up what he'd just seen, noting that in the film, entitled *The Apple Knockers and the Coke*, the actress:

> wears a longish dress with scooped neckline
> peels down top
> lies down ... pulls kisrt [skirt] to thigh ... gets up ... stands and drops dress altogether ...
> wearing enormous cover-up knickers ... poses thus ... tickles tits with a potted plant ... grins absurdly ... rolls apple in tits ... rolls knickers down ... takes coke bottle ... drinks ... spills on tits and belly ... sucks coke bottle ... finally seen from rear lying down with bare bum ... but's that's all we see[3]

Again, disappointment! The young woman cavorting with a piece of fruit and a bottle of a popular American soft drink was not Marilyn Monroe, but Arline Hunter. Born in 1931, she made a career out of her resemblance to Marilyn; for years *The Apple Knockers and the Coke*, thought to have been shot in 1948, was rumoured to be a genuine Marilyn flick. In 1970, the short featured in *Hollywood Blue*, a compilation of 'stag films', and sold as the 'Private Erotic Films of the Stars!' Three years later, when the film was released in Japan, the designers of the poster used an image of Marilyn – half-naked and in a swimming pool – taken on the set of her last, unfinished film *Something's Got to Give*, and the myth of Marilyn starring in *The Apple Knockers and the Coke* persisted well into the late 1980s.

Opportunists and flesh merchants have long understood the high value of Marilyn's image. In 1997, Mikel Barsa, a Spanish events promoter, claimed that he was acting as an agent for a collector who wanted to sell a six-minute, silent pornographic film that he'd had in his possession for two decades. 'This is a hard-porn film,' he said of the black and white movie that he claimed Marilyn had made in 1947.[4] Barsa said that he sold the short 16mm film – which he alleged showed her masturbating and having sex with a man – to a collector for $1.2 million in 2001. Then in 2011 he tried to sell an 8mm copy of the same film in Buenos Aires for a starting price of $500,000, expecting it to fetch at least twice that amount. News of the auction prompted the Authentic Brands Group, which owns Marilyn's image rights, to release a strong statement, denying that the actress in the porn film was Marilyn. If such a sale went ahead it would, according to ABG, perpetuate 'a fraud on the public, violating the Monroe estate's exclusive rights to her image and other claims of intellectual property infringement'. When the film failed to sell, Barsa blamed ABG. 'It's foul play,' he said. 'They know it's Marilyn.'[5]

Scott Fortner, the Marilyn historian and collector, analysed the footage of the erotic film and compared the images with photos taken of her in 1947 and found a number of obvious differences. 'The "porn star" has a very squared, pronounced, and almost masculine jawline, as compared to Norma Jeane's much more feminine appearance,' he said. The actress was much heavier than Norma Jeane, who 'was being photographed regularly in the mid to late 1940s, and there are no images from this period in which she is heavy or overweight ... Perhaps the most significant variance, other than facial, teeth and body weight differences, is a glaringly apparent distinction between the hairline of the "porn star" and Norma Jeane Baker. It's quite well known that Norma Jeane/Marilyn had a very distinct widow's peak her entire life, and this is documented in countless images of the screen legend, as a child, a teenager, and throughout her entire career until her death.' The woman in the porn film does not have a widow's peak. Says Fortner: 'In my personal opinion ... the "porn star" hairline has spoken: "No widow's peak, no Marilyn."'[6]

Another sex tape allegedly starring Marilyn – this one apparently showing her giving oral sex to a man – surfaced in 2008. This was uncovered by New York-based memorabilia collector

Keya Morgan, who has a penchant for taking selfies with the rich and famous. He maintained that he came into possession of the 16mm film, which showed an unidentified man being pleasured, through the son of a deceased FBI agent. 'The FBI agent that I interviewed said J. Edgar Hoover was completely obsessed,' said Morgan, who claimed he uncovered the footage while researching a documentary about the actress, '[to] see if that was really President Kennedy'. Although Morgan said he sold the 15-minute film for $1.5 million to a New York businessman, there was no way of verifying its authenticity – or even its existence – because its new owner didn't want to release the tape in case it damaged the image of Marilyn. 'The gentleman who bought it said out of respect for Marilyn he's not going to make a joke of it and put it on the internet and try to exploit her,' he said. 'That's not his intention and I would never get my name involved if that were to happen.'[7] Soon after Morgan made these claims, a website called The Smoking Gun reproduced a redacted FBI document which related how, in February 1965, a government agent investigating the interstate transportation and distribution of obscene material had visited an unnamed individual in New York City who had 'exhibited a motion picture which depicted deceased actress MARILYN MONROE committing a perverted act upon an unknown male. According to [name redacted] claimed that former baseball star JOSEPH DI MAGGIO in the past had offered him $25,000 for this film, it being the only one in existence, but that [name redacted] had refused the offer.' The Smoking Gun highlighted the contradictions between Morgan's statement – that the tape was in the possession of the FBI or one of its agents – and the FBI report itself, which confirmed that it never left the hands of its original owner. When presented with the evidence, Morgan apparently replied, 'It doesn't matter what it says in the documents.' As a result of their investigation, The Smoking Gun concluded that on balance the film was nothing but a 'hoax'.[8]

NBC News also conducted its own investigation into Morgan's claims that the FBI in Washington and New York had analysed the film. The news organisation reported that a team of FBI agents had spent thirty-two personnel hours searching through databases and archives, and that 'the records show no indication we ever had such a film'.[9] Morgan insisted that the footage was real. 'You see instantly that it's Marilyn Monroe – she has the famous mole,' he said. 'She's smiling, she's very charming, she's very radiant, but she's known for being radiant.'[10]

In 2014, William Castleberry, a bodyguard turned memorabilia collector, claimed that a tape featuring not only Marilyn and JFK, but the president's brother Robert Kennedy too, was seized from his home in Tulare, California, by debt collectors. 'It's real,' he said. 'I had it for years and I never released it out of respect for Joe DiMaggio ... I'm just sick about it and I'm desperately trying to raise money to get it back ... They demanded a $90,000 payment I couldn't afford and that is when the sheriff came in and seized the sex tape and all of my other memorabilia I have been collecting my entire life.' However, the auction of the 8mm footage of the threesome was cancelled when it was reported that a mysterious – and convenient – benefactor settled Castleberry's debts.[11] The news was a disappointment for those hoping for a quick thrill. As the gossip website TMZ reported, 'Castleberry says he knows people think he's a fraud, but insists it's definitely MM on that film. He says he's trying to raise the $200k to pay off his debt before the film is sold. Just a hunch, but most of the world is hoping Castleberry fails.'[12]

Porn sites are awash with actresses in blonde wigs dressed up as Marilyn having sex with randy men in suits. For some, the 2022 Netflix film *Blonde*, starring Ana de Armas and directed by Andrew Dominik, performs the same exploitative function: at one point, the character of Marilyn is forced to have oral sex with the president as he's talking on the phone. 'Dirty slut – oh, oh, you dirty slut,' says the leader of the free world as he ejaculates into her mouth. After watching the film, Manohla Dargis, the chief film critic of the *New York Times*, observed, 'if Dominik isn't interested in or capable of understanding that Monroe was indeed more than a victim of the predations of men, it's because, in this movie, he himself slipped into that wretched role'.[13] In his defence, Andrew Dominik maintained that he was pleased that the film had offended so many people. In his view, the problem was that the audience wanted to see Marilyn represented as an 'empowered' woman. 'And if you're not showing them that, it upsets them.'[14]

50

MARILYN AND ELLA

Of course, the actress was more than just a sex symbol, as Ella Fitzgerald recalled. 'I owe Marilyn Monroe a real debt,' the singer told *Ms* magazine in 1972. 'It was because of her that I played the Mocambo, a very popular nightclub [in LA] in the '50s. She personally called the owner of the Mocambo [Charlie Morrison], and told him she wanted me booked immediately, and if he would do it, she would take a front table every night. She told him – and it was true, due to Marilyn's superstar status – that the press would go wild. The owner said yes, and Marilyn was there, front table, every night. The press went overboard ... After that, I never had to play a small jazz club again.'

Versions of this story have been told repeatedly over the years. In June 2020, a tweet, which claimed that Fitzgerald couldn't get booked by clubs because 'she was black' until Marilyn stepped in, went viral, with over 424,000 likes. The message concluded with 'That's how you use your privilege for good.'

The anecdote has also been used as the basis for a 2008 musical play – Bonnie Greer's *Marilyn and Ella* – which, in the words of the *Guardian*'s theatre critic, dramatised the 'documented fact that it was Monroe who in 1955, when racial prejudice was still entrenched, persuaded the owner of Hollywood's Mocambo club to book Fitzgerald for a week'.[1] And a photograph of the 'Blonde Bombshell' and 'The First Lady of Song' sitting next to one another in a nightclub is frequently captioned as being taken at the Mocambo.

There's no doubt that Marilyn was a huge fan of Fitzgerald. She had been introduced to her music by voice coach Hal Schaefer, who instructed her to buy some of the singer's albums. 'That was her homework – and she did do it,' he said.[2] Fitzgerald did indeed appear at the Mocambo, the club on Sunset Strip, for a ten-day run starting on 15 March 1955. Many celebrities came to watch her perform: the list includes Bob Hope, Dinah Shore, Eartha Kitt, Frank Sinatra with Peggy Connolly, and Judy Garland with husband Sid Luft.

But Marilyn was not there. She was in New York.

So how did this story originate? Marilyn did attend a Fitzgerald concert at the Tiffany Club, on West 8th Street, in Los Angeles, in November 1954. The photos of Marilyn and Ella supposedly taken at the Mocambo were in fact shot here. It seems as though Fitzgerald confused the two concerts, but also, either consciously or unconsciously, invested Marilyn with the status of what we would now define as a 'white saviour'. Prior to this date, many Black artists had played both the Tiffany Club (Julia Lee, Nat 'King' Cole, Nellie Lutcher, Slim Gaillard, Louis Armstrong) and the Mocambo (Lena Horne, Eartha Kitt, Dorothy Dandridge, Joyce Bryant). If any resistance to book Fitzgerald came from the management of the Mocambo, it's likely that this was motivated not by racism but by prejudicial attitudes towards Fitzgerald's size and perceived lack of 'glamour'. However, the March gig was such a hit that Fitzgerald was booked again later that year.

When writer and Hollywood historian April VeVea first investigated this story for her blog classicblondes.com – and presented the carefully gathered evidence to show that Marilyn did not in fact strong-arm the owners of the Mocambo to book Fitzgerald – she was attacked. 'I have had people tell me I am a horrible person and that I should just let sleeping dogs lie,' she told the *All Things Marilyn* podcast.[3]

Although the Fitzgerald–Mocambo story has been exposed as an urban myth, Marilyn was appalled by segregation and racial prejudice. 'Marilyn was passionate about equal rights, rights for blacks, rights for the poor,' said her therapist's daughter Joan Greenson.[4] Marilyn's appeal is summed up in a quote from someone W. J. Weatherby identifies only as Christine, a young Black woman whom the journalist said he met when he travelled from the set of *The Misfits* to New Orleans in 1960. 'She's been hurt,' said Christine of Marilyn. 'She knows what the score is, but it hasn't broken her . . . She's someone who was abused. I could identify with her. I never could identify with any other white movie star. They were always white people doing white things.'[5] Weatherby went on to detail his intimate interracial relationship with 'Christine' in his 1966 book *Love in the Shadows*; in reality, however, 'Christine' was a Black man. It's unclear whether Marilyn ever knew Weatherby was gay. Despite what Sidney Skolsky said about Marilyn's indifference towards gay liberation, she voiced her support for the actor Montgomery Clift. 'People who aren't fit to open the door for him sneer at his homosexuality,' she said. 'What do they know about it?'[6]

As a Hollywood star, Marilyn was supposed to be living the embodiment of the American dream. But as writer and academic Jacqueline Rose has pointed out, her complex persona – the way her biography leaches through the shiny surface of her films and attaches itself to her audience – demands the necessity of a more radical rereading. 'I have great feeling for all the persecuted ones in the world,' Marilyn wrote in a private note from 1962,[7] and as Weatherby observed, the actress had a natural affinity for the underdog, the dispossessed, the abandoned. In the course of their conversations, Marilyn is asked for a quarter by a 'wino with a black, ravaged face'; after giving him one, she turns back and instead presses a dollar into his hand.[8]

'If Monroe offers an image of American perfectibility,' writes Jacqueline Rose, 'we shouldn't be surprised to find behind that image, as its hidden companion, a host of other images through which that same – perfectible – America indicts itself'.[9]

51

'I NEVER HEARD THAT SHE WAS PRODUCING GOLD WHEN SHE PEED'

On Sunday 27 March 1955, a few days after Marilyn attended the opening night of Tennessee Williams's *Cat on a Hot Tin Roof* at the Morosco Theatre in New York, she was invited to a tea party on the roof terrace of the St. Regis hotel to meet the playwright's mother Miss Edwina. The intellectual headcount was high, with guests including Truman Capote, Gore Vidal and Carson McCullers, whom Marilyn already knew as a fellow resident at the Gladstone Hotel, her Manhattan pied à terre that spring. The writer and actress Elaine Dundy, who was married to influential theatre critic Kenneth Tynan, was there that day and described the buzz of Marilyn's arrival in her autobiography *Life Itself*:

> Everybody stopped what they were doing, freeze-framed with their drinks, hors d'oeuvres or cigarettes halfway to their mouths. They were all looking in one direction. A path had been cleared, and walking through it was Marilyn Monroe. She was wearing what anyone else would have called an underlap, a simple, unadorned black slip with thin shoulder straps and clearly nothing under it. Her skin was a luminous alabaster with pearly blue and rose tints such as I have never seen outside paintings by the Old Masters. She was more astonishingly beautiful in the flesh than on celluloid and we all stared silently in our reverence.[1]

There were others, however, who chose not to mythologise the star in this way. Brownie McGhee, the American blues singer, recalled how he'd met Marilyn in 1955 at a rehearsal for *Cat on a Hot Tin Roof*. She had come into the theatre on West 45th Street with her friend and former lover Elia Kazan, the director of the production. 'I didn't think of her as anything other than just a show woman,' he said. 'I don't know why they placed Marilyn on a pedestal ... Shit, she was just a woman. As far as I was concerned I never heard that she was producing gold when she peed.'[2]

52

Marilyn and the pink elephant

Marilyn is spilling out of her tight circus-girl outfit – half woman, half bird – balanced atop a real elephant painted bright pink. The 8,000-strong crowd at Madison Square Garden are roaring and cheering and calling her name. 'Sweet baby,' she whispers into the elephant's enormous ears, as she ignores the nagging pain from a pin that pricked her thigh during the costume fitting. Instead, she smiles and dazzles, her diamond earrings and necklace sparkling in the light from the photographers' flash bulbs.

The event, on 30 March 1955, was Marilyn's first public appearance since her divorce from Joe DiMaggio; although the two were no longer together, they remained close until the end of her life. 'I've always been able to count on Joe as a friend after that first bitterness of our parting faded,' she told a journalist in 1962. 'I just like being with him.'[1] Indeed, Joe was there watching that night. Marilyn's Fox contract – which still had not been resolved by Milton Greene and the lawyers – barred her from making money from paid events, but the Ringling Brothers and Barnum and Bailey was a charity gala, in aid of the New York Arthritis and Rheumatism Foundation. Entitled 'Dream Show', the event – directed by Michael Todd, with comedian Milton Berle as ringmaster – portrayed the 'major holidays of the year' and also featured personalities such as Sammy Davis Jr, Jeanette MacDonald, James Cagney and the Keystone Cops.[2] 'Animals, wild and domesticated; color, gaudy and glittering; death-defying suspense and the fantasies of childhood reasserted their say over the circus last night at Madison Square Garden,' reported the *New York Times*.³

But it was Marilyn who stole the show. 'Everyone cheered her and, when I looked up toward the balcony, it was the strangest sight,' remembered Amy Greene. 'All I could see were open mouths, right up to the rafters.'⁴ And despite the pain she was in, Marilyn enjoyed the evening because of the special affinity she felt with animals. 'I became quite fond of the elephant, he was very nice,' she said.⁵

Milton thought the event would be great publicity, and he was right: the bank of photographers took hundreds of dazzling images that were wired all around the world, images that rankled with Zanuck and Fox studio executives back in LA.

Watching in the crowd – and snapping away with his own Rolleiflex camera alongside veteran photographers such as Weegee – was 15-year-old budding journalist Marvin Scott. 'She was bigger than life,' remembers Scott, who went on to become an Emmy Award-winning television journalist.

> For a fifteen-year-old kid with raging hormones it was quite a moment. How did I get in? I went to the press department at Madison Square Garden and I told them I wanted to cover her appearance for my High School newspaper in the Bronx. I showed them my High School press pass and they bought it! I put on a jacket, a tie, and really dressed nicely. And I walked in like I really belonged, showed my High School press pass and here I was with the paparazzi. I elbowed my way in with my Rolleiflex, which I still have to this day, and popped pictures. First, there were pictures of her getting up and being positioned on the elephant. She was wearing this skimpy outfit. She was radiant – radiant. I often said Marilyn toyed with a camera the way a kitten might toy with a spool of wool. She was magnetic with every click of the shutter . . .

I remember the photographer Eve Arnold told me that Marilyn was the animal trainer and the photographer was the beast. She had a love affair with the camera. And I can say with my experience that it is so true.[6]

53

A HUMMINGBIRD IN FLIGHT

Constance Collier, the British-born theatrical grande dame turned influential Hollywood acting coach, described Marilyn as a beautiful child. 'I don't mean that in the obvious way – the perhaps too obvious way,' she told Truman Capote before her death, age seventy-seven, in April 1955. 'What she has – this presence, this luminosity, this flickering intelligence – could never surface on the stage. It's so fragile and subtle, it can only be caught by the camera. It's like a hummingbird in flight: only a camera can freeze the poetry of it.'

Collier, who had made the transition as an actress from the era of silent films to talkies (her films included roles in *Stage Door*, *Kitty* and *Rope*), had been introduced to Marilyn through Capote, and had spotted something special about her. According to Capote, Collier only accepted professional actors as her students, and 'usually only professionals who were already "stars"': her famous pupils included Colleen Moore, Audrey Hepburn, Vivien Leigh and Katharine Hepburn. Collier had never seen any of Marilyn's films; she was only aware that she was 'some sort of platinum sex-explosion who had achieved global notoriety'. Yet she recognised raw talent when she saw it; she referred to her new pupil as her 'special problem' and told Capote, 'anyone who thinks this girl is simply another Harlow or harlot or whatever is *mad*. Speaking of mad, that's what we've been working on together: Ophelia. I suppose people would chuckle at the notion, but really, she could be the most exquisite Ophelia.'[1]

One day Collier had been talking to her friend Greta Garbo – the two women had starred in the 1935 film adaptation of *Anna Karenina* – about Marilyn's talents. Garbo had seen two of Marilyn's films – 'very bad and vulgar stuff' – but had been so excited about the younger actress's potential that she dreamed of casting Marilyn opposite her in a film of Oscar Wilde's *Portrait of Dorian Gray*. 'With her [Greta] playing Dorian, of course,' said Constance. 'Of course, Greta is a consummate artist, an artist of the utmost control. This beautiful child [Marilyn] is without any concept of discipline or sacrifice. Somehow I don't think she'll make old bones. Absurd of me to say, but somehow I feel she'll go young. I hope, I really pray, that she survives long enough to free the strange lovely talent that's wandering through her like a jailed spirit.'[2]

It's impossible to know whether Constance actually had a sense of foreboding about Marilyn's premature death or whether Capote invented these portentous words, safe in the knowledge that neither Collier nor Marilyn could object. He wrote them in his essay *A Beautiful Child*, which appeared in 1979 and takes the form of a reported conversation between himself and Marilyn on the day of Collier's funeral, 28 April 1955. The portrait of Marilyn that emerges is of a woman who is neurotic, insecure, funny and foul-mouthed: she relates how she went to a 'half-ass party' where she saw Errol Flynn 'whip out his prick' and use it to play 'You Are My Sunshine' on the piano.

In the essay, Capote describes how he arranged to meet Marilyn at the chapel of the Universal Funeral Home on Lexington Avenue and 52nd Street. Marilyn is late for Collier's service because she has spent time getting ready – applying eyelashes, putting on lipstick – before she became anxious that her glamorous appearance might not be appropriate at a funeral and so had to wash off her make-up. She is dressed entirely in black: a black dress that was 'loose and long', black silk stockings, a black chiffon scarf covering her hair, 'vaguely erotic' black high-heeled shoes and black sunglasses that 'dramatized the vanilla-pallor of her dairy-fresh skin'. When she takes off her glasses to reveal her blue-grey eyes full of tears she looks, writes Capote, like a 12-year-old 'pubescent virgin who has just been admitted to an orphanage and is grieving over her plight'.[3]

After the service is over, the friends stay in the chapel and talk about their shared love of New York and hatred of Los Angeles, which Marilyn likens to 'one big varicose vein'; her fascination with Elizabeth Taylor – 'what is she *really* like?' she asks Truman; and her hatred of funerals – 'I'm glad I won't have to go to my own,' she says. 'Only, I don't want a funeral – just my ashes cast on waves by one of my kids, if I ever have any.'[4] From the chapel they make their way from Lexington Avenue, down Third Avenue, past P. J. Clarke's, which Marilyn rejects because it is the hangout of gossip columnist Dorothy Kilgallen, whom she believed wrote spiteful things about her. (In one syndicated column, in July 1953, Kilgallen – who herself would die of an alcohol and barbiturate overdose in November 1965 – reported a rumour that Marilyn had been killed in a California plane crash. 'Strange how those rumors start . . . and are passed on as absolute fact,' wrote Kilgallen.[5])

As Capote and Marilyn stop to look in the window of an antiques store, she spots a display case containing a line of rings. She tells Truman that she wishes she could wear rings, but thinks her hands are too fat. She is like Elizabeth Taylor in that regard, she says, but 'with those eyes, who's looking at her hands?' She confesses that she likes to dance naked in front of a mirror and watch her 'titties jump around. There's nothing wrong with them.' The sight of a grandfather clock makes her come over all maudlin. 'I've never had a home,' she says. 'Not a real one with all my own furniture.'[6]

They continue to walk and talk until they stop to drink champagne in an empty Chinese restaurant on Second Avenue, where

Capote questions her about her private life. According to his account of that day, Marilyn confesses about how she enjoyed a good sex life with Joe DiMaggio – 'He can hit home runs. If that's all it takes, we'd still be married' – how she'd enjoyed a recent fling with Wall Street financier Paul Shields and how she's started a relationship with a 'secret lover'. When Truman correctly guesses the identity of the man – Arthur Miller – she becomes upset; she thought she'd managed to keep the affair secret. Marilyn is so annoyed with Truman that she says if he ever blabs about her new relationship she would have him killed. 'I know a couple of men who'd gladly do me the favor,' she says.[7]

After they finish their champagne – Marilyn is too upset to drink another bottle – the couple take a taxi south through Manhattan, travelling through the Bowery, with its pawnshops, doss houses, dingy bars and clutches of homeless people. At South Street, they emerge to feed the seagulls with a bagful of fortune cookies Marilyn has taken from the Chinese restaurant. As they walk towards the South Street Pier, gazing at the Brooklyn skyline across the East River, Marilyn stops and bends down to stroke a dog, a chow. When its owner tells her that she shouldn't touch strange animals she replies, 'Dogs never bite me. Just humans.'[8]

54

The Method

'Since I came here to New York, I feel accepted, not as a freak, but as myself, whoever the hell that is,' Marilyn told Susan Strasberg in 1955. The two women had met the previous year on the Fox lot where Marilyn had been filming the 'Heat Wave' number from *There's No Business Like Show Business*. Susan, who was fifteen when they met, was immediately taken by her presence, describing her as seeming 'to flicker like a flame giving off a nimbus of light'. She assumed this was some trick of lighting until she stood next to the older actress and she realised that Marilyn glowed, radiating 'sex and innocence together'.[1]

Under the intense klieg lights, Marilyn perspired and runs of sweat and frustration streamed down and through her thick pancake make-up. As she lip-synched her way through the dance number, she repeatedly fluffed each take, and finally she misplaced a step and fell hard 'smack on her ass'.[2] While in her dressing room, Marilyn told the teenage girl that one day she hoped to be able to study acting with Susan's father Lee. 'She was gorgeous, the American dream,' recalled Susan. 'I was sure I would never see her again.'[3]

She was wrong. One day, in the early spring of 1955, Susan came home early from school to her parents' apartment in New York, and heard voices coming from the living room, which also doubled as her father's study. Her mother Paula, who was also an acting coach, told her to be quiet as she didn't want Lee to be disturbed. Who was the pupil? Susan asked. Her mother was not forthcoming. Finally, at dusk, as 'smoky light' cast the apartment in a kind of chiaroscuro, Marilyn – all blonde hair, pearlescent skin, surrounded by what looked like a 'halo' – emerged from the darkness of the room. As Susan watched the actress talk to her parents – it was obvious that her father was already enamoured with the star – she noticed how Marilyn had changed since the last time she had seen her. The Marilyn she had encountered on the Fox lot was an exaggerated, overblown, erotic creature – 'like an alien from another planet'[4] – yet the woman before her seemed shy and extremely fragile. This quality was also noticed by Susan's younger brother John, born in 1941. 'When I looked into her eyes, it was like looking into my own, they were like a child's eyes,' he said. 'My feeling was she had less ego or was less narcissistic than most of the actors who never really bothered with me . . . She was so open, so loose, and her sensuality as such was so totally innocent, nothing dirty in it at all . . . She was quiet, too, I remember, like an animal is quiet.'[5]

Lee Strasberg, whose star was in its ascendant due to the success of pupils including Marlon Brando, Kim Stanley, Paul Newman and Shelley Winters, recognised Marilyn's potential immediately. 'She has a phenomenal degree of responsiveness [and] the greatest sensitivity,' he said.[6] Although Marilyn told everyone that she wanted to help Strasberg make her a 'real actress', she was, in his view, one already, 'but she didn't know it'.[7] Lee went on to tell his daughter that it was necessary to look beyond Marilyn's glitzy Hollywood image, ignore the 'bad mannerisms and habits' she may have picked up while making films, and peel away the layers of superficiality to uncover the well of talent beneath.[8]

For her part, Marilyn trusted Lee implicitly. She was grateful that he was one of the few people who seemed to take her seriously. 'I've always wanted for people to see *me*, not the actress, the real person. Your daddy does,' Marilyn told Susan.[9] In early 1955, when she had first announced the formation of Marilyn Monroe

Productions, journalists had laughed at her when she said she would like to play Grushenka in *The Brothers Karamazov*. 'I could really have played her. You know why I make fun of myself? So I'll do it before they do.'[10] One day, on the way to the Actors Studio with Eli Wallach – whom she had met after seeing his Broadway performance of *The Teahouse of the August Moon* in 1955 – Marilyn passed a billboard advertising *The Seven Year Itch*, with the iconic photograph of her standing over a subway grille, her skirts billowing up around her shoulders. 'You see that?' she said, pointing to the image. 'That's all they want me to do in films.'[11]

Marilyn and Lee met three times a week for acting lessons at the family's apartment. Susan became immune to hearing the sounds of the famous star laughing, weeping or shouting that emanated from the living room. Strasberg also invited Marilyn to sit in and watch the carefully choreographed sessions he held twice a week at the Actors Studio.

Each masterclass was almost ritualistic in its intensity. Strasberg always sat in the front row, with Paula next to him. A secretary would hand him a card on which was written the details of a scene and the name of the actor playing the role. As he watched, Lee's face would remain solemn, and at the end of the scene he would ask the actors, 'What were you trying to do?' After listening to the responses from the actors, Strasberg then turned to the students in the audience and asked them for their analyses. Once the discussion was over, Lee then furnished the group with his own critique, words captured on audio tape and scribbled down furiously by his legion of adoring pupils. 'He was a stern and devoted father and, equally, a loving mother who assumed a near total responsibility for the welfare of her family,' said Kazan, one of the founders of the Actors Studio. 'He was also a tribal chief leading a movement that was to change the art of acting in our theatre. His sessions had the intimacy of a family gathering but also the intimacy of a cabal.'[12]

On 9 March 1955, Marilyn served as an usher, alongside Marlon

Brando, at a benefit performance of Kazan's *East of Eden* at the Astor Theatre to raise funds for the Actors Studio; the money helped purchase a permanent base at 432 West 44th Street. She attended classes regularly, sitting silently at the back of the room, absorbing everything. She didn't put on any airs or graces, never played the star card and was often charmingly self-effacing. 'It took guts for that lamb to walk into the lions' den,' an unnamed member of the theatre group told a reporter. 'They were ready to rip her to shreds – politely, of course. But she just sat there in the dark with the rest of us, watching the performances onstage, saying nothing, dead serious and then going out to a cafeteria afterward, listening some more, saying what she thought when she was asked. In a couple of weeks she belonged.'[13]

After almost a year of studying with Strasberg, Marilyn worked up the courage to play a scene from Eugene O'Neill's *Anna Christie* in front of fellow students from the Actors Studio; her partner on stage would be Maureen Stapleton. As the clock ticked down to the moment she was to step on stage, Marilyn felt increasingly nervous. 'It's one thing to do a part that's not too well known, so that your interpretation can be judged essentially on its own merits,' commented Stapleton. 'But to do Anna Christie, a role that's been done by a dozen wonderful people [including Garbo in the 1930 film], means that you'll be compared to them and, what's worse, that everyone in a professional audience will have his own idea of how it should be played.' Witnesses thought that Marilyn's stage fright was so intense they feared the actress might collapse. 'I couldn't see anything,' Marilyn said, 'I couldn't feel anything, I couldn't remember one line. All that I wanted to do then was lie down and die. I was in these impossible circumstances and I suddenly thought to myself, "Good God, what am I *doing* here?" Stapleton even suggested that Marilyn have a copy of the play script to hand in case she forgot her lines, but she refused the prompt. 'I can't,' she told her. 'If I do it this time, I'll do it the rest of my life.'[14]

Perhaps Marilyn was picking up some of the waves of negativity emanating from the audience. It may have been standing room only in the 120-seat arena, but there were plenty who had turned up expecting to see her fail – spectacularly. Some of the other actors viewed Marilyn as a symbol of Hollywood superficiality. 'Many even condemned her for being a success, for being beautiful and sexy,' said Susan, who watched in trepidation as Marilyn began the scene, her hands trembling as she picked up a glass.[15] 'It's my Old Man I got to meet,' she said, tapping into her own painful memories of an absent mother, a non-existent father and unhappy relationships with men. 'I ain't seen him since I was a kid – don't even know what he looks like – just had a letter every now and then ... But I ain't expecting much from him. Give you a kick when you're down, that's what all men do.'[16]

When the scene ended, there were a few moments of intense silence, followed by rapturous applause, which was according to Susan a 'rare phenomenon' at the Actors Studio.[17] But despite the praise from respected actors such as Kim Stanley, Marilyn still felt she had let herself down and disappointed Strasberg. 'You're worn out when it's over, and somehow you always feel you've done something awful and embarrassing,' she said.[18]

Lee Strasberg was so impressed by Marilyn's performance that he suggested she play challenging roles such as Lady Macbeth, and the prostitute Sadie Thompson in *Rain*, an adaptation of a Somerset Maugham short story that had been turned into a play with Jeanne Eagels in the lead, and into three films, each starring a queen of the silver screen: Gloria Swanson in 1928, Joan Crawford in 1932 and Rita Hayworth in 1953. After watching Marilyn rehearse Sadie's scenes from *Rain*, Strasberg became convinced that his star pupil could carry the lead in a television special. 'It is one of my deep sorrows that the public never was able to see her in that and other plays which we had the good fortune to see her in at the Actors Studio and in my private classes,' he said. 'It was my feeling that she would have come close to creating both the earthiness and sensuality and the strange striving that Jeanne Eagels had originally created in that part.'[19]

However, there were some close to both Marilyn and Lee who believed that the acting coach did not have her best interests at heart. Elia Kazan observed how Strasberg took her under his wing, but then fed her false hopes and polluted her judgement with delusions of grandeur. In his view, the problem was that Strasberg had cast himself as the leader of a cult-like institution. 'The more naive and self-doubting the actors, the more total was Lee's power over them,' he said. 'The more famous and the more successful these actors, the headier the taste of power for Lee. He found his perfect victim-devotee in Marilyn Monroe.'[20] Kazan also believed that Marilyn's presence at the Actors Studio bred resentment among the other students. They regarded Lee as something of a 'star-fucker' – not in the sexual sense of the word, more the fact that he seemed overawed by the blinding power of celebrity.[21] Billy Wilder told friends, 'The Strasbergs didn't do Miss Monroe any good, but she worshipped them like a religion.'[22]

Marilyn, for her part, did not see it this way. From 1955 until her death, she became increasingly dependent on the Strasbergs: Paula, always swathed in a mass of dark clothes, and Lee, whom she referred to as 'The Great White Father'. Marilyn made sure that Paula was employed as her acting coach on the sets of all her films from *Bus Stop* in 1956 to her final, unfinished movie *Something's Got to Give* in 1962, often earning between $3,000 and $5,000 a week, sometimes more than Marilyn herself. Even towards the end of her life, Marilyn was hoping that Lee would take a role in a production company she wanted to set up with Marlon Brando. On 1 June 1962 – her thirty-sixth and last birthday – she wrote to the Strasbergs in New York from her home in Brentwood, Los Angeles. The letter, which is typed in capitals, expresses her deep love and respect for the couple whom she considered had changed her life for the better:

> THIS IS THE TIME I WANT TO TELL YOU STRAIGHT OUT THAT THE MOST IMPORTANT THING IN MY LIFE IS MY WORK, MY WORK WITH YOU. THE ACTORS STUDIO IS MY HOME ... I WONDER IF YOU REALIZE WHAT THE WORK HAS MEANT TO ME. ASIDE FROM THE WORK AS AN ACTRESS AND WHAT YOU, LEE, CALL <u>MY</u> PARTS, WHAT IT HAS MEANT TO ME AS A HUMAN BEING ... THANK YOU LEE, FOR BEING MY FRIEND AND MY TEACHER. THANK YOU PAULA, FOR BEING WITH ME AND REALLY TRULY DIRECTING THE GOOD AND RIGHT MOMENTS ON FILM. THANK YOU LEE, FOR LETTING PAULA BE WITH ME AND WORKING WITH ME.
>
> WHEN I THINK OF HOME IT IS NEW YORK AND THE ACTORS STUDIO. THAT IS WHERE I CAN EXIST IN THE HUMAN RACE.
> LOVE,
> MARILYN.[23]

One of Susan's most striking memories of her time with Marilyn comes from the summer of 1955, when Marilyn visited the Strasbergs at their rented house on Fire Island where the two women shared a room. Susan remembered waking up early to see Marilyn standing naked by the window, her body caressed by gentle sunlight. She watched as the star proceeded to shave her legs and bleach her pubic hair. Marilyn looked up, perhaps sensing that she was being studied, at which point Susan, embarrassed and blushing, blurted out that she wanted to be just like her. 'Oh no,' replied Marilyn. 'Oh no, Susie. I wish I were like you. I'd love to have your family.'[24]

55

ON THE COUCH

When Lee Strasberg started work with Marilyn he recommended that she also begin regular psychoanalysis; this kind of deep therapy, he believed, helped an actor get in touch with his or her inner feelings and led to performances of greater depth and authenticity. Marilyn had already seen a therapist, Dr Abraham Gottesman, in Los Angeles between 1951 and 1954. During the making of *Gentlemen Prefer Blondes*, Jane Russell tried to introduce her to Christianity, but Marilyn politely declined, saying that instead she had tried to convert Russell to Freud. As part of her quest to reinvent herself in New York, Marilyn was keen to continue to explore the mysteries of her interior world. Of course, there was no shortage of shrinks in Manhattan in the 1950s; many of the Freudians who had escaped the rise of Nazi Germany settled in and around New York, where they helped calm the nerves of a populace suffering the stresses and strains of the so-called Age of Anxiety.

In early 1955, Marilyn began psychoanalysis in New York with Dr Margaret Hohenberg, a Hungarian immigrant who had studied in Vienna, practised in Prague and emigrated first to London and then to America. The 57-year-old therapist with her 'tightly wound braids and a Valkyrian bosom' was recommended to Monroe by one of her other clients, Milton Greene.[1] Marilyn saw the psychoanalyst as often as five times a week at her office on East 93rd Street, and although she didn't discuss with Amy the details of her conversations, she began to record something of the results of the therapeutic process in her notebooks. Central to many of the entries from 1955 is the theme of internalised shame and its effect on Marilyn's thinking and behaviour. She singles out the figure of 'Ida' – which could be her foster mothers Ida Bolender, Ida Martin, or a combination of the two – as a representation of everything that has repressed and stifled her over the years.

> Ida – I have still
> been obeying her –
> it's not only harmful (inhabits myself, inhibits my work, inhabits thoughts)
> for me to do so[2]

In the same extract, which runs over a number of pages – apart from two sheets that have been ripped from the notebook – Marilyn makes a list of self-affirmations, objectives which seem to have resulted from her work with her therapist. She is determined not to be punished for her desires, her sensitivity or her sexuality:

> or be afraid, or ashamed of my genitals being
> exposed, known and seen ...
> I do have feeling,
> very strongly sexed feeling
> since a small child.[3]

Finally, she concludes that she will continue to work 'analytically' despite the pain this may cause. She singles out the qualities of discipline and concentration as being essential to her progress, before singing out, loud and proud:

> my body is my body
> every part of it.[4]

Yet running alongside this ambition to become confident, more open to the possibilities of joyful living, is an underlying sense of self-doubt and shame. 'I always have this secret feeling that I'm really a fake or something, a phony,' she confessed.[5] Written on the stationery from the Waldorf-Astoria Towers – Marilyn lived in the hotel, in a luxurious three-room suite on the twenty-seventh floor from April to September 1955 – she scribbles a reminder to tell Dr Hohenberg about her dream of meeting a repulsive man in an elevator, a man so physically repugnant he looked as though he was suffering from a venereal disease. The stranger stood too close to her and she felt as though she was about to lose control – 'my panic and then all my thoughts dispiseing [despising] him – does that mean I'm attached [or attracted] to him,' she asks.

Below this, on the same page in the notebook, a disturbing entry reads like the transcription of another dream or a stream of consciousness style. Marilyn sees herself lying on an operating table in a clinically white room, with Lee Strasberg acting as the surgeon, and Dr Hohenberg serving as both diagnostician of her mysterious condition and her anaesthetist. The aim of the procedure is 'to bring myself back to life and to cure me of this terrible dis-ease, whatever the hell it is'. As the operation begins, the two figures merge, so Strasberg is standing there next to her but with 'Hohenberg's ass'. When they open Marilyn up, her mentors discover the problem: there is nothing there; she has no self, no soul, no identity. Strasberg realises his mistake: instead of the teeming mass of complexities and sensitivities that he assumed existed beneath her surface, there is nothing but finely cut sawdust, like the filling from an old rag doll. Marilyn's therapist, seeing the spill of sawdust on the floor, is disheartened, while the man who would become her third husband, Arthur Miller, who is also in the dream, is left feeling disillusioned at the discovery she is nothing but a hollow vessel.

Strasberg's dreams & hopes for theater are fallen, Dr H's dreams & hopes for a permant phyicatrcic [permanent psychiatric] cure is given up – Arthur is disappointed – let down.[6]

56

THE 'EGGHEAD' AND THE 'HOURGLASS'

They are sitting across from one another in a $1,000 a week suite on the twenty-seventh floor of the Waldorf-Astoria, the lights of New York sparkling below. They are anxious about being spotted out together. Marilyn can't emerge from the building without being photographed, and Arthur Miller is still very much a married man, so their relationship has to remain a secret. As a result, during the spring and summer of 1955, the three-room suite, 2728, becomes something of a gilded prison. They have long talks about their childhoods, their relationships, their work, their possible futures. At times, the conversation stalls and they lapse into silence. He asks himself: can he make this work? After all, the match seems an improbable one: to the outside world he is a Pulitzer Prize-winning playwright, celebrated for his intellect and sense of moral purpose, while she is the caricature of the dumb blonde; he is all New York intense interiority, while she is all LA superficiality; he is (as later summed up in a famous *Variety* headline on the Monroe–Miller marriage) a stereotypical 'Egghead', while she is nothing but an 'Hourglass'. Yet, he senses there is something there, a spark that cannot be ignored.

'But beneath the clash of dissimilarities there seemed a dark carpet of wordless being on which we could walk at our ease together,' Miller wrote in his 1987 autobiography *Timebends*.[1] Marilyn and Arthur had kept in touch since they had first met in Hollywood in 1951. Back then, it had been hard for Miller to control his desire; although his biographer Christopher Bigsby suggests that the playwright had had an affair with an unnamed woman the year before, he was still trying to make his marriage to Mary Slattery work. They had married in 1940 and had two children, Jane and Robert, yet a deadening staleness had crept into the relationship. In a revealing letter he later wrote to his parents, Miller outlined how he had first met Marilyn and the impact she'd had on him, maintaining that despite the desire he felt for the actress, nothing untoward had taken place. 'To everyone else, apparently, she was the sexy dame,' he said. 'To me she had a face bathed in tears, was scared to death, and could barely talk above a whisper.' He saw her, he said, only three or four times over the course of three days, but they were never alone together.[2]

On their last day together in Los Angeles, it was difficult for Miller to wrench himself away from Marilyn. Yet he knew he had to step away. 'I made no big advances toward her, because I knew I was susceptible,' he said. 'And I didn't want to start anything that I would regret.'[3]

Decades later, Miller could recall every detail of that moment that day at the airport. As he watched Marilyn – wearing a white satin blouse and a beige skirt, her hair, parted on the right, hanging down to her shoulders – walk back through the terminal building, he felt something akin to pain. 'I knew that I must flee or walk into a doom beyond all knowing,' he wrote. An internal battle raged inside him: he'd always been shy, too timid and repressed, but now he was forced to acknowledge desires that frightened him. Perhaps he could retreat behind the cloak of respectability, a mask that disguised and concealed the intensity of his real emotions. As he flew back to New York, the trace of perfume on his skin, he realised that his 'innocence was technical merely'.[4] Yet his brief encounter with Marilyn had given him a lasting gift: the knowledge that he could, after all, lose himself in a newly discovered sensuality, a sign that he could write something new and exciting. Elia Kazan remembered Miller wrote to him 'in the most rapturous tone about certain feelings he'd been having, awake and asleep, dreams of longing ... He was a young man again, in the grip of a first love, which was – happily – carrying him out of control.'[5]

Miller's appearance in Marilyn's life seems like some kind of manifestation; a wish fulfilment made real. In a 1952 colour image, taken by the silent comedy film star and daredevil stunt performer turned photographer Harold Lloyd, Marilyn poses in front of a bookcase containing a copy of Miller's 1949 play *Death of a Salesman*. In 1954, she told Sidney Skolsky that one day she would marry the famous playwright, a proclamation that came just a few days after she had married Joe DiMaggio, whom Miller would later describe as 'a cruel and stupid man'.[6]

After that initial meeting in Los Angeles, Marilyn sent messages to Miller in New York, letters written in her 'strangely meandering handwriting' that snaked its way around the paper, up one margin and down another, often written with two or three different pens, sometimes with the additional marks of a pencil. She told him that she would fly over and meet him in Manhattan, but Miller – still playing the role of the respectable husband – wrote back and told her that he 'wasn't the man who could make her life happen as I knew she imagined it might'. Yet secretly, he dreamed of taking his car, jamming his foot on the accelerator and heading west. His letters to her were polite, full of encouragement in her attempt to educate herself, and recommendations for further reading: he knew that she was interested in the figure of Abraham Lincoln (Marilyn thought Miller resembled the sixteenth President of the United States) and singled out Carl Sandburg's biography, which she duly bought. He also sent her a note of caution about the perils of stardom. 'Bewitch them with this image they ask for,' he wrote, 'but I hope and almost pray you won't be hurt in this game.'[7]

Marilyn understood Miller's predicament and empathised with his suffering. She wrote to Kazan, compelling him to try to cheer up his friend. 'Make him believe everything isn't hopeless,' she said.⁸ One day, she even flew across the continent to meet Arthur in a hotel room, but he didn't show up, a rejection that left her devastated. 'I knew how wounded she'd been because I'd seen how high her hopes were that morning,' said Kazan.⁹

And so when the two finally did meet again, at a New York party in April 1955, there was already a sense of inevitability about the romance. Marilyn had arrived in Manhattan to start a new life. She was single, on a mission to stimulate her intellect and immerse herself in culture. Arthur was looking for a way out of a failing marriage, keen to revitalise a somewhat etiolated sexuality and find a muse who would perhaps imbue his writing with a new sensuality. He was also bolstered by a sense of empowerment, brought on by his recent success in the theatre: he'd had three hit plays, *All My Sons* (1947), *Death of a Salesman* (1949) and *The Crucible* (1953), while *A View from the Bridge* would open in New York that September. 'With success like that you get feelings of omnipotence, a little touch of it, you know,' he said. 'You think you can do anything. You invariably begin to feel a kind of impact of power which is sexual, which is financial, which is everything ... People now were talking to me differently – women, men – they were looking at me like an icon of some kind.'¹⁰

Their union seemed like an absurd one, to the outside world at least, but each of them had their reasons. For Marilyn – open, honest, sometimes childlike Marilyn – the appeal was simple: 'He is the nicest man I ever met,' she said. 'He is sensitive, and intelligent, with a sense of humor.'¹¹ When questioned much later on this subject by Alan Yentob for the BBC's *Omnibus* in 1987, Miller's response was both more analytical – and tortuous – than Marilyn's. 'There was an unlikely quality to it, sure, from a cultural point of view, if you want to call it that, but in a way, we were both trying to do the same thing, which was – I was desperately trying all my life to unify experience,' he said. 'And the very inappropriateness of our being together was to me the sign that it was appropriate, that we were two parts, however remote, of this society, of this life. One was sensuous and life loving, it seemed, while in the centre of it, there was a darkness and a tragedy, that I didn't know the dimensions of at that time ... So it wasn't that crazy.'[12]

Miller immediately responded to Marilyn's sense of innocent wonder. 'Most people never notice what's in front of them,' he said. 'Marilyn always does ... She has enormous variation in her ability to react honestly and sensitively.'[13] Towards the end of his life, Miller was questioned by his daughter Rebecca about his attraction to Marilyn. 'I thought she was total honesty – that's what knocked me out,' he said. 'She seemed utterly without guile, completely honest about herself and about anything she looked at, whereas the society I came from was very guarded, judgemental.' Arthur could also appreciate Marilyn's wit; she made him laugh, and she had a talent for 'being cute and making fun of being cute at the same time'.[14]

Yet one night in the Waldorf-Astoria in 1955, Miller sensed something tragic about Marilyn that perhaps he should have taken as a warning sign. After a particularly long and heavy silence between them he told her what he was thinking. 'You're the saddest girl I've ever met,' he said. Initially, Marilyn interpreted this remark as an indication that the relationship was doomed; men, she once said to him, only wanted girls who were happy. But then, when she realised that Miller did not want to end their relationship, and that he actually meant this as a kind of compliment – a symbol of the depths of her personality – she smiled, and replied, 'You're the only one who ever said that to me.'[15]

57

MARILYN ON A BIKE

The couple, possessed by love, cycled through the busy city streets of New York and the green of Central Park, across Brooklyn Bridge, to the neighbourhood where Miller had grown up after his parents had lost their money in the Depression. They explored the city, seeing it afresh through one another's eyes. Arthur was passionate about this new mode of transport, telling his friend Robert Whitehead, the theatrical producer, 'You gotta get a bicycle, Bob. It's the only way to get around New York.'[1]

Marilyn adored the freedom cycling gave her; the feel of the summer breeze through her hair; the fact that no one expected a movie star to travel like this and so she could move through the city like an ordinary person. It wasn't just a passing fad: photographs taken in the summer of 1956 in England, when Marilyn was filming *The Prince and the Showgirl*, show the married couple cycling through Windsor Great Park. In July of that year, the *Daily Sketch* had given her a bike; the newspaper published one image of her, deliberately taken from behind so as to emphasise the curves of her bottom. The photograph cheekily expressed the well-known pun from Constance Bennett, who starred with Marilyn in *As Young as You Feel*, and who is supposed to have quipped, 'There's a broad with her future behind her.'

Arthur, however, was determined to see beyond and beneath the superficialities of Marilyn's screen persona. Each day, as he walked down to 42nd Street for rehearsals of his forthcoming production of *A View from the Bridge*, he would pass a gigantic cut-out image of her advertising *The Seven Year Itch*, her mouth open, her white skirts billowing up around her body. The image was something of a prison, he realised. 'Of course sex and seriousness could not exist in the same woman,' he said, in a damning critique of the presiding misogynistic culture, 'and this American illness was not about to end or so it seemed.'[2]

Miller and Marilyn certainly shared a sense of excitement and optimism about their new relationship. Although their four-year marriage would end in a bitter separation during the filming of *The Misfits*, and then divorce, in early 1961, Marilyn always kept Arthur's love letters. When questioned in 2002 about whether he'd kept anything from his time with her, Miller pointed to the actress's bike that he stored in his garage, at the same house they once shared in Roxbury, Connecticut. 'It's been hanging up in there for forty years,' he said.[3]

58

Love letters

'Poppy you said that I was dear to you,' Marilyn wrote to Arthur Miller towards the end of April 1956, addressing him using a favourite nickname, 'partly because I had not lived the life of propriety and so-called morality – but my darling don't you understand I was never once offered that and maybe if it was possible for me – I might have gone down that road – in other words – there was no choice to make – the same road was <u>always</u> before me. So when you speak of my nobility it really wasn't so noble – but my dear dear dear – that you love me makes so much that has happened to me and is happening to me (in the worst case) unreal – and still I know from all my nerves and muscles and mind that they did happen – so you see how it's doubly difficult to understand that you – the finest, dearest, most beautiful human being chose me – to love.'[1]

Marilyn, who was staying at the Chateau Marmont hotel in LA while filming *Bus Stop*, sent this letter to Arthur in Pyramid Lake, Nevada, where he had gone to live for six weeks in order to get a quick divorce from his first wife. Miller was worried about news of their relationship breaking before he had a chance to introduce Marilyn to his two children, Jane, eleven, and Bob, nine. In one letter, Miller enclosed a sprig of sage which he suggested she place under her pillow. He also made it clear his desire for her knew no bounds: his letters are full of sexual fantasies, imaginings of their erotic encounters when they were reunited.

On 9 May, Miller wrote to his parents outlining his reasons for wanting to divorce Mary and telling them of his love for Marilyn. The letter – which was closely guarded by the Miller family until 2022 – reveals in stark terms the barrenness of Arthur's marriage, describing how Mary was 'a vindictive, punishing woman' and that had he not made the break, he would have had to abandon his career as a writer. 'I cannot write when I am full of hate and surrounded by hate ... My home was a tomb,' he explained. By contrast, Marilyn was an inspiration: a source of joy, a fount of happiness.[2]

Over the course of the next week, a nervous Miller waited for a response from his 'conventional' parents. He'd been afraid that they would judge him as being immoral and reject him. On 17 May 1956, Miller drove into Reno to the post office, where he picked up a letter from his mother, which he read to himself in the public square. The letter from Augusta Miller, which he forwarded to Marilyn, was full of reassurance and acceptance, a document that Arthur said prompted something of a magical reawakening. Finally, he felt secure in his sexuality and free to express the joys of physicality that came from loving Marilyn.

Miller's mother's words crystallised a number of things in his mind: that he had embarked on a correct course of action, that his love for Marilyn was deep and pure and real, and that she was essential for his future well-being. 'You have given me back my soul, Darling,' he wrote to Marilyn. As he composed the letter, he realised he was near to tears; that day was like another rebirth, said Miller. Marilyn had liberated him from the conventions that had stifled him. He went on to talk about possible dates for their wedding and how he couldn't wait to reunite. Arthur signed the letter, 'The World's Luckiest Man Since Adam.'[3]

59

'You know he never really asked me'

On 21 June 1956, Arthur Miller was called before the House Un-American Activities Committee in Washington and was asked if he was a communist. 'I was never under Communist Party discipline,' he replied, but he did admit that he had made a 'great error' by sympathising with various communist causes in the early 1940s. He explained that the ideology 'suited my mood in those days'. But he would not, he insisted, give the committee any names of other communist sympathisers, a standpoint that risked him being charged with contempt. The committee claimed that it had decided to question Miller because it was investigating the possible misuse of American passports that they believed might help the cause of international communism. They knew that Miller needed a passport so that he could accompany Marilyn to London to film *The Prince and the Showgirl*. The relationship between the playwright and the actress had become public knowledge that spring.[1]

Just before the hearing, Miller's lawyer Joseph L. Rauh Jr received a message from Francis Walter, who chaired the committee. The playwright was told that he would not have to appear before the committee if he could persuade Marilyn to pose for a photograph with Walter. That was 'how dangerous he really thought I was', said Miller.[2] When he refused, a charge of contempt was issued against Miller, a citation that was eventually discharged.

The dry question and answer format of the committee proceedings was enlivened by the following interchange:

> Richard Arens: Now, your present application for a passport pending in the Department of State is for traveling to England. Is that correct?
> Arthur Miller: To England, yes.
> Arens: What is the objective?
> Miller: The objective is double. I have a production which is in the talking stage in England of *A View from the Bridge*, and I will be there to be with the woman who will then be my wife. That is my aim.[3]

Marilyn told friends that this was how Miller proposed – in front of a committee. 'Have you heard?' she asked Norman and Hedda Rosten. 'He announced it before the whole world! He told the whole world he was marrying Marilyn Monroe. Me! Can you believe it? You know he never really asked me.'[4]

There were others, such as director Joshua Logan, who were suspicious of Miller and thought that he had ulterior motives. In Logan's words, 'he used her just to get his chance to go to Europe, you know, and get his passport'.[5]

60

A FATAL CHASE

It's 29 June 1956. A white Chevrolet sedan is being driven at high speed through the country lanes of Roxbury, Connecticut. It's following a green Oldsmobile, a car that contains one of the most famous women in the world and her prospective husband.

The already frenzied media interest in the union has risen to a level approaching the hysterical: camped out in front of Miller's home are around four hundred reporters, photographers and newsmen. Marilyn 'was a native of that queer country in which it is taken for granted that one's personal life exists to be exploited for the titillation of the masses,' wrote Maurice Zolotow, who was present that day. 'But Miller was like a foreigner going into the jungle and having to get used to the growl and howl of jungle beasts and the frightful tropical bird screams.'[1] The novelist William Styron, Miller's neighbour, described the invasion of journalists into the normally sedate and tranquil setting of rural Connecticut as 'a gawking procession of shortshirted, Pontiac-ensconced, growling cretins such as you would never have imagined'.[2]

The chase is turning messy, dangerous. Driving the white Chevrolet is 18-year-old Ira Slade, assistant to his brother, the photographer Paul Slade, while his passenger is the New York bureau chief for *Paris Match* magazine, the Russian Princess Mara Scherbatoff. At the wheel of the Oldsmobile is the playwright's cousin Morton Miller, who as a resident of Roxbury knows the twists and turns of the roads, and who is driving Arthur and Marilyn back from picking up their marriage licence.

As he approaches a hairpin bend near where Tophet Road turns into Gold Mine Road, Morton Miller slows down, before picking up speed again. Slade, in hot pursuit, and keen to gain an exclusive, takes the bend at top speed, but loses control of the car. Panicking, he tries again to steady the Chevrolet, but it's too late: the car shoots off the road and smashes into a large tree. Scherbatoff is thrown into the windscreen. The force of the impact cuts open her face from her forehead to her lips, takes out a number of her teeth and severs an artery in her neck.

The three passengers in the Oldsmobile hear the terrifying smash, stop, and turn around to see if they can help. What they witness is a scene of destruction. There is blood everywhere. Although Ira has escaped with minor injuries, it's clear that Scherbatoff is seriously injured. Miller helps carry the photographer and the journalist from the wreckage, and then the group return to the house, where they telephone for help. The closest hospital is in New Milford, and Miller is told an ambulance will take hours to arrive. 'There's been an accident,' Morton Miller tells the crowd of journalists outside the house. 'It's bad ... There was a photographer and a girl ... We tried to do what we could for them. She's bleeding ... God, she's cut all over.'[3] Marilyn is hysterical. 'A girl has been terribly hurt,' she says. 'It's awful.'[4]

Sensing a sensational story, a messenger from a photo agency jumps on his motorbike to take some shots of the scene, but when he returns he tells his colleagues, 'My stomach wasn't strong enough. I put a blanket on her. The bleeding ...' An image published the following day shows the full horror of the accident's aftermath, with Scherbatoff lying prostrate by the smashed-up car. Other, unpublished photographs show her with her ribcage exposed, the flesh torn from her face. The 47-year-old journalist dies later that afternoon at the hospital in New Milford.

The accident only serves to increase the seemingly insatiable appetite of the media representatives. The reporters and photographers swarm 'like flies to a carcass' to the scene of the accident and then back again to the house. When Arthur, dressed in a V-neck sweater over a white shirt, and Marilyn, in a gold blouse and a cinch-belted black skirt, step out of the house, the press lunge towards them. 'It was chaotic,' admitted Zolotow.[5]

Unedited newsreel footage reveals the tension between the soon-to-be-married couple and the media pack. Marilyn looks nervous and whispers something inaudible into Milton Greene's ear, before coming to stand by Miller. Drawing on her years of experience as an actress, she does her best to compose herself and blinks away the anxiety. But then a reporter asks whether Miller wishes to be questioned or whether he would prefer to make a statement saying that he's sorry about the accident. 'Somebody should question you people,' snaps Marilyn. A journalist asks about where and when they will be married. Arthur lights up a cigarette before he speaks. 'We just had a terrible accident on this road as a result of the mobs that have been coming by here. I knew that was going to happen, at least I suspected it was, because these roads were made for horse carts and not for automobiles, and people who don't know them often times smash up around here. And I asked the press to assemble all at once today so that the pictures could be taken that were wanted, in the hope that that can be avoided.'[6]

The couple were frightened that more people might get hurt. 'It's got to stop,' said Marilyn to Arthur. 'How do we stop it?' he asked. 'Give them what they want,' she said. 'Get married.'[7] The couple decided to bring their marriage forward and later that night, at a courthouse in White Plains, New York, they were married in a civil ceremony. Marilyn had turned thirty just a few weeks before; Arthur was forty.

But the death of Mara Scherbatoff cast a shadow over the union. 'Yes, I remember it too well,' Marilyn said when asked about the accident four years later. 'When we returned to our car, I saw a blood stain on my skirt and I thought, "It's a bad omen."'[8] In

Miller's autobiography, he wrote of how 'a pall of disaster' fell over them after the accident. Over time he watched how the tree on Gold Mine Road gradually died from the impact of the car. 'The struck tree slowly rotted and after a half a dozen years finally toppled over, leaving a stump that my eye could not avoid looking for in the weeds whenever I drove past,' he said.[9]

61

'I want to be a Jew'

'Honey, you know we are married now, even in the eyes of my religion,' Arthur told his new bride, soon after the civil ceremony. 'I want to be a Jew,' Marilyn replied. 'I want it now, before we go to England [where she was to film *The Prince and the Showgirl*] ... This doesn't change anything. I only want it more.'[1]

On Sunday 1 July 1956, Marilyn and Arthur had a second marriage ceremony. This Jewish wedding – at the Westchester home of Miller's agent and friend Kay Brown – was carried out by Rabbi Robert Goldburg, the spiritual leader of Congregation Mishkan Israel in Hamden, Connecticut. A couple of months before the ceremony the rabbi had met with Miller, who informed him of Marilyn's desire to convert to Judaism. 'He made it clear to me that in no way did he make this demand on Marilyn,' wrote Goldburg in a letter. 'A meeting was arranged and I met Marilyn and Arthur at her apartment in New York at Sutton Place and 57th Street ... I was struck by her personal sweetness and charm. She seemed very shy but said that she had no religious training other than some memories of a Fundamentalist Protestantism which she had long rejected.'[2]

Marilyn told the rabbi that she felt drawn to Judaism through the many Jews that she had known and respected, not least Arthur himself. A year before she married Miller, Marilyn had volunteered to help raise funds for the United Jewish Appeal. She also told the rabbi that she had read extracts from Albert Einstein's essay collection *Out of My Later Years,* a book which Arthur owned.

Einstein was something of a 'hero' to her, she said, a man who represented 'the great scientist-humanist-Jew-Socialist dissenter'.[3]

Marilyn also told the rabbi that she was 'impressed by the rationalism of Judaism – its ethical and prophetic ideals' – and she read a number of books that the spiritual leader gave her. 'Marilyn was not an intellectual person, but she was sincere in her desire to learn,' said Goldburg. 'It was also clear that her ability to concentrate over a long period was limited.'[4]

Before the actual wedding ceremony, the rabbi carried out Marilyn's conversion. He had already explained to her that as the Millers defined themselves as Reformed Jews, she wouldn't have to be bound by the strict laws that were followed by Orthodox Jews. Personal choice was at the heart of the approach – she could be 'as Jewish as she wanted to be'. 'Is it of your own free will that you seek admittance into the Jewish fold?' Rabbi Goldburg asked her. 'Do you renounce your former faith?' 'Do you pledge loyalty to Judaism?' 'Do you promise to cast in your lot with the people of Israel amid all circumstances?' 'Should you be blessed with children do you agree to rear your children according to the Jewish faith?' Marilyn answered 'yes' to all the rabbi's questions.[5]

One of the guests at the ceremony was Marilyn's close friend, the poet Norman Rosten, who himself was Jewish. 'She participated with touching seriousness,' he recalled. 'Those who had secretly laughed at or mocked her desire to adopt the Jewish faith were moved to silence.'[6] Rosten's wife Hedda had suggested the shade of Marilyn's wedding dress – which was described as 'bone-colored' – and organised the dyeing of her veil with a solution of tea leaves.[7] Norman observed how perfectly Marilyn played her part – how she delivered her lines, how she followed the ancient Jewish ritual, how she lifted her veil to sip from the goblet of wine. 'She spoke her "I do" in a clear if shaky voice, exchanged rings, was kissed by the groom, and then received dozens of kisses by some twenty-five friends, relatives, and a few reporters. A giddy delirious day. It was a fairy tale come true. The Prince had appeared, the Princess was saved.'[8]

As well as the security of marriage, Marilyn was desperate for an extended family she could call her own. 'Marilyn had a yearning to belong,' wrote Miller later.[9] His parents Isidore and Augusta had not felt comfortable with the Catholic faith of Arthur's first wife Mary, but when they knew that Marilyn wanted to convert, they welcomed her into their home. 'She opened her whole heart to me,' said Augusta of her new daughter-in-law.[10] Marilyn was also keen to learn the art of Jewish cooking and asked her new mother-in-law to show her how to make typical dishes such as chopped liver, potato pierogi, gefilte fish and chicken soup with matzo balls. By the end of their first month of marriage, Arthur said that his new wife had mastered borscht, declaring it to be 'authentic'.[11]

There's an apocryphal story about the day when the new couple had been invited to Friday night supper at Isidore and Augusta's home in Brooklyn. 'Gee, Arthur, these matzo balls are pretty nice,' Marilyn is alleged to have said. 'But isn't there any other part of the matzo you can eat?'[12] Marilyn would often playfully drop Jewish expressions or phrases into the conversation. 'Hi Bubuleh,' she would say. 'Oy vay, what tsures.'[13]

Years after Marilyn's death, Miller would define his former wife's conversion as superficial – it was, he claimed, nothing more than 'a conversation with a rabbi friend of mine with whom her connection was less religious than political and social'.[14] It's true that Goldburg shared Marilyn's passion for civil and human rights. In 1961, the rabbi was arrested, along with Martin Luther King, at a demonstration in Albany, Georgia; the two men went on to share a jail cell and later King spoke at Goldburg's temple in Hamden.

Despite what Miller said subsequently, Marilyn – who regarded herself as 'an atheist Jew'[15] – did feel a deep connection to the Jewish people. After her divorce from the playwright in 1961, Marilyn told Goldburg that she had no plans to renounce Judaism and the two continued to correspond for the rest of her life. On the mantelpiece of her last home, in Brentwood, Los Angeles, Marilyn displayed a menorah given to her by her mother-in-law; the multi-branched candelabra was fitted with a mechanism that played 'Hatikvah', Israel's national anthem.

Marilyn didn't go on to study or practise the religion but she said that ultimately she felt a deep and profound identification with the Jewish people. 'Everybody's always out to get them, no matter what they do, like me,' she said.[16]

62

THE WORLD GOES MAD FOR MARILYN

Marilyn and her new husband had survived twelve hours in a propeller plane over the Atlantic and a press conference at which they were besieged by 400 journalists. 'At one point the camera flashes formed a solid wall of white light that seemed to last for almost half a minute,' remembered Arthur Miller, 'a veritable aureole, and the madness of it made even the photographers burst out laughing.'[1]

They had travelled to England in July 1956 to film *The Prince and the Showgirl*. Marilyn Monroe Productions had paid $275,000 for the film rights of Terence Rattigan's 1953 play *The Sleeping Prince*. Laurence Olivier was to direct and reprise his role as Charles, the Prince Regent of Carpathia, for a fee of $100,000. Marilyn – whose fee was $50,000 plus expenses – was to play the role of Elsie Marina. When the film was first announced, Joshua Logan, who had directed Marilyn in *Bus Stop*, proclaimed that the Marilyn–Olivier match was 'the most exciting combination since black and white'.[2]

The presence of the star on English soil drove the nation into a state of mass hysteria. 'She is a form of longing in the public's imagination, and in that sense godly,' wrote Miller.[3] *Time* magazine reported that Marilyn received 5,000 letters a week from around the world. Miller said that women wanted to know how to be more like her; some people asked for money; many men asked for sexual favours; the occasional letter contained faeces; and 15 per cent of them were 'quite insane: several offered to put her out of her misery free of charge in some cases, for a fee in others'.[4] In

Turkey, one young man 'went so daft' after watching *How to Marry a Millionaire* that he felt compelled to slash his wrists. In Japan, her infamous nude calendar photograph was displayed in municipal assembly buildings in a mission 'to rejuvenate the assemblymen'. And, according to a 1956 report in *Time*, her image was displayed on the Table of Elements inside the radiation control lab of the world's first atomic submarine.[5]

The night of their arrival – 14 July – the couple collapsed into bed at their rented home, Parkside House, Englefield Green, Surrey, which backs onto Windsor Great Park. Miller dreamed that he and his new wife were being serenaded by an angelic choir. The music was almost unbearably beautiful, so sublime he felt as though it had the power to lift him up and carry him through the air. But, in the early hours of the morning, as he woke, he realised that he could still hear the sound. Was he going mad? he wondered. He got out of bed, drew back the curtains and saw, standing in the moonlight, a few hundred boys and young men dressed in blazers – most probably the scholars from nearby Eton College – all of them gazing up at the window and singing 'knightly lyrics' in a reverential tone, almost as if they were performing for a queen or some goddess.

Arthur woke Marilyn, who came to look. Both of them stood there at the window, completely naked but shielded by the curtains, and wondered what to do, until gradually the boys began to leave and fade away into the night. At the airport, a Scotland Yard detective had warned the couple that there were 'all kinds of crazies' in England and that it would be best if Marilyn avoided large groups of people at all costs unless she had her bodyguards protecting her.[6] A few weeks later, when she visited a Marks and Spencer's store in London, officials had to close the shop for her, 'for fear of an uncontrollable stampede of people trying to get a look at her,' said Miller. 'She shattered a thousand years of British imperturbability.'[7]

63

Problems on – and off – set

Arthur and Marilyn thought of their arrival in England as something of a new start. Miller likened the atmosphere in America to a 'pressure cooker'. Marilyn was looking forward to working with Olivier, regarded as the best actor of his generation. She was keen to prove herself as an actress and demonstrate the techniques she had learned with the Strasbergs, that she was more than just the dumb blonde of popular perception. And she was excited about the prospect of married life with her new husband.

Yet it wasn't long before the problems started. Reportedly, soon after filming at Pinewood commenced, Marilyn began to arrive late on set and fluff her lines. Instead of turning to her director, Olivier, for guidance, she relied on her acting coach Paula Strasberg, who was being paid an astonishing $25,000 for ten weeks' work. 'The truth came to light with uncanny speed,' wrote Olivier in his autobiography. 'Paula knew nothing, she was no actress, no director, no teacher, no adviser – except in Marilyn's eyes, for she had one talent: she could butter Marilyn up.' On a car journey, Olivier overheard Paula giving her most famous student a pep talk that lasted over an hour: 'My dear, you really must recognize your own potential,' she said, 'you haven't even yet any idea of the importance of your position in the world, you are the greatest sex symbol in human memory, everybody knows and recognizes that and you should too, it's a duty which you owe to yourself and to the world, it's ungrateful not to accept it. You are the greatest woman of your time, the greatest human being of your time; of any time, you name it; you can't think of anybody, I mean – no, not even Jesus – except you're more popular.'[1]

When Olivier had first met Marilyn in Manhattan in February 1956, he was so taken by her beauty, charm, intelligence and sexual allure that he thought he might fall in love with her. He imagined that, during the process of filming, he would have to tell his second wife Vivien Leigh that he was going to leave her for Marilyn just as he had told his first wife Jill Esmond that he was leaving her for the *Gone with the Wind* star. Yet, within a matter of weeks his infatuation turned first to annoyance – he found Marilyn's dependence on 'the Method' frustrating and self-defeating – and then to something approaching hatred. 'I think that when he [Olivier] first met her, and agreed to do the film, he thought he could have an affair with her,' wrote Colin Clark, the 23-year-old third assistant director on the film, to his friend Peter Pitt-Millward in November 1956. 'But after a few weeks on the set, he would gladly have strangled her with his bare hands.'[2]

After visiting the set, Olivier's son Tarquin recalled how Marilyn alienated everyone involved in the film.[3] Her acting was poor – in his words, 'Marilyn was as subtle as a schoolgirl throwing up'[4] – while Olivier told his son that the actress had the 'shape and mind of an amoeba'.[5] Later, in his autobiography, Olivier wrote, 'You would not be far out if you described her as a schizoid.'[6]

For her part, Marilyn thought Olivier was patronising. On one occasion, early in filming, he told her in an offhand manner to 'Be Sexy', an instruction that baffled and infuriated her in equal measure. It was, in the words of Lee Strasberg, 'the wrong thing to say to her at that moment. Whatever she did *sexy* was natural, spontaneous. It came out of her relation to what she was in contact with.'[7]

Miller observed how, on the set, his wife was left confused by Paula Strasberg's advice. On the first morning of filming, Olivier's heart sank as he tried to direct Marilyn in a scene in which her showgirl character meets his prince. 'We had spent the whole time trying to inject a scintillating spirit into the scene of our first meeting,' he said.[8] However, there was one nugget of motivational guidance that seemed to work wonders: Strasberg told Marilyn just to think of Frank Sinatra and Coca-Cola. 'Needless to say, it worked; enough to make a man cut his throat, enough for this man, anyway,' recalled Olivier.[9]

Elaine Schreyeck, who was born two years before Marilyn in 1924, was the script supervisor in charge of continuity. 'I found her to be like a little girl – she seemed completely lost,' she told me. 'I used to hold my breath hoping she'd remember her lines. You wanted to help her all the time. You wanted to give her confidence without this woman [Paula Strasberg] who was always saying, "Oh, you're wonderful, everything is marvellous." When you saw the rushes the next day, you held your breath, hoping everything would be fine. But she really was amazing – as soon as she got in front of the camera, it was magic.

'At times she thought that everybody was against her which was stupid. "Well, you know, *you're* on their side," she once said to me. "There is no side to it, Marilyn," I said, "we're all making the same picture." But she was often late and there was one occasion when Sir Laurence said, "You've kept everybody waiting and you should apologise." And she did.'[10]

Marilyn's timekeeping and absenteeism were a problem for the film-makers throughout the shoot. On 9 January 1957, Hugh Perceval, the movie's production manager, wrote a letter marked 'private and confidential' to Cecil Tennant, Olivier's agent at MCA in London, which set out how much her late starts and no-shows had cost the film. In a detailed log, he outlined how on 7 August, the first day of filming, Marilyn was twenty minutes late. Although it may seem insignificant, he said such delays added up, as it cost the production an estimated £5 per minute, totalling £100 for this first day, or £450 during the first week. In addition to the lateness on set, Marilyn was not available at all on 22, 23, 24 or 31 August, 3, 4, 5, 6, 7 or 28 September, 11, 23, 24 or 29 October, or 2 or 8 November.

'Although we cannot prove it, we are convinced that if she had been present on all the days she was required, and was really on the ball, we could have shot the picture in 3 weeks less, i.e. a total of 12 weeks which was Sir Laurence's original estimate,' said Perceval. 'And as I'm in a computing mood, I calculate that in order for the producer to recover his loss of £38,000, an extra 2,000,000 people must pay 2/6d each to see the film. This is based on the estimate of the producer receiving 3/- from every £1 into the box office. Will Monroe productions guarantee to produce these extra paying customers?'[11]

Marilyn also thought that Olivier was trying to steal the limelight, competing with her, as Miller wrote in his autobiography, 'like another woman, a coquette drawing the audience's sexual attention away from herself'.[12] Miller's biggest mistake, in hindsight, was to side with Olivier over what he began to regard as the wild imaginings and neurotic anxieties of his wife. In fairness, Arthur took a pragmatic approach: he wanted what was best for Marilyn, but he also realised that what some regarded as her increasingly erratic behaviour threatened the completion of the film. 'She couldn't trash him [Olivier] too much or where would she be?' Miller told his biographer in 2002. 'She would be left with nobody on the set. And so I found myself defending him, and that was the worst possible thing I could have done.'[13]

At some point during the filming of *The Prince and the Showgirl*, Miller scribbled something in his journal that expressed his doubts about his new wife. While the exact wording of the note is unclear, its existence is not, as Miller confirmed in an interview in the 1980s. 'She was aware of a grinding frustration in me,' he said, 'and in that note there was an allusion to the fact that I was unable to help her and I was not of any use to her or myself.'[14]

When Marilyn came across Miller's note in the journal – which was lying open on a desk in Parkside House – she was devastated. 'I rarely snoop and I certainly didn't intend to read it,' she later told her masseur and close friend Ralph Roberts. 'You know how sometimes your eyes become riveted to some printed word in a newspaper? Well, he had written the most dreadful things about me. I couldn't believe what I saw. I made a terrible scene. I was torn in half.' Marilyn said that reading the note took her back to the worst days of her childhood. 'All of a sudden I was back in that preacher's foster home, accused of singing before breakfast, which was considered a sin. Punished. But as bad as that had been, this was infinitely worse.'[15] Marilyn was due to be up early the next morning and, in a panic, she took a sleeping pill, which she said did nothing, and so she took another, which also seemed to have little effect. According to the film's production files held in the Olivier archive in the British Library, Marilyn did not turn up on set on 22, 23 or 24 August, which most likely dates the discovery of Miller's journal to the night of 21 August.

The Strasbergs, who paid a visit to Marilyn at Parkside House, later told their daughter Susan of what they encountered there. Marilyn said that Arthur 'was ashamed of me, ashamed to love me, how at first he thought I was an angel, and now he'd realized how he was wrong, I'd disappointed him'.[16] Lee Strasberg recalled what the actress had told him – in Marilyn's words, 'That his first wife had let him [Miller] down, but I had done something worse. Olivier was beginning to think I was a troublesome bitch and that he [Miller] no longer had a decent answer to that one.'[17]

In Miller's 1964 play *After the Fall* – which is generally considered to be a semi-autobiographical portrait of the couple's marriage – the Marilyn character, Maggie, discovers just such a note, a 'letter from hell', from her husband Quentin. In that document, Quentin writes, 'The only one I will ever love is my daughter.' Maggie recalls how when she first read the note, she fainted and how it nearly 'killed' her. In turn, Quentin reveals what prompted him to write it: 'you suddenly turned on me, calling me cold, remote, it was the first time I saw your eyes that way – betrayed, screaming that I'd made you feel you didn't exist ... I wanted to face the worst thing I could imagine – that I could not love.'[18]

In his autobiography *Timebends*, Miller wrote, 'She had no means of preventing the complete unraveling of her belief in a person once a single thread was broken.'[19] The couple tried their best to patch up their differences, but for Marilyn the discovery of the note and its harsh contents so soon after their wedding would continue to cast a shadow over the marriage. 'I would say that when you have a person so distraught we have to rush her to a psychiatrist to try to get her straightened out, that is considerable impact,' recalled Lee Strasberg. 'That's when this whole terrible problem really began.'[20]

In a poem written on Parkside House stationery and thought to have been composed around this time, Marilyn articulated her deep sense of despair and alienation. She was terrified at the prospect of what lay in store for her, and her role as a wife. In a line from the poem she wrote,

> *since I know from life*
> *one cannot love another,*
> *ever, really.*[21]

64

MISCARRIAGE?

Laurence Olivier: Why can't you get here on time, for fuck's sake?
Marilyn Monroe: Oh, do you have that word here in England, too?[1]

There was another reason suggested for Marilyn's absence on the set of *The Prince and the Showgirl*: a possible pregnancy. Rumours started to appear in the press, and later it was discovered that the Hungarian couple who worked for the Millers had been selling snippets of gossip to the newspapers. On 5 September 1956, the *Daily Sketch* alleged that while the official story put out by the studio was that Marilyn was suffering from an attack of gastritis, the actress had consulted a gynaecologist because she believed she might be pregnant. 'There's been speculation more than a week on the set,' an unnamed source told the newspaper. 'She seems queer (ill) in the mornings but perfectly fit after lunch.' Reportedly, the gynaecologist arrived before lunch on 4 September and stayed for three-quarters of an hour.[2]

The rumour of the star's pregnancy was almost immediately denied. 'Marilyn Monroe's tummy ache is simply an overdose of acting orders from Sir Laurence Olivier,' reported the *Daily News*.[3] When, on 5 September, Arthur Miller arrived back at London Airport from an eight-day trip to Paris and America, he said, in a comment that was widely syndicated, that the story of his wife's pregnancy was 'Absolutely rubbish. There is no truth in it.'[4]

Colin Clark, the third assistant director who later wrote the memoir *My Week with Marilyn*, claims that he was there – on Marilyn's bed – when she started to experience the first signs of a miscarriage. '"It was Arthur's," Marilyn said, between sobs. "It was for him. He didn't know. It was going to be a surprise. Then he would see that I could be a real wife, and a real mother."'[5]

In Clark's version of events, a doctor arrives – possibly Dr Arthur Blackall Connell – who confirms that Marilyn had been about three weeks pregnant but that she had miscarried. 'But she can always try again,' he says. 'It isn't the end of the world.'[6]

However, questions arise over this account. First of all, Clark lists the date when this incident is supposed to have taken place as 18 September 1956, yet the production schedule doesn't list this as a day when the actress was absent from the set. The young man's encounter with Marilyn – when he claims he spent the night in her bedroom – is supposed to have taken place when Miller was away in America. Yet we know the playwright returned to London on 5 September.

In the extract, Clark tells us that he is surprised that Marilyn is pregnant. Yet, the news was splashed across the newspapers earlier that month. And in Clark's earlier book, *The Prince, the Showgirl and Me* (published in 1995), he tells us that he recorded the following in his diary, under the date 2 September 1956: 'Last night, after an excellent dinner, Tony [Bushell, the associate director] told me of a rumour that MM was pregnant!'[7] Then, on 8 September 1956 – a full *ten days* before the encounter described in *My Week with Marilyn* – he wrote, 'Plod [a retired policeman employed to guard Monroe's house] called me over to Parkside for a chat. He could say nothing directly, but he hinted that MM had been pregnant but had now miscarried. The baby must have been no more than a month.'[8]

The mix-up over the dates could be interpreted as a simple lapse of memory; after all, Clark admits to not keeping a diary for a nine-day period in September 1956. Others have accused Clark of wilful invention. In 2011, on the release of *My Week with Marilyn*, the film adaptation starring Michelle Williams and Eddie Redmayne, Sarah Churchwell, author of *The Many Lives of Marilyn Monroe*, told National Public Radio, 'He [Clark] does claim that she [Marilyn] told him all kinds of intimate details, which coincidentally appear in virtually every biography of her. So, there's nothing in these books specifically about Marilyn that he couldn't have found out. And more importantly, he waited some forty years after the fact to publish them, which does make one think, you know, having read all of these biographies, that he capitalized on her fame and her familiarity and wrote a couple of books claiming a little bit more than happened.'[9]

In the introduction to *My Week with Marilyn*, Clark himself describes the experiences recounted in the book as a 'fairy story, an interlude, an episode outside time and space'.[10] He confesses that, as the son of Kenneth Clark, the renowned British art historian and broadcaster, he had been brought up in a world of 'make believe'. Yet despite this, he insists what he recorded was 'real'. Indeed, there are others who trust the essence of his account, particularly the details he provides of Marilyn's 1956 pregnancy and subsequent miscarriage. Arthur Miller's biographer Christopher Bigsby is one; his book confirms the miscarriage. According to Marilyn's biographer Donald Spoto, two doctors had confirmed that Marilyn was pregnant, 'but that she was afraid she will lose the baby'.[11]

Although Clark's account is unreliable, most of the evidence taken together suggests that the actress did suffer a miscarriage at this time.

65

IN THERAPY WITH ANNA FREUD

Such was the seriousness of Marilyn's mental distress that on 28 August 1956, her psychoanalyst Dr Margaret Hohenberg was flown over from New York to London. The day before, Arthur Miller had left England to travel to New York, where he was due to meet his children. Her new husband's absence, combined with the discovery of his harsh journal entry about her, the ongoing conflicts with Laurence Olivier, her insecurities over her acting, her anxieties over a possible pregnancy and fears that perhaps she could not trust those closest to her, led to a psychological crisis.

It was easy for those on the sidelines to make cruel judgements about Marilyn's appearance, her lateness and absenteeism, and her lapses of memory, but they were not privy to the very real struggles that Marilyn endured during the making of *The Prince and the Showgirl*. 'She is constantly having to test what she hasn't been able to put together yet,' said Hedda Rosten, who worked as her secretary during the summer of 1956.[1] The comment is a perceptive one; Hedda, married to the poet Norman Rosten, had experience working in psychiatric social care. The observation, which she relayed to Arthur Miller, articulates Marilyn's battle to understand the fragmentary nature of her identity and the courage with which she forced herself to explore the dark, uncharted geography of her psyche.

That summer Hohenberg referred Marilyn to Anna Freud, the therapist who specialised in the treatment of child trauma from the house in Hampstead she had shared with her father Sigmund until his death in 1939. The little we know about Anna Freud's sessions with Marilyn is from a biography of Freud's housekeeper Paula Fichtl, who had lived with the family since 1929, first in Vienna and then in London. According to the 1987 book *Alltag bei Familie Freud: Die Erinnerungen der Paula Fichtl* by the journalist Detlef Berthelsen, Marilyn turned up at the house one summer's day wearing a simple blue gabardine coat, a floppy hat, sunglasses and no make-up. Each day for a week, she underwent analysis with Anna Freud, who described her as 'very simple, not at all conceited, she looked a little scared, but when she smiled you could really like her'. She told Anna that she had read Sigmund Freud's classic work *The Interpretation of Dreams*, when she was twenty-one and that she was particularly taken by his description about dreams of nudity; indeed, a compulsion to undress in public was reportedly one of Marilyn's own psychological quirks. According to Fichtl, the Freud archives contain a note that she claims refers to Marilyn, under a disguised name, in the following terms: 'Adult patient. Emotional instability, exaggerated impulsiveness, constant need for external approval, inability to be alone, tendency to depression in case of rejection, paranoid with schizophrenic elements.'

Anna Freud invited the actress to handle and play with marbles, a type of play therapy she sometimes used with her young patients. Freud interpreted the manner in which Marilyn passed the marbles towards her as an indicator of 'desire for sexual contact'. Marilyn was so grateful for Freud's help that a few months later she sent her a cheque for a 'considerable sum'.[2] The actress always held the therapist in such high regard that, in 1960, when John Huston was making a film about Sigmund Freud and offered her the prestigious role of Cecily, partly based on Anna O, one of Freud's most famous case histories, she turned it down because she believed Anna Freud did not approve of the project. (The role went to Susannah York, with Marilyn's friend Montgomery Clift as Freud. Jean-Paul Sartre had worked on an early draft of the script; he was disappointed that Marilyn chose not to take part because, according to Huston, the philosopher considered her to be one of the greatest actresses alive.)

In early 1957, Anna Freud recommended a new therapist for Marilyn: New York-based Dr Marianne Kris, whose father Oskar Rie had been a collaborator and friend of Sigmund's, and also the paediatrician to his children. Kris, who was born in Vienna in 1900, trained as a doctor and psychoanalyst – she was analysed by Freud – and after escaping Austria with her psychoanalyst husband Ernst, she worked in London and then emigrated to America.

Marilyn often had as many as five sessions a week with Kris at her office-apartment on Central Park West – in the same building as the Strasbergs' home – and worked closely with her over the next four years. Central to their sessions was the long shadow cast by the suffering the actress had experienced in childhood. In 1959, Marilyn asked a lawyer, John F. Wharton, to look into organisations that 'provided psychiatric assistance to children' as she was thinking of setting up her own foundation; Wharton's first recommendation was the Anna Freud Foundation in New York.

Although Marilyn did not succeed in making such a bequest during her lifetime, in 1990, twenty-eight years after her death, a Manhattan judge ordered that a share of her estate could go to the Anna Freud Centre for the Psychoanalytic Study and Treatment of Children, in London. The settlement came after a series of lengthy and protracted legal battles. Under the terms of Marilyn's 1961 will, she left a quarter of her estate to Marianne Kris, who in turn willed that share to the Anna Freud Centre. However, in August 1980, the Surrogate's Court in New York heard Kris's claims that the Monroe estate had dwindled from $1.6 million to $101,229, due to the mishandling of funds. During that hearing, an executor of the estate, Aaron Frosch, stated that at the time of her death in 1962 Marilyn had been $372,136 in debt and that since then most of the remaining money had gone on taxes and lawyers' fees.

Although the court ruled that a quarter of that $101,229 should go to the Anna Freud Centre, the legal battle was not over, because Marianne died only three months later in November 1980, while visiting Anna Freud at her house in Hampstead. Kris's will was challenged by Anna Strasberg, the third wife and widow of Lee Strasberg, who had inherited the bulk of the Monroe estate. 'Mrs Strasberg had challenged the Freud Centre's right to the money, saying Kris's rights to the estate ended when she died,' reported the *Guardian*. However, Strasberg lost the case and the money went to the institution in London. 'There's been an explosion in the revenue,' said Bernard Green, the lawyer for the Anna Freud Centre at the time. 'It's not an insubstantial amount.'[3]

Marilyn's wish to give money to a foundation specialising in child mental health had finally come true.

66

Hope for the future

'A child of her own was a crown with a thousand diamonds,' wrote Arthur Miller.[1] He and Marilyn had rented a house, Stony Hill Farm, in Amagansett, Long Island, for the summer of 1957. Miller spent the morning writing: his short story *The Misfits*, which he would later rework into a screenplay, was published in the October issue of *Esquire*. Marilyn, who had turned thirty-one on 1 June, enjoyed playing Mrs Miller, as she called herself, busying herself with domestic tasks and walking along the shoreline. The ordeals during the filming of *The Prince and the Showgirl* were, for the most part, behind them. Yet Arthur worried about his wife's sensitivity. One day he watched her as she ran up and down the beach attempting to capture – and throw back into the sea – a few dozen gasping fish that had been discarded by local fishermen. Miller would later rework this incident into his 1960 short story *Please Don't Kill Anything*. 'She took off one sandal and went to a fish that was writhing and tried to flip it into the water, but it slipped away,' writes Miller, who is Sam in the story. 'Sam came over and picked it up and flung it into the sea. He was laughing now, and she kept saying, "I'm sorry. But if they're alive . . . !"'[2]

That summer Marilyn learned that she was pregnant, news that transformed her. Miller remembered a new 'quietness of spirit' in his wife,[3] while according to Susan Strasberg, Marilyn was 'euphoric'. 'I hope my kid's as happy about getting me as I am about getting him,' the actress said to her friend. It was clear she wanted a boy.[4]

The local community in Amagansett found themselves swept along by the good news. According to a report in *Modern Screen*, everyone was excited to play 'armchair godmother and godfather to a baby who was still seven months away but whom everyone was waiting for as if the baby was their own – because they had come to love the baby's parents so much already'.[5]

On the morning of 1 August, Miller heard a cry from the garden. Marilyn was doubled over in pain. He contacted a doctor, who in turn called an ambulance to take her 100 miles from eastern Long Island to the Doctors Hospital in Manhattan. The playwright informed waiting reporters that his wife had been pregnant for five or six weeks and that the baby was expected at the end of March 1958. 'My wife is fighting off a threatened miscarriage,' Miller told Louella Parsons.[6] However, when the actress was examined, doctors discovered that the pregnancy was ectopic – the foetus was growing outside the womb, in one of the fallopian tubes. Studies show that sufferers of endometriosis have a much higher incidence of ectopic pregnancies. Marilyn had to undergo emergency surgery to remove the foetus; one report claimed that if it had been left longer than six hours it's most likely she would not have survived. 'The baby was unsavable and it was urgent to protect the life of the mother,' said the surgeons.[7]

The locals in Amagansett gathered at the grocery store to listen to the radio; when the news finally came through that Marilyn had lost her child, the residents experienced a collective grief. 'It was a sad, touching thing to see the way the news affected these people,' said one neighbour. 'One old woman was shopping, right alongside me, and when she heard it began to cry. She told me that she'd talked to Marilyn right there in that store only two days earlier; that she'd told Marilyn she'd heard the wonderful news and had started to sew a surprise for the baby, which she'd give to Marilyn at the end of the summer. That Marilyn had been so delighted and happy she'd kissed her.'[8]

Despite whatever private pain she was experiencing, Marilyn continued to support and express her love for Miller's two children, Jane and Robert, from his first marriage. On 9 August 1957, while still in hospital, she wrote a tender and light-hearted note to 'Janie' about the family dog, Hugo, a basset hound. 'He got kicked by that donkey. Remember him? His nose swelled up with a big lump on top and it really wrecked his profile. I put an ice pack on it and it took several days for it to go down but the last time I saw him it was pretty well healed. Bernice [the maid] is taking care of him and the house while I am at the hospital. We are going home tomorrow and then I will write you by hand.'[9] The same day she wrote to Robert, or Bobby as she called him, who was away at summer camp. 'Guess what? I planted some flowers and Hugo loves them,' she writes. 'I mean he doesn't bother them. He doesn't even pee on them ... Your Daddy misses you very much and so do I. Sometimes Hugo is thinking of you. I can tell because he smiles.'[10]

With the end of the pregnancy, Marilyn believed that she had somehow failed her husband and felt consumed by an irrational fear that he would abandon her – 'a fear that was incredible to me,' said Miller. The three-hour journey back in the ambulance from Manhattan to the house on Long Island was interminable; the couple sat mostly in silence as they contemplated the news given to them by the doctors, that there was no guarantee another pregnancy would prove successful. 'Somehow, the past once again seemed to be reaching out its dead hand to drag her down,' Miller wrote. 'There were no words anymore that could change anything for her.'[11]

According to Susan Strasberg, Marilyn was so devastated at the loss of the baby that she took an overdose. After finding her in a comatose state, Arthur rushed her to hospital. 'After all she'd been through, to lose that baby, I could understand why she'd try to numb herself,' said Susan.[12]

In the spring of 1958, Marilyn faced a dilemma: should she

take on another role in a movie, or should she stay at home and try to get pregnant again? 'That's what I want most of all, the baby, I guess, but maybe God is trying to tell me something, I mean with all my pregnancy problems,' she told Norman Rosten. 'I'd probably make a kooky mother, I'd love my child to death. I want it, yet I'm scared. Arthur says he wants it, but he's losing his enthusiasm. He thinks I should do the picture.'[13] Marilyn wrote a letter to Norman and Hedda Rosten around this time, telling them that she thought she might be two or three weeks pregnant. Her breasts, she said, 'have been too sore to even touch – I've never had that in my life before also they ache – also I've been having cramps and slight staining since Monday – now the staining is increasing and pain is increasing by the minute.' The day before she hadn't eaten at all, but 'last night I took 4 whole amutal [amytal] sleeping pills – which was by actual count really 8 little amutal sleeping pills. Could I have killed it by taking all the amutal on an empty stomach? (except I took some sherry wine also) What shall I do? if it is still alive I want to keep it'.[14]

The pregnancy was a false alarm. For some close friends, the news came as something of a relief. Susan Strasberg questioned how she would have coped with the demands of a child; after all, if Marilyn had given birth, she would have been forced to interrogate her relationship with her own mother, whom she never mentioned but whose presence was 'omnipotent'. According to Susan, it was clear Marilyn never wanted to be 'anything like her own tormented, mad mother'.[15]

Marjorie Plecher, wardrobe assistant at Twentieth Century-Fox and wife of Allan 'Whitey' Snyder, maintained that Marilyn wanted a baby more than anything. 'I think if she could have conceived a child and had it she would given up her movie career and been the happiest lady alive,' she said.[16]

*

Marilyn started working on *Some Like It Hot* in Los Angeles in the summer of 1958. She was in an emotionally and physically vulnerable state, with an ear and throat infection which Miller said was 'so serious that a specialist forbade her to work at all until it was cured'.[17] When she arrived at Los Angeles International Airport on 8 July she was met by waiting reporters and photographers, one of whom asked her how she felt about being 'definitely chubby'. Marilyn tried to laugh off the comment. 'It's still in the right places, isn't it?' she responded. 'My weight goes up and down like everyone else's, but I'll be in good shape in two weeks because I intend to do lots of walking and exercising.'[18] But the question must have stung. On 16 July, Marilyn wrote to her stepdaughter Jane. 'Thanks for helping me into my white skirt. I almost didn't make it – but now that I'm busier I'll start losing weight – you know where.'[19]

Marilyn felt isolated and alone. On 7 September, Hedda Hopper wrote her gossip column about how the new film was something of a 'comeback' for the actress, as if she were some fading star desperate for a career lift.[20] In a poll carried out for a summer 1958 issue of *Photoplay*, Marilyn's name didn't appear in a list of the top twenty-five stars; in the same poll carried out in 1953 she had taken the number one spot. Arthur Miller was over 2,400 miles away on the East Coast, busy looking after his two children and trying to work. On 12 September, the playwright wrote to his wife – his 'Darling Girl' – who was staying at the Bel Air Hotel. In that letter, Miller – who had recently started having therapy again – expressed his deep sense of longing for his absent wife; without her the bed they normally shared was as empty and as wide as a field, he said. 'Everything I am and feel always turns toward you,' he wrote, before flying out to California to be with her.[21]

That September, Marilyn discovered she was pregnant again.

67

'It's me, Sugar ... It's Sugar, me!'

According to director Billy Wilder, one scene in *Some Like It Hot* – in which Marilyn had to say 'Where's that bourbon?' – took nearly fifty takes. 'There was the whole afternoon trying to get it, because she cried after every take, because she didn't get it, and then she had to be made up again,' recalled Wilder. 'And then also we lost the morning because she didn't show up, and we lost the afternoon because she didn't remember the line.'[1] Another simple line, where Monroe had to say 'It's me, Sugar', reportedly took even more takes to get right. 'I had signs painted on the door: IT'S. ME. SUGAR,' said Wilder. '"Action" would come and she would say, "It's Sugar, me!" I took her to the side after about take fifty, and I said, "Don't worry about it." And she said, "Worry about what?" [Shakes head.] The fiftieth take, that was, and then there was the fifty-first, and the fifty-second ... I've got an old aunt in Vienna who would say every line perfectly. But who would see such a picture?'[2]

Once again the men working with Marilyn didn't understand why she might be late on the set or repeatedly fluff her lines. Marilyn's two co-stars Tony Curtis and Jack Lemmon – who had to spend most of the time filming dressed in drag – were furious when she kept them waiting. Curtis later complained about how uncomfortable it was to hang around on location in the heat wearing 3-inch heels; tubs of ice were on hand so the two men could soak their feet when they took off their shoes. It was also, he observed, hard on the bladder. 'You had to piss, but it was impossible to do it with those metal jock straps they fitted on us,' he said. 'I never had any trouble, but it bothered Jack a lot. He said, "Why in hell don't you ever have to take a leak?" He complained to Billy, too, but Billy only said, "Don't drink too much before you go to makeup." Curtis's secret was to have a pipe fitted through his clothes so he could urinate at will.[3]

Arthur Miller told Billy Wilder about Marilyn's pregnancy and informed him that this would mean she would be unable to work a full day; he suggested she turn up on set at eleven rather than early morning. Wilder responded, 'I say, "Before eleven o'clock? She's *never* on the set before eleven o'clock! I wish you would be directing it – you would be tearing out your hair, you would slit your own throat, because she's never there!"'[4]

On 24 October 1958, Marilyn was admitted to the Cedars of Lebanon Hospital in Los Angeles, where she stayed for three days. When the hospital's gynaecologist Dr Leon Krohn examined her, he was alarmed to discover that his famous patient was still drinking alcohol and taking barbiturates even though she was pregnant. According to Krohn, Marilyn felt she needed to take something to ease the tension brought about by the stress she felt in her marriage. Krohn recalled being shocked by what he described as 'the biggest change ever in her'; he believed that Marilyn and Miller were trapped in a 'kind of Pygmalion story', where the playwright was trying to 'make a sophisticate' out of her. Krohn warned Marilyn about the danger to the foetus and told her that 'she was going to kill it with the drink and pills ... it's impossible to tell when just one drink will set things off'. Marilyn did not receive this medical advice well: she was furious and accused Krohn of bad practice, that he was 'only saying these things because Mirisch [the producer of *Some Like It Hot*] was a friend of his' and that he only 'wanted her to finish the picture'. The doctor – whom Marilyn had been seeing since 1952 – told her, quite calmly, that if that was how she truly felt then there was no point them continuing their professional relationship. Three hours later, Miller turned up at Krohn's office in Beverly Hills and successfully pleaded with him not to drop his wife as a patient.[5]

Four years later, Marilyn was still thinking about the clash with Dr Krohn and his warning about the dangers of drinking and taking drugs in pregnancy. On Wednesday 1 August 1962, just a few days before her death, she tracked down the gynaecologist to the Hillcrest Country Club in Beverly Hills where he was playing a round of golf. After being paged, he walked inside the clubhouse to discover that it was Marilyn on the phone. 'Are you still angry with me – about the baby?' she asked.[6]

According to Arthur Miller, twelve hours after the last day of filming on *Some Like It Hot* – 7 November 1958 – Marilyn miscarried again, although the loss of the baby would not be announced publicly until 17 December. Miller was not only angry with Wilder for working his wife so hard and ignoring medical advice, but he was furious with the director's negative comments about her in an interview with Joe Hyams, published in the *New York Herald Tribune*. How was Wilder now the shoot was over? asked the reporter. 'I am eating better,' answered the director, who had been suffering from back pain during filming. 'I have been able to sleep for the first time in months. I can look at my wife without wanting to hit her because she's a woman.' He went on to mock Marilyn for her timekeeping, her frequent absences from the set and her problems with delivering her lines. Would he, the reporter asked, ever work with Marilyn again? 'I have discussed this project with my doctor and my psychiatrist and they tell me I'm too old and too rich to go through this again,' he said.[7] No doubt Wilder thought he was being amusing, but his rude and misogynistic comments hurt both Marilyn and Arthur. On seeing the interview, Miller dashed off a series of telegrams to Wilder. 'You choose [*sic*] to ignore this fact [the doctor's warning about his wife's pregnancy] during the making of the picture and worse yet, assiduously avoided mentioning it in your attack on her,' he wrote. 'Fact is, she went on with the picture out of a sense of responsibility not only to herself but to you and the cast and producer . . . Now that the hit for which she is so largely responsible is in your hands and its income to you assured, this attack upon her is contemptible . . . Your jokes, Billie, are not quite hilarious enough to conceal the fact. You are an unjust man and a cruel one. My only solace is that despite you her beauty and her humanity shine through as they always have.'[8]

Wilder sent back a telegram almost immediately in which he outlined his own position and, in the strongest possible terms, defended himself against charges of cruelty. From the first day of filming, he said, he'd had to bat off requests from both national and international journalists who had heard about Marilyn's 'unprofessional conduct'. He rejected the accusation that Marilyn had lost her baby because of the treatment she received by him or his staff. 'The fact is that the company pampered her, coddled her and acceded to all her whims,' he wrote. 'The only one who showed any lack of consideration was Marilyn, in her treatment of her co-stars and her co-workers right from the first day, before there was any hint of pregnancy . . . Her chronic tardiness and unpreparedness cost us eighteen shooting days, hundreds of thousands of dollars, and countless heartaches.' He went on to relate an incident that occurred on a day when Marilyn had shown up two and a half hours late clutching a copy of Thomas Paine's *The Rights of Man*. When the second assistant director knocked on her dressing room door and asked her if she was ready, said Wilder, 'her humanity shone through and she replied, "Drop Dead!"' Others have reported that her real words were, 'Go fuck yourself!' Wilder said he knew that Marilyn had issues, but 'her biggest problem is that she doesn't understand anyone else's problems'. A quick poll of cast members and crew would reveal that Marilyn was far from popular, said Wilder, and if Miller himself had worked on the film he too would have been forced to conclude that the only option would have been to 'have thrown her out on her can, thermos bottle and all, to avoid a nervous breakdown'.⁹

The interchange of cables between the two men continued until Wilder, adopting the role of a reluctant peacemaker, decided to draw a line under the spat. 'I hereby acknowledge that Good Wife Marilyn is a unique personality and I am the beast of Belsen,' he wrote. He ended the telegram by referencing the last words of *Some Like It Hot*: 'Nobody is perfect.'¹⁰

68

A HOUSE OF DREAMS

Just as Marilyn was recovering from the miscarriage, the December 1958 issue of *Photoplay* hit the newsstands. Inside there was an interview with her entitled 'The Empty Crib in the Nursery'. The article, which was flagged up as 'Marilyn's first magazine interview since the loss of her baby', had been conducted in the summer while she was staying at the Bel Air Hotel and filming *Some Like It Hot*. She was full of hope for the future. 'I'd say there's only one … one cloud on our happiness,' she told journalist Radie Harris, referring to her ectopic pregnancy and subsequent loss of the baby in 1957. 'We do long so much for a child. That will come, I'm sure. We've built a new wing on our country house, and we've christened it, out loud, "the nursery".'[1]

The last time Harris had seen the star before this interview was in November 1957 at an off-Broadway production of Noël Coward's *Conversation Piece*, starring Miller's sister Joan, when Marilyn had told her that she and Arthur intended to build a 'modern ranch house in Connecticut'. Miller had sold his old house at 153 Tophet Road, Roxbury, and in October 1957 had bought a nearby farm, the Leavenworth estate, at 232 Tophet Road, with 110 acres. Marilyn had extravagant tastes: she wanted a swimming pool even though there was a natural spring pond within 200 yards of the house, a place where Miller would swim over the course of the next fifty years.

Marilyn wanted to enlist the services of Frank Lloyd Wright – the famous architect of the Guggenheim Museum, a project he started in 1943 and finished in 1959 – and she called on him at his apartment in the Plaza Hotel, New York. 'With his capes and kingly bearing and mile-high starched collars, Wright existed on a plane more Olympian than any other celebrity's,' wrote one of the architect's biographers.[2] Wright – who was a spry and athletic ninety years old – was intrigued by Marilyn and gladly took on the commission. One grey autumn morning in 1957, he settled himself in the back of Miller's car for the journey to the site and promptly went to sleep, awaking a few hours later at his destination.

After taking one look at the existing house, built in 1783, Wright, whom Miller described as 'theatrically handsome' with a manner of delivery similar to the comic actor W. C. Fields, said in a rather dismissive tone, 'Ah, yes, the old house. Don't put a nickel in it.' Marilyn, Arthur and Frank shared a lunch of smoked salmon and bread, after which Miller took him on a tour of the land and up to the top of a hill where the fantasy house would be built. Although the playwright informed the architect of what he and Marilyn were looking for – they wanted something they could actually live in comfortably, not a statement house – Wright did not seem to listen. When the plans arrived – in the form of impressionistic sketches done in watercolour – the couple were disheartened to see that their vision for a dream house looked as though it had been designed for the headquarters of a corporation. The 60-foot circular sitting room, complete with a domed ceiling, was interspersed with a series of 5-foot-thick ovoid columns fashioned from fieldstone. The 70-foot-long swimming pool that jutted out from the hillside was supported by a 20-foot-high wall, which would necessitate, in Miller's opinion, 'heavy construction on the order of the Maginot Line'.[3] When Arthur asked about the cost, Wright replied that it would be in the order of around $250,000, but Miller estimated that this sum would just about cover the building of the swimming pool.

The house – which was never built – came to symbolise the

difference between Marilyn's and Miller's attitudes towards money. Marilyn liked to spend liberally, while for Arthur money meant the 'freedom to write'.[4] After they rejected Wright's plans, the couple began to renovate the existing house, employing a team of carpenters, electricians and plumbers. 'I looked at it [the house] and thought how it had been standing there, weathering everything, for more than 180 years,' said Marilyn. She liked the idea that the house had been lived in by generations of families – 'it's as if some of their happiness has stayed there even after they went away, and I can feel it around me,' she said.[5]

69

THE JOY OF COOKING

While married to Miller, Marilyn took it upon herself to learn how to cook. She worked her way through *The New Fannie Farmer Boston Cooking-School Cook Book* and *The New Joy of Cooking* by Irma Rombauer and Marion Rombauer Becker. The two books owned by Marilyn – which sold at the Christie's auction in 1999 for $13,800 and $29,000 – are full of her handwritten shopping lists, recipes that she ripped out of newspapers, and eating plans. She prided herself on making bread and serving up a chicken dish with a special seasoning that was a favourite of her husband's.

'I started from scratch,' she said. 'In fact, from *below* scratch ... When I was a kid, I learned to do a lot of things. I could scrub marvelously. I could dust, I could clean anything; but they never let me near the food – that was too valuable. So that's why I say I started from below scratch ... Now, when I go into the supermarket, I know just what I want. I make a list before.'[1]

Although Marilyn loved *The New Joy of Cooking*, she had one criticism: its recipe for home-made pasta. She told a journalist her problem:

> I roll the dough out very thin, then I slice it into narrow strips – like this – *then*, the book says, 'Wait till they dry.' We were expecting guests for dinner. I waited and waited. The noodles [pasta] didn't dry. The guests arrived: I gave them a drink; I said, 'You have to wait for dinner until the noodles dry. Then we'll eat.' I had to give them another drink. In desperation, I went

and got my little portable hairdryer and turned it on. It blew the noodles off the counter, and I had to gather them all up and try again. This time I put my hand over the strips, with my fingers outspread, and aimed the dryer through them. Well ... the noodles finally dried. So they *do* leave out a few instructions.[2]

Recipes that Marilyn liked include this one for cheese lasagne that she tore out of the *New York Post*. It took about forty minutes to prepare, made about six portions and cost about twenty cents per serving:

- 8 ounces lasagne noodles or any wide [pasta] noodles
- 2 eight ounce cans tomato sauce
- 2 cups creamed cottage cheese
- ½ teaspoon basil
- 1 teaspoon salt
- ¼ teaspoon Worcestershire sauce
- ¼ cup finely chopped onion
- ½ pound cheddar cheese, thinly sliced
- ¼ cup grated Parmesan or Romano cheese
- ½ cup buttered bread crumbs

Cook noodles [pasta] according to directions on package. Drain.

Mix the tomato sauce with the cottage cheese, basil, salt, Worcestershire sauce and onion. Arrange alternate layers of noodles, cheddar cheese and the sauce mixture in a buttered two and one-half quart casserole. Top with crumbs that have been mixed with grated cheese. Bake in a moderate oven (375 degrees) for about 25 minutes.

70

Enter Dr Greenson

On 11 February 1960, Marilyn – now back in Los Angeles – started to see a new psychoanalyst, Dr Ralph Greenson. He was a distinguished Hollywood psychiatrist, former army doctor, expert on the condition that would come to be called post-traumatic stress disorder, and a man who would play a key role in her life over the course of the next two years.

After complaining to Greenson about her insomnia and her problems on the set of her new film, the musical comedy *Let's Make Love*, Marilyn began to reveal her true feelings for her husband. Dr Greenson's case notes indicate that she felt 'disappointment' and 'resentment' when Miller did not, as she saw it, give her the support she needed in her work. She related a long list of grievances she held against Arthur, such as her belief that he was 'attracted to other women', dominated by his mother, neglectful of his father, not particularly nice to his children, and – most importantly, noted Greenson – 'doesn't love her enough and is inconsiderate'.

Marilyn told Greenson how she suffered from a particular form of perfectionism where the high standards she set for herself in every single scene of a film resulted in anxiety. 'As her anxiety increases, her co-workers become her mistreaters,' wrote Greenson in 1960 in an unpublished letter to Marilyn's New York therapist Dr Marianne Kris. Not all of this was paranoid behaviour, stated Greenson, as some of Marilyn's suspicions proved to be true. She found herself trapped in a never-ending vicious circle: as her anxiety levels rose she began to act more like the abandoned waif or orphan of her past, which then in turn provoked her colleagues to treat her with disrespect. In response, Marilyn saw her co-workers on set not as part of her professional network but as symbols of the foster parents who had treated her so badly. It was important, Greenson told her, that she try to view herself not as an abandoned child or waif but rather as a more 'robust' adult personality. Initially, this seemed to work, and Greenson likened this suggestion to a kind of 'magic charm'. There was, however, a setback after only two more days on *Let's Make Love* when Marilyn began to experience menstrual cramps, fatigue and anxiety about not sleeping. She sought out more medication from one of her doctors, and had an 'unpleasant' conversation with Arthur Miller, who was in Ireland working on the script of *The Misfits* with director John Huston.[1]

Miller had started this work in the immediate aftermath of Marilyn's ectopic pregnancy in August 1957 in the hope that it would serve as a kind of filmic *billet-doux*. The playwright believed that, in the words of his biographer, the screenplay 'could be a gift to his wife, not merely a way of raising her spirits in the short term but a means both of offering the acting challenge she craved and of bringing the two of them together'.[2] Yet almost from the beginning, he sensed a certain reluctance in Marilyn to play the role of Roslyn, a part he had written specially for her.

One of Greenson's first tasks was to assess Marilyn's medication. He was concerned that she was consulting two other doctors – one only known as Dr R, and the other, the Fox studio physician Dr Lee Siegel – which made it difficult to keep track of exactly what she was taking. He asked her to choose only one of these two doctors: she decided on Dr R. When Greenson contacted him, he told Greenson that Marilyn had responded well to injections of Phenergan, an antihistamine often used to help sedate patients. Greenson agreed that Dr R could also prescribe some non-barbiturate sedatives. When her psychiatrist questioned Dr

R and Dr Siegel, they told him that although Marilyn seemed to resemble an addict, she did not fit the usual pattern. They observed that she could absorb an enormous quantity of drugs into her system, but she could give up the medications suddenly, and also go without them with apparently few signs of withdrawal. However, the medics were worried about the possibility that one day she would become a true addict. One of the problems was that her star status gave her almost unlimited access to prescription drugs. 'Unfortunately, Mrs M. only uses doctors who are experienced with movie people, and as long as she uses such doctors, she will get into similar situations,' noted Greenson.

Towards the end of February 1960, Marilyn experienced something of a crisis. Over the course of a week, she failed to turn up for her appointments with Greenson, who initially was not unduly worried. However, when he was finally contacted by Miller, who had returned from Ireland to find his wife in the middle of a mental health crisis, Greenson paid Marilyn a visit. He found the actress in a depressed state, confined to bed, 'slightly woozy', and desperate for increasing amounts of medication (she had gone behind Dr R's back and contacted Dr Siegel at the studio). It took Greenson five hours to quieten her and get the two doctors to agree on a future course of treatment; it was important, he stressed, to remember the dangers of giving too much medication to a patient like Marilyn.

Greenson learned how the previous day, a Thursday, Marilyn had worked hard on the set of *Let's Make Love*, but she had become increasingly anxious again as she felt that Miller was not giving her the amount of support she needed. She was so out of control that she felt she needed a shot from the studio doctor – she often received intravenous Demerol from him, and she also self-medicated with alcohol. As Greenson talked to Marilyn, he became astounded by her knowledge of pharmaceuticals. In addition to Demerol, she knew all about phenobarbital and intravenous sodium amytal.

Marilyn begged Greenson for an injection of sodium amytal or sodium pentothal, a strong anaesthetic sometimes used as a truth serum or one of the drugs administered during the process of lethal injection on death row. It was her wish to be 'knocked out', he said. Greenson refused such an intervention and warned her of the serious dangers of intravenous treatments. 'I promised she would sleep with less medication if she would recognize she is fighting sleep as well as searching for some oblivion which is not sleep,' he said.

On the evening of Thursday 10 March, after several days of not seeing her, Greenson was called again by Miller. Marilyn had been doing well until she experienced, once again, feelings that her husband was neglecting or not supporting her, which made her angry, anxious and depressed, and which resulted in her need to get a shot from the studio doctor. It seems as though the emotional pain was too much and she wanted Greenson to give her another injection so she would temporarily lose consciousness. The psychiatrist was adamant: he would not enable her whims, he would not stand by and allow himself to be used in this way, as a kind of 'accomplice' in her ongoing battle with her husband. He would help treat her in a professional manner, but he maintained he would 'not help her kill herself or spite her husband or rush into oblivion'. After talking this through with Marilyn, he gave her two Seconals and she went to sleep.

Greenson then turned his attention to Miller. The writer confessed that while he had a great deal of respect and admiration for his wife, he was beginning to feel that he was reaching the end of his tether and that he sometimes lost his temper with her. 'There's an underlying feeling that Mrs M. is on probation,' wrote Greenson. The therapist told Miller that it was important to provide Marilyn with unconditional support and love and encouraged him to take advantage of the break in filming due to a Screen Actors Guild strike and return to New York, where the actress could see Marianne Kris again. As Greenson wrote to Kris, in a detailed case history of his twenty or so sessions with Marilyn, from his analysis he considered that she was not schizophrenic but suffered from episodes of paranoia that were 'masochistic and an acting out of the orphan girl rejections'. He liked Marilyn and felt sorry for her – he admired the fact that she had succeeded despite her 'terrible, terrible background'.

There was another issue too. In the same case file, Greenson noted 'the fact that the leading man [in *Let's Make Love*, Yves Montand] reminded her of her second husband [Joe DiMaggio] and she felt guilty to have erotic reactions toward him'.[3]

71

LET'S MAKE LOVE

'I was a million miles from thinking that anything whatsoever could happen between Marilyn and me,' said Yves Montand.[1] After a number of Hollywood stars such as Gregory Peck, Cary Grant and Rock Hudson had turned down the male lead in *Let's Make Love*, Marilyn suggested that the Italian-born French actor and singer – best known for his films *Le Salaire de la peur* and *Les Sorcières de Salem*, an adaptation of *The Crucible* – would be perfect for the role. She had seen Montand's one-man show in New York in September 1959, where he presented himself as a charming Gallic combination of Charlie Chaplin and Fred Astaire. 'He sings with his body,' she said.[2] Arthur and Marilyn met Yves and his wife, actress Simone Signoret, soon after the hit Broadway show, and by the time rehearsals started for *Let's Make Love*, in January 1960, they had all become firm friends. The two couples, who during filming occupied adjoining bungalows at the Beverly Hills Hotel, found they had a great deal in common and they bonded over their shared political beliefs.

'If I was thinking of falling in love with anything, it was the English language,' recalled Montand. His part in *Let's Make Love*, directed by George Cukor, called for him to play a millionaire Frenchman whose English was not only fluent but learned in the best schools and universities. 'It was the hardest time I've ever had in my acting career,' said the actor, whose English was limited.[3] Miller was also professionally involved, as he was brought in to rewrite the script, a decision he later regretted.

On the first day of filming, after Marilyn arrived late, she apologised to Montand with the words, 'You're going to see what it means to shoot with the worst actress in the world!' Picking up on her insecurity, Montand voiced his own fears. 'So you're scared,' he said. 'Think of me a little bit. I'm lost.' The confession – that he was petrified because of his obvious lack of English – 'liberated' her and they soon began rehearsals in private together. She corrected his pronunciation, while he tried to boost her confidence. Yet when he witnessed Marilyn behaving in what he thought was an inconsiderate way – she didn't turn up on set one day and gave no indication of when she would return – he let it be known that this was unacceptable. After knocking on the door of her bungalow and receiving no answer, he left a note that read, 'Don't leave me to work for hours on end on a scene you've already decided not to do the next day. I'm not the enemy, I'm your pal. And capricious little girls have never amused me.' Marilyn was so upset by the letter that she called her husband, who was away working in Ireland. Miller telephoned Montand and told him that his wife was too ashamed to come out of her room. Yves and Simone did their best to comfort Marilyn, who was in floods of tears and who kept repeating to herself the words, 'I'm bad, I'm bad.'[4]

Montand's harsh words had hit Marilyn hard, and from then on she did her best to turn up on set and behave in a more professional manner. 'My affection for her grew once I realized her vulnerability, her lucidity, her true sadness at not being given a real part to play in our movie,' said Montand.[5] He thought she was beautiful, but for those first few months of 1960 he didn't desire her. 'All I felt was this powerful radiation, the impact of this amazing charisma,' he said.[6]

All that changed in late April 1960 when Marilyn and Yves were left without their partners in Los Angeles. Simone Signoret, who had just won a Best Actress Oscar for *Room at the Top*, had filming commitments in Italy, while Arthur Miller was busy with his work on *The Misfits*. For his part, he didn't think he need worry. 'Anyone who could make her smile came as a blessing to me,' he said.[7]

At the end of one busy day, Yves went into Marilyn's bungalow. As he bent down to kiss her goodnight, she turned her head towards his. 'It was a wonderful, tender kiss,' he remembered. 'I was half stunned, stammering. I straightened up, already flooded with guilt, wondering what was happening to me. I didn't wonder for long.' The next day, their scenes together were invested with a new kind of energy – 'total symbiosis' was how Montand described it – and they spent the night together again. 'Not for a moment did I think of breaking with my wife, not for a moment,' he recalled, 'but if she [Simone] had slammed the door on me, I would probably have made my life with Marilyn. Or tried to. That was the direction we were moving in. Maybe it would have lasted only two or three years. I didn't have too many illusions. Still, what years they would have been!'[8]

The couple couldn't keep their affair secret for long. Gossip columnist Dorothy Kilgallen started the rumours with the question about which 'actress whose name came up at this year's Oscars is currently having marital problems'. The European tabloids began to print reports of the scandal. 'The press undertook to transform into an "event" one of those stories that can occur in any enterprise, big or small, any apartment house, big or small,' recalled Signoret in her autobiography, published in 1978. 'It's now in the hands of the buyers of newspapers. And consequently it becomes the "business" of the paper merchants. It's sad. And abysmally stupid.'[9] The hate mail that Signoret received because of her public support for Algerian independence was full of ill-informed poison harvested from the scandal sheets. 'They generally said that my husband had been quite right to prefer a gorgeous blonde to me,' she wrote. 'They suggested I go back to the Arabs, whose amorous aptitude is so well known. They often added that it served that Jew Miller right.'[10]

The press reported torrid – and invented – scenarios of Marilyn turning up at Montand's bungalow wearing nothing but a mink coat, and of Miller surprising the two lovers in bed after he returned to the room to get his pipe. The painful truth was that this was not a light erotic farce to be played out for the public's titillation and entertainment: Marilyn had developed deep feelings for her co-star. 'Arthur and I have long since just been marking time,' she told Ralph Roberts in September 1960. 'Working with Yves was such fun ... Glamorous. For the first time, I could see how two people acting together could let that fine line be crossed.'[11]

At the end of June 1960, after filming had finished, Monroe flew to New York in the hope of reuniting with Montand, who was stopping over on his way to fly to Paris. Although she had booked a hotel suite under an assumed name, her offer was declined by Montand; instead, he agreed to meet her in an air-conditioned limo. Over champagne and caviar in the back of the car, the actor broke the news that their affair was over. 'The public and many of my friends thought I was mainly flattered by the relationship,' he wrote in his memoir. 'I was certainly flattered. But to a much greater degree, I was touched. Touched because it was beautiful and because it was impossible.'[12]

Back in France, Montand explained everything to his wife, who handled her husband's internationally publicised dalliance with typical French insouciance. When a British television crew came to interview Signoret about winning an Oscar and questioned her about Montand's affair with Marilyn, she said, 'Do you know many men who would sit still with Marilyn Monroe in their arms?' Montand said he was proud of his wife's response, as it sent a clear message to the world: 'Okay, Simone's man had cheated on her, but with the most beautiful girl in the world.'[13]

For her part, Marilyn seemed to recognise that her affair with Montand served as a sign that her marriage to Miller was in its final stages. Reflecting on the 'understanding' that appeared to exist between Yves and Simone – 'he can flirt and then go back', she said of Montand – she outlined her own position on fidelity. 'Well, when I was interested in it, in my husband, I wasn't interested in anyone else. I don't see how a marriage can last if you run around.'[14]

In September, the night before Yves Montand was due to fly from Los Angeles to Paris to meet his wife again, gossip columnist Hedda Hopper received a tip-off that he was in residence at one of the bungalows of the Beverly Hills Hotel. She had been told that if she knocked on the door, Montand would talk to her. 'I did precisely that,' she said. As soon as she stepped into the room, the telephone started to ring. Marilyn was on the phone. Hoping to get a scoop, Hedda encouraged him to talk to her. 'You'll probably never see her again,' she said. 'Go on.' But Montand could not be persuaded to answer the phone, and so the gossip-monger did the next best thing: she mixed him 'one hell of a martini to get him talking'. Hopper later reported their conversation in her autobiography.

>   Hedda Hopper: You deliberately made love to this girl. You knew she wasn't sophisticated. Was that right?
>   Yves Montand: Had Marilyn been sophisticated, none of this ever would have happened. I did everything I could for her when I realized that mine was a very small part. The only thing that could stand out in my performance were my love scenes. So, naturally, I did everything I could to make them good.[15]

Montand sipped his martini and continued to talk; Hedda listened. Although she'd missed out on eavesdropping on his side of a telephone conversation with Marilyn, she knew that his confession would still make a terrific scoop. Sure enough, the next day – 2 September 1960 – her column led with the headline, 'Montand Denies Divorce Plan Over Marilyn Monroe'.

'I think she is an enchanting child,' Montand told Hopper. 'And I would like to see her to say good-by [sic]. But I won't talk to her on the telephone. She has been so kindly to me but she is a simple girl without any guile. Perhaps I was too tender and thought that maybe she was sophisticated as some of the other ladies I have known ... I've never met anyone quite like Marilyn Monroe. I enjoyed working with her very, very much. She is known throughout the world, but she is still a child. Some women show you only their outside, others show you their deep inside. Perhaps she had a school-girl crush. If she did, I'm sorry. But nothing will break up my marriage.'[16]

After starting work on *The Misfits* in Reno, Nevada, Marilyn was struggling with her health. She returned to LA and had now been admitted to the Westside Hospital for a week-long course of barbiturate detoxification. 'Did Marilyn come down from Reno after she started *The Misfits* to see you?' asked Hopper. 'Yes she did but I did not see her,' replied Montand.[17]

72

The Misfits

In July 1960, Marilyn started work on filming *The Misfits*, a screenplay adapted by Arthur Miller from his own short story, and directed by John Huston. Huston recalled meeting Marilyn for costume tests.

> She was not the fresh little girl that I'd known. She'd put on pounds – she was overweight and going to have to slim down. Very soon we were aware that she was a problem. It wasn't drink, it was the drugs that was the problem. She'd be late on the set, always. She would be difficult, she'd come to the set and be in her dressing room – we were on location [in Reno] – and sometimes the whole morning would go by. Occasionally, she'd be non compos mentis. I knew she was under psychiatric care, but I didn't know at that time that she was having difficulties with Miller, which I discovered during the course of the picture. I remember saying to Miller one day – I was talking to him, it was almost an accusation against *him* – I said, if she went on at the rate she was going then she would be in an institution in two or three years or dead. Anyone who allows her to take a narcotic or drug ought to be shot. It was in a way an indictment against Miller and then I discovered he had no power over her. She was increasingly rude to Miller in front of people, and I found myself on Miller's side.[1]

One day, after filming on location in Nevada, Huston was about to drive back from the isolated stretch of desert when he came across Miller standing alone; neither Marilyn nor her retinue had offered him a lift back to Reno. 'If I hadn't happened to see him, he would have been stranded out there.'[2]

The advance buzz about the film was overwhelmingly positive: United Artists had invested heavily in the production, then said to be the most expensive black and white film ever made, with a budget of $4 million. The cast was starry: Clark Gable as ageing cowboy Gay; Eli Wallach as his widowed best friend Guido; Montgomery Clift as the psychologically and physically damaged rodeo rider Perce; and Monroe as Roslyn, who is in Reno to get a divorce. 'Each one has their aria of pain and they're all explaining their pain to this woman, who is in pain as well,' said Eli Wallach.[3]

The plot centres around the men's mission to track down a group of wild horses that they hope to be able to sell for dog food. 'It's sort of an Eastern Western,' Miller told Gable after the actor expressed some initial doubts about his script. 'It's about our lives' meaninglessness and maybe how we got to where we are.'[4] At the beginning of filming, Miller maintained that he believed the project could still save his marriage to Marilyn. 'And Roslyn's dilemma was hers, but in the story it was resolved,' he wrote in his memoir.[5]

The shoot was challenging: the temperature was often as high as 110 degrees Fahrenheit; forest fires led to power cuts which meant that for a few days there was no electricity at the Mapes Hotel, in Reno, where the cast and crew were staying. There were tensions and divisions on set between those who cast their lot in with Marilyn and her camp of devotees, such as Paula Strasberg (known as 'Black Bart' on the set because of her penchant for black clothes and black cone-shaped hat), and others who sympathised with and supported Arthur Miller. Miller kept rewriting the script, unusually shot in sequence, which meant that the actors – including

Marilyn – often had to learn new lines overnight. Arthur had trouble settling on the ending of the film, particularly whether to let Roslyn and Gay (symbolic stand-ins for Marilyn and himself) separate or drive into the sunset together. The irony of the situation was not lost on Miller: while he had conceived the story of *The Misfits* in a spirit of 'hopefulness', as filming progressed he realised that he had to accept that his marriage to Marilyn was over.[6] When he talked to Marilyn about the ending, she was clear: 'What they really should do is break up at the end,' she told him.

'Sometimes I had the eerie sense that we were in another dimension – that we were hearing Marilyn's own cry against the brutal violations of her life,' said John Huston.[7] At times, during filming, she heard herself uttering lines that came directly from her own past – moments she had shared with Arthur Miller and which he had then transposed into the script. 'What makes you so sad?' asks Gay. 'I think you're the saddest girl I ever met.' It was the same question Miller had posed to Marilyn in the early days of their courtship when the two were holed up at her apartment at the Waldorf-Astoria. Reliving the memory was so hard for Marilyn that she burst into tears. Her friends on the set rushed to help her, but she brushed them away. '"I don't want makeup or hair! I don't want any of that!" Marilyn tearfully begged Huston to stop the scene and let her go for the day,' said Eli Wallach, who witnessed the outburst. 'He agreed to do so. The episode seemed to set a pattern for what was to come over the next weeks. Marilyn seemed to feel that the camera could detect her innermost thoughts.'[8] Wallach expanded on this point in an interview in 2006. 'She felt that the cameras were like X-ray machines, and they'd go right through her eyes into her brain so they'd know what she was thinking,' he said. 'It made it terribly difficult.'[9]

At times, it must have been painful for Marilyn to tease apart the realities of her life from the reworking of her experiences as imagined by Miller in the screenplay and then reconstructed by

Huston. Susan Strasberg, who visited the set, recalled how upset Marilyn had been with Miller's vampiric tendencies. 'He'd used things she'd told him, personal things about her life, out of context,' she said.[10]

In one scene, Roslyn shows Guido into the remodelled bedroom she now shares with Gay and opens a closet to display a set of photographs of herself pinned to the door. In Miller's text, he describes these images as 'girlie photos for the doorway of a second-class nightclub, herself in net tights, on her back, in bizarre costumes'.[11] In the film, these seedy photographs are represented by iconic studio stills from some of Marilyn's most famous movies and publicity shots. The scene may have been conceived as a light-hearted meta-filmic joke between Miller and Huston, but did the blurring of the boundaries between memory and make-believe begin to have an impact on Marilyn's mental health?

After four years of marriage, Miller found it difficult to read his wife during this time, as she seemed to veer between extreme solipsism, incapable of noticing or relating to anyone around her, and extreme sociability; he didn't know how to judge her mood until the moment she opened her mouth. In effect, Miller was witnessing a manifestation of Marilyn's mental illness, the exact diagnosis of which remains open to question. 'She wasn't acting very much,' Miller told his biographer. 'Off-screen she was a lot like on-screen excepting that she got angry. She wouldn't show that, excepting I had her do it in the last scene of *The Misfits*, when she was furious at them for capturing the horses. Then she was quite a different person, and she became herself: quite paranoid.'[12]

Eli Wallach – and his wife, actress Anne Jackson – noticed the change that had come over Marilyn. They had first met Marilyn in 1955 and had become so close to her that they often asked her to babysit their children. In an unpublished autobiography, Jackson – who was trained at the Actors Studio and nominated for a Tony Award for her role in Paddy Chayefsky's *Middle of the*

Night – writes fondly of her memories of meeting the star. 'I stared at that alabaster skin and her baby blue eyes thickly lashed,' she recalled. 'Her mouth seemed always parted to reveal porcelain white teeth ... perfectly lined up like those in an old fashioned china doll ... Her bottom lip and top lip touched and it was as if she kissed herself ... or maybe the lips touched for reassurance ... There was also I noticed just a hint of blue vein running down the side of her face. She seemed all white and pulsating.'

The two women were introduced after Eli brought Marilyn back to the family's New York apartment to meet his baby daughter Roberta, born in August 1955, and 4-year-old son Peter. Anne was conscious that, as a new mother, she looked rather different to this movie goddess; she had talcum powder on her skirt, the sheen of baby oil on her hands, traces of warm milk on her wrist. 'Seeing Marilyn off screen life size in my living room affected my balance,' she wrote. 'I was aware of trying to act normal. There she was before me in a wiggle as you walk dress, her famous bosom swaying and barely contained, arms bare.'

Despite her sexualised image, it was obvious that Marilyn was 'nobody's fool'; she talked deals, business, contracts and money. She was 'not yet victimized in that area', Jackson said. And although there were rumours that Eli and Marilyn had had an affair, the truth was that the actors were just good friends. 'I like her like a sister,' Eli told his wife.

Marilyn was particularly good with children. After Marilyn's problems trying to get pregnant and subsequent miscarriages, Anne felt a great deal of pain and guilt around her for having such a happy and healthy family (in July 1958 she gave birth to her third child, Katherine). By the time Anne met Marilyn again during the filming of *The Misfits*, it was obvious that she had changed. 'Eli says Marilyn was transformed from friendly to nasty,' she recalled.[13]

The whole family arrived on location in Reno, where Anne and the three children visited a local store and got kitted out in cowboy outfits: jeans, colourful shirts, boots and hats. Peter was particularly keen to see Marilyn, whom he hadn't seen since she babysat him; he wanted to show her his new costume. 'But the moment we got to her trailer, she looked out and when she saw us, she shut the door,' said Wallach.[14]

In 1960, Marilyn told the journalist W. J. Weatherby that she knew she could be a 'monster'; it was a side of herself few ever saw. 'You know how sometimes you try to be the person people want you to be?' she said. 'Some of my friends want me to be innocent and shy, and I find that's the way I am with them. If they saw the monster in me, they'd probably never talk to me again. Sometimes I think that's what happened in my marriage to Arthur. When we were first married, he saw me as so beautiful and innocent among the Hollywood wolves that I tried to be like that. I almost became his student in life and literature, the way I'm Lee's student for acting. But when the monster showed, Arthur couldn't believe it. I disappointed him when that happened. But I felt he knew and loved all of me. I wasn't sweet all through. He should love the monster, too. But maybe I'm too demanding. Maybe there's no man who could put up with all of me. I put Arthur through a lot, I know. But he also put me through a lot. It's never one-sided. You can't have two people trying to make it together without that, without a lot of pain.'[15]

One day, Miller watched as Marilyn and Gable shot a scene by Pyramid Lake. As he stood there, observing his wife at work, he realised that he was looking down on the spot near where he had lived four years ago when he had arrived in Nevada to seek a divorce from his first wife so he was free to marry Marilyn. His journey from optimism to despair was almost complete. But there was one final drama to witness: Marilyn's breakdown, which resulted in the temporary shutdown of the film.

When Lee Strasberg had arrived on the set and called Miller up to his room, the acting coach, dressed in a straight-out-the-box cowboy outfit, started to tell the playwright about the need to have a serious conversation, as the situation had got out of control. The writer could not agree more, but he was shocked to discover that Strasberg was referring not to Marilyn's severe psychological problems, her lateness on set, her inability to remember her lines, and her drug issues, but to Huston's cold disdain for his wife Paula. Strasberg demanded that Miller try to smooth over the differences and attempt a reconciliation; if not, then he would have to insist that Paula withdraw from the film, an action that would bring about Marilyn's defection too. Miller stood his ground and told Strasberg that it was important for him to talk to Marilyn as she was in a bad way.

Miller wasn't privy to the conversation Lee Strasberg eventually had with Marilyn, but one thing was clear: nothing had changed and she still felt unable to work. After Lee returned to New York, Arthur checked on Marilyn, who had vacated the hotel apartment they shared in Reno to move into one with Paula Strasberg. What he saw shocked him. Marilyn was sitting up in bed, a doctor by her side searching for a vein in her hand into which he could inject amytal, which Dr Greenson had warned her against taking. When Marilyn saw her husband – who wanted to stop the doctor from injecting her with the strong sedative – she began to scream at him to leave the room, which he did.

The medic expressed astonishment that his patient remained relatively animated after the injection; the dose he had just administered was equivalent to one someone would receive just before undergoing a major operation. He told Miller that he would not inject Marilyn again; he feared for the actress's life if she were to be given any more shots. As Arthur watched his wife gradually calm down and close her eyes, he began to wonder about the impossibility of the role he had cast for himself – that of Marilyn's saviour. It was too late. The drugs, the complex mass of chemicals that she had been ingesting and injecting for years, had removed her from him, transported her to another dimension completely out of his reach. He realised that he was 'worse than useless to her now, a bag of nails thrown in her face'. His presence, his mere existence, was a stark reminder of her 'failure to pull herself out of her old life even when she had at last truly loved someone'.[16]

Could Marilyn save herself, Miller wondered, if she withdrew from the film world completely? Yet without her status as a movie star, did she have any identity at all? Miller realised the impossibility of these hypothetical questions as 'her stardom was her triumph, nothing less; it was her life's achievement,' he later wrote.[17] Since Marilyn had first begun dreaming of being a Hollywood actress, she had cultivated a relationship with the public. Dismantling the image from the woman would come with terrible consequences. His conclusion was devastating: *'She was "Marilyn Monroe", and that was what was killing her,'* he wrote.[18]

Marilyn herself was acutely conscious of the gilded cage that she – together with the studio bosses and the general public – had created. In *The Misfits* Miller was supposed to gift her something special – a role that would show the world she was more than just blonde hair, the sexy body, the wiggle, the breathy voice of popular perception. But as she saw it, he had just fallen into the same trap. Worse, he had taken elements from her real life – tender moments, shared experiences, snatched words – and melded them together with her star image. 'All my life I've played Marilyn Monroe, Marilyn Monroe, Marilyn Monroe,' she told Henry Hathaway, who had directed her in *Niagara*, and who came across her crying during a break in filming of *The Misfits* when the crew relocated to a sound stage in Los Angeles. 'I've tried to do a little better and find myself doing an imitation of Edie Adams [a comedian known for her grotesque impersonations of Marilyn] doing an imitation of me. I try to do a little better, but then I do an exaggeration of myself doing the same thing. I want to do something different. That was one of the things that attracted me to Miller when he said he was attracted by me. When I married Miller, one of the fantasies I had in my mind was that I could get out of Marilyn Monroe through him ... And here I find myself back here on the stage, and I just couldn't take it, I had to get out of there. I just couldn't face having to do another scene of trying to do something with Marilyn Monroe.'[19]

It's no wonder that Marilyn's already fragile mental health began to worsen. In an interview Miller gave to his biographer in 1995, the playwright explained that despite his wife being under the care of two of the best psychoanalysts in America – Dr Kris in New York and Dr Greenson in Los Angeles – she could not be helped. 'The self-destruction was terrifying, and certainly it was beyond me to master it,' he said. 'I could never do it, but I doubt that anybody could have.'[20]

John Huston – who himself faced his own addictions to gambling and alcohol, often so drunk or hungover he would fall asleep on set – was forced to make the difficult decision to temporarily close down the picture. 'Marilyn continued heavily into the drugs, and finally the young doctor on location refused to give her any more, even though he feared he might lose his job by not catering to her desires,' he recalled. 'She got drugs elsewhere, however, and eventually she broke down completely and had to be sent to a hospital in Los Angeles ... The picture closed down. There were no holidays to help us, so we had to pay the entire crew for every working day lost. This added enormously to our costs – which already were staggering.'[21]

One night at 4:30 a.m. during the location shoot, a telephone call woke Sheldon Roskin, who worked on the film's public relations. A journalist from New York was on the line and wanted to verify a rumour. 'We're just calling to check a news flash that Marilyn Monroe has committed suicide,' said the reporter.[22]

73

'SHE HAD THIS OBSESSION ABOUT BEING NUDE'

Angela Allen, the script supervisor in charge of continuity on *The Misfits*, is one of the dwindling number of people still alive with memories of Marilyn. Born in London in 1929, she had previously worked with John Huston on films such as *The African Queen* (1951), *Beat the Devil* (1953), *Moby Dick* (1956) and *Heaven Knows, Mr Allison* (1957). Her recollections of Marilyn, however, are far from positive. 'I didn't think she was particularly beautiful, not in the flesh,' she tells me during an interview in 2021. 'I remember asking the men on the crew, "Do you find her extremely sexy?" and they said, "Have you lost your marbles?"

'It was a very difficult shoot, and one didn't quite realise it at the time, but we were watching the disintegration of a marriage. She was never on time and she was totally, totally dominated by Paula Strasberg, who was a really evil woman, and who turned her against everybody, including Arthur.

'She had a scene which involved her wearing a bikini and coming out of the water. But we all tried to put off filming this because she was getting fatter. She kept asking, "When am I doing my scene?" but we managed to find something else to do in the hope that she might get a bit thinner. Gable was very diplomatic. She tried her wiles on him one day, but he certainly wasn't interested.

'One day she was being particularly bitchy. John [Huston] said he would tell me all about it later that evening. It turned out that she had accused me of having an affair with Arthur. I knew where she got that idea from. John would have Arthur rewriting every day, and one day I was standing with Arthur in the room looking at the script and I sensed a presence in the room. I said, "I think your wife wants you," and I walked out. As I used to say to John, "If I'm having the affair, am I enjoying it? I'd love to know." She may have felt guilty about her own affair with Yves Montand. I think she thought Montand was going to leave his wife. But why would Yves Montand leave Simone Signoret for her – it would be mad. I'm sure Simone knew Yves was having an affair, she'd gone through that before. But she knew how to handle things.

'I never confronted Marilyn about the false rumour about the affair. Some time ago, Eve Arnold, who was a friend and who took photographs on the shoot for Magnum, got hold of this script of a play being put on in Manchester. [*Misfits* by Alex Finlayson at the Royal Exchange, in 1996. 'Could you make a boring play from this material?' asked Paul Taylor in his review for the *Independent*. 'Only too easily, it seems.'] It was calling me something like a horse-faced bitch, and accused me of having an affair with Arthur. I contacted the director and I said, "I am still alive, and if you are going to use my name in this way then I'm going to be suing you." All they did was change my name.

'I never saw Marilyn as a victim. She probably did have a somewhat deprived childhood, but I don't think she was ever starving. And as for the idea that every man was supposed to find her intellectual depths – the great brains that she had? Well, I think they failed perhaps because it wasn't there.

'I didn't know anything about pills – I mean, I'm not a pill taker – but she was on downers and uppers. She couldn't learn lines and did scenes and only got three or four words right. We were way over schedule and it was proving incredibly expensive. I remember us doing a scene when she was supposed to cling to Clark Gable, but she kept hitting him on the chest. We did a few more takes, but she couldn't get it right. That's when we stopped shooting and Marilyn got sent away. John said, "I've been accused of many things in my life, but I'm not going to be accused of her death."

'In my estimation, and looking at her behaviour in another age, she would have been a prostitute. Yes – not even quite as high as a courtesan. She was a whore at heart – that may sound brutal, but that's the way I see her. She had this obsession about being nude – she never wore any underwear. And I can tell you that in that sort of heat, I'm glad that I wasn't the wardrobe woman having to deal with her clothes, which you couldn't wash. She had this silk dress – well, you'd have it hose it down with chemicals.'[1]

74

THE LOST FOOTAGE FROM *THE MISFITS*

In August 2018, it was revealed that a fourteen-second clip of Marilyn letting a bedsheet drop away from her breasts to reveal her naked body – shot on the set of *The Misfits* – had been discovered. The news of the existence of this lost footage, said by some to be the first nude scene starring an American actress in a feature film, went viral. The man who now possesses the film – which ended up being cut from the movie because of strict censorship rules – is Curtice Taylor, the son of *The Misfits*' producer Frank Taylor. Curtice, thirteen at the time of filming, lived on location with his mother Nan and his father, who in the 1940s had been Miller's editor.

'There's this scene in the cabin together,' says Curtice, describing what happened on the shoot. 'Clark [Gable] appears fully dressed at the door of the bedroom, where Marilyn is lying in bed. He walks in and stands over her, comes down to lie on her, whispers something in her ear and says something like, "I've got a surprise for you." He kisses her, she smiles and it's quite touching and lovely. And then she sits up in bed. John [Huston] says, "When you sit up, Marilyn, make sure you use the sheet to cover your body." They'd do a couple of takes, and every second take she'd drop the sheet and her beautiful breasts would fall out. At the end of every day of filming they would watch the dailies and this one scene comes up which is amazing – her smile is bigger and they really lock lips together. She's just so happy to be alive and to be in love. But then the sheet is dropped and her breasts are exposed.

'John says that you can't print that one. But my dad says, "But it's the best take." John knows it's the best take, but he's conscious of the censors. You've got to remember the crazy censorship rules still applied. Also, Huston was weird about sex. He was a famous womaniser – my God, I mean, *legion*. But there's almost no sex in his films, not even men and women kissing. He was sort of prudish in an odd way.

'Gable – who was watching the dailies – then chimed in and said he thought it was the best take too. So, they print both takes. The story my dad told about what happened then was not accurate – that a fight happened between him and John, and my dad stormed into the editing booth and took the film off the projector and stormed out. What happened is this. The scene – with Marilyn's breasts exposed – was left in, as was the scene in her negligee when she is drunk and she embraces a tree. The Legion of Decency [the powerful Catholic group that monitored indecent content in films] came back and declared that scene to be obscene – they said the character was masturbating against a tree – and also said the one in which her breasts are exposed had to be deleted too. John then said, "What if we just drop the one with her breasts?" since the scene with the tree is much more important to the overall film. So that's when my father went into the editing suite and said, "Give me the film." He marched out of there with it and kept it in a file drawer for years.

'I know there are Marilyn fanatics out there who would probably give me half a million dollars for it. After all, it's the only nude shot of Marilyn in a finished movie. That's why the story went viral, even though it's tawdry and sad.

'Going back in time, when Arthur Miller first wrote *The Misfits* he asked my dad – who had been a publisher and had edited a book of Miller's non-fiction and a novel – for advice. Arthur said why don't you bring your family up to Roxbury for the day and I will go over the manuscript with you. Maybe he didn't realise what the family comprised – in addition to him, and my mother, there were four boys that ranged in age from sixteen down to six. And we were going up to meet Marilyn Monroe. My adolescent brothers were sort of wet in the back seat, and I was around eleven years old, so I was more intrigued than aroused. She didn't appear for the longest time. We just heard the sound of vacuuming from upstairs. Evidently, Marilyn was nervous and when she was nervous she would house clean.

'When she came down she was marvellous with us kids. I'd been out in the fields and so I joined the group a little late, but when she saw I had no place to sit she said, "Why don't you sit with me in the hammock?" My older brothers were seething when she said that. But then she had each of us go over and swing in the hammock with her. But what was interesting is that she picked up on the fact that one of my brothers, Mark, was dyslexic, rebellious and had a learning disorder. But Marilyn spotted this immediately and she gave him the most attention. She liked the wounded, she *understood* the wounded.

'I remember on another occasion I went up with my father and brother to visit Arthur Miller and Marilyn Monroe's estate in Roxbury. Like many artists living on a farm, he leased some of the land out to a farmer, a dairy farmer. I recall that I was there with my brother when he came across a cow in the process of giving birth. The calf was still in its sack when we went to call for Marilyn, because we knew she would appreciate it. She came out wearing the exact same outfit she would later wear in *The Misfits* – blue jeans, an oversize men's shirt, probably Arthur's, tied to show off her midriff, and her hair in pigtails. She thought the scene of the mother cow and calf so wonderful, but then the farmer turned up, who when he discovered it was a male calf said he would deal with it. He went and got a gunny sack from his truck and proceeded to stuff this calf into the sack. And of course, Marilyn went *insane*. She said he couldn't take the calf away from its mother, that she would give him money for it and so on. In *The Misfits* this scene is reproduced with the horse and foal standing in for the cow and calf. I can't say that the film was based on that scene from real life because Miller had already written it at that point. But it's pivotal in my opinion.

'I often say to people if you want to get a full picture of Marilyn – and Arthur, God knows, could paint a good picture – take *The Misfits* and shuffle in *After the Fall* [Miller's 1964 play which contains a thinly veiled portrait of Marilyn]. And you'll see a pretty clear picture of who she was. *The Misfits* is about the wounded, naive, sweet, sexy person. And *After the Fall* is about the mess that ensues.'[1]

75

LOCKED UP

In October 1960, Dr Greenson wrote another letter to his East Coast colleague Dr Marianne Kris outlining Marilyn's state of mind. 'The situation with her husband has worsened again,' he wrote, adding that Marilyn considered Arthur to be possibly 'cruel and destructive to herself. He has become the mistreater ... Her husband is more or less resigned to the situation because he feels helpless to change this role she has cast him in as the villain, the mistreater etc.'[1] According to Greenson, the marriage broke down mainly because of a fundamental sexual incompatibility: 'He suffered from feelings of inadequacy and she from frigidity ... [she] found it difficult to sustain a series of orgasms with the same individual.'[2]

Greenson updated Dr Kris about Marilyn's recent mental health crisis. One of the central problems facing the actress, he said, was a tendency towards 'severe depressive reactions' and the concomitant 'impulse desires' that followed on from these.[3] He told Dr Kris about how Marilyn had spent a week in Westside Hospital during which the medics had weaned her off barbiturates. By the time she returned to the set of *The Misfits* she was only prescribed chloral hydrate to help her sleep (one of the drugs found in her system after her death). However, when she returned to Los Angeles to complete the film in the studio, she managed to secure a fresh supply of barbiturates. Greenson was conscious he didn't want to precipitate another crisis by denying Marilyn her medication, but he advised her not to take too many of the drugs. She also told him about her future plans: after finishing the film she wanted first to return to New York and then go to Mexico to get a quick divorce from Miller. The realisation that she wanted a permanent separation from her husband of four years gave her a new sense of liberation. 'She no longer has to drown him out with the medication,' said Greenson.[4]

However, the news of the sudden death of Clark Gable – from a heart attack on 16 November 1960, at the age of fifty-nine, and only twelve days after finishing shooting *The Misfits* – affected Marilyn's mood. Then gossip columnists began to suggest that her erratic and unpredictable behaviour on set had contributed to his premature death. 'I feel completely drained,' Marilyn told Ralph Roberts.[5] Roberts supported her during this difficult time, often giving her massages in the middle of the night. It was a period he described as an 'utter hell'.[6] While living in New York, where she cleared the East 57th Street apartment of Arthur's possessions, she saw Dr Kris for therapy on a regular basis: twenty-four times in December 1960 and twenty-three sessions in January 1961. At times, she seemed to lose touch with reality; once she called up Arthur and asked him when he was coming home.

On a flying visit to Mexico, Marilyn filed for a divorce on 20 January 1961, the same day that President John F. Kennedy delivered his inaugural address. No doubt Marilyn, and her PR team, hoped that by scheduling the divorce hearing for this date they could minimise the press coverage. 'Arthur is a brilliant man,' she told Louella Parsons. 'A wonderful writer. Maybe it wasn't his fault that he was a much better writer than he was a husband.'[7]

It's likely that at this time Marilyn learned of Miller's new relationship with the Austrian-born Magnum photographer Inge Morath. Although the couple had met on the set of *The Misfits*, they didn't become close until mid-December, after completing the film. On 31 January 1961, Marilyn attended a preview of the movie at the Capitol Theatre in New York with Montgomery

Clift. The reviews were poor. 'Miss Monroe – well, she is completely blank and unfathomable,' wrote Bosley Crowther in the *New York Times*. 'But there is really not much about her that is very exciting or interesting ... Characters and theme do not congeal ... the picture just doesn't come off.'[8] After the preview screening, producer Frank Taylor invited Miller and Inge Morath – whom Arthur married in February 1962 – to a dinner at his brownstone.

The next day, Marilyn began to talk to Marianne Kris about her suicidal thoughts. On 5 February, she was hospitalised at Manhattan's Payne Whitney Clinic, under the name Faye Miller. Marilyn considered her experience there to have been the most traumatic of her life. The actress assumed that she was being admitted to the clinic for rest and to help her system withdraw from a bout of excessive barbiturate use. What she encountered she described as the stuff of her worst nightmares: her ward was locked; she was trapped. Surely, she thought, there must be some kind of misunderstanding as this was, as she immediately realised, a unit for '*very disturbed*, depressed patients'. Wasn't she happy here? asked one of the attendants. 'Well, I'd have to be nuts if I like it here!' Marilyn responded. They suggested that she try a little occupational therapy with the other patients – sewing, playing checkers or cards, perhaps knitting? She told the staff that '*the day I did that they would have a nut on their hands*'.[9]

Why did she think she was different to the other patients? 'I just am,' she said. On the first day, Marilyn did talk to a fellow patient, she said, a young woman who had repeatedly cut her throat and wrists, who informed her of the existence of a telephone in the hospital. As she was waiting in line to phone for help to get her out, she was spotted by a guard who told her that she could not use it. Marilyn returned to her room and sat on her bed.

In a letter she wrote to Dr Greenson, Marilyn claimed that her ensuing behaviour was a considered reaction to the question: what would a character do if she was presented with the situation in an acting exercise? 'I got the idea from a movie I made once called *Don't Bother to Knock*,' she wrote. She picked up a chair and slammed it against a glass wall until it smashed into pieces. She picked up a slither of glass and smuggled it into her room, and waited for an attendant or doctor to check on her. 'If you are going to treat me like a nut I'll act like a nut,' she told them, stressing that if they didn't let her out she would cut herself. In reality, she told Dr Greenson, she would never hurt herself this way, as she knew the importance of her appearance to her star appeal. 'Remember when I tried to do away with myself I did it very carefully with ten seconal and ten tuonal [Tuinal, a sedative] and swallowed them with relief (that's how I felt at the time),' she said. That day at the Payne Whitney Clinic, she refused to cooperate with the staff and so two men and two women picked her up and carried her up to the seventh floor. 'I just wept quietly all the way there,' she said.

Marilyn was swiftly confined to what she described as a 'cell', constructed of cement blocks, its walls daubed with the stains and markings of former patients, its windows protected by bars. She waited until a psychiatrist came in to talk to her. This doctor told her that she was a 'very, very sick girl and had been a very, very sick girl for many years'.[10]

With each day Marilyn felt increasingly desperate, unable to sleep because of the sound of patients screaming, feeling as though she was 'in some kind of prison for a crime she hadn't committed'. She must have thought that her worst fear – that she was going mad like her mother, like her grandmother, like her grandfather – was coming true. 'I can't tell you how terrified I felt,' she told Ralph Roberts. 'My mind was in a turmoil. Was my mother really sick when she was placed in an institution?'[11]

Gloria Romanoff – wife of the Beverly Hills restaurateur Mike Romanoff – later claimed that Marilyn told her that, while she was restrained in her bed, a steady procession of medical staff would come into her room and touch her under the bed clothes. 'It was a nightmare ... I was a curiosity piece, no one had my interests at heart,' said Marilyn.[12] Although Gloria maintained that she believed Marilyn was telling the truth, the anecdote seems fantastical: if this had happened, it's likely that Marilyn would have described it in her long and detailed letter to Dr Greenson.

She talked a nurse into giving her a sheet of notepaper, on which she scribbled a message for Lee and Paula Strasberg. She told them that Dr Kris had confined her against her will to the care of 'two idiotic doctors' and how if she stayed locked up at the clinic she was sure 'to end up a nut too'.[13] But as the Strasbergs weren't next of kin or authorised to act on Marilyn's behalf, they were powerless. On 9 February, Marilyn managed to get access to a phone and called Joe DiMaggio, whom she had grown close to again after her divorce from Miller. DiMaggio – who immediately flew up from Florida, where he was employed as a coach for the Yankees – threatened to tear down the hospital 'brick by brick' if the clinic did not release his former wife. His intervention worked and the next day she was free.

Marilyn was furious with Dr Kris, who was forced to admit that she had done a 'terrible thing' in admitting her to Payne Whitney. It wasn't that the actress did not need help – it was obvious she was still in the grip of a mental health crisis – but rather the place and method of treatment were inappropriate. After a night back at her New York apartment, Marilyn was admitted to a private room at the Neurological Institute of Columbia-Presbyterian Medical Center, where she stayed for three weeks. She was allowed regular visitors including Joe DiMaggio, who saw her daily, as well as the Strasbergs and the Rostens. 'She lifted her hand weakly and smiled; her energies seemed at a new low,' recalled Norman Rosten. 'She was ill, not only of the body and mind, but of the soul, the innermost engine of desire. That light was missing from her eyes.'[14]

On 10 February, her former publicist Rupert Allan sent Marilyn a telegram that read, 'I don't want to be a sockeyed salmon. Please get me out of this too dam [sic] cold Trukee [sic] River soon. I'm with you always, and I want to get on those meadows again with you.'[15] The telegram's reference to salmon reflects a conversation Allan had with Marilyn when the two were on location filming *The Misfits*. One night the two friends were looking out over the Truckee River when Allan told her about the life cycle of salmon: how the fish swim up-river to breed, only for thousands of them to die. Marilyn said that she could identify with the salmon; she told him about how she had contemplated suicide by jumping out of a New York window. Allan too confessed how he had sometimes thought of ending it all and the two came up with an arrangement: if either of them had black thoughts and contemplated suicide, they were to contact the other immediately. Their code phrase would be 'Truckee River'.

Newsreel footage shows Marilyn leaving the Columbia-Presbyterian hospital, flanked by a team of security guards, and her press agents John Springer and Patricia Newcomb. As she battles her way through the crowd of around four hundred reporters and photographers, all jostling to get a snatched comment or a quick snap, Marilyn keeps her composure. Her expression is one of calm bewilderment. She responds to questions politely and with good humour. How are you feeling? 'I feel wonderful, thank you,' she says. 'I had a nice rest.'

The coverage of Marilyn's discharge from hospital after four weeks of treatment focused more on her appearance than the state of her mind. The reporter from United Press International, which supplied syndicated news to titles across America, described her as 'smiling as radiantly as an Oscar winner ... Miss Monroe was a vision in beige-champagne. Her cashmere sweater, sheath skirt and shoes all matched her new hairdo.'[16] John Pascal of the *New York Journal-American* went one step further, and penned a report that today reads like a sexual fantasy, laced with a heavy dose of casual misogyny typical of the period. 'All's well with the world, men, so fear not, fear not,' it begins. 'Marilyn's face still has the ethereal rose-petal texture, the smile's as delicately soft as ever, the figure – ah, yes, the figure – and best of all they've untied the knots in her nerves.' Pascal obsessed over her appearance, noting that she was 'paler and a bit thinner' than when he had last seen her. 'By common agreement, she was an absolute knockout,' he continued. 'Her cashmere sweater was open at the neck and the sheath skirt was just snug enough to be interesting.'[17]

Mara Scherbatoff, New York bureau chief for *Paris Match* magazine, lies on the ground after a high-speed crash in Connecticut on the day of Marilyn's wedding to Arthur Miller in June 1956. The journalist would die of her injuries hours later.

Arthur on Marilyn: 'I thought she was total honesty – that's what knocked me out.'

Marilyn embarked on an affair with actor Yves Montand (left) during the filming of *Let's Make Love*. When he ended the relationship, Marilyn was left devastated.

The cast of *The Misfits*: Montgomery Clift, Marilyn, Clark Gable, Eli Wallach, together with screenwriter Arthur Miller and director John Huston.

Marilyn's last – and most important – psychoanalyst Dr Ralph Greenson, who rejected couch-based therapy for a more unconventional approach. 'I did what I thought was best, particularly after other methods of treatment apparently hadn't touched her one iota,' he said later.

A poignant shot from Bert Stern's 'The Last Sitting' series of photographs taken in 1962.

© Associated Press/Alamy

© Cecil Stoughton/THA/Shutterstock

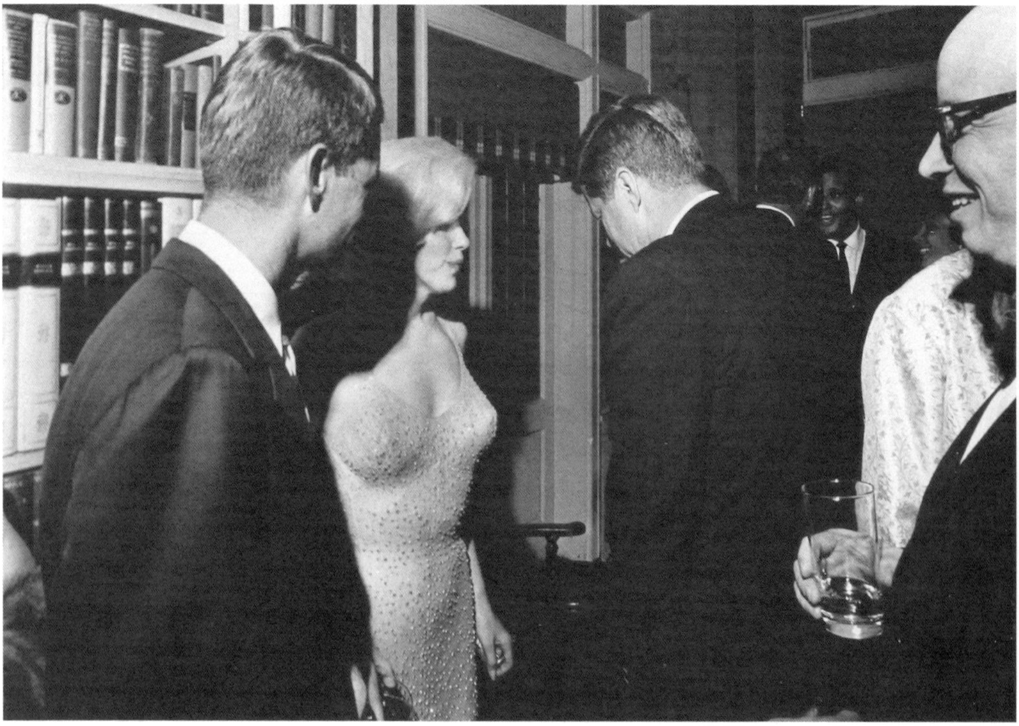

Marilyn talking with President John F. Kennedy and attorney general Robert F. Kennedy soon after her 'Happy Birthday' performance at Madison Square Gardens in May 1962.

© Kobal/Shutterstock

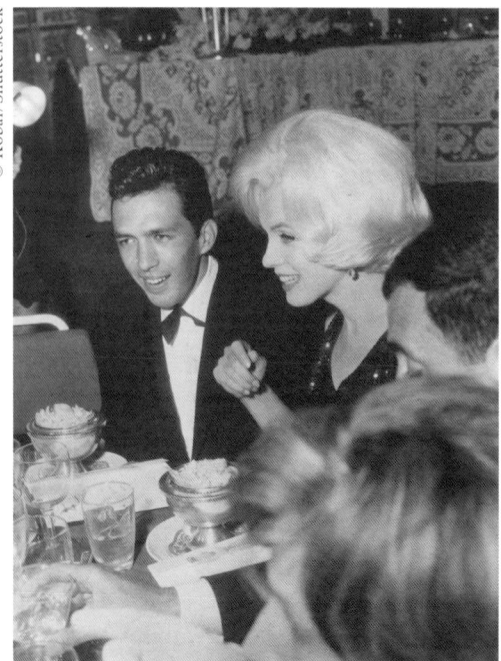

Marilyn with Mexican screenwriter José Bolaños, whom she met in February 1962. According to one witness, she called him 'the greatest lover in the world.'

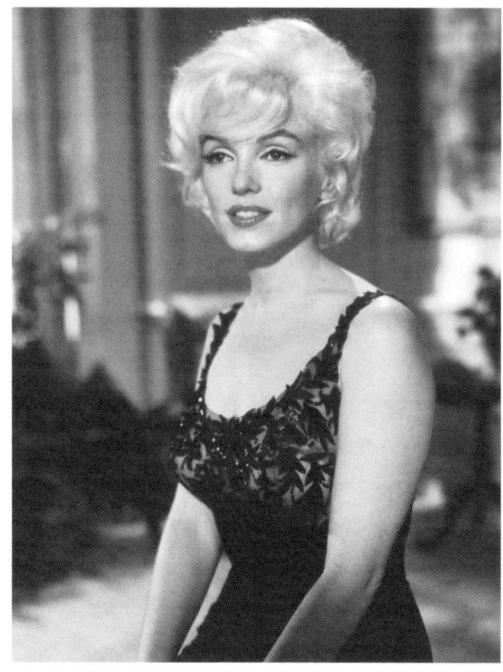

A still from Marilyn's last – unfinished – film, *Something's Got to Give*. When she was fired from the movie, the star suffered a severe depressive episode.

Marilyn's bedroom on the night her body was discovered. During the last two months of her life, she had been prescribed 830 units of medication, enough to kill several people several times over.

Eunice Murray, Marilyn's 'devoted assistant'. According to the official version of events, in the early hours of 5 August 1962, Mrs Murray woke up and discovered the star's body. 'I saw Marilyn lying on the bed – face down, nude,' she said.

Pat Newcomb, Marilyn's publicist and close friend. When she arrived at Marilyn's house, she was so angry at discovering a mob of pressmen that she screamed, 'Keep shooting, vultures!'

© Keystone Press/Alamy

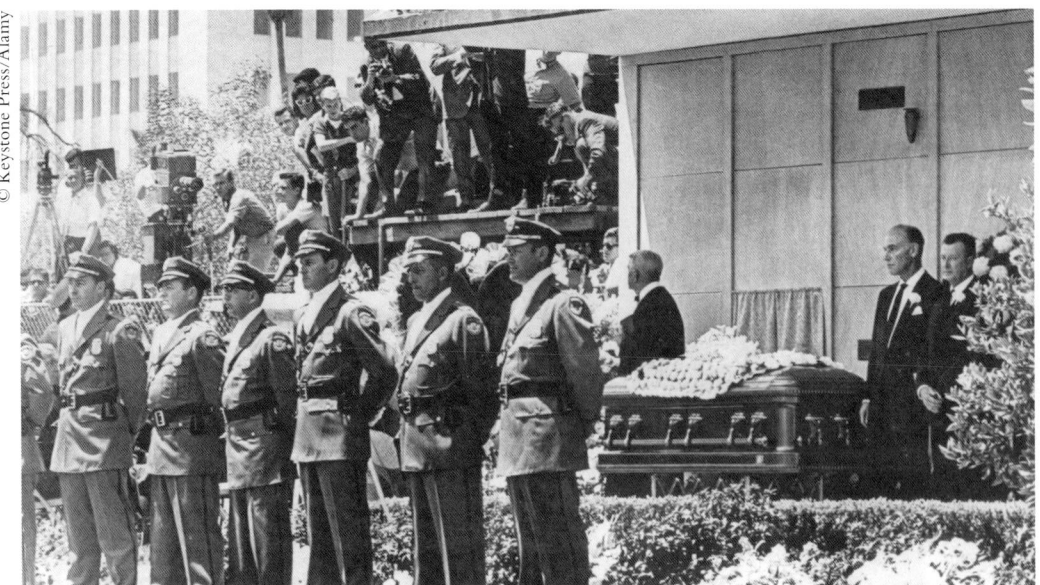

Marilyn's funeral, 8 August 1962. 'About 200 persons, mostly reporters and photographers, managed to enter a parking lot adjoining the cemetery, where they climbed on cars and boxes to try to see over the cemetery wall,' wrote one reporter.

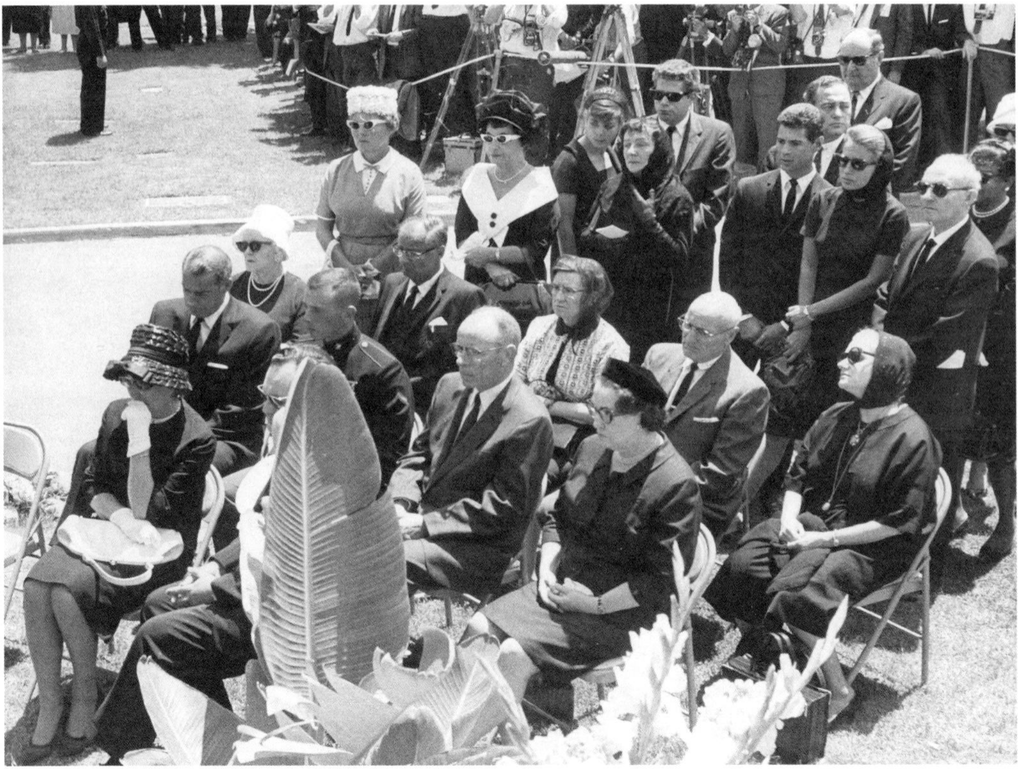

Held at Westwood Memorial Park, the funeral was an intimate affair, attended by fewer than thirty people, including ex-husband Joe DiMaggio, Marilyn's half-sister Berniece Miracle, the Greenson family, the Strasbergs, Patricia Newcomb and members of the star's staff. Arthur Miller chose not to attend.

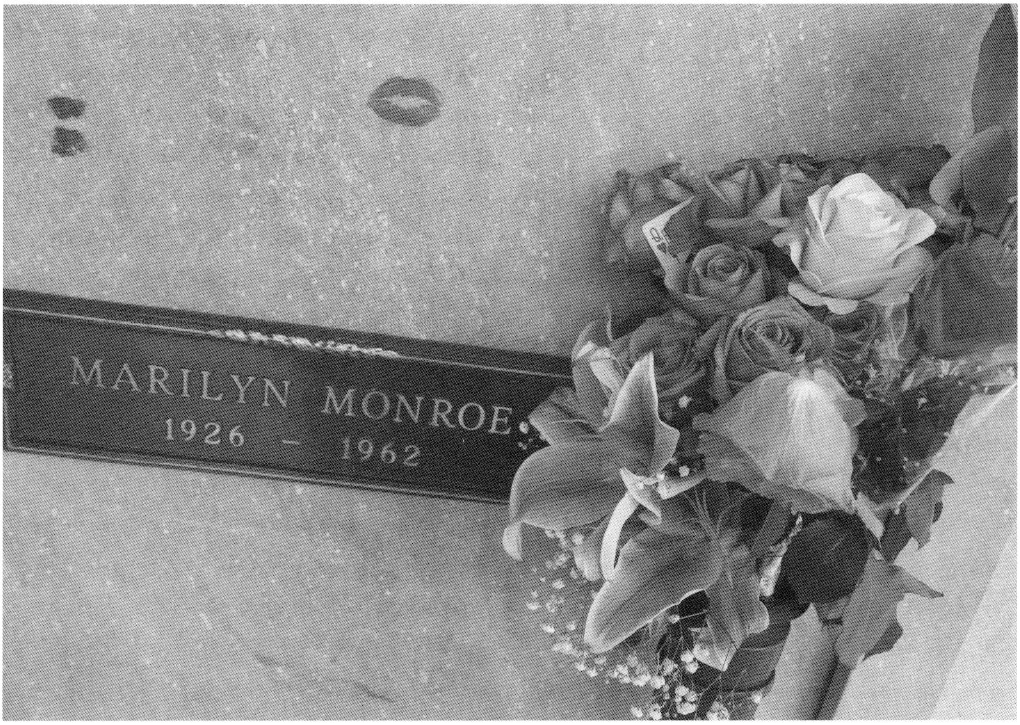

© Barry King/Alamy

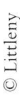

Devoted fans leave lipstick traces at Marilyn's final resting place at Westwood Memorial Park.

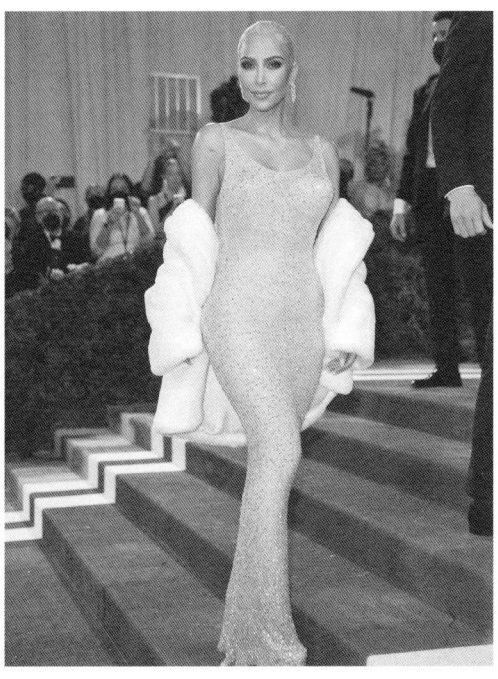

Kim Kardashian wearing Marilyn's famous 'Happy Birthday Mr President' dress at the Met Gala in May 2022. The dress now has an estimated value of $10 million.

© Littleny

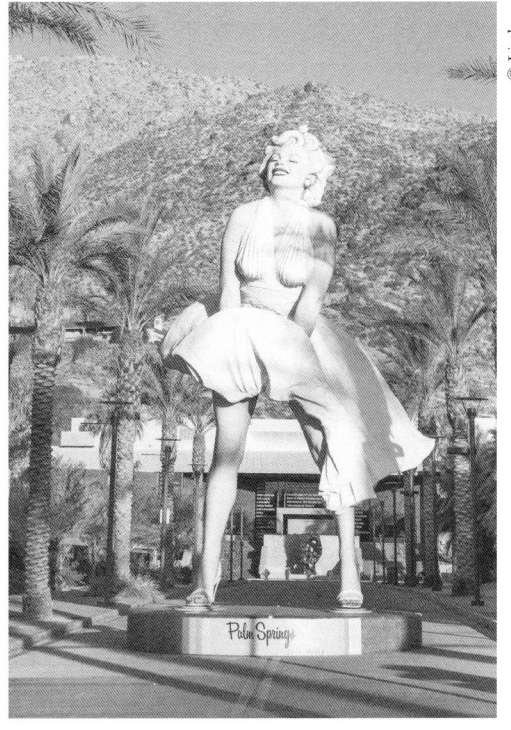

The controversial *Forever Marilyn* statue in Palm Springs, California.

© JUSTIN LANE/EPA-EFE/Shutterstock

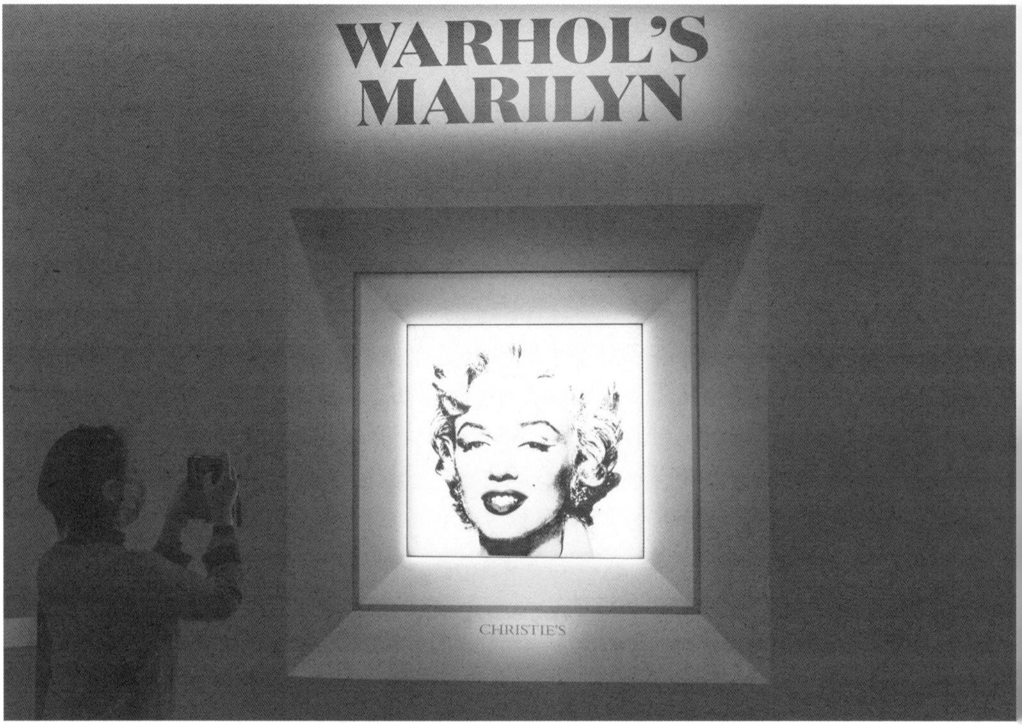

In 2022, Andy Warhol's 1964 *Shot Sage Blue Marilyn* sold at Christie's for $195 million.

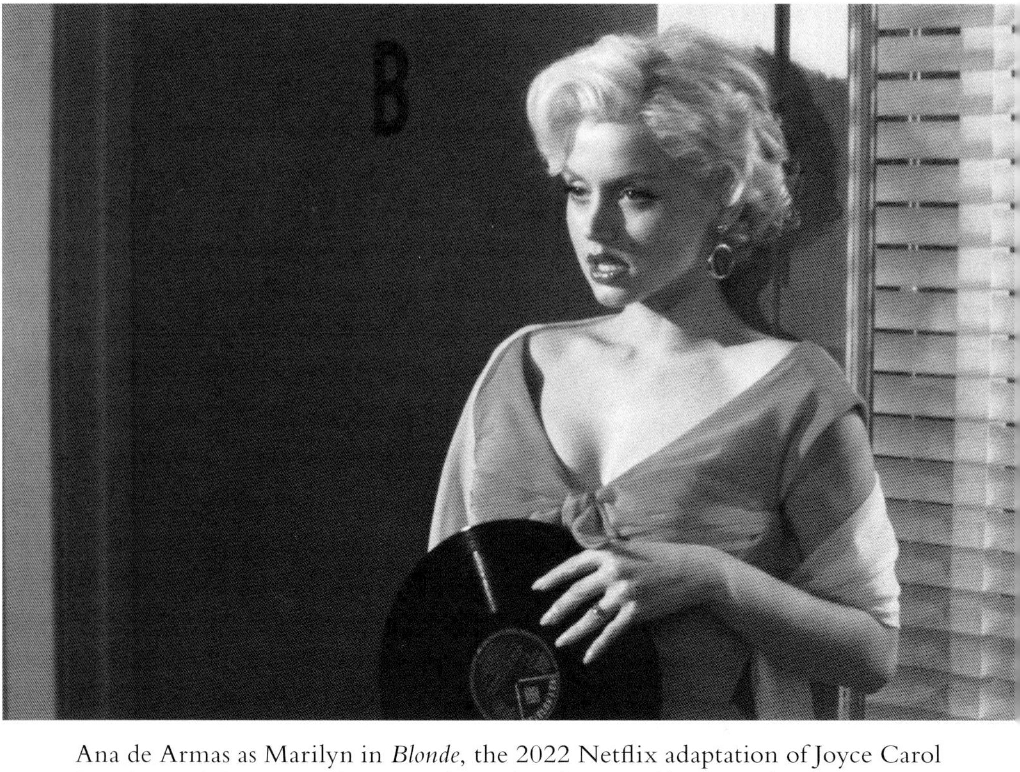

Ana de Armas as Marilyn in *Blonde*, the 2022 Netflix adaptation of Joyce Carol Oates's novel. 'Being in the same places that she was, filming in her house, it was a very strong sensation,' said the actress. 'There was something in the air.'

76

FRANK

When Marilyn came out of hospital in March 1961 she seemed to have a new zest for life. 'Things are going to work out,' she told her New York maid Lena Pepitone. 'I can feel it. This is gonna be my year.'[1] She went on holiday to Florida with Joe DiMaggio, was excited to be starring in an NBC television production of Somerset Maugham's short story 'Rain' (a project she eventually pulled out of); attended Judy Garland's legendary Carnegie Hall concert; and she began a relationship with Frank Sinatra, who had visited her during her stay at Columbia-Presbyterian Medical Center.

The two had known each other since around 1954: Marilyn had been selected to star with Sinatra in a handful of movies (though the productions never went ahead), while the singer and actor had been a close friend of DiMaggio's. Any tension that lingered over Sinatra's involvement in the 'wrong door raid' of 1954 had long been forgotten. Marilyn loved his music and would often play his records both at home and on set. 'He helps me get in the mood for acting,' she told Ralph Roberts. 'Frees me.'[2] By this point Sinatra had become a huge star, having released albums such as *Songs for Young Lovers* (1954) and *Come Fly with Me* (1958) and won awards and praise for roles in films such as *From Here to Eternity* (1953), *Guys and Dolls* (1955), *High Society* (1956) and *Ocean's 11* (1960).

Sinatra and Marilyn also had a connection through two doctors. He counted Dr Leon Krohn, Marilyn's gynaecologist, as one of his close friends and, in 1953, Dr Greenson treated him for three months. However, when Marilyn mentioned Sinatra's name to

Greenson, the psychiatrist was sceptical about the future of their relationship. In a letter written to Greenson, on 2 March 1961, Marilyn described how, in the past, Greenson would 'frown with your moustache' and raise his eyes to the ceiling whenever she mentioned the name of an unidentified man, who was clearly Sinatra. 'He has been (secretly) a very tender friend,' she said. 'I know you won't believe this but you must trust me with my instincts. It was a sort of a fling on the wing. I had never done that before but now I have – but he is very unselfish in bed.'[3]

The two became closer that spring. While Marilyn knew that DiMaggio would never marry her again – 'He loves me, but that's it. We can't agree about the movies,' she told Lena Pepitone – she had hopes that Sinatra might become her fourth husband. 'Frankie wouldn't expect me to be a housewife,' she said. 'We can both have our careers.'[4] Marilyn realised that if she wanted to pursue her relationship with Sinatra – as well as make more movies – she would have to spend more time in Los Angeles. And so in the summer of 1961, she returned to Hollywood, where she rented the small apartment on Doheny Drive where she'd lived back in 1953.

On 7 June, Sinatra invited Marilyn as his guest to the Sands Hotel and casino in Las Vegas (one of the locations for *Ocean's 11*) to celebrate the forty-fourth birthday of fellow singer and actor Dean Martin. Staff were ordered to respect the privacy of the couple – who shared a suite – and not to disturb them before 2 p.m. Heavy drinking was the order of the day, but it was clear that Marilyn couldn't handle the excessive amounts of alcohol she consumed. 'All eyes were on Marilyn as she swayed back and forth to the music and pounded her hands on the stage, her breasts falling out of her low-cut dress,' recalled actor Eddie Fisher, who was sitting at the same table with his wife Elizabeth Taylor. 'She was so beautiful – and so drunk. She came to the party later that evening, but Sinatra made no secret of his displeasure at her behavior and she vanished almost immediately.'[5] Elizabeth Taylor, observing her rival's lack of control, took full advantage to show off: as she picked up a martini, downing it in one, she declared, 'Now me, *I* know how to hold my liquor.'[6]

A few days later, the news of the Sinatra–Marilyn relationship was all over town. Journalist Earl Wilson wrote to the actress telling her how everyone in Hollywood was gossiping about the couple. In August, a few weeks after surgery in New York to remove her gall bladder, Marilyn and Frank, together with Dean and Jeanne Martin, enjoyed a weekend trip together in California on the yacht that belonged to Gloria and Mike Romanoff, who ran a fashionable LA restaurant. Photographs show Marilyn, free of make-up, relaxed and happy. Yet her girlfriends remembered that she spent the weekend in something of a drugged-up haze. Gloria Romanoff watched as Marilyn would retire to the cabin at about 10 p.m. and she'd sleep for thirteen or fourteen hours. Jeanne Martin recalled that one night at 3 a.m. she saw Marilyn stumble around the deck, desperately searching for 'reds' – barbiturates. She classified the affair with Sinatra as superficial, as the two stars 'were both too narcissistic' for it to develop into anything deeper or more meaningful. 'She was lazy, like a child, terribly irresponsible,' said Martin.[7]

Dr Greenson, who was seeing Marilyn for therapy in LA as often as five or six times a week from spring 1961, also compared her to an adolescent girl. In a letter he wrote to Dr Kris, he was astounded by the emptiness of her narcissistic existence. His main mission, he said, was to 'help her not to be so lonely, and therefore to escape into the drugs or get involved with very destructive people, who will engage in some sort of sadomasochistic relationship with her'. Although it seemed as though Marilyn was responding well to his sessions with her, 'this does not prevent her from cancelling several hours to go to Palm Springs with Mr. F. S.,' he wrote.[8]

In September, Marilyn asked Lena Pepitone to fly from New

York to LA with a $3,000 sequinned emerald green Norman Norell gown to wear to a party at Romanoff's restaurant. 'I've already told Frankie and he's all excited about seeing me in it,' said Marilyn.[9] It was obvious to Pepitone that the couple were enamoured with one another. 'They kissed like two people truly in love,' she said. Sinatra gave Marilyn a pair of emerald earrings, which he said had cost $35,000. When she turned up at the event – hosted by Harold and Lottie Mirisch in honour of Billy Wilder – her entrance on the arm of Frank Sinatra was so dazzling it was mentioned in the *Hollywood Reporter*. 'Poured into a Norell gown of emerald sequins, she really didn't need her diamond and emerald earrings, because no one's eyes strayed further north than her neck!' wrote journalist Radie Harris. 'And it wasn't only the male contingent who ogled in appreciation but every rival glamor puss in town.'[10]

Even though Marilyn knew Sinatra was dating other women, the news in early January 1962 of his engagement to actress and dancer Juliet Prowse – whom he had met on the set of the 1960 film *Can-Can* – left her feeling despondent and signalled the end of their relationship. Juliet, who was ten years younger than Marilyn, was said to have the best legs in Hollywood. Back in New York, Lena Pepitone caught Marilyn, now aged thirty-five, looking at her own legs. 'They're too short and fat,' she said. 'They're horrible.'[11] Since her gall bladder operation Marilyn had become increasingly critical of the way she looked: her breasts were getting flabby, she thought; there were stretch marks on her buttocks; her face was showing signs of crow's feet and lines. Unlike her friend Montgomery Clift – whose looks were damaged in a car accident in 1956 and by increasing alcohol and drug misuse – she believed that her limited acting skills meant that she had to rely on her surface beauty alone. 'When my face goes, my body goes, I'll be nothing ... nothing ... all over again,' she said.[12]

Yet Marilyn was philosophical about the split with Sinatra: she realised that while marriage to Frank was now out of the question, she was determined they would remain friends. 'I can't tie him down, not Frankie,' she said, 'but I'll always love him.'[13]

Marilyn had a constant reminder of Sinatra in the form of a dog he gave her in 1961, soon after her release from Columbia-Presbyterian Medical Center. Maf — reportedly named after a jokey reference to Sinatra's alleged Mafia connections, but which could also stand for 'Marilyn And Frank' — was a white Maltese poodle bought from dog breeder Maria Gurdin, Natalie Wood's mother. 'This is my baby, mine and Frankie's,' Monroe told Lena Pepitone. When Marilyn first christened the dog, Sinatra objected to its name. 'Why not Fifi or Pierre,' he suggested, 'you know, something French?' He also thought the name damaged his reputation. 'But I told Frankie, "Nothing can make you look bad," so he let me keep the name,' said Marilyn.[14] When, in the summer of 1961, she made the move back from New York to Los Angeles, she arranged for Maf to go into kennels in Roxbury, Connecticut. Then, on 14 December, Maf flew out on American Airlines to join his mistress in LA. 'Maf has outgrown his basket, and he might have chewed it en route,' wrote Constance Hutchinson of Southdown Kennels to Marilyn. 'Hope he is adjusting!'[15]

Marilyn always felt a special bond with animals. Over the years there had been her childhood dog Tippy, who lived with the Bolender family; Muggsy, a collie bought by Jim Dougherty to keep his wife company, and who died of a 'broken heart' after Norma Jeane left home to work as a model;[16] Josefa, the chihuahua given to Marilyn by Joseph Schenck; a cat, Mitsou, which she owned in New York in the mid-1950s; Hugo, the basset hound, who continued to live with Arthur Miller in Connecticut after the couple's separation; and a couple of talking parakeets.

'Marilyn was coming out here [to the West Coast] to make

Some Like It Hot and she fell in love with my birds, my parakeets that could talk, and she decided she would like to have one too,' recalled Inez Melson, Marilyn's business manager from the early 1950s until the end of the actress's life. Her favourite was a bird called Butch. 'He had more trips back and forth to New York than any other bird. You couldn't get birds on a plane, but Marilyn could. She a had a little cage, covered in a plastic bag, inside the luggage she took on board. During the flight, at some point over Nevada or some place, it started to say, "I'm Marilyn's bird!" She loved those birds as she loved her little dog Maf.'[17]

In 2010, the Scottish writer Andrew O'Hagan wrote a comic novel entitled *The Life and Opinions of Maf the Dog, and of His Friend Marilyn Monroe*. The book is narrated from the perspective of the little white dog, who comes to see himself as the star's friend and protector. 'Marilyn was a strange and unhappy creature, but at the same time she had more natural comedy to her than anybody I would ever know,' says Maf. 'More comedy and more art.'[18]

When a lot of six colour photographs of Maf came up for sale at Christie's in 1999, the estimate was $600–$800; in the end the set went for $222,500. O'Hagan was at the auction of Marilyn's possessions in New York that day and saw the frenzy of the bidding first-hand. 'As I was watching all the people frantically waving their paddles and trying to get a hold of this seemingly crucial piece of art from the twentieth century – that's how they behaved – I felt I could hear the dog's voice,' he told the *Paris Review*. 'My ambition was to take on the most written-about woman of the twentieth century, a woman who had somehow been erased as a woman and replaced with mythology. And I thought Maf would give me an opportunity; that the small domestic details witnessed from floor level would reinstate themselves through the dog's eyes and would revive her humanness.'[19]

At Marilyn's last home, 12305 Fifth Helena Drive, Los Angeles, Maf slept in the guest room, on a white beaver coat that Arthur

Miller had bought for his wife after she had suffered one of her miscarriages. 'I live here all alone with my snowball, my little white poodle – he was given to me by my dear old friend Frank Sinatra,' Marilyn told the photojournalist George Barris in the summer of 1962. 'I call him Maf. Oh sure, it gets lonesome at times living alone; I'd rather be married and have children and a man to love – but you can't always have everything in life the way you want it. You have to accept what comes your way. I live alone and I hate it.'[20]

77

LOOKING FOR A FAMILY

When Marilyn moved back to Los Angeles in 1961 she committed herself to regular therapy sessions with Dr Greenson, whom she called her 'Jesus'.[1] She told Lena Pepitone of his qualities: how he stimulated her intellect, how he boosted her confidence, how he enthused her with a new-found sense of courage. If Marilyn was away from Greenson, she would call him several times a day. But what would happen if she couldn't reach him? asked Lena. 'I'd be in trouble,' replied the star.[2] In May 1961, Greenson had written to Marianne Kris about Marilyn's progress: 'All in all there's been some improvement, but I do not vouch for how deep it is or how lasting.'[3]

Greenson embarked on a highly unconventional form of treatment: instead of the traditional method of analysis (fifty minutes on the couch, strict boundaries and an interpretative approach), the psychotherapist decided to open up the professional–patient relationship so that it was more fluid and porous. 'There are so many different schools of thought on how you treat patients who are that severely disturbed and upset,' Greenson said of his work with Marilyn in a 1973 interview with *Medical Tribune*. 'There are so many divisions of thought that I don't think you can get any consensus that what I did was right or wrong or terrible or marvelous or whatever. It is controversial, I know that. Nevertheless, I have practiced for some 35 years and I did what I thought was best, particularly after other methods of treatment apparently hadn't touched her one iota.'[4]

Before and after sessions in the soundproofed office of his Mexican-style house at 902 Franklin Street, in Santa Monica, Marilyn was encouraged to socialise with Greenson's family: his wife Hildi; their son, USC medical student Danny, who sometimes dropped by; and particularly Greenson's daughter Joan, then in her early twenties and studying for a four-year Master's of Fine Arts degree at the Otis Art Institute and living at home. In an unpublished memoir, Joan writes of her father's famous client in a sensitive, non-sensational way that captures many of Marilyn's contradictions: she was, for instance, an extremely glamorous movie star who seemed in many ways to behave like a child. Although Marilyn was fourteen years older than Joan, often the younger woman would give the actress advice about life.

Joan got to know Marilyn gradually; after her father had told the actress off for being late for sessions, she made a special effort to be on time. On many occasions, Marilyn turned up before Dr Greenson arrived home, and so she and Joan would take walks around Santa Monica. She noticed that Marilyn didn't speak in the affected, breathy way of many of her screen roles. She also seemed a lot thinner than she did on screen. After her gall bladder operation, Marilyn had to stick to a low-fat diet and dropped 25 pounds; the weight loss meant that many of her dresses were now too big for her. Sometimes, Dr Greenson asked his daughter to drive to Marilyn's Doheny Drive apartment and pick her up. This was nothing like the movie star home of popular perception. Rather, it was small – the living room doubled as the bedroom, complete with a large bed, and black-out drapes, but absent of any personal possessions, paintings, awards or mementoes. It was, noted Joan, as if Marilyn had tried to wipe away all traces of her past.

Marilyn clearly thought she was benefiting both from the therapy sessions and the regular social contact she enjoyed with Dr Greenson and his wife and children; she would stay for dinner, help wash the dishes, and drink 1952 Dom Pérignon champagne in the kitchen. 'Marilyn was always looking for a family,' said her publicist Pat Newcomb.[5] She loved opening a bottle of champagne on the staircase in the kitchen, watching the cork pop, revelling in the spray of fizzy wine trickling down the stairs. On 1 June 1961, the day of her thirty-fifth birthday, Marilyn sent a telegram to Greenson that read, 'In this world of people I'm glad there's you. I have a feeling of hope though today I'm three five.'[6]

Joan noticed that Marilyn had a very black and white view of the world. Her views were strongly held. She believed in total loyalty and if she felt an acquaintance had slighted one of her friends, her judgement would be fierce. Sometimes, the group would debate politics. It was clear Marilyn's sympathies lay with the workers – she was passionate, Joan said, about civil rights. When Joan's brother Danny first met Marilyn he viewed her as little more than a one-dimensional stereotype, yet another superficial actress flitting her way through the fake LA world. 'I hated Hollywood,' he said. 'In fact, I found the whole thing to be obnoxious and terribly offensive. My family knew enough Hollywood people – during my high school and college days I would bump into them here and there. I met movie stars at parties and at times people would try to fix me up with starlets. These people were phonies, narcissistic characters and even though I didn't know the word back then – hedonistic. Looking back, it was clear I had a chip on my shoulder about the whole business. So when I heard my dad was seeing Marilyn, I thought she would be a spoiled rich bitch. As I started to talk to her my opinion about her changed. Those first conversations with her were about politics, I think. Although my parents were both open-minded and liberal, I was very much the left-winger; that's the part I played in the family. As we got into these conversations about politics, I discovered Marilyn to be very much on my side. I was involved in a protest demonstration at Berkeley against the House Un-American Activities Committee, which was investigating alleged communism within the teaching profession and students. Although Marilyn was uneducated and unsophisticated, her instincts were always with the underdog. A friendship developed between us and I began to recognise that there was more to her than meets the eye. She wasn't at all like a typical Hollywood person. I never saw her in make-up – the only time I could have seen her like that was when she was in her casket [coffin]. I'd never seen her dressed up, never saw her acting like the Marilyn Monroe out of the movies. She seemed very nice, very warm, very genuine, and slightly hysterical, but that seemed to be the real her.'[7]

By December 1961, according to a letter Dr Greenson wrote to Anna Freud, Marilyn exhibited all the signs of a 'borderline paranoid addict'.[8] She suffered a 'severe depressive and paranoid reaction' because he had challenged some of her irrational beliefs: her distrust of those around her, her view that some in her circle were using her, her feeling that she was being persecuted. 'I did not deny the fact that I was somewhat impatient, but she took this to mean that I too, could someday throw her out,' Greenson wrote to Dr Marianne Kris. The fear of potential abandonment left her feeling desperate. 'She talked about retiring from the movie industry, killing herself etc. I had to place nurses in her apartment day and night and keep strict control over the medication, since I felt she was potentially suicidal.'[9]

Marilyn invited Joe DiMaggio to Los Angeles to spend the Christmas of 1961 with her. 'He had come down there to spend Christmas with her in part because she was in need,' remembered Danny Greenson.[10] What was the nature of their relationship? When, in 1962, a journalist asked Marilyn whether they were romantically involved, she replied, 'I've always been able to count on Joe as a friend after that first bitterness of our parting faded. Believe me, there is no spark to be kindled. I just like being with him, and we have a better understanding than we've ever had.'[11]

Joan Greenson recalls how, two days before Christmas 1961,

Marilyn went out and bought a tiny tree just 2 feet tall, which she arranged by the windows in her apartment that looked out onto the deck. The normal-sized fairy lights had all sold out and so the actress had had to make do with a string of enormous bulbs designed for outside. The result was rather incongruous, thought Joan, and the tree drooped under the weight of the heavy lights. Yet it was obvious that the tree was something of a symbol for Marilyn; perhaps as she looked at it, she was reminded of the happy times she had enjoyed around the Christmas tree with her mother just before Gladys's final breakdown in January 1935, and also the moment Joe had surprised her with a tree back in 1952. Joan remembers how Marilyn kept the small tree for months afterwards, long after it had died.

78

'I AM FINISHING MY JOURNEY'

Marilyn was keen to establish a base in Los Angeles. She loved Dr Greenson's home and, with the help of Eunice Murray – who, together with her late husband John, had built the therapist's house on Franklin Street, and who from November 1961 was employed as the actress's 'devoted assistant' – she started to look for something similar. 'The doctor thought that the house would take the place of a baby or a husband, and that it would protect her,' said Murray.[1]

Over the course of thirty-five years Marilyn had lived in over fifty different places – houses, apartments, hotels – and as a result her peripatetic existence had fostered a sense of not belonging. Once, at a reception, she had inscribed in the column marked 'Address': 'None.'[2] When she purchased 12305 Fifth Helena Drive in early 1962 it was the first time she had ever bought a property in her own name. 'My work is the only ground I've ever had to stand on,' she said that same year. 'Acting is very important. To put it bluntly, I seem to have a whole superstructure with no foundation. But I'm working on the foundation.'[3]

One of the most important considerations for Marilyn was privacy. Before she bought the modest house – in a small cul-de-sac located only five minutes' drive from Dr Greenson – she enquired about the immediate neighbours and drove around Brentwood to see whether anyone could spy on her from the nearby hills. The single-storey property – situated behind a high white wall, with three bedrooms and a small kidney-shaped swimming pool – cost

$75,500. Marilyn put down a sum of $42,500 and arranged a fifteen-year mortgage with the City National Bank of Beverly Hills, paying $320 a month. She instructed builders to renovate the house: she wanted a new kitchen and bathrooms, and hoped to return the property to its original hacienda style, complete with Mexican tiles and furniture. 'I could never imagine buying a home alone,' she said. 'But I've always been alone, so why couldn't I imagine it? ... It's better to be unhappy alone than unhappy with someone – so far.'[4]

The purchase boosted Marilyn's self-esteem, as Dr Greenson had hoped. 'The biggest spurt in her treatment came when she began to furnish such a house, which in many ways was similar to mine,' he said. He felt able to reduce their therapy sessions from seven days a week to their regular meetings on Saturday and Sunday, 'when she was particularly lonely or depressed'.[5]

Marilyn was keen to fill her new house with life and encouraged friends over for dinner, to use her pool, and for extended visits. On 2 February, she wrote to Arthur Miller's son Bobby, begging him and his sister Janie to come and stay. 'As I told you, it is an authentic little Mexican house, but it's got a gigantic swimming pool, and it looks just like Mexico,' she wrote. 'You would just love it. I have two guest rooms, plus a large playroom, plus lots of patios, and a big Mexican wall goes all around the place with big high Mexican gates (that's to keep the intruders out, in case anybody gets intrusive).'[6]

Set into the tiled doorstep was a coat of arms and an inscription that read, 'Cursum Perficio'. The translation from the Latin means: 'I am finishing my journey' or 'My journey ends here'. When Marilyn explained this to photographer George Barris, she said, 'I hope it's true.'[7]

79

'THE GREATEST LOVER IN THE WORLD'?

In February 1962, while in Mexico to buy furnishings, textiles and paintings for her new home, Marilyn met screenwriter José Bolaños. She had just arrived in Mexico City, together with a party that included her publicist Patricia Newcomb and housekeeper-assistant Eunice Murray. The circumstances of the meeting with Bolaños are unclear: one source places this at the rooftop bar of Marilyn's hotel, the Hilton Continental; another witness claims they met in a furniture shop. Reportedly, Bolaños – known for his 1959 film *La Cucaracha* – was interested in Marilyn starring in a possible adaptation of Fellini's *Nights of Cabiria*.

Within days Marilyn and José were lovers. He was brooding but not particularly handsome, she said, but she liked him because of his wonderful manners and his performance in the bedroom. She called him, according to her maid Lena Pepitone, 'the greatest lover in the world'.[1] In 1983, when Bolaños was interviewed by Anthony Summers, he boasted (like many men before him) that he played the part of Marilyn's liberator – he was, he claimed, the first man to give her true sexual fulfilment. According to one of his other lovers, the actress Elsa Aguirre, Bolaños had the ability 'to make you feel like the only woman in the world'.[2] Monroe herself voiced the same opinion – he made her feel 'like I'm the only woman on earth,' she said. But his behaviour could be unpredictable: one minute he was laughing and upbeat, the next he seemed possessed. 'I never know what he's thinking,' said Marilyn. 'And if he sees another man even looking at me, he wants to kill him. If I looked back, gee, I don't know what he'd do to me. But it's exciting, being scared. It's sexy.'[3]

Marilyn's new friends in Mexico – the political writer Frederick Vanderbilt Field and his Mexican wife Nieves – did not take to Bolaños. On 23 February, three days after arriving in Mexico, Field and Nieves drove Marilyn and José to the traditional market in Toluca, outside the city. According to Field, 'it was quite evident that MM and José had spent the night together'. Field – born into the wealthy Vanderbilt family but now a committed communist – was so worried by Bolaños's behaviour that day that he was determined to check out this man he described as a 'thoroughgoing nogoodnik'. From his contacts he discovered that Marilyn's new lover was 'an unprincipled opportunist, an unsuccessful director', someone 'not trusted by his colleagues', while Nieves 'had picked up other unsavory items about his womanizing habits'. He was, in Field's opinion, a 'louse', and possibly even an FBI plant.[4]

Marilyn's presence in Mexico – and the fact that she spent a significant amount of time socialising with those believed to be involved with the American Communist Group in Mexico – was recorded by the FBI. Indeed, the security agency had a long-standing interest in the actress and her alleged left-wing views: their files on her date back to her first involvement with Arthur Miller. 'The atmosphere of the Cold War was unpleasant, to say the least,' wrote Field in his memoir. 'You had to assume that your telephone was tapped, your mail opened, your private life spied upon and reported to the federal police. You didn't make a date by telephone to go to the movies without supposing that a reference to such and such a picture or such and such a restaurant would be interpreted as Aesopean language for some sinister rendezvous.'[5]

Field expressed some of his suspicions about Bolaños to Marilyn – 'nothing more than the political risks involved,' he said – but when this did not work he tried to put some distance between the two lovers. On 24 February, he and his wife drove

Marilyn and Eunice Murray to Taxco, for some more shopping. All the hotels were full and so they checked into a small inn, Los Arcos. That night, as everyone had retired to bed, Bolaños turned up with a number of mariachi bands he had hired from Mexico City. The noise woke everyone up – including Marilyn, who was forced to step out onto her balcony to try to calm the musicians. 'In the patio below, the group in their bright costumes smiled up at her, dark eyes intent on her every moment,' recalled Eunice Murray. 'Marilyn waved them away with outspread arms, her expression one of delight, but crying out, "Go away, you crazy Mexicans. Go away!" . . . The most amazing response came in the morning when Marilyn said, "You know, I didn't take any sedation last night. I just fell asleep."'[6]

She flew back to Los Angeles on 3 March, but she did not have to spend long without her lover: two days later he was her date at the Golden Globe Awards. On 5 March, at the Beverly Hilton Hotel, Marilyn accepted the 1961 Henrietta Award for the world's favourite actress – with a trophy that would sell for $250,000 in 2018. Susan Strasberg witnessed Marilyn and José's entrance that night. As the actress walked into the room, in a dress so fitted she could hardly move, some of the other stars stood on chairs to catch a glimpse of her. Susan thought Bolaños looked like all the gigolos she had met in Italy, while Marilyn appeared drunk, out of control, her make-up too theatrical. When she accepted her award her voice seemed slurred. 'Watching her weave in front of the microphone like a hypnotized cobra,' wrote Susan in her memoir, 'I tried to reconcile that befogged woman with the clear-eyed, agile-witted, sensitive person I knew was hovering just beneath the surface.'[7]

80

SOMETHING'S GOT TO GIVE

It's Friday 1 June 1962, Marilyn's thirty-sixth birthday; she doesn't know it's her last. She's at work filming the light comedy *Something's Got to Give*; she is also not aware it will be her final day on set. She has one last film to do in order to fulfil her Fox contract, but Marilyn has had her doubts about the project from the start. She's scribbled notes on her script, comments like 'This is funny?' and 'Would she come right out with this sort of thing?'[1] Next to some other pages of dialogue, she has written, 'Some changes should be made but not like this. Either they have to trust me to play the scenes with heart or we are lost.'[2]

At the end of the day, Marilyn's stand-in Evelyn Moriarty presents her with an enormous birthday cake, complete with a doll in a bikini swimming in a pool – a reference to the nude bathing scene Marilyn had filmed. She's received numerous telegrams, including one from Joe DiMaggio that reads, 'Hope today and future years bring you sunny skies and all your heart desires.'[3] She has flowers from Marlon Brando, Robert Wagner and Jack Lemmon, and a crate of champagne from Patricia and Peter Lawford. She laughs when she sees her specially designed card, showing a cartoon image of her wearing a robe, and smiles as she reads some of the messages inside, such as 'To the most beautiful girl ... If only I was the marrying type.'[4] She passes out glasses of Dom Pérignon and asks photographer George Barris to help cut the cake, pieces of which she gives to Eunice Murray, Patricia Newcomb and some other members of the cast and crew. One of her favourite presents is a champagne glass engraved with 'Marilyn' inside. 'Now, I can see who I am while I drink my champagne,' she jokes.

Later that night, Marilyn throws the first ball at a charity baseball game held at Dodger Stadium, talks to a group of children suffering from muscular dystrophy, and poses for some photographs – the last ever taken of her in public. Although she is smiling in the photographs – both those taken at the stadium and those on set – when she looks at the images she knows that they show how she is really feeling inside: empty and hollow. 'There was a smile on my face, but look, my eyes are dead,' she tells Joan Greenson.

To the outside world it seemed as though Marilyn had so much going on in her life. She looked better than she had in months. 'In the last part of her life, since she had her gall bladder taken out, she was in absolute, perfect shape,' said Pat Newcomb. 'She was very secure about how she looked.'[5]

She had a new lover, José Bolaños. She had a new home she adored. She had lots of future projects lined up. She had hopes of forming a new production company with Marlon Brando and Lee Strasberg, something she wrote about on her thirty-sixth birthday. She still wanted to make a movie about Jean Harlow. There was the prospect of another Billy Wilder film, co-starring Peter Sellers – *Kiss Me, Stupid* (which was eventually made with Dean Martin and Kim Novak in the lead roles). She planned on splitting her time between LA for work, and New York, the city she loved. And yet, at times, she felt hopelessly lost, completely without purpose, suffering from a depression that ate away at her.

That weekend, Joan and Danny Greenson received a call from Marilyn, who sounded drugged up. Their father Dr Greenson was out of the country, on a work trip to Israel, combined with a holiday in Europe, and Marilyn was feeling angry that he had abandoned her. When Joan and Danny arrived at Fifth Helena Drive, they were shocked by what they saw.

'It was in the middle of the afternoon and she was in bed,' recalled Danny. 'She had one of those lone ranger masks over her eyes to shut the light out. She was lying in bed and she was goddamn naked. I was red-blooded, but this was the least erotogenic experience one could possibly have. She talked about how terrible she felt about herself – that she was worthless, nobody likes me, I don't have anybody, there's no point in living and the stuff that I now know are the symptoms of someone who is in the midst of a profound depression. She talked about not having kids, how she felt ugly, and how people only wanted what they could get off her, not just physically.

'I tried to reassure her, I told her that she had friends, that she was a person of substance, that people admired and liked her, and that she was attractive. The more I talked to her, the more she seemed to be entrenched in these feelings of worthlessness, hopelessness and uselessness. She felt as if she was a nothing. She was trying to go to sleep – but she had this dread, this phobia that she wouldn't be able to. Now, as a psychiatrist [Danny became a doctor like his father], I realise how sick she really was.'[6]

The Greenson children called Dr Milton Wexler, who was looking after Marilyn in Greenson's absence, and he came and removed the bottles of pills by her bedside. On Sunday 3 June, she sought treatment for sinusitis at the Cedars of Lebanon Hospital and suffered from a high fever. (She'd been suffering from a virus, with occasional temperatures of 101 degrees, since early May.)

When Marilyn didn't turn up for work on *Something's Got to Give* that week, the executives at Fox manoeuvred to get her fired from the picture. They were furious that she had taken off for New York to appear at President Kennedy's Madison Square Garden birthday gala when she had repeatedly called in sick. Yet the publicity firm, Arthur P. Jacobs, surmised there was something else at play. Its notes within its Marylin Monroe files, suggest that the studio was in deep trouble – Fox's *Cleopatra*, starring

Elizabeth Taylor, was already hugely over budget – and they felt they could cast Marilyn as a scapegoat. Despite assurances from Dr Greenson – who cut short his trip to Europe – that he could get Marilyn back on set in two days, Fox fired her. Marilyn tried to defend herself by issuing a statement via her publicist – 'The studio is obviously in a panic having over-extended themselves on *Cleopatra* and are now blaming me,' she said – but it was no use.[7]

Arthur P. Jacobs' notes state that the studio started to feed negative stories about Marilyn to the press. *Life* magazine reported that *Something's Got to Give* was already $1 million over budget, and it was clear that Marilyn was to blame: she had turned up for work only twelve days out of thirty-two, and during this time she had only been able to produce seven-and-a-half usable minutes of film (a blatant lie). Marilyn sent out a series of telegrams to the cast and crew, stating, 'Please believe me, it was not my fault. I so looked forward to working with you.'[8]

The news of her dismissal, and the way that Fox chose to spin the story, impacted Marilyn to such an extent that she suffered a serious depressive episode and confined herself to bed. Production on the film – which had cost the studio $2 million – was suspended on 11 June, after her co-star Dean Martin refused to work with any other actress besides Marilyn, and legal action was launched against her. If this was not enough, Peter Levathes, the executive vice president of the studio, released a statement that Marilyn must have interpreted as a stinging reference to her own battle with mental illness. 'The star system has got way out of hand,' he said. 'We've let the inmates run the asylum and they've practically destroyed it.'[9]

On 19 June, Hedda Hopper declared that the actress's career was over. 'Marilyn is emotionally disturbed, and for that reason I feel desperately sorry for her,' she wrote in her gossip column. She presented a neat summary of Marilyn's most recent failures: her bad behaviour on the set of *The Misfits* angered Clark Gable, who died soon after; the failure of her third marriage, to Arthur Miller, was 'a terrible blow' from which she never fully recovered; her last two films had bombed at the box office; her affair with Yves Montand resulted in her ending up in hospital, by which point he couldn't bring himself to talk to her on the phone. 'The last time I talked [to] Marilyn she was an extremely nervous girl,' wrote Hopper. 'She seems unable to control herself. She knows that what she is doing is bad for her, but she can't stop herself.' She interpreted Marilyn as a tragic figure — both at the beginning of her life and now at what appeared to be the close of her career. Her behaviour on the set of *Something's Got to Give* was particularly inexcusable. On the few days she did bother to turn up for work, 'her performance was bad,' wrote Hopper. 'She behaved as if she were in a trance — as one of the movie's top men put it, "as if she were acting under water".'[10]

The words could have been dictated by George Cukor, the film's director, whom Marilyn had never trusted and who now launched a vicious publicity campaign against her. After her death, he said, 'I think she was quite mad ... She was very sweet, but I had no real communication with her at all. You couldn't get at her ... I think it was the only ending for Marilyn, and I think she knew it.'[11]

On 7 June 1962, Marilyn — under the name of Joan Newman — turned up at the office of Dr Michael Gurdin complaining of facial swelling and tenderness to the nose. Accompanied by Dr Greenson, Marilyn told the Beverly Hills cosmetic surgeon that she had fallen in the shower at some point between two and three in the morning. Dr Greenson was worried that she had broken her nose, but after an examination and a series of X-rays, it was concluded that she had just bruised it.

There are some who believe that the injury was caused by

something other than a fall. Indeed, according to Dr Gurdin himself, 'it is possible that she could have been struck on the face'.[12] According to Joe DiMaggio's biographer Richard Ben Cramer, the baseball star had heard of his former wife's problems with the studio while on a trip to Europe. Playing the part of her rescuing saviour, Joe booked the first flight from London to Los Angeles. On arrival, he tried to persuade Marilyn that her dismissal from *Something's Got to Give* could work in their favour. If Marilyn could be forced to step away from the movie industry he hated, a business that clearly treated her with contempt, they would be free to marry again. 'And she looked at him like he was from Mars,' writes Cramer. '*What was he talking about? No one was going to sink her!* . . . And then it turned into a terrible fight.'[13]

If Marilyn's resistance to Joe's narrative of domesticity did indeed result in the re-emergence of domestic violence, this would put paid to the rumour that she was toying with the idea of re-marrying DiMaggio at the end of her life. 'I don't believe that they were going to remarry,' super-fan James Haspiel told Larry King in an interview in 2001. 'Joe DiMaggio had a problem with . . . violence, and that had obviously been gone for many years after their divorce, but it re-emerged a month before Marilyn's death. And so there couldn't have been a marriage.'[14] Yet it was obvious that Marilyn still harboured feelings for Joe right until the very end. Discovered in her possessions after her death was an unfinished letter she wrote to him, in which she states, 'If I can only succeed in making you happy, I will have succeeded in the biggest and most difficult thing there is – that is, to make one person completely happy.'[15]

Whatever happened on 7 June, the incident left Marilyn in such a state of high anxiety that Dr Engelberg, the medic who worked with Dr Greenson and who was in charge of her drugs, felt the need to prescribe one hundred chloral hydrate and fifty Librium pills (he also issued an additional prescription for another fifty Librium pills the day after).

The amount of drugs Marilyn had in her possession was extraordinarily excessive: during the last two months of her life she had been given prescriptions for 830 units of medication, enough to kill several people several times over. These included Valmid, Librium, Sombulex, Parnate, Percodan, Dexedrine, Seconal, Tuinal, Darvon, Sulfathallidine, Lomotil, Phenergan, and the two drugs found in her system at the point of death: chloral hydrate and Nembutal.

Delos V. Smith Jr, a friend of Marilyn's from her days at the Actors Studio in New York, was always worried about her consumption of sleeping pills. It would take five pills to sedate her, he said; the problem was, if she took seven, that would kill her. 'She was living for years, two pills away from the lethal dose,' he remarked.[16]

81

THE LAST NIGHT

Subject: The death of Marilyn Monroe
Location: 12305 Fifth Helena Drive, Brentwood, Los Angeles
Date: Saturday 4 – Sunday 5 August 1962
Key Characters:

- **Eunice Murray**: 'Marilyn's devoted assistant' and housekeeper
- **Dr Ralph Greenson**: Marilyn's psychiatrist
- **Dr Hyman Engelberg**: Marilyn's doctor, in charge of overseeing her prescriptions
- **Pat Newcomb**: Marilyn's publicist, employed by Arthur P. Jacobs; she was also a close friend
- **Peter Lawford**: British-born actor, husband of Marilyn's friend Patricia Kennedy Lawford (sister of John F. Kennedy and Robert F. Kennedy)
- **Mickey/Milton Rudin**: Marilyn's attorney, also Dr Greenson's brother-in-law
- **Milton Ebbins**: Peter Lawford's manager
- **Arthur P. Jacobs**: head of his own publicity company which looked after press for Marilyn
- **Natalie Trundy**: actress, Arthur P. Jacobs' date for the night of 4 August, later his wife
- **Jack Clemmons**: sergeant with the LAPD, and the first police officer to arrive at Marilyn's house
- **John F. Kennedy**: President of the United States from January 1961 until his assassination in November 1963

- **Robert F. Kennedy**: brother of John F. Kennedy, Attorney General of the United States from January 1961 to September 1964; New York Senator and presidential hopeful from January 1965 until his assassination in June 1968

It's 4 August 1962, Marilyn's last day alive. She hasn't slept well, partly because of an argument she had with Pat Newcomb the night before. Marilyn invited Pat to stay over at Fifth Helena Drive because her publicist turned close friend is suffering from bronchitis and the actress thought a little rest and sunbathing would benefit her. That morning, Marilyn takes some more sleeping pills that leave her feeling groggy. At 9 a.m. she eats a grapefruit – or, according to another account, drinks a glass of grapefruit juice – and chats to Eunice Murray, who is due to spend the day at the house. The actress does a little light gardening and takes delivery of a bedside table and some fruit trees that Eunice Murray will plant in the garden. At around 10 a.m. photographer Lawrence Schiller drops by to show Marilyn some nude shots he took of her on the set of *Something's Got to Give*, which he hopes to sell to *Playboy*. (In a letter to Marilyn from Pat Newcomb, the publicist recommended that the actress not work with Schiller; she said that although he was a good photographer, she wouldn't trust him as far as she could throw him, and he was quite a 'chubby fellow'.[1])

At around noon Marilyn's former father-in-law Isidore Miller – to whom she was still close despite the divorce from Arthur – phones the house, but Mrs Murray tells him Marilyn is dressing and will call him back. 'She never got that message,' Isidore said later. 'If she had, she would have talked to me. She always interrupted even a business conference to talk to me.'[2] Marilyn spends some of the morning in her bedroom, talking on the telephone. She receives many calls congratulating her on her interview with Richard Meryman for *Life* magazine, which had just hit the newsstands. There are other projects that need her attention: she is intrigued by the idea of the lead role in an Arthur Jacobs production of *What a Way to Go!* (a part that was eventually taken by Shirley MacLaine). She is interested in a possible musical production of *A Tree Grows in Brooklyn*, composed by Jule Styne, co-starring Frank Sinatra and Dean Martin. And there's even talk of her being reinstated on *Something's Got to Give*.

Just after noon, Pat emerges from the guest room, having had over twelve hours of sleep, a luxury beyond Marilyn's wildest imaginings and something that seems to enrage her. Pat enjoys an omelette cooked by Mrs Murray made with herbs from the garden, but Marilyn eats nothing. The two women continue to bicker.

At some point during the early afternoon, Marilyn asks Eunice Murray whether there is any oxygen in the house, a question that strikes the housekeeper as so strange that she rings Dr Greenson to ask for his advice; he tells her he will call by at some point later. At 4:30 p.m. Marilyn, sounding depressed, telephones Dr Greenson herself and he makes the short trip over to the house. 'She was unhappy and complained about her girlfriend [Pat Newcomb] again, about not sleeping well, but after I had spent about two and a half hours with her, she seemed to quiet down,' he wrote in a letter to Norman Rosten.[3] Greenson suggests that it would be better if Pat leave the house, which she does. According to Eunice Murray, Pat Newcomb flounced out as if she had been insulted. 'I'm assuming that the two of them [Marilyn and Pat] had controversial discussions,' said Murray later. 'It might have had to do with taking too many tablets, or whatever. They both took sedation in order to sleep. They both had psychiatrists. There was a good deal of what I'd call contention between them. And he [Greenson] must have gathered that this disturbed Marilyn very much and if she [Pat Newcomb] left, perhaps she'd feel better.'[4]

Between 5 and 6 p.m. masseur and close friend Ralph Roberts telephones the house. Dr Greenson picks up the phone and when

Roberts asks to speak to Marilyn he informs him she isn't at home and hangs up. After the session with Greenson is over, Marilyn tells him that she'd like to go for a walk on Santa Monica pier — she says it is a place that brings back the few happy memories from her childhood — but the psychiatrist warns her that she is too groggy. Before he leaves, at around 7:15 p.m., he is so worried about Marilyn that he asks Mrs Murray to spend the night at Fifth Helena Drive, something she didn't often do, as she had her own apartment on Ocean Avenue. Greenson makes Marilyn promise to call him the next morning. About half an hour later, he receives a call from her sounding much brighter — she tells him that she is pleased because DiMaggio's 20-year-old son Joe DiMaggio Jr had just rung to inform her that he wasn't going to marry 'some awful girl' and she felt 'relieved about that'.[5]

During the same conversation with Greenson, Marilyn asks the psychiatrist if he has taken away her bottle of Nembutal. 'I was surprised that she asked me that,' he wrote in a letter to Marianne Kris. 'I did not know she was taking Nembutal. She had stopped taking barbiturates for three weeks.' Dr Greenson denies removing the sleeping pills, at which point Marilyn changes the subject. 'I thought perhaps she was just confused,' he said. 'Anyway she sounded pleasant on the phone, although somewhat depressed, but by no means acutely so.'[6]

Mrs Murray hears Marilyn talking on the phone first to and then about Joe DiMaggio Jr, and believes her employer's mood has improved. 'She said that was the most wonderful thing that happened to me in a long time,' recalled Mrs Murray. 'She was in good spirits. Then she turned around and said, "I think we'd better not go for that ride after all, Mrs Murray," the one that Greenson suggested. She closed the door and that was the last time I saw her alive.'[7] For his part, Joe DiMaggio Jr, a marine stationed at Camp Pendleton, said, 'If anything was amiss, I wasn't aware of it. She sounded like Marilyn.'[8]

The late afternoon into the early evening continues with a complicated game of telephone tag. At some point between 7 and 8 p.m., actor Peter Lawford calls Marilyn. Earlier on in the day he had invited her to a small dinner party at his Malibu Beach house and he wants to check whether she's still coming. During the conversation her voice seems to 'fade out' and when he tries to call back her line is busy. Lawford is so concerned by what she says – 'Say goodbye to Pat, say goodbye to Jack [the president], and say goodbye to yourself because you're a nice guy' – that he contacts his manager Milton Ebbins, who advises him not to go to Fifth Helena Drive – after all, not only has Lawford been drinking but he is the brother-in-law of the president. Ebbins, in turn, at 8:30 p.m., leaves a message for Milton Rudin to call him. Fifteen minutes later the two men talk over the phone and Ebbins relates what he's heard from Lawford. At 9 p.m., Rudin rings the house at Fifth Helena Drive and Eunice Murray picks up the phone. He asks about Marilyn and Mrs Murray reassures him that she is in her bedroom and that she is 'alright'. This is a key moment of the night, one of the points when Marilyn's life could perhaps have been saved. During the course of the evening, she takes a large dose of both chloral hydrate and Nembutal. The people around her do not know about the overdose, yet there are a number of alarming signs that should have served as a warning that something was wrong.

When Milton Rudin was interviewed by the police a few days later, the report stated, 'Believing that Miss Monroe was suffering from one of her despondent moments, Mr. Rudin dismissed the possibility of anything further being wrong.' The contradiction built into this sentence is so alarming it's extraordinary that no one has picked it out for analysis: rather than seeing Marilyn's despondency as a warning sign, Rudin takes it as a sign that she is OK.

To give Rudin the benefit of the doubt, Marilyn's habit of drinking and taking sleeping pills had become so habitual that he considered it normal behaviour, and it was usual for her to feel low or depressed. Yet the very same word – 'despondent' – was used by both Dr Greenson (in the Mortuary Report, dated 5 August 1962) and Peter Lawford (in an interview with the LA police) to describe her state of mind on 4 August. It was obvious that Lawford was worried about Marilyn. Why else would he have contacted Ebbins, who in turn called Rudin? Yet perhaps if Lawford had spoken directly to Rudin himself – and emphasised just how concerned he was about Marilyn – that may have made a difference. Certainly, the Chinese whispers didn't help.

Eunice Murray – who later described herself as the star's 'protector'[9] – could also have checked on Marilyn at 9 p.m. when Rudin called. Why didn't she? This is her explanation: 'Rudin said, "Is Marilyn there?" and I said, "Yes she is, she's in her room – shall I call her?" There was a leading question there – could I do something about it? – and he didn't tell me he was concerned in any way. He said, "Oh no, don't bother." He didn't mention the call he'd had from Lawford.'[10]

At some point that evening, Mrs Murray hears the telephone ring in Marilyn's room. 'I don't remember what time the call came in, and I don't know who it was from,' she told the *LA Times* a few days after the star's death. 'But knowing Marilyn as I do, I think that if this call waked her up she might have taken some more sleeping pills.'[11] Later, Mrs Murray would tell biographer Anthony Summers, 'Marilyn had a phobia about sleeping, anything that would deter sleeping, especially after she had taken some sedation, and then she would have to take more – and that's dangerous, she told me that.' Marilyn was so neurotic about not being disturbed that Mrs Murray would not knock on the actress's door in case it woke her. 'Marilyn would become enraged if awakened from a sleep,' said Dr Greenson.[12]

In the guest bedroom, Eunice Murray watches television and reads before she turns out her light and goes to sleep. At around midnight she wakes up and, after stepping out of her room, notices that the cord for one of the telephones is still under the star's bedroom door. (Marilyn had two lines: one of her night-time rituals – to ensure she was not disturbed – was to take the telephones out of her room.) What happens next is unclear. According to the testimony of Sergeant Jack Clemmons, the first police officer on the scene, Mrs Murray told him that Marilyn's body was discovered at around midnight. This is important because official reports give the time of discovery as around 3:30 a.m. According to one of the most widely believed conspiracy theories, this delay of three or four hours in reporting the death would give Monroe's supposed murderers time to clear the house of any incriminating evidence and get out of Los Angeles.

When Anthony Summers interviewed Eunice Murray about this key moment in the chronology, the interchange went as follows.

> Anthony Summers: You said twice that you woke up about midnight?
> Eunice Murray: Well, that's possible, *about* is the important word there because I didn't know what time it was. I'm sorry I said that, I had no idea that it was going to be so important. It was after midnight, certainly, I had a feeling it was in the middle of the night. I'm sure it was later than midnight. But this would be a record with the police department ...
> Summers: That was going to be my next question: how long, roughly, was it between the time that you called Greenson to alert him, and ... when the police were called?
> Murray: Well, that's the thing, when you're in panic – when I'm in panic – I know now time has no ... you're just not concerned about time. I was thinking just wildly

about this horrible, how awful, what on earth is everybody going to do next.[13]

Mrs Murray's account is plausible; sometimes people in traumatic situations do lose all sense of time. But her opaqueness – and her surprising failure to note the time on the night of Marilyn's death – left police investigators so suspicious that they wrote in one report filed a few days later, 'Mrs Murray was vague and possibly evasive in answering questions pertaining to the activities of Miss Monroe during this time. It is not known whether this is, or is not intentional.'[14] When this specific point was put to her later, Mrs Murray replied, 'I wasn't sure myself of what had happened. I mean I was not someone who was in charge there. I was only the person who took up a hem occasionally and saw that Marilyn was . . . did whatever she thought I could do to help her.'[15]

Another possibility that might explain what exactly happened at midnight could lie in the confusion over what Eunice Murray overheard that night. According to Dr Greenson's private correspondence, he estimated the time of Marilyn's death to be 'around midnight'.[16] Could Mrs Murray have relayed this information to Sergeant Clemmons, who misunderstood her and instead became convinced that Marilyn's body had been *discovered* at midnight? Or did Clemmons deliberately twist Mrs Murray's words so as to cast a shadow over the official version of events?

82

Saturday night, Sunday morning

According to the official version of events, Mrs Murray woke up again at around 3:30 a.m. and saw that the phone cord was still under Marilyn's door. At this point, she didn't check whether the door was locked because she was still worried about incurring Marilyn's wrath in case she woke her up. Instead, she went outside, looked through the window and saw something that shocked her. 'I saw Marilyn lying on the bed – face down, nude,' she said. 'It was not a warm night, the light was on, and so everything was wrong. I was really in panic.'[1] She rushed inside and, using the second telephone, rang Dr Greenson, who told her to call Dr Engelberg. When Greenson arrived shortly after, and finding the bedroom door locked, he took a poker from the fireplace, went around to the side of the house, broke one of the panes of glass in a window not covered by *rejas* (Spanish/Mexican-style security grilles), opened the window to Marilyn's room and climbed in. She was lying face down on the bed, with her shoulders exposed; it was obvious to him that she was dead – 'and as I got closer I could see the phone clutched fiercely in her right hand,' he wrote in a letter to Norman Rosten. Greenson assumed that, in her last moments of consciousness, she was trying to telephone him, as she often did in moments of crisis.[2]

When Dr Engelberg arrived, he took out his stethoscope, checked Marilyn's pupils and confirmed that she was dead. The two doctors noticed that rigor mortis had set in. They also saw that Marilyn's bedside table was cluttered with bottles of pills, including an empty one of Nembutal, which Dr Greenson noted had not been there when he visited the day before. Engelberg related to his colleague that on Friday 3 August, when Marilyn had received her regular vitamin injections, she had told him that Greenson had given her permission to ask for a prescription of Nembutal. The truth was rather different: Greenson did not know she was taking the drug; indeed, he assumed that she was free of all barbiturates. Dr Greenson monitored her intake of drugs and, according to his daughter Joan, he would often search her house and take away any he thought were potentially dangerous. Yet on this occasion, Marilyn's possession of Nembutal – which Engelberg had prescribed – passed him by. What she had told Dr Engelberg was, in Dr Greenson's words, 'one of Marilyn's childish lies'.[3]

As the two doctors stared at Marilyn's lifeless body on the bed, they didn't know what to do; perhaps this explains why they didn't report the death to the police until 4:25 a.m. Whose fault was it that Marilyn had died? Certainly, both of them had to take some share of the blame. Dr Engelberg didn't check with Dr Greenson about the Nembutal as he was meant to; he was going through a difficult divorce at the time, and his mind wasn't on his work. 'Dr Engelberg was supposed to tell Dr Greenson if Marilyn ever asked for barbiturates,' said Pat Newcomb. 'Otherwise Dr Greenson might have been a little more alarmed about Marilyn that last time he saw her.'[4]

For years afterwards, Dr Engelberg would deny that he ever prescribed the chloral hydrate that was found in Marilyn's body, and one of the drugs listed on her autopsy record. In 1982, during an interview with Alan Tomich, an investigator with the Los Angeles County District Attorney's Office, which opened an investigation into the star's death, Engelberg maintained that he only supplied her with Nembutal. For the record, he stated, 'I was surprised to see at the side of her bed a large number of other sleeping pills ... I knew nothing about any chloral hydrate. I never used chloral hydrate.'[5] Yet in 2011, at Julien's Auctions in Los Angeles, one of Marilyn's prescriptions for chloral hydrate (dated 7 June 1962) came up for sale, which bore Engelberg's signature. In addition, the coroner's report of chemical analysis, dated 6 August 1962, showed that Engelberg had prescribed chloral hydrate on 25 July 1962, refilled on 31 July 1962. In addition, yet another doctor – Lee Siegel, the medical director at Twentieth Century-Fox – had issued a prescription for twenty-five Nembutal pills that was dispensed on 3 August.

Dr Engelberg's denial implies his guilt – if he thought he'd done nothing wrong, why not tell the authorities the truth about the prescription of chloral hydrate? He should also have been aware of the toxic – and potentially fatal – nature of Nembutal taken together with chloral hydrate. Writing in 2016, Dr Howard Markel, director of the Center for the History of Medicine and the George E. Wantz Distinguished Professor of the History of Medicine at the University of Michigan, analysed the prescription drugs that killed Marilyn, singling out the dangerous interaction between Nembutal and chloral hydrate: 'This is a particularly lethal cocktail, not only because each of these drugs increase, or potentiate, the power of the other, but also because people who take this combination often forget how much they previously consumed, or whether they took them at all, and soon reach for another dose.'[6]

If such a case happened today, there's little doubt that Dr Engelberg – like Conrad Murray, the doctor who was pop star Michael Jackson's physician at the time of his death in 2009 and who prescribed the singer a powerful anaesthetic to help him sleep – would be charged with involuntary manslaughter.

Dr Greenson ignored some of the warning signs too. He failed to pursue why, on Saturday 4 August, Marilyn asked Eunice Murray whether there was any oxygen in the house. Marilyn could have been wondering whether it might relieve Patricia Newcomb's bronchitis. Yet it's likely Marilyn knew that an overdose of barbiturates causes respiratory depression, which in turn results in a lack of oxygen reaching the heart. Oxygen could also be used as a way of trying to revive a patient who had taken an overdose of the drug. Was she sending a coded signal to Greenson? If so, he ignored it, just as the psychiatrist ignored Marilyn's question about whether he had taken her bottle of Nembutal, which he dismissed as merely a symptom of the actress's confused state of mind.

Dr Greenson may have satisfied himself that there was no Nembutal in Marilyn's room that afternoon, but he failed to search the house. He was well aware of Marilyn's crippling insomnia and the devastating effect it had on her. As she wrote to him in March 1961, 'Sometimes I wonder what the night time is for. It almost doesn't exist for me – it all seems like one long, long horrible day.'[7] She was also plagued by horrific nightmares, populated by the same demons and monstrous creatures as painted by Goya. 'I know this man very well, we have the same dreams,' she said of the artist. 'I have had the same dreams since I was a child.'[8]

In 1960, Marilyn told the journalist W. J. Weatherby about her use of sleeping pills: 'It can become a habit, but if you can't sleep, what are you supposed to do? You feel so lifeless next morning. Nobody's really ever been able to tell me why I sleep so badly, but I know once I begin thinking, it's goodbye, sleep. I used to think exercise helped – being in the country, fresh air, being with a man, sharing – but sometimes I can't sleep whatever I'm doing, unless I take some pills. And then it's only a drugged sleep. It's not the same as really sleeping.'[9] However, she admitted to her psychiatrist that she enjoyed swallowing these pills in large doses because it gave her what she described as a 'womby tomby' feeling.[10]

Is that what she was searching for the night she died? Temporary oblivion? The guaranteed certainty that she could forget about everything for a few hours? And if she had the sleeping pills with her in the house, why hadn't she slept properly the previous night, Friday 3 August?

83

The silent woman

Patricia Newcomb, born in 1930 and still alive at the time of writing, has not given a full and detailed interview about Marilyn for the last thirty years. 'Norman Mailer is one of the few people I have talked to, and it didn't seem to do much good,' she told Robert Slatzer in 1972.[1] Facts are ignored, she said, and the truth is deliberately distorted. So what's the point of granting more interviews?

Even those who have questioned Newcomb say that she has been far from forthcoming on the subject of Marilyn and what happened on that last night. This has led many to believe – falsely – that Newcomb (who started her career as a talented publicist adept at shaping and manipulating public images, and who was close to the Kennedy family) covered up for either JFK or RFK, or both. Marilyn's connections to the two brothers and the ensuing conspiracy theories will be examined in later chapters.

It's likely that the truth is a far simpler – but sadder – affair. This is Newcomb in her own words, from an unpublished interview with Robert Slatzer before the publication of *The Life and Curious Death of Marilyn Monroe* in 1974. 'The small argument ... that she and I had that day, it was a very brief comment – she was angry that I had been able to sleep all night and she hadn't,' she said. 'I was asleep with my door closed [on the Friday night] – she apparently had been up wandering around. She just couldn't stand not being able to sleep.'[2]

Newcomb herself, in an unpublished interview, confessed, 'I

did take one of the pills, not one of the Nembutals.'[3] Dr Greenson expanded on the devastating consequences of this seemingly innocent act in an in-depth conversation with Maurice Zolotow in 1973. The psychiatrist felt compelled to talk to the journalist and biographer after the publication of Norman Mailer's sensationally bad book on Marilyn, in which the writer suggested, without providing any proof, that the star may have been murdered. In the Zolotow interview, published in the *Daily News* in September 1973, Greenson states, 'I think the fight [between Marilyn and Pat Newcomb] may have been because Pat Newcomb had taken the pills away.' Yet excised from the printed interview is this sentence: 'It is possible that in her confused state, which seemed to be centered on sleep, she [Marilyn] decided to get into some sleep competition with her friend [Pat Newcomb] and [had] taken a bottle of sleeping pills.'[4]

It's true that Marilyn had a competitive relationship with her friend. When Newcomb first worked with Marilyn as a publicist — for *Bus Stop*, back in 1956 — it was often remarked how much she resembled her client. Fred Guiles, who interviewed Newcomb for his biography of the actress, said that, 'They were almost exactly the same height (nearly five feet six); her [Pat's] thick hair was medium blonde and hung loose to her shoulders . . . She seemed poised, but there was a controlled restlessness in her, a jungle cat in repose. Marilyn seemed to like her on sight, and they immediately became good friends, frequently eating together and giggling together.'[5]

However, their friendship suffered when they became — in Marilyn's eyes at least — 'sexual rivals'. Guiles related how one day in Phoenix, Arizona — where the director Joshua Logan was shooting a rodeo scene for *Bus Stop* — an unnamed man in his thirties became so smitten with Marilyn he asked her out on a date. When he arrived at her hotel room he found not Marilyn but Patricia Newcomb 'not quite dressed — the two women often wandered between their suites with little on'.[6] Reportedly, the star interpreted her publicist's behaviour as sexual competitiveness and Newcomb was swiftly replaced. 'I didn't know how to cope with it, and Arthur Jacobs told me I'd better get out of there at once,' said Newcomb later.[7] Rupert Allan, whom Marilyn knew from his days at *Look* magazine and who took over the role of publicist from Newcomb, said, 'Pat had this competitive thing against Marilyn, I don't know why.'[8]

When, in 1960, Rupert Allan went to Europe to work for Princess Grace of Monaco, he passed the publicist role back to Pat Newcomb. Over the course of the next two years Marilyn and Pat became close again, so close in fact that Newcomb would write postcards and letters to the star when she went travelling, or when the two were on different coasts, notes signed 'Love, Pat'. Marilyn's nickname for Newcomb was 'Sybil' – jokingly referring to the sibling rivalry that existed between them – but towards the end of her life, as the star became increasingly paranoid, Marilyn began to look at her friend in a different, more suspicious, light. She told Dr Greenson how furious she became one day when Pat returned from the hairdresser's with a platinum streak in her hair – the same shade as Marilyn's own hair. Marilyn, in Greenson's words, 'accused her [Newcomb] of trying to rob her of her most valuable possession'.[9] This incident, and perhaps others, sparked what can only be described as a kind of homosexual panic on Marilyn's part. At times, she did not trust certain men and women she believed were gay; however, she had a number of close homosexual friends, including Montgomery Clift.

At the heart of the matter was her warped idea that homosexuality signalled some sort of twisted desire for possession. She had a fear that homosexuals of both sexes wanted to *be* her. Dr Greenson tried to untangle Marilyn's fears, but found it difficult to understand, as he wrote in a letter to Marianne Kris shortly after his client's death. In that August 1962 letter, he outlined how, in December 1961, one of the reasons why Marilyn plunged into a severe depression was because he had challenged her on her irrational feelings about homosexuality. Perhaps he expressed himself too forcefully, he said; maybe he was too impatient, but he thought it was right for him to try to adjust her skewed perspective on the issue. But Marilyn had reacted so badly to what she saw as Greenson's rejection of her that she threatened suicide.

Reflecting back on the case, Greenson became convinced that these two strands – Marilyn's irrational fear of the threat homosexuality posed for her, and her negative emotions towards him, together with a fear that he would leave her – contributed to her death.

'Two things became very clear to me in her treatment,' he wrote to Kris. 'One was that she couldn't bear the slightest hint of anything homosexual. She had an outright phobia of homosexuality and yet unwittingly fell into situations which had homosexual coloring, which she then recognized and projected on to the other, who then became her enemy.' Dr Greenson tried to explain the varied spectrum of human sexuality to Marilyn, and how he believed everyone had homosexual as well as heterosexual components to their psyche. 'Marilyn reacted as though this were a revelation and a catastrophe,' he said. To reassure her, he stressed that he was certain her psychosexual make-up was 100 per cent heterosexual, or at the very least 99 per cent.

So was some of this going through Marilyn's mind the night she died? According to Dr Greenson's letter to Kris – one of the key documents that helps explain the mystery surrounding her death – 'She sensed instantly that identification means homosexual possessiveness.'[10] Did Pat Newcomb's simple act of taking a sleeping pill lead to Marilyn's death? Did Marilyn feel that her publicist and close friend was over-identifying with her? Did she feel threatened in some way? Did she think Newcomb was attracted to her? Or was it all a delusion? After all, it has to be emphasised that during the last months of her life, Marilyn had become increasingly paranoid and out of touch with reality. When Anthony Summers showed Pat Newcomb the contents of Dr Greenson's letter to Dr Kris, the publicist maintained that the star 'never spoke of homosexual worries'.[11] Yet when Greenson was interviewed by the Suicide Prevention Team – a group of doctors who investigated the actress's psychological state – shortly after Marilyn's death, he stated that his patient was 'jealous' of Pat Newcomb. Marilyn had exhibited 'unconscious conflicts about homosexuality (though Greenson was unaware of any actual homosexual link between them, nor that MM had ever had a lesbian experience)'.[12]

Pat Newcomb went on to marry Gareth Wigan, a British-born producer and Hollywood studio executive, in 1982; yet within Hollywood circles it was rumoured that she had slept with women. When the news of Newcomb's marriage was shared with George Barris, the photographer and friend of Pat's quipped, 'I didn't think she was the type.'[13] In an entry dated 5 October 1968, Richard Burton wrote in his diary, 'Eliz [Taylor] tells me that the latest scandal about the above-mentioned Pat Newcomb is that she has decided that she is a lesbian and has moved in with Liz Smith who is a journalist of some distinction.'[14]

Gossip columnist Liz Smith, who later in life made no secret of her bisexuality, wrote of Pat Newcomb in her memoir *Natural Blonde* that she was 'a delightful creature with a dazzling smile and a brain to match ... Then, she had been close to Ethel and Bobby Kennedy after JFK died, and she was given a job under Edward R. Murrow with the U.S. Information Agency. There were rumors that Pat had been "paid off" by the Kennedys to keep quiet, but the reality is that Miss Newcomb was a natural clam about her famous friends and clients. She is another one of the few who has never tried to cash in on what and who she knows.'[15] In March 1992, Liz Smith, writing in the *LA Times* in response to a false story on the television show *Hard Copy* – an allegation that the

Kennedys had 'more or less bribed' Newcomb to keep quiet about what really happened on the night of Marilyn's death — said that despite her best efforts she had been unable to extract 'any lurid tidbits or scandal' from her 'longtime friend'. The team from *Hard Copy* had asked Newcomb to participate in a two-part special investigation into the death of Marilyn Monroe, claiming that the producers were in the business of 'making history'. 'This is not history!' she replied.[16]

Pat Newcomb repeated the story to Liz Smith of how she had learned of Marilyn's death. At around 4 a.m. on Sunday 5 August, Mickey Rudin phoned her and informed her that Marilyn had died. She immediately went over to Fifth Helena Drive, where she encountered a mob of camera- and pressmen; she was so infuriated by their behaviour that she screamed, 'Keep shooting, vultures!'[17] In a taped — and unpublished — telephone interview with Robert Slatzer, Newcomb said, 'I was naturally upset, as anyone would be ... I think everybody was in such a state of shock you don't always think rationally at a time like that. Mrs Murray was in as bad a state as I was, so was Dr Greenson ... I went home and talked to just under five hundred journalists from all over the world. That was my job as her public relations representative; whether she was dead or alive it was my job to do what I could for her.'[18]

Newcomb told Liz Smith that that night she knew no more about the details of how Marilyn had died than anyone else; her view was that it had been an accidental overdose. 'It could easily have happened,' she said. 'I have never believed she meant to kill herself.' In response to the particular allegations surrounding JFK and RFK, and whether her silence had been bought, she responded, 'The Kennedys never gave me a dime, never offered me anything, and never made a job available to me.'[19]

84

An alternative timeline

There is another important witness whose testimony blows apart the official timeline of events, but whose account deserves to be taken seriously: Natalie Trundy, a respected young actress who was publicist Arthur P. Jacobs' date for the night of 4 August. (Jacobs was head of his own press agency that represented a number of Hollywood stars, including Marilyn. He would marry Natalie in 1968 and the couple were together until his death in 1973.) Trundy's version of what happened that Saturday also calls into question the recollections of Pat Newcomb, who was employed by Jacobs' press agency to look after Marilyn.

Natalie would tell two biographers, Anthony Summers (in 1985) and Donald Spoto (in 1992), that she and Jacobs had attended a concert at the Hollywood Bowl that night. Towards the end of the evening – as she listened to the Henry Mancini Orchestra and the piano duo Ferrante & Teicher – a message was brought to Jacobs' seat. 'It was about ten-thirty when the message came that Marilyn was dead,' said Natalie, who would celebrate her twenty-second birthday on 5 August 1962. 'We got the news long before it broke. Pat Newcomb was already there.'

Jacobs immediately rushed to Fifth Helena Drive and asked the other members of the party, the producer-director Mervyn LeRoy and his wife Kitty, to drive Natalie home. 'I don't think I saw him for two days after that,' Natalie remembered. 'He had to deal with the press – my husband fudged everything off. He kept everyone in abeyance. I cannot tell you why – he is no longer with us. But

I mean, if you were my friend and I committed suicide today, you would keep the press at bay. [The official version of events] is not true, because my husband was there. He also had to deal with Pat Newcomb — Pat adored Marilyn and went to pieces. Arthur did not fire her [contrary to some of the reports at the time]. She just couldn't cope and had to leave [the agency]. I thought Pat Newcomb was going to commit suicide herself."[1]

It's conceivable that Arthur Jacobs did indeed 'fudge' the details of that night and interfered with the official timeline of events, by arriving first on the scene and orchestrating what happened next. If Mrs Murray contacted Jacobs first — and not Dr Greenson — he could have pushed the discovery of Marilyn's body from the late evening of 4 August into the early hours of the next day. This would also explain some of Mrs Murray's confusion about exactly when Marilyn had been found dead.

Dr Greenson told the authorities that he arrived soon after Mrs Murray called him at 3:30 a.m., an account that has been questioned. But perhaps he never knew anything of Arthur Jacobs' earlier arrival on the scene, nor the possibility of a clean-up.

What would be the reason for Jacobs' fudging? Certainly, it would have bought him, the studio and perhaps other interested parties a bit more time to clean up, both Marilyn's body and her image. Perhaps it was all done with the best of intentions. 'I think she just got loaded and forgot how many pills she'd taken,' Jacobs told journalist Earl Wilson.[2] An overdose, after all, can be a messy affair and — as the one responsible for Marilyn's public persona — Jacobs no doubt felt that it was his duty to stage this one last piece of promotional wizardry for his brightest star. How could Jacobs have known the consequences of his actions? For into this black hole of these few empty hours — the time between 10:30 p.m. on Saturday night when Natalie Trundy says she and Jacobs were told about Marilyn's death and the official discovery of her body, first by Mrs Murray at 3:30 a.m., and shortly after by

Dr Greenson – conspiracy theorists have injected a thousand wild conjectures.

Central to the question of the alleged cover-up is Marilyn's involvement with the Kennedy family.

85

DIGGING UP DIRT ON THE KENNEDYS

Six weeks after Marilyn's death, Sergeant Jack Clemmons, who had been the first police officer on the scene, met with two men who – like him – had a vested interest in digging up dirt on the Kennedys. Clemmons was a director of the right-wing Fire and Police Research Association of Los Angeles – 'If you haven't time to learn more about and to fight communism today,' runs the tagline for one of the organisation's newsletters, 'you'd better start getting ready to learn how to live under it tomorrow!'[1] Jim Dougherty, Marilyn's first husband, was a colleague of Clemmons's at the LAPD, where Jack was known for his extreme right-wing views. 'The old rascal, he hates the Kennedys,' said Dougherty. 'He's so far right, I can't tell you, if he stuck out his head he'd hit himself in the right eye ... He would paint the Kennedys as black any way he could. We would turn him on in the mornings and tell him what wonderful people the Kennedys were and he was ready to spit fire. We'd have to cool him off before he met the public. He was way out right – and those people can be just as dangerous as those people who are way out left.'[2]

Clemmons's co-conspirators in a battle to bring down the liberal Kennedy clan – whom they thought were too sympathetic to far-left causes – were Maurice Ries, president of the anti-communist Motion Picture Alliance for the Preservation of American Ideals, and private detective turned right-wing propagandist Frank Capell.

At that initial meeting in September 1962, the three men

discussed the possibility of using Marilyn's death to besmirch the Kennedy brothers. Ries had heard a rumour – nothing more – that Marilyn had been having an affair with Robert Kennedy; according to hearsay, the attorney general had promised to marry her, but when he changed his mind she was so angry and bitter she threatened to expose him. In order to shut her up, so the story went, Kennedy had her murdered.

Clemmons and Capell joined forces to investigate Marilyn's death, determined to start a smear campaign. The result was the slim but poisonous pamphlet *The Strange Death of Marilyn Monroe*, written by Capell, and published by the Herald of Freedom, a 'national anti-Communist educational bi-weekly', in July 1964. Capell presented himself as a 'patriot and a dauntless crusader' against communist activities – in the late 1930s and early 1940s, he was a confidential investigator and then chief of the Subversive Activities Department for the Sheriff of Westchester County, New York.[3] Yet, in 1943, while working as an investigator for the War Production Board, he was arrested and indicted on counts of bribery. He was found guilty two years later and given a suspended prison sentence and a large fine.

A year after the publication of *The Strange Death of Marilyn Monroe*, Capell was in trouble with the law again when he was found guilty of libelling Californian Senator Thomas Kuchel for suggesting – falsely – that the politician had been arrested for committing a homosexual act with another man while drunk in a car. Although he was a Republican, Kuchel was considered too liberal for Capell. At the end of the trial, Capell was found guilty of libel, fined and given a suspended sentence. One of the other men named in the libel case against Kuchel was none other than Jack Clemmons.

When Clemmons and Capell discovered from Marilyn's autopsy – carried out by Thomas Noguchi on the morning of 5 August – the seemingly significant detail that no residues from the pills were found in the star's stomach, the two men believed they had stumbled upon evidence of foul play. (In fact, they misunderstood and misinterpreted the physical evidence: not all of those who die by overdose have traces of the drugs left in their stomachs.) And so the fantastical murder plot was hatched. Like in a terrible whodunnit, Clemmons and Capell gathered together their suspects in the fetid drawing room of their dark imagination. 'When a person has become a liability or is getting out of hand, the Communist Party has no compunction in ordering his or her liquidation,' wrote Capell. 'Many "suicides" and "heart attacks" and "accidental deaths" are in reality murders ordered by the Communist Party. Marilyn was deeply involved with left-wingers and identified Communists and her death has many suspicious aspects to it which we shall attempt to bring out by presenting documented evidence.'[4] Capell calls out many in Marilyn's life as known or suspected communists – Arthur Miller, Dr Hyman Engelberg, Lee and Paula Strasberg, Norman and Hedda Rosten – but he leaves the reader in little doubt who was to blame for Marilyn's death: Robert Kennedy.

'If Marilyn's death were really murder dressed up to look like an accident or suicide who would have wanted her out of [the] way?' Capell asks. 'The most likely [suspect] would be an ambitious man, already important but wanting to become more important and knowing that a serious scandal might ruin his chances for the biggest job of all. Would he take a gun and shoot her or personally involve himself in the dirty work? No, he would be devious as always and utilize the forces best qualified for the job – the Communist Conspiracy which is expert in the scientific elimination of its enemies. Marilyn, already surrounded by doubtful people, was easy game.'[5]

In an unpublished letter, written to lawyer and fellow right-wing activist Helen Clay, Capell admitted to using the Monroe case for his own political ends. He hoped that the resulting bad publicity 'would bring home to the New York Voters the truth about Bobby Kennedy'. He believed that if Kennedy was elected senator, 'I am afraid he will become the un-official "Dictator" in Congress, since he has the support of every known left-winger group, liberal group etc, etc ...'[6]

On its publication, *The Strange Death of Marilyn Monroe* generated little serious media interest, apart from the occasional mention by Walter Winchell, one of Capell's stooges (and not a fan of Marilyn since the star's divorce from his friend Joe DiMaggio). Winchell, in his syndicated gossip column, called the book an 'eyebrow-raising breath-taker – even if the chronicler can never be confirmed'.[7] In June 1967, Winchell heard a story from New York press agent Lenny Traube about the rumoured publication of a number of Marilyn's love letters, taken from the star's home after her death. 'The signatories included some important lawyers, medics, and politicians,' wrote Winchell. 'One is a U.S. Senator.'[8] Capell picked up on the story and hoped to include details of the letters from Robert Kennedy in a revised edition of his book. His intention was to scupper Kennedy's chances at the presidency.

Robert Kennedy had made many powerful enemies, including J. Edgar Hoover, the director of the FBI. Kennedy – whose 1960 book *The Enemy Within* documented his battle with corrupt labour unions – believed that Hoover used his connections to the mob to try to dig up dirt on the Kennedy family. Hoover was so thrilled by Capell's central allegation that he took the trouble to write Robert Kennedy a memo that read, 'Mr. Capell stated he will indicate in his book that you and Miss Monroe were intimate, and that you were in Miss Monroe's apartment at the time of her death.'[9] However, in the same cache of FBI files, it maintains that 'the allegation concerning the Attorney General and Miss Monroe has been circulated in the past and has been branded as utterly false'.[10]

Throughout the 1960s, Hoover was on the look-out for anything that he could use to besmirch Robert Kennedy, but no matter how hard he searched, he couldn't find anything. 'Although Hoover was desperately trying to catch Bobby Kennedy red-handed at anything, he never did,' said William Sullivan, deputy director of the FBI. 'Kennedy was almost a Puritan. We used to watch him at parties, where he would order one glass of scotch and still be sipping from the same glass two hours later.' Sullivan then went on the record to state the truth of the matter. 'The stories about Bobby Kennedy and Marilyn Monroe were just stories,' he said. 'The original story was invented by a so-called journalist, a right-wing zealot [Frank Capell] who had a history of spinning wild yarns. It spread like wildfire, of course, and J. Edgar Hoover was right there, gleefully fanning the flames.'[11]

86

NORMAN MAILER'S OBSESSION

The shadowy godfather of the Marilyn conspiracy theorists, Frank Capell, 'a heavy-set man with dark hair, [and] glasses', passed his hit list down to a litany of followers.[1] The first – and flashiest – of this rabid cabal who turned Marilyn's death into a full-blown (and highly profitable) industry was Norman Mailer, the Pulitzer Prize-winning novelist and 'bad boy of American letters'.[2]

Mailer had long been fascinated by Marilyn and in 1955 he published a novel, *The Deer Park*, which featured a thinly disguised portrait of the star. 'She seemed to bounce when she walked, her shoulders swayed in a little rhythm with her hips, her neck curved, her hair tumbled in gold ringlets over her head, and her husky voice laughed at everyone's jokes,' writes Mailer of his central character, blonde actress Lulu Meyers.[3]

Mailer had lived only 5 miles from the Connecticut house that Marilyn had shared with Arthur Miller. Yet the couple had kept their distance from him, perhaps sensing Mailer's predatory mindset: in his 1973 book on Marilyn, he revealed that he had wanted to seduce her. Writing about himself in the third person, Mailer said: 'One of the frustrations of his life was that he had never met her, especially since a few people he knew had been so near to her. The playwright and the novelist had never been close . . . Nor could the novelist in conscience condemn the playwright for such avoidance of drama. The secret ambition, after all, had been to steal Marilyn.'[4]

Mailer's *Marilyn* had started out as a photographic project featuring a series of lush images of the actress, and overseen by Lawrence Schiller, who had taken a series of semi-nude photographs on the set of *Something's Got to Give*. ('You're already famous, Marilyn,' he said to her. 'Now you can make me famous.' He went on to sell the photos to *Playboy*.) After the success of the exhibition 'Marilyn Monroe – The Legend and The Truth', which showcased the work of twenty-four photographers, Schiller decided the project could be turned into a coffee table book. The publishers needed a star writer to bash out 25,000 words as a preface and, after various names were considered, Grosset & Dunlap approached Norman Mailer.

The offer came just at the right time. 'I had some debts,' Mailer told *Time* magazine in July 1973. The only problem was that he had to turn the book around within a couple of months. The more Mailer learned about Marilyn, the more obsessed he became, and the initial preface (for which he was paid $50,000) turned into a long-form essay and then a 90,000-word book. However, just before publication, Monroe biographers Zolotow and Guiles raised concerns about just how much Mailer had lifted from their books. Zolotow had agreed that Mailer could use sixteen passages from his book, amounting to around 3,500 words. When Zolotow discovered that Mailer had actually used 169 additional passages and 20,000 words, he threatened to sue Mailer for $6 million.[5]

In Britain, W. H. Allen, the publisher of both the Zolotow and Guiles books, claimed that over 250 sections of the two biographies had been used by Mailer without permission. 'He has taken nearly one quarter of Mr. Guiles's book and lifted it without requesting permission from the publisher,' said Mark Goulden, chairman of W. H. Allen.[6] When Mailer learned of Goulden's statement he went into fighting mode, not unusual for a man who was both a fan of boxing and domestic violence (in November 1960 he was arrested for stabbing his wife Adele with a penknife during a drunken party at their Manhattan apartment). 'No one is going to call me a plagiarist and get away with it,' snarled Mailer. 'If I'm going to steal from other authors, let me use Shakespeare or Melville. I don't have to steal from Fred Guiles.'[7]

On the inside sleeve, the volume was advertised as a major biography, but within the first few pages Mailer himself reclassified it as a 'novel biography'. Certainly, there is a fictional quality to Mailer's manic prose, but his short deadline meant that he did not have enough time to check basic facts. To cover himself, Mailer – with typical chutzpah – invented in *Marilyn* a new word, one that has entered the lexicon: the factoid. He defined the term as 'facts which have no existence before appearing in a magazine or newspaper, creations which are not so much lies as a product to manipulate emotion in the Silent Majority'.[8]

The irony is Mailer himself fell victim to this pernicious trend – that a lie may become truth through its repetition – within the pages of his own book. At the end of *Marilyn*, Mailer outlines his theory that the star was murdered by a right-wing group (such as factions within the FBI or CIA) in order to discredit her reputed lover Bobby Kennedy, or to gain some political advantage over the powerful family.

On 13 July 1973, Mailer was interviewed by Mike Wallace on the CBS show *60 Minutes*. 'All Hollywood was gossiping about Marilyn having an affair with Bobby Kennedy, which I believe she was not having, although they were dear and close friends,' he said. 'So, if she could be murdered in such a way that it would look like a suicide for unrequited love of Bobby Kennedy, it would be a huge embarrassment for the Kennedys.' Wallace proceeded to question Mailer. Was Marilyn having an affair with Robert Kennedy? Was he at Fifth Helena Drive on the night of her death? Was she murdered? Mailer backtracked, stumbled over his answers, insisted that he didn't know, before finally confessing that he didn't believe Robert Kennedy was with Marilyn at her home during that last weekend. The real problem, he maintained, was that no one wanted to talk. At this point, Wallace brought on his star witness: Marilyn's housekeeper Eunice Murray, whom Mailer had not interviewed because he believed she was either dead or in hiding. Mrs Murray was not difficult to find – her name was in the phone book – but then, backtracking even further, Mailer insisted that he and his publishers had made a conscious decision not to interview important witnesses. 'I hate that way of getting facts,' said Mailer. 'I – I don't believe in fact gathering . . . I was coming down to a deadline. I had something like twenty thousand words to finish in the last week.'

Although Mailer himself described the book as 'half-finished' and said that he had done 'a superficial job', his speculation and lazy research did not affect the book's success.[9] The first printing of *Marilyn* was for an order of 320,000 copies; the publisher sold serial rights and it spent nine weeks on the *New York Times* bestseller list. Lawrence Schiller told journalist Lloyd Shearer 'we stand to make worldwide about a million and a half bucks. Norman gets one-third of the royalties and the photographers get two-thirds . . . The interest in Marilyn is still fantastic.'[10]

87

'The Toad'

Hot on the heels of Mailer's 'biography in the form of a sustained masturbatory reverie' came another book from a fantasist who went one step further.[1] Robert Slatzer – author of *The Life and Curious Death of Marilyn Monroe* – was a man who claimed he and Marilyn were not only lovers but once man and wife.

According to Slatzer's account, published in 1974, he first met Marilyn in the summer of 1946, while he was working as a freelance writer in Hollywood. One day, while waiting in the reception of Twentieth Century-Fox, he started chatting to Norma Jeane, whom he described as 'a cute girl with brown hair ... carrying a huge portfolio'. At this time she was in the midst of her divorce from Jim Dougherty. By the time Marilyn starred in *Niagara* – or so Slatzer declared – the two were so close they had started to talk about marriage. Indeed, a photograph in Slatzer's book shows the couple snuggling up to one another on a bridge overlooking the Falls, together with an inscription that reads, 'To Bob, Luck & Love, Marilyn'. And, in September 1952, in a guest spot taking over from syndicated gossip columnist Dorothy Kilgallen, Slatzer wrote how he was educating Marilyn by recommending literary works such as Thomas Wolfe's *Look Homeward, Angel*.

When Slatzer published *The Life and Curious Death of Marilyn Monroe*, the world widely believed the story he told: that in October 1952 the couple drove down to the Mexican border town of Tijuana and married. He said that the marriage only lasted two days, because once they were back in Los Angeles

Marilyn realised that she was in love with Joe DiMaggio, whom she was dating. Slatzer alleged they then returned to Mexico where they bribed an official to destroy their marriage certificate. 'She was happy with me, but not happy being married to me,' he wrote. 'She was afraid of Joe, of what the studio would say, and of Natasha Lytess [her acting coach], who was very jealous and possessive and who had a tremendous influence over her. It just wasn't going to work.'[2]

Slatzer claimed he had managed to keep news of this union a secret until the early 1970s when he began to think about writing a book to cash in on the renewed interest in Marilyn. On 30 August 1972, he wrote to journalist and author Will Fowler to ask whether he would be interested in collaborating with him on a project about Marilyn. The proposal – described as a 'fictional book project' – was called *The Beautiful Loser*, the same title as the first chapter of *The Life and Curious Death of Marilyn Monroe*. Tellingly, at this stage there was no mention of a wedding between Slatzer and Marilyn. The twelve-page outline detailed, in a rather anodyne fashion, how Slatzer and Marilyn went to see a film, *Any Number Can Play* (1949), at the Pantages Theatre in Hollywood, drank champagne and talked about films, books, Hollywood and her future as an actress. After buying a ripe watermelon that exploded over their clothes, the two went back to Slatzer's room at the Hollywood Plaza Hotel, where Marilyn washed his trousers and her own shoes and tights, before they fell asleep on the bed. 'Hope this is what starts things off ... am I feeding it to you the right way?' Slatzer asked Fowler. 'It's tough to recall everything but my memory is efficient and these recollections are the highlights.'[3]

In February 1973, a contract was drawn up between Slatzer and Fowler and none other than Frank A. Capell (who for his share in the deal agreed that the book could include the sleaze and unfounded innuendos about the Kennedys from his 1964 pamphlet).

'We used Mr Capell's 80 pages to give some *backbone* to what I was desperately trying to form into a book,' said Fowler later.[4]

According to the terms of the contract, the three men would share equally in the profits from the book but it was imperative that while 'Robert F. Slatzer will receive full credit for the writing of this WORK, Frank. A. Capell and Will Fowler's names will remain secret'.[5]

At some point during the ghostwriting process – as Slatzer regurgitated whatever he could remember about meeting Marilyn – Fowler made a passing remark. 'Then, the most terrible words came from me in pure innocence,' wrote Fowler later in an unpublished letter. 'I said to Mr Slatzer, "It's too bad you weren't married to Marilyn Monroe, then we'd [have] a *great* book." At this time, Mr Slatzer skulked off following having several drinks with me ... And some time later (days? No longer than eight), he returned as if in Confession and told me that HE HAD BEEN MARRIED TO MARILYN FOR "A WEEKEND".'[6]

Slatzer would later claim that the marriage had been witnessed by Noble 'Kid' Chissell, the boxer and bit-part actor; indeed, Chissell's statement was reproduced in a number of biographies of Marilyn. But this turned out not to be true, like many other aspects of the story. Joseph Jasgur, who had taken a series of photographs of Marilyn in 1946, was a friend of Chissell's, and one day, when Jasgur bumped into Chissell, he asked him about the marriage. Jasgur blew apart Slatzer's claim in a 1991 letter to Will Fowler. 'There wasn't a wedding between Bob Slatzer and Marilyn Monroe. He [Chissell] told me Bob Slatzer offered him some money (I believe he said it was $100) to sign a statement stating he was a witness to their "supposed" wedding in Tijuana. "Kid" also told me he never received the money or any money promised him by Bob, and the wedding never happened.'[7]

A definitive piece of evidence that exposes Slatzer's lies is an innocuous sale receipt for $313.13, dated 4 October 1952 – the date of the alleged wedding – from Jax, the Beverly Hills boutique favoured by Marilyn. When she was supposed to be marrying Slatzer in Mexico, she was in fact shopping in Los Angeles.

Even Marilyn's scrawled signature on the cheesy photograph of her and Slatzer cosied up together in Niagara Falls was a fake. 'When I first saw the photo, it was not autographed,' said Fowler, 'but before I left off with the book, I later saw it inscribed in tall, nearly unreadable words which nowhere match MM's writing.'[8]

Whole conversations are reproduced by Slatzer in his book in which Marilyn is reported to have made some extraordinary claims. Journalists took his account seriously, including his allegations that Marilyn had been having a sexual relationship with Robert Kennedy and that she had been murdered. The book opens with a conversation in which Marilyn tells him, 'Bobby Kennedy promised to marry me. What do you think of that?'[9] Slatzer also claimed that Marilyn had kept a diary – red leather, he said – in which she had noted down some of the things Bobby had told her: that the CIA were plotting to assassinate Fidel Castro of Cuba; the attorney general was determined to imprison the powerful union leader Jimmy Hoffa, who had connections to organised crime; and that the Justice Department had made a series of deals with mobsters Sam Giancana and Johnny Roselli. When Bobby Kennedy rejected her – so Slatzer's theory goes – Marilyn threatened to hold a press conference on Monday 6 August 1962 in order to 'blow the lid off this whole damned thing'. Slatzer alleged, 'Marilyn said she would reveal all at her press conference and that decision probably sealed her fate.'[10]

In 1974, the world took Slatzer's story seriously because he claimed he'd had a close friendship with Marilyn; even after the supposed brief marriage, he said he maintained regular contact with the star until her death and acted as her confidante. Slatzer made a career out of his apparent association with Marilyn: his first book was adapted into a terrible 1991 television movie *Marilyn and Me*. In 1992, Slatzer published *The Marilyn Files*, which was turned into a two-hour investigative special; part of the studio for the live broadcast was transformed into a replica of the bedroom where the actress died.

But the truth is that Slatzer never had a relationship with Marilyn.

'Why has it always been in life that no one ever *saw* Slatzer with MM with the exception of the only time he ever met her, on the *Niagara* set in Niagara Falls?' asked Will Fowler. 'This came about when Slatzer, then a newspaper space ad salesman on *Ohio*, posed as a columnist to 20th Century-Fox unit publicist on *Niagara*, Frank Neill. This was when Neill allowed him to have his picture taken with MM "to be printed" in Slatzer's paper. This was the only time Slatzer met MM. But with a single color photo of Slatzer hugging MM from behind on the *Niagara* location, he has based his entire false career about himself with the actress.'[11] After working closely with Slatzer over a number of months, Fowler was in no doubt 'that Robert Slatzer was simply a Monroe fan who had gotten carried away by his imagination'.

In today's cultural landscape, Slatzer would be regarded as an obsessive celebrity stalker. In the Marilyn fan community, he is simply referred to as 'The Toad'.[12]

88

The 'missing' diary

In October 1975, the journalist Anthony Scaduto – using the pen-name Tony Sciacca – wrote an article entitled 'Who Killed Marilyn Monroe?' for the soft-porn magazine *Oui* (cover lines for the issue read: 'Latest Sex Kink: Women Who Rape' and 'Sex Tapes: How I Lost My Virginity'). Scaduto, quoting heavily from Robert Slatzer, alleged that the LAPD, together with the LA County Coroner's office, had taken part in an operation to cover up Marilyn's murder in order to protect Robert Kennedy.

Central to Scaduto's case was his belief in the existence of a 723-page report in the vaults of the LAPD, labelled 'MARILYN MONROE – MURDER', a claim first made by Slatzer. The document alleged that Marilyn had been secretly taping conversations with both Kennedy brothers. Scaduto claimed that on 4 August 1962, Robert Kennedy went to see Marilyn at Fifth Helena Drive, where she became so hysterical that he had to slap her to calm her down. The attorney general is then supposed to have called a doctor who injected her with phenobarbital and another substance. 'The evidence of the murder was suppressed to protect John and Robert Kennedy,' wrote Scaduto. 'Almost certainly, both had been her lovers.'[1]

After the publication of the *Oui* article, the LAPD ordered the city's Organized Crime Investigation Division to examine Scaduto's claims. The police interviewed Robert Kennedy's brother-in-law Peter Lawford – who told the authorities that Kennedy was not in Los Angeles on the day of Marilyn's death – and Thomas Noguchi, who had carried out Marilyn's post-mortem in August 1962. After examining the evidence, the LAPD dismissed the claims in *Oui* by selecting a sentence from Scaduto's own article and turning it against him: 'Some of the evidence is as thin as Depression food line soup.' Indeed, the supposed file in the LAPD vaults has never surfaced.[2]

In 1982, LA private investigator Milo Speriglio – who had been employed as a detective by Robert Slatzer – published *Marilyn Monroe: Murder Cover-Up*. The book's central premise was that Marilyn's house had been bugged by the infamous wiretapper Bernard Spindel for the benefit of labour boss Jimmy Hoffa – who hated Robert Kennedy – and that the secret recordings were meant to prove that the star had been murdered. Speriglio claimed that one of the voices on the alleged tapes says, 'What are we going to do with the body?'[3] Speriglio stated that he knew the identities of Marilyn's killers, one of whom was still alive in 1982.

> He was one of the two men in her house the night she died, and she invited them there, knowing both of them quite well. One was a high-ranking political appointee. His feet often walked over the carpeting of the White House. The other is a well-known star of motion pictures ... I for one do not like being tagged as subscribing to a conspiracy theory; but professionally, in this case, regardless of who killed her, I know that there was a very clever and clandestine cover-up. She did not – and could not – take her life as has been reported in the media of the world for the past two decades. Now I believe we know the real identities of her killers and we are closer now than ever before to revealing those names to the world. When those tapes are played, it will be a devastating shock to all who hear them.[4]

The tapes never materialised.

In August 1982, Speriglio announced that he would pay a

reward of $10,000 for the red diary purportedly kept by Marilyn, an offer that was soon trumped by a Beverly Hills art dealer who raised the sum to $150,000. The news generated interest around the world: in addition to tip-offs from thirty-seven US states, the private detective said that he received calls from Australia, Germany, Canada, Britain and the Philippines. One caller stood out: at 8:30 a.m. on 4 August, Speriglio spoke to a man over the phone who said that his name was Ted Jordan, an actor who had once worked at Twentieth Century-Fox. Jordan maintained that he could retrieve the diary from a box stored inside the garage of a friend. However, soon Jordan began to change his story, claiming that the book in his possession was not a diary full of personal revelations but a journal made up of Marilyn's love poems. When asked to produce it, Jordan alleged that the book had been stolen from his car. 'I'm not going to buy that, no way,' said Speriglio.

Then in 1985, Jordan claimed that he had sold the diary to *Penthouse* publisher Bob Guccione for $100,000 and also alleged that Marilyn had been killed by an injection into her arm. 'If I had exposed everything and everyone before, I would never have worked again,' he said. 'Now I am retired and I don't care.'[5] The diary was never found. And in his 1989 book *Norma Jean: A Hollywood Love Story*, Jordan stated that she was not murdered but died from an accidental overdose. That same year Jordan was charged and pleaded guilty to two counts of misdemeanour for making threatening and obscene phone calls to Robert Slatzer and Milo Speriglio. Jordan was fined $1,000, served two days in jail, followed by three years' probation. It's ironic that Robert Slatzer — who himself had a questionable relationship with the truth — said of Jordan, 'He is a liar and I challenge the authenticity of any facts he claims.'[6]

Yet the industry that has built up around the idea that Marilyn Monroe was murdered is littered with liars and men on the make. In August 1982, the Los Angeles County Board of Supervisors launched a new investigation into her death – and the alleged subsequent cover-ups – after concluding that a recent explosion in media coverage could not be ignored. Clustered around the twentieth anniversary of the star's death, there was a rash of articles about the so-called missing red diary; comments from Milo Speriglio (pushing his new book); a seven-part series in the *New York Post*; and – perhaps the most significant – 'shocking' new information from a former coroner's aide, Lionel Grandison.

Grandison said that he had been forced to sign Marilyn's death certificate against his will; stated that her red diary, full of potentially dangerous secrets, was removed (probably by the CIA) from a locked safe at the coroner's office two days after it had been checked in; and that key elements of the original report had been either doctored or deleted. It's no surprise that a reporter from United Press International wrote at the time, 'The enduring legend of sex goddess Marilyn Monroe, dead two decades of a drug overdose, has taken on elements of a movie thriller – complete with international intrigue, CIA assassins and hypodermic needles.'[7]

Despite the fantastical – if not downright bizarre – nature of some of the claims, the District Attorney's Office was determined to take the matter seriously.

By the end of December – after three and a half months, forty interviews and a re-evaluation of the files from law enforcement agencies, including the FBI – the District Attorney's Office concluded its investigation and revealed that no foul play had been uncovered. Marilyn's death, said Deputy District Attorney Ronald 'Mike' Carroll, was the result of either suicide or an accidental drug overdose. But what about the fact that no drug residue had been found in her stomach? Surely if Marilyn had swallowed the barbiturates, they would have left some trace? After all, Nembutal leaves a tell-tale yellow stain and should still be visible. Toxicology tests carried out back in 1962 showed that Marilyn had about twice as much barbiturate residue in her liver as her bloodstream, due to 'an advanced stage of the metabolic process'. And although her stomach was never chemically tested, 'the respective blood and liver level indicated that her body had time to disperse much of the barbiturates from her stomach to other organs before she died'. And what about the theory that she had died from an injection? Again this scenario proved to be false because 'a needle injection would have produced a much higher blood level of barbiturates than the toxicologist's tests showed, a much more rapid death and a much lower level of barbiturates in Monroe's liver.'[8]

Addressing next the allegations of Lionel Grandison, Carroll said that there was no evidence that the coroner's office had ever taken possession of Marilyn's diary – or whether a journal even existed; he questioned whether the actress had the capacity to keep one at this stage of her life as she was 'in almost daily need of psychiatric support to accomplish ordinary tasks'. It was also revealed that in December 1962, Grandison, then twenty-two, was found guilty of stealing the credit card from the body of a 76-year-old man who was lying in the morgue. He was given six months in jail, placed on probation for five years, an offence that resulted in his resignation from his position as a coroner's aide. Grandison also confessed to having read Slatzer's *The Life and Curious Death of Marilyn Monroe* before making any public statements about the issue. In conclusion, said Carroll, 'The homicide hypothesis must be viewed with extreme skepticism.'[9]

89

INSIDE MARILYN

It might seem as though the private detectives, reporters and (some) biographers were digging deep into the Marilyn story in the spirit of public service journalism. But beneath the surface, there was something rank and rotten about the nature of their pursuit. Many of the investigators zoned in on the insides of Marilyn's body, believing – like some haruspex at an ancient augury – that the state of the star's entrails could offer some extra insight into how she died, details not provided by the official autopsy carried out by Thomas Noguchi.

During his work as ghostwriter on Robert Slatzer's book, Will Fowler made a note to himself to ask Frank Capell about Noguchi's description of Marilyn's colon as having a 'purplish discoloration'. What did this mean? he asked. Was it something to do with the pooling of blood in the body in the hours after death? 'Or does this point to nechrophilia? [sic],' noted Fowler. 'No record of a smear for semen was taken to verify this. Necrophilia is common among undertakers and grave diggers. [There] is one on record from the Westwood Memorial Park [the cemetery where Marilyn was buried] of a grave digger, about 15 years ago, who dug up the body of a young girl buried a few months earlier, and his defiling her body, then burying her again.'[1]

Lionel Grandison also alleged that Marilyn's body had been interfered with while at the coroner's office, but again there was no evidence to prove this. And so the legion of conspiracy theorists sought to look for other ways of explaining the discolouration of

Marilyn's colon. Could the barbiturates have been administered by means of a suppository or enema? She had been in the habit of using enemas or colonics to help with quick weight loss and constipation – a side effect of some sleeping pills – while they could also have been used to relieve the symptoms of ulcerative colitis, another condition it's known she suffered from.

The enema theory has been seized upon by a number of biographers: for instance, in his 1993 biography Donald Spoto alleged that Dr Greenson ordered Eunice Murray to give the actress an enema of chloral hydrate on the night of her death to sedate her (not knowing that she had already taken Nembutal). According to Spoto's speculative thesis – he has no evidence for this imaginary scenario – Greenson and Murray panicked when they realised that the combination of the drugs had killed Marilyn and they then tried to cover up the accidental death.

Spoto also maintained that Eunice Murray was seen using a washing machine at Fifth Helena Drive in the early hours of 5 August, soon after the discovery of Marilyn's body (possibly to clean the soiled bed linen). Recently, however, this theory has been debunked – the only (unreliable) witness was Sergeant Jack Clemmons, and in fact there was no washing machine or dryer installed at Fifth Helena Drive. When pressed on this point for the 1985 television documentary *Say Goodbye to the President*, Eunice Murray – in a segment that was never broadcast – said, 'I certainly wasn't doing the washing.'[2]

However, the most enema-fixated figure connected with the Marilyn story has to be John Miner, who was the LA County's deputy district attorney back in 1962. He surfaced again three decades later when he attempted to sell off a batch of notes he claimed he'd made after listening to a tape of Marilyn engaged in free association. This is his version of how the star died, reproduced from the *LA Times* in August 2005:

Marilyn Monroe took or was given chloral hydrate to render her unconscious. Someone dissolved Nembutal in water by breaking open 30 or more capsules. That person then administered the Nembutal loaded solution by enema to Miss Monroe using an ordinary fountain syringe or enema bag. As the drug was slowly absorbed, the tissues of the large intestine reacted to the trauma of exposure to the poisonous substance by an inflammatory response producing congestion and a marked purple color. That congestion and purple color were in evidence when the body was opened at the autopsy. Never regaining consciousness, Marilyn Monroe died. It must be concluded from the medical evidence alone that Marilyn Monroe was killed by person(s) unknown.[3]

However, when Marilyn biographer Lois Banner investigated Miner for her 2012 book she uncovered a sordid tale of sexual exploitation and strange fantasies. Miner seemed to be obsessed with enemas: he extolled their virtues to Banner and 'had been convicted of suggesting to several women in the district attorney's office that he perform enemas on them', resulting in the suspension of his licence to practise law for a number of years. Before she knew this about him, Banner suggested that he should write the story of his extraordinary life, but Miner told her that this would be impossible because he had done too many 'horrible things' to women. 'There were also his stories about being the featured speaker at a convention in Las Vegas on sadomasochists, discussing those who used enemas as well as whips and chains,' said Banner. 'After all he told me, I concluded that he had made up the transcript, which represented his sexual interests, not Marilyn's.'[4]

If only the subscribers to the enema theory had bothered to read the easily available post-mortem results, they would have seen that Marilyn's bowels were not empty. This point was raised in 1982, when Ronald 'Mike' Carroll, who led the reinvestigation into her death in 1982, interviewed Thomas Noguchi, the man who carried out the autopsy twenty years earlier. 'Another story that is going around that doesn't make sense when you read your autopsy report is that she had an enema, a hot shot enema,' said Carroll. 'The reason that doesn't make sense to me is you found a formed stool in the colon. It seems to me, if you give someone an enema, they don't have a formed stool in their colon, do they?'

Noguchi answered with one word: 'No.'[5]

90

THE RISE AND FALL OF A STAR WITNESS

In 1983, Deborah Gould, Peter Lawford's third wife, told biographer Anthony Summers of a conversation she had once had with her husband; it too involved enemas. Lawford had been 'kind of high', but then as he started to talk about his memories of Marilyn, he broke down. Sobbing into his wife's lap, Lawford – in a cryptic and melodramatic fashion – gave her a clue about the manner of the actress's death: 'Marilyn took her last big enema'.[1]

Many people assumed that because Deborah Gould had been married to Peter Lawford – albeit only for a few months in 1976 – she might have some special insight into the mystery of Marilyn's death, particularly the involvement of the Kennedy brothers. After all, she claimed to have heard exactly what happened on the night of 4 August 1962 from her husband, the brother-in-law to both Attorney General Robert Kennedy and President John F. Kennedy. She was a star witness and she was prepared to go on record – and on camera – to describe to the world exactly what she knew about the murky affair.

On 25 October 1985, the BBC aired the documentary *Say Goodbye to the President*, with interviews conducted by Anthony Summers; it was broadcast in the US under the title *The Last Days of Marilyn Monroe*. The film tied in with the release of Summers' bestselling biography *Goddess: The Secret Lives of Marilyn Monroe*. During the course of his research, Summers interviewed over 650 people and uncovered many shadowy aspects of the star's life;

when the biographer came across Deborah Gould, he must have been ecstatic. Her revelations were astonishing.

Gould told Summers that Lawford introduced Marilyn to John Kennedy and that they began their affair before Kennedy became president. 'It was a relationship, a sexual relationship, for sure, but much deeper than that, if you know what I'm saying,' said Deborah on the documentary.[2] The liaison, Gould told Summers, ended when JFK asked his brother Robert, his 'messenger boy', to break the news to the actress that he'd had enough of her. 'Marilyn took it quite bad and Bobby went away with a feeling of wanting to get to know her better,' claimed Gould. 'At the beginning it was just to help and console, but then it led into an affair between Marilyn and Bobby. From what Peter told me, he fell head over heels.'[3]

According to Gould's testimony in *Say Goodbye to the President*, Robert Kennedy – who was married with children when all this is supposed to have happened – then broke off his relationship with Marilyn because he was afraid of potential future pressure from the mob. 'He [Lawford] mentioned gangster type of enemies, people that had a big pull, that had actually some information, and if they got hold of anything like this [a relationship between RFK and Marilyn] it could ruin his career forever, and not only his but his brother's who was president at the time,' she said. Marilyn did not take the news well – after all, now she had been rejected by both brothers. 'She told Peter, "This is it, that's enough, I'm going public with everything. I've been hurt enough. I've been used – nothing but a person who has been thrown from one man to another. I've had it and I'm going public with everything."'[4]

In Gould's version of events, Robert Kennedy did visit Marilyn on the afternoon of 4 August 1962. 'Marilyn was, from what Peter told me, she knew then that it was over – that was it, over, final,' said Gould. 'And she was very distraught and depressed and perhaps even suicidal at the time.'[5] Gould said that, later that night,

Lawford managed to arrange for Robert Kennedy to fly from LA to San Francisco by helicopter.

According to Deborah Gould, Marilyn did leave a suicide note. What did it say? 'I don't know,' she told Summers in the documentary. 'It was destroyed.' Who destroyed it? 'I'm sure Peter did, he told me he did.'[6] Gould said Lawford did this to 'protect loved ones involved' – his friends and brothers-in-law JFK and RFK. It was his job 'to cover up all the dirty work, and take care of everything,' she said.[7] The Kennedy brothers would make sure, she added, that there would be no full or proper investigation in the future.

Gould's story reinforced the idea of a massive cover-up at the very top of the American system. Only there was a problem. The story she told had come from Peter Lawford and Lawford was still alive. Responding to Gould's claims, Lawford said, 'It's all a fabrication. You can put me on a lie detector right now and tell me about that and the needle won't move.' Lawford – who died in December 1984 at the age of sixty-one – denied all of his former wife's allegations. 'It didn't happen the way she's talking,' he maintained.

Of course, conspiracy theorists would claim that – even towards the end of his life – Lawford was still protecting the powerful Kennedy family, decades after the assassinations of both John and Robert. 'Even if those things were true, I wouldn't talk about them,' he said. 'That's just the way I am. Plus the fact, I have four children. I'm not going to embarrass them. I'm not going to embarrass the rest of the family.'[8]

But then the foundation stones of the Monroe–Kennedy conspiracy theory edifice were blown apart when Anthony Summers learned, long after publication of *Goddess*, that – by her own admission – nothing Deborah Gould had told him in her interview for the biography or the documentary could be relied upon. He felt he had no choice but to remove all reference to Gould from future editions of the book.

91

MARILYN AND JFK

In the months leading up to her death, Marilyn was asked – in a Q & A interview – to name figures who inspired her. She singled out Eleanor Roosevelt for her 'devotion to mankind'; the poet Carl Sandburg, with whom she was photographed stretching and dancing in January 1962; Greta Garbo 'for her artistic creativity and her personal courage and integrity'; and President Kennedy and his brother Robert because 'they symbolize the youth of America – in its vigor, its brilliance and its compassion'.[1] From this statement it does not sound as though Marilyn had anything to hide about her relationship with the two brothers; in fact, it only speaks of her respect and admiration for them.

The rumour about Marilyn having an affair first with JFK and then RFK has been branded upon our collective consciousness. Their relationships have been represented and re-represented in films, books and on television with such frequency and dramatic power that this continued repetition has mutated from hearsay and speculation to become established fact. Images such as those taken by artist Alison Jackson – whose grainy black and white shots show a lookalike Marilyn embracing JFK, snatched through windows and shutters – are sometimes mistaken as authentic photographs.

So what *is* the truth about Marilyn and the Kennedys? Towards the end of her life, she told Dr Greenson that she was romantically involved 'with some v. important men'.[2] The psychiatrist was concerned that she might be being used, but felt it wasn't his place to dictate who she could and could not see. However, he advised his famous patient that she should be certain that these relationships were 'valuable' to her and not continue to maintain them if she felt under any kind of pressure. Later, in 1983, Dr Norman Tabachnick, one of the experts charged with producing a 'psychological autopsy' back in 1962, assumed that these powerful men were the Kennedy brothers.[3]

The first documented evidence of Marilyn and John F. Kennedy being in the same room together is from 12 April 1957 when they attended a charity event, the Paris Ball at the Waldorf-Astoria, in New York. Both were with their respective spouses – Marilyn with Arthur Miller, Senator Kennedy with his wife of three years, Jacqueline. There are no photographs of Marilyn and Kennedy together from that evening, and it seems likely that they didn't even talk to one another that night. The next public event was JFK's birthday celebration, and Democratic gala fundraiser, at Madison Square Garden on 19 May 1962, when Marilyn sang 'Happy Birthday' in front of a crowd of fifteen thousand people. 'I can now retire from politics after having had Happy Birthday sung to me in such a sweet, wholesome way,' joked the president.

Afterwards, Marilyn – together with her date for the evening, Isidore Miller, Arthur's father, and her publicist Patricia Newcomb – attended a party at the Manhattan townhouse of Arthur and Mathilde Krim. This is where the famous photograph of Marilyn, JFK and RFK was taken, the only one known of the three together. In the image it looks as though the president and his brother might be ogling the star, gazing down at her breasts. Often, in reproduction, the photo is cropped to show only Marilyn and the two Kennedy men, but in reality they were surrounded by a number of other guests.

It's often been alleged that the actress and the president spent that night together at his apartment at the Carlyle Hotel – one persistent rumour has it that the couple escaped the party through a secret tunnel that led to the hotel. However, the Krims' house on East 69th Street is seven blocks from the Carlyle on East 76th Street. Also, receipts from Marilyn's car service, Exec-U-Car, show, in detail, the actress's movements that night. She left the party with Isidore Miller, drove with him to his home in Brooklyn, and before she dropped him off, asked him whether he would like to accompany her back to LA the next day. 'Later, Marilyn,' he said. 'Maybe in November.' (It was the last time he saw her.[4]) From Brooklyn, Marilyn then returned to her apartment building on East 57th Street, where she was spotted by superfan James Haspiel. 'I can tell you with *authority*, that I was with Monroe at her apartment ten minutes to four in the morning,' he said. 'Categorically, Marilyn was not asleep at the Carlyle Hotel, and I didn't notice the president anywhere near us, either!'[5]

It's clear that if Marilyn and the president – who, despite his philandering nature, had a public image as a happy family man – were conducting an affair, they would want to keep it out of the public eye. In various biographies there have been dozens of witnesses – some more reliable than others – who have testified that Marilyn and JFK had been lovers. The statements of Marilyn's friends such as Henry Rosenfeld, Ralph Roberts and Susan Strasberg – all of whom confirmed such a relationship between the two – should be taken seriously.

Rosenfeld maintained that Marilyn's relationship with JFK started after he became president – 'she was so excited you'd think she was a teenager' – but that the sexual contact between them was confined to 'a very, very few times'. According to Rosenfeld, the couple used to meet up at a place on 53rd Street in New York, and that Marilyn travelled to Washington a couple of times, although she never made it into the White House itself.[6] 'She would say, "I'm going to be with You Know Who again – he's so important",' said the wealthy New York dress manufacturer. 'She was going to bed with the President of the United States. She was awed by big names.'[7] On the Thursday before she died, she phoned

Rosenfeld and asked him to accompany her to Washington for a pre-Broadway tryout of the new musical *Mr President* – she had heard that John Kennedy had been invited to a production on 25 September (on that occasion he was accompanied by the First Lady). 'I'm going, Henry,' she told him, 'I'm going to Washington, and I want to go with you!'[8]

According to masseur Ralph Roberts, Marilyn called JFK 'the Gentleman Caller'. At the end of March 1962, she phoned Roberts to tell him that the president had invited her to spend the weekend of 24–25 March in Palm Springs. Initially, the venue was going to be Frank Sinatra's house, but this was changed at the last minute to Bing Crosby's estate. 'I'm not sure that I want to go,' Marilyn told Roberts. 'I've gotten to know the Gentleman Caller's sister [Patricia] quite well. She's a remarkable girl. I think she's fantastic. We have a lot of laughs together.' The next day, Marilyn rang Roberts again and told him that she had changed her mind, and that she was going to travel in disguise, as she often did. 'I'm wearing the black wig, carrying an attaché case. I have an identification card with a picture of me wearing the wig. Guess what my name is? Tony Roberts.' She went on to say that the president was anxious that she might be identified by her trademark sexy walk. 'He says I would be recognized in the deepest part of Africa from it,' she said.

From Palm Springs, Marilyn telephoned Roberts again and told him about a conversation she had with the friend – whom he took to be President Kennedy – about her walk and her knowledge of physiology. During the call, she passed the phone to the president – Roberts recognised JKF's voice – and the masseur and the leader of the free world (and a sufferer of back problems) had a brief chat about the psoas muscle. 'He [Kennedy] said that the little massaging I did on his back worked wonders,' she told Roberts on another occasion. 'I replied that I'd learned from a master. He remarked, "Well, he might be the master, but you added a touch

I bet he doesn't have.'"[9] When Susan Strasberg met the president at a White House dinner for the French minister of culture, she thought him to be 'charming, charismatic and witty. I could see why MM was crazy about him.'[10] At the Krims' party, Susan had the chance to study JFK as he in turn observed Marilyn. 'Those two glittering, charismatic Geminis were fascinating together, and apart,' she said.[11]

The testimony of Natalie Jacobs – who was married to Marilyn's press agent Arthur Jacobs – is also worth noting. She confirmed to Anthony Summers that Marilyn had had a fling with the president; this was not a rumour or hearsay, she maintained, it was a fact. The relationship lasted at least five months, she said, and it was an on–off affair.

In the weeks before her death, according to Natalie Jacobs, the actress had been telling people that she had been pregnant, but that she had suffered a miscarriage. The truth of this pregnancy is difficult to establish – Arthur Jacobs did not believe Marilyn; he thought she was in the grip of a delusion.

During the interview with Anthony Summers, Natalie Jacobs also revealed something else. On the night of 4 August, Marilyn was trying to get in contact with the man she said was the father of that miscarried child – John F. Kennedy himself. Even if the pregnancy was nothing more than a fantasy on Marilyn's part, it's not surprising that Arthur Jacobs, a PR maestro, felt the need to take control of the situation and do his best to clean up Fifth Helena Drive. Who knows what he took away with him?[12]

92

Marilyn and RFK

And what about Robert Kennedy? The first documented meeting between Marilyn and the attorney general occurred at a dinner party on 1 February 1962, at the house of Peter Lawford and his wife Patricia Kennedy Lawford. Kennedy, who was thirty-six, was there with his wife Ethel, thirty-three; the couple, who married in 1950, were due to embark on a near-month-long trip to Asia and Europe as part of a 'goodwill' tour. Danny Greenson – the medical student son of Marilyn's psychotherapist whose political views were located to the left of the Kennedys' liberal agenda – remembered helping Marilyn prepare for the night.

'I was in the dining room [of his parents' house] one day, and she [Marilyn] talked about going over to the Lawfords' house,' recalled Danny. 'She said, "Goddamnit, Kim Novak is going to be sitting there, talking about a new house up in Big Sur, and I wanted to have something to talk to him [Robert Kennedy] about." And so we talked about some political questions which we thought might be interesting. They were left of centre criticisms, about Vietnam, the House Un-American Activities Committee, the Freedom Rides and civil rights – things like that. She wanted to impress him [RFK] and she ended up writing the questions down and putting them in her purse. At some point [that night] he caught on to the fact that she was looking into her purse before she'd asked the questions. And so she took out the list and showed it to him.'[1]

The next day, at noon, Marilyn wrote a letter to Bobby Miller, whom she continued to regard as her stepson even after her divorce from his father, and told him about the evening. 'Oh, Bobby, guess what: I had dinner last night with the Attorney-General of the United States, Robert Kennedy, and I asked him what his department was going to do about Civil Rights and some other issues,' she wrote. 'He's very intelligent, and besides all that, he's got a terrific sense of humor. I think you would like him. Anyway, I had to go to this dinner last night as he was the guest of honor and when they asked him who he wanted to meet, he wanted to meet me.' Impressed by her questions, Kennedy asked whether she had been attending any meetings or discussions. 'I laughed and said "no, but these are the kind of questions that the youth of America want answers to and want things done about." Not that I'm so youthful, but I feel youthful. But he's an old 36 himself which astounded me because I'm 35. It was a pleasant evening, all in all.'[2] Marilyn also wrote to Isidore Miller, telling him of the encounter, describing Robert Kennedy as 'rather mature and brilliant for his thirty-six years', but having a 'wonderful sense of humor'.[3]

After dinner, the Lawfords played some music and Marilyn taught Robert Kennedy how to do the twist. 'He isn't a bad dancer either,' she said.[4] Then, at some point in the evening, Robert made a phone call to check on his father Joe, who had suffered a brain haemorrhage and was no longer able to talk or walk. Correspondence continued between Marilyn and the Kennedys, including an invitation from Robert and Ethel to visit their estate, Hickory Hill, in Virginia, and attend a dinner held for Peter and Patricia Lawford. 'Unfortunately, I am involved in a freedom ride protesting the loss of the minority rights belonging to the few remaining earthbound stars,' Marilyn wrote on 13 June, in a tongue-in-cheek telegram, referring to her recent firing from *Something's Got to Give*. 'After all, all we demanded was our right to twinkle.'[5]

Marilyn must have written to Joe Kennedy because in an undated note to Marilyn from Jean Kennedy Smith – sister to JKF and RFK – she thanks the star for her kindness in corresponding with her father. It is this note that has been interpreted – almost certainly wrongly – as proof that not only was Marilyn having an affair with Robert Kennedy but it was evidence to show that she had been accepted by the Kennedy clan. 'Understand that you and Bobby [RFK] are the new item!' wrote Jean. 'We all think you should come with him when he comes back East!'[6] The tone of the letter, and the context in which it was written, surely suggest that the note illustrates the fact that the two were *not* having a relationship. The ironic way Jean Kennedy Smith describes Marilyn and Bobby as 'the new item' most likely refers to either their spirited performance on the dance floor at the Lawfords' house when they did the twist in front of a crowd of people – including RFK's wife Ethel – or the jokey rumours that were perhaps already doing the rounds.

In July 1962, while Ralph Roberts was giving Marilyn a massage at her house at Fifth Helena Drive, the actress asked her friend whether he had heard the gossip about the supposed affair between her and Robert Kennedy. That was all Hollywood was talking about, said Roberts. 'You know it isn't true,' she maintained, explaining that the politician wasn't her type.[7] 'I do admire him tremendously,' she told Roberts. 'I like him. I am stimulated by his conversation, but ... he's so puny.'[8] Marilyn also told Danny Greenson that 'as opposed to the other members of the Kennedy family, Bobby was a straight shooter – Bobby didn't fuck around, while all the rest of them did. I took it to mean that she wasn't involved with Bobby.'[9]

One night, Marilyn and Joan Greenson had a heart to heart. After Joan talked to her older friend about her new boyfriend, Marilyn began to share details about her own relationship, 'somebody that was important'. She told Joan that she didn't want to 'burden' her with the knowledge of the man's name so as a form of shorthand she would call him 'the General'. Joan knew that

Marilyn wanted to disguise the man's real identity, and so it made no sense to her when people later claimed that Marilyn's secret lover had been Bobby Kennedy. What was the point of having a mysterious codename if Marilyn simply shortened the moniker from Attorney General to 'the General'? In an interview with Anthony Summers, Joan Greenson stated that she believed the man to be John rather than Robert Kennedy.[10]

As the last person to see Marilyn alive, housekeeper Eunice Murray was the figure people turned to for answers about the supposed relationship between Marilyn and RFK. Yet at times Mrs Murray seemed confused and muddled. In the BBC documentary *Say Goodbye to the President*, Mrs Murray claimed that Robert Kennedy first phoned Marilyn and then came over to her house the day she died. When questioned about this – after all, this important detail was missing from the 1975 book *Marilyn: The Last Months* that Eunice wrote with her sister-in-law Rose Shade – Mrs Murray replied, 'It became so sticky, that the protectors of Robert Kennedy, you know, had to step in there and protect him.'[11]

It seemed that Mrs Murray was now confirming – for the first time – that not only was the attorney general present at Fifth Helena Drive on 4 August, but that his 'protectors' had had to take some kind of drastic action in order to handle the potentially explosive situation. Yet, excised from the broadcast is an exchange that proves the opposite – that Robert Kennedy *wasn't* at Marilyn's house that day. Eunice Murray – who was eighty-three at the time of the interview – remembers that she went out shopping, leaving Marilyn alone with Robert.

> Q: And when you came back from your shopping he was not at the house – he wasn't there?
> A: Er – I really, to be – right now – kind of fuzzy . . . No, no, I'm not withholding. I don't really remember that.
> Q: But you'd remember if it . . .

A: Would I? If I read my book I could remember it.
Q: Well, it's not in your book, of course.
A: Isn't it?
Q: No, because you—
A: I knew Kennedy wasn't there. Oh, I – I'm getting the time [mixed up]. *I thought this was a day when he was there when everything was very nice.*[12]

93

'LISTEN – TALK TO BOBBY KENNEDY'

Those who believe the theory that Robert Kennedy killed Marilyn Monroe – or had her murdered – often cite a taped conversation between Dr Ralph Greenson and magician turned celebrity photographer Billy Woodfield, one of the first media representatives to turn up at Fifth Helena Drive in the early hours of 5 August 1962. (Woodfield was there with Laurence Schiller on the set of *Something's Got to Give* when Marilyn swam naked; he said that their photographs of her nude made them $175,000.) Working with journalist Joe Hyams of the *New York Herald Tribune*, Woodfield started to 'play detective'. The week after Marilyn's death he claimed that he'd discovered from a pilot's log in Santa Monica that a helicopter had been ordered to pick up a passenger from Peter Lawford's beach house in the early hours of 5 August and take them to Los Angeles Airport. 'It showed clearly that a helicopter had picked up Robert Kennedy at the Santa Monica Beach,' Woodfield said.[1] Woodfield and Hyams realised that if this were true, they had a big scoop on their hands and requested a comment from Robert Kennedy's office, which reportedly asked them not to run the story. Hyams wrote it up anyway and offered it to his newspaper, which decided not to publish it.

Woodfield did not pursue the story until the German magazine *Stern* contacted him in 1964 to check out the allegations contained in the Frank Capell book, *The Strange Death of Marilyn Monroe*. During his research, Woodfield tracked down Dr Greenson and recorded their subsequent telephone conversation. The tape – which was featured on *Say Goodbye to the President* – became famous for the following quote from Dr Greenson: 'I can't explain myself or defend myself without revealing things I don't want to reveal. You can't draw a line and I'll say, "I'll tell you this, but I won't tell you that." ... It's a terrible position to be in to have to say I can't talk about it because I can't tell the whole story ... Listen – talk to Bobby Kennedy.'[2]

The implication was clear. Dr Greenson's taped testimony suggested that Robert Kennedy was the person to blame for Marilyn's death. However, an examination of the whole taped conversation, instead of this edited segment, casts the so-called revelation in an entirely different light.

After Greenson tells Woodfield about the moral and ethical difficulties involved in talking to a journalist, he adds, 'the stories of the gossips are quite fantastic', a quote missing from the final broadcast. Woodfield asks Greenson whether he will sit down with him for a proper interview. The news of the Capell book is going to break soon, he says, and Greenson replies that nobody will listen if it's just read by a few people in the John Birch Society, a reference to the right-wing group. (Little did Greenson realise then that the Capell book would be used as a kind of twisted Bible for a thousand conspiracy theories.) *This* is the subject they are talking about when Greenson makes his famous 'Listen – talk to Bobby Kennedy' comment. They are not discussing who is responsible for Marilyn's death or anything to do with Marilyn. Rather, they are discussing the possible impact of Capell's pamphlet. Here is the transcript:

> Billy Woodfield: It's [the Capell book] going to break all over New York City just before the election. [Bobby Kennedy was standing to be New York Senator, a position he secured in November 1964.]
> Dr Greenson: Well, when that happens – listen – talk to Bobby Kennedy.[3]

Believers in the Bobby Kennedy conspiracy theory often cite the fact that Marilyn placed a series of phone calls to the attorney general's office that last summer. Surely this was evidence of a love affair between them? There is, perhaps, a more prosaic interpretation. Might it be that Marilyn had an introduction to the highest lawyer in the land and used it to ask him about her legal position after being fired from *Something's Got to Give*? Or, RFK may have actually wanted to seek *her* advice. As she told Ralph Roberts, 'Bobby is trying to break up MCA [the talent agency] and he asked me to help him.'[4] Marilyn – as a former MCA client – was in a good position to provide inside information to Kennedy, who in his role as attorney general was in the process of investigating the agency for alleged anti-trust violations and the monopolisation of certain sections within the entertainment industry. (The issue was resolved in September 1962.) It's also possible that Kennedy – whose book *The Enemy Within* had been bought by Twentieth Century-Fox in February 1961 – wanted to pick Marilyn's brains about how best to deal with the studio.

The strongest evidence that Robert Kennedy was nowhere near Fifth Helena Drive on 4 or 5 August 1962 is a set of fifteen photographs taken over the course of that weekend. These photos place the attorney general, Ethel and their four children (including Robert Kennedy Jr), together with their hosts, John and Nancy Bates, at a ranch in Gilroy, northern California – over 300 miles away from LA. The Kennedy family arrived at the country home of Bates – a prominent Californian lawyer and a friend of JFK's from his navy days – on Friday 3 August and stayed until Sunday 5 August.

One photograph, taken on the Saturday morning, shows Robert with the foreman of the ranch, saddling up ready for a three-hour ride; another shows the whole group on horseback. Another shows them by the pool, yet another captures Kennedy, dressed in white shorts and a white sweatshirt, with a herd of cows. We also know from an interview John Bates gave to the makers of *Say Goodbye to the President*, and from a letter he wrote in October 1986, that every hour of Kennedy's time can be accounted for that weekend. For instance, after lunch, they spent time around the pool, and then, at the urging of Kennedy, they went on a 2-mile hike to the top of a hill, where they played touch football. Back at the ranch, the Kennedys and the Bateses relaxed by the pool again, and some of the kids got thrown in the water. That evening the children ate first, and then the adults settled down to dinner at around 8:15 p.m.; the conversation centred around the speech the attorney general was due to give to the American Bar Association in San Francisco on Monday. Between 10:30 and 11 p.m. – around the time Marilyn may have taken her last breath – the guests retired to bed. On the morning of Sunday 6 August, the Kennedy family attended mass in Gilroy; they returned to the ranch and then John Bates drove them to San Francisco, where they spent the night at the apartment of Paul B. Fay, under-secretary of the navy and a close friend of JFK's.

In that 1986 letter Bates wrote to the photographer Bruno Bernard – known for his images of Marilyn taken in the 1940s and 1950s – he dismantled the conspiracy theories. 'There was no way that Bob [Kennedy] could have left our ranch at any time that weekend, gone to Santa Monica and returned to the ranch,' he said. 'Even if he had attempted such an impossible feat, we certainly would have known about it.'

Bates finished the letter with a rallying cry not to believe the people he assumed were possessed by a desire to make money, seek fame, or were in the grip of a powerful episode of unexplained mass hysteria. 'Those purported eyewitnesses who claim to have seen Bob Kennedy in southern California on Saturday are either lying, victims of hallucinations, or they have been victimized by falsely crafted theories,' he wrote.[5]

The Bobby Kennedy–Marilyn Monroe conspiracy theory started

by Frank Capell, and expanded by Robert Slatzer, Norman Mailer and others was also blown apart by an interview Milton Ebbins gave to United Press International in October 1985. Ebbins – Peter Lawford's manager and friend – outlined how he had talked to Lawford on the night of Marilyn's death. He maintained that Lawford never left his Santa Monica beach house that night, and that Robert Kennedy never stepped foot in Los Angeles that weekend. He described the sequence of events – how Lawford was concerned by Marilyn's 'fuzzy' voice on the phone; how Lawford tried to call her back, but was told by the operator that the phone was off the hook; and how he talked Lawford out of going over to Fifth Helena Drive.

'This was no conspiracy to kill Marilyn, you know, involving Mickey [Rudin] and Mrs. Murray, for God's sake,' said Ebbins. 'Peter called me twice more when he was getting a little drunk, expressing his fear that Marilyn was very ill. Peter called me once after midnight and he was bombed.' At around 4 a.m., Ebbins got another call from Rudin. 'And I asked him, "How's Marilyn?" He said, "Not good. I'm here with Dr. Greenson and Dr. Engelberg (Marilyn's personal physician). We broke into her bedroom. They pronounced her dead. We just called the police."'

This is the first time that anyone closely involved in the scandal had placed Mickey Rudin – Marilyn's lawyer – at Fifth Helena Drive that night.

'Peter was guilt-ridden because he hadn't gone to Marilyn's house,' recalled Ebbins. 'I told him that Marilyn was doomed. She had tried to commit suicide five or six times previously. This time she made it. I never heard Bobby's name mentioned, much less about him arriving at Peter's house in a helicopter that night ... That is the unadulterated story of the night Marilyn died. The rest of that stuff is pure fantasy.'[6]

It's time to finally bury the conspiracy theories. As Marilyn's friend and publicist Pat Newcomb stated in an unpublished interview, 'Everyone tried to make something out of the most glamorous people of that particular era. That was what they decided to invent ... I do not think she was murdered. I am certain she was not murdered. I do not think she meant to kill herself. I think it was an accidental suicide – period.'[7]

94

THE LAST GENTLEMAN CALLER

One of the last people who claimed to have spoken to Marilyn on the night of 4 August was her Mexican lover José Bolaños. He said he called her at Fifth Helena Drive sometime between 9:30 and 10 p.m. At the end of the conversation, Marilyn didn't hang up but just laid the receiver down, something José said was not out of the ordinary.

Bolaños had recently rented an apartment in Los Angeles and had last seen Marilyn in person about three weeks before the weekend of her death. He always maintained that he was the last man in her life, her last lover; there were even some reports that the couple planned to marry in Cuernavaca in September. Later, Bolaños described her as 'the golden one – I never found another one like her'.[1] However, if they were engaged and living in the same city, why did the couple not see one another during late July and early August?

After all, back in February and early March, it seemed as though they could barely keep their hands off one another. At the time of Marilyn's death, it was reported in Mexican newspapers that the relationship between them had cooled. Perhaps this explained Pat Newcomb's dismissive comment about the couple, as reported on 16 August, nearly two weeks after Marilyn's death, that 'there was nothing serious between them ... there was no talk of marriage, no plans for marriage'.[2] It was no secret that Bolaños was a notorious womaniser, a well-known 'Lothario'.[3] Could Marilyn have discovered the truth about him? Or had he become insanely jealous of her very public seduction of the president at the Madison Square Garden birthday event in May 1962 and her secret meetings with JFK? She had told Lena Pepitone that she was scared of José, fearful of what he might do if she even so much as looked at another man.

When Bolaños met biographer Anthony Summers in Mexico City in September 1983, he refused to reveal the exact details of that last conversation with Marilyn. It was, he hinted, something that would shock the world, yet it had nothing to do with any sexual or political scandals. If Summers wanted to hear the truth, Bolaños told him, it would cost him – to the tune of $100,000. Then, without prompting, Bolaños raised his hand and made a cutting movement, as if slicing into his chest. What did the gesture imply? Was he the one responsible for her death? Had she killed herself because he broke her heart? There were those close to Marilyn who thought the match was not a good one, fearful that he would let her down, afraid that the relationship would end in misery. When José spoke to Pat Newcomb she told him, 'You were bad for Marilyn,' and, 'You did a bad thing to Marilyn.'[4] In an official report sent to the district attorney in 1982, Dr Robert Litman – one of the medics in charge of the original psychological autopsy – wrote that Marilyn had told Dr Greenson of her 'considerable dissatisfaction with the fact that here she was, the most beautiful woman in the world and she did not have a date for Saturday night. She had had no date the previous Saturday night, likewise.'[5] Was this one rejection too many for her?

'In summary, the psychological picture emerges of a very dependent woman who felt abandoned by the men in her life,' concluded Dr Litman. 'She had obtained secretly, and through some subterfuges, a large and lethal stock of Nembutal and chloral hydrate. The best inference is that she ingested approximately 25 100 mgs Nembutal capsules and approximately 20 chloral hydrate capsules around 9 o'clock Los Angeles time.'

This is around the same time that José Bolaños phoned Fifth

Helena Drive. Marilyn then drifted into unconsciousness and, as Dr Litman suggested in his report, lay in a coma for four to five hours before she died. 'This might explain why none of the drug was found in her stomach,' he said. 'Apparently, it had all been absorbed. Did she have it in mind that this amount of drug, taken all at once might very likely be fatal? The best inference is yes.'[6]

When Bolaños heard of Marilyn's death, he said he had to be placed under sedation for four days. He was not allowed to attend the funeral – Joe DiMaggio refused to let him in – but on 13 August he was photographed at Marilyn's crypt, wearing sunglasses and a sharp black suit. 'It was a terrible thing to take this girl who was show business itself and put her away in a drawer in an abandoned cemetery,' he told a journalist at the time. 'If this girl had died in Mexico, she would have had a state funeral.'[7] Soon after, Bolaños returned to Mexico without speaking to the authorities about that last phone call or the circumstances leading up to the star's death. The doctors at the Suicide Prevention Team, carrying out an investigation into Marilyn's psychological state, did not have the power to force Bolaños to help with their enquiries. Yet a Mexican newspaper at the time seemed to have no doubts about the reason why the star decided to end her life: its headline read, 'Marilyn Monroe Killed Herself Over a Mexican'.[8]

95

THE WORLD WAKES UP TO MARILYN'S DEATH

The news of Marilyn's death made headlines around the world in that first week of August 1962.

> Emotionally whatever she touched turned to ashes . . . but she is alive no more and the appalling shattering tragedy – that sudden stab at the very heart of Hollywood – will be felt as painfully thousands of miles from Sunset Boulevard.
> – *Daily Mirror*, London

> The sad and ironic realization is that Miss Monroe sincerely aspired to creativity and quality in the films and perhaps in the theater. But the effort to overcome the many obstacles to professional expansion that were in her way was apparently too great for her. Therein lies her tragedy and the tragedy of Hollywood.
> – *New York Times*

> The little girl who had nothing suddenly had everything, and then discovered she had nothing after all.   – *New York Mirror*

> Somehow she was fated to be sad.   – *Daily Sketch*, London

> The world took her completely to its heart, and now the world seems a heartbeat the poorer.   – *Frankfurter Abendpost*

> She is the victim of the glaring lights, the too severe demands, the cracking whips, the cheers and the juggling in the big circus tent of movies. — *Dagens Nyheter*, Stockholm

> She was one of the most fascinating figures that have appeared on the screen. — *Hoja del Lunes*, Spain

> This woman was a product and a recent victim of Hollywood... A human being of prefabricated fame made to live and yet frightened by the hullabaloo of publicity in the higher hells of manufactured film notoriety. — *Die Welt*, Hamburg

> Who killed her? If we look ourselves in the face we are forced to answer: We did. We who have tried to kill Brigitte Bardot and Elizabeth Taylor, we people who go to the movies, we who in a time without idols, without crowned kings and ermined queens have felt the compelling need to construct scapegoats for our daily consumption. — *Il Tempo*, Rome[1]

News of Marilyn's death came just as an eight-page *Vogue* fashion shoot with Bert Stern — which had taken a year to organise — was about to go to press. The editors debated whether it would be possible to remove the photographs from the issue, but as they waited for a response from their printers they decided to publish. 'For these were perhaps the only pictures of a new Marilyn Monroe — a Marilyn who showed outwardly the elegance and taste which we learned that she had instinctively,' wrote journalist Joan Didion, in a hastily written, uncredited short piece to accompany the images. 'She has given a warm delight to millions of people, made them smile affectionately, laugh uproariously, love her to the point of caring deeply — often aggressively — about her personal unhappiness. That she withstood the incredible, unknowable pressures of her public legend as long as she did is evidence of the stamina of the human spirit.'[2]

Those who knew Marilyn personally found it difficult to take in the news. 'Cannot believe that Marilyn M. is dead,' wrote Truman Capote in a letter. 'She was such a good-hearted girl, so pure really, so much on the side of the angels. Poor little baby. God bless her.'[3] Cecil Beaton – who in February 1956 took what Marilyn said was her favourite photograph of herself, an image of her lying on a bed, holding a flower – maintained that she 'was doomed to a sad end'. Beaton added, 'She was a desperate creature, pitchforked into a world she knew nothing about. Though she stood up to it well on the surface, deep down she just could not cope.' Edith Sitwell echoed his view. 'If anyone had asked me to compile a list of people I thought might commit suicide, I would have put her name on it,' she said.[4]

Marilyn's death sent shockwaves not only through the entertainment industry but through the whole of society. 'Do you remember when Marilyn Monroe died?' recalled Marlon Brando. 'Everybody stopped work, and you could see all that day the same expression on their faces, the same thought: "How could a girl with success, fame, youth, money, beauty ... how could she kill herself?" Nobody could understand it because those are the things that everybody wants, and they can't believe that life wasn't important to Marilyn Monroe, or that her life was elsewhere.'[5]

Gay Talese reported that the number of suicides in New York jumped to a record high of twelve in one day in the week following Marilyn's death. According to David Phillips, a sociologist at the University of California at San Diego, the actress's death by her own hand led to a 'copycat effect' or 'suicidal contagion', with a rise in suicides by as much as 12 per cent during the month after her demise.[6]

The effect was felt on the other side of the Atlantic too. On 7 August 1962, 28-year-old 'chorus girl' Patricia Marlowe – born Anita Wimble – was found dead in her mews house in Mayfair, London, after taking an overdose of drugs. 'Pat talked to me on the phone yesterday about Marilyn Monroe,' said the actress's friend Gerry Calvert. 'She knew her well after they met in Hollywood. She was upset about Marilyn's suicide and said she could understand why she did it. I suppose it could have influenced her.'[7]

On the night of 24–25 August, 29-year-old shorthand typist June Cavanagh took an overdose of sedatives at her flat in Hough Green, Chester. A bottle of pills found by her bedside had contained Nembutal, one of the drugs that had killed Marilyn. 'Last time I saw her she was talking about Marilyn Monroe,' said her father Herbert.[8]

Writing in *Life* magazine in 1964, Clare Boothe Luce concluded, 'Those suicides who identified with her [Marilyn] may have felt "doomed", as she felt herself to be, to a suicidal solution of their problems. Others, depressed over their lack of money, fame, youth, or sex, may have asked themselves, "If she, the woman who had 'everything' had nothing to live for, what do I, with so much less, have to live for?"'[9]

96

The funeral

The funeral – at 1 p.m. on 8 August 1962, held at Westwood Memorial Park, 1215 South Glendon Avenue, Los Angeles – was an intimate affair, attended by only twenty-three people. The three who organised the service – Marilyn's half-sister Berniece Miracle, her business manager Inez Melson and ex-husband Joe DiMaggio – issued a statement to the press which explained why they felt they had to limit the number of guests.

> We hope that each person will understand that last rites must of great necessity be as private as possible so that she can go to her final resting place in the quiet she has always sought. We could not in conscience ask one personality to attend without perhaps offending many, many others and for this reason alone, we have kept the number of persons to a minimum. Please – all of you – remember the gay, sweet Marilyn and say a prayer of farewell within the confines of your home or your church.[1]

There were many who felt angry at being excluded, including a host of Hollywood stars: Peter and Patricia Lawford, who had flown across America from Hyannis Port, Massachusetts, planning to attend; and Frank Sinatra, who hired a team of security men who tried unsuccessfully to get him into the service. A crowd of about one thousand people were kept at bay by police and private security guards. 'About 200 persons, mostly reporters and photographers, managed to enter a parking lot adjoining the cemetery, where they climbed on cars and boxes to try to see over the cemetery wall,' wrote Florabel Muir in the *Daily News*. 'Another 50 or so watched from the top floor of a new building going up across the street.'[2] Joan Greenson, who attended with her parents, recalled the sound of camera shutters and motor drives being so loud that it drowned out normal conversation. The service, led by Lutheran Minister A. J. Soldan, was non-denominational Christian – even though Marilyn had regarded herself to be an atheist Jew since her marriage to Arthur Miller, who chose not to attend ('to join what I knew would be a circus of cameras and shouts and luridness was beyond my strength,' he said).[3] The reverend read Psalm 23 and based his sermon on the reworked quotation from Psalm 139, 'How fearfully and wonderfully she was made by the Creator.' During the service, the organist played 'Over the Rainbow' from the 1939 film *The Wizard of Oz*.

Marilyn, dressed in a green Pucci sheath dress, lay in an open, satin-lined casket at the front of the chapel. Her trusted make-up artist Allan 'Whitey' Snyder did his best to make her look presentable. Years before – when Marilyn had been shooting the 1953 film *Gentlemen Prefer Blondes* – the star had said to him, 'If anything happens to me, promise me you'll make me up.' Snyder had jokingly replied, 'Sure, bring the body back while it is still warm and I'll do it,' and in the same spirit of jest Marilyn gave him a Tiffany gold money clip engraved with the words, 'Whitey Dear:/While I'm still warm/Marilyn'.[4]

Lee Strasberg – in a shaky, uncertain voice – began his eulogy with the words, 'Marilyn Monroe was a legend. In her own lifetime she created a myth of what a poor girl from a deprived background could attain. For the entire world she became a symbol of the eternal feminine.' However, he said he did not want to talk about that Marilyn Monroe, the public image; today he wanted to address Marilyn, his friend and colleague. She was, he said, 'a warm human being, impulsive and shy, sensitive and in fear of rejection, yet ever avid for life and reaching out for fulfilment'. He talked of her talents, her sensitivities, her ambitions, her appeal. 'Others were as physically beautiful as she was, but there was obviously something more in her, something that people saw and recognized in her performances, and with which they identified,' he said. 'She had a luminous quality – a combination of wistfulness, radiance, yearning – that set her apart and yet made everyone wish to be part of it, to share in the childish naïveté which was at once so shy and yet so vibrant.'

He regretted that the public would never see her on stage; he had no doubt that she would have proved herself to be one of the greatest theatrical actresses of the time. 'I cannot say goodbye,' he said, only just managing to get his words out. 'Marilyn never liked goodbyes. But in the peculiar way she had of turning things around so that they faced reality – I will say au revoir. For the country to which she has gone, we must all some day visit.'[5]

At the end of the prayers, Inez Melson bent over the casket and 'showered the face of the dead woman with kisses and tears'.[6] When Joe DiMaggio approached the coffin he was broken with grief, and as he kissed the body of his former wife he whispered, 'I love you, I love you, I love you.'[7] Sitting at the front of the chapel, Joan Greenson recalled seeing a strand of blonde hair fall from the open casket. Her parents were led forward to pay their last respects, but Joan did not want to look at her friend's body in the coffin, instead choosing to remember her in her prime.

In New York, Norman and Hedda Rosten and a small group of people who had known Marilyn opened a bottle of Dom Pérignon in her honour. 'It seemed right, and she seemed to be with us,' wrote Rosten to Dr Greenson. Rosten also told his friend of a phone conversation Marilyn had had with Hedda, in which she told her that the Strasbergs were trying to persuade her to step away from Dr Greenson's therapy and, instead, '"work out" her problems' through acting, and 'that analysis would hurt her creatively'. He recalled the pact he'd once made with Marilyn about how, if one of them was feeling suicidal, they would reach out for support from the other. 'I believed her promise, yes I did, but she fooled me and I'm still shaking my head over it,' he wrote. '(I'm angry.)'[8]

Dr Greenson was left devastated by the loss. 'It's still so hard to believe that we will never see her again,' he wrote to Rosten on 15 August. 'She was always so lively and I guess that makes it so difficult to believe that she is anything more than absent temporarily.' He detailed the events of that last weekend, and the fall-out from Marilyn's death, including the barrage of vicious letters he received accusing him of being a murderer or a coward, before concluding, 'There are some things in life you never get over and I know I will never get over this ... I'm sure the cranks will stop their yammering, the phoneys will stop their exhibitionist glorification and self pity, and a few [of us] will feel sad for her, sad because we miss her and sad because we wanted her to have a chance to live and to laugh and to find joy.'[9]

From England, Marianne Kris – who was staying with her friend Anna Freud in Walberswick, Suffolk – wrote to Dr Greenson expressing her sadness at the news of Marilyn's death. Although Kris felt guilty for referring such a difficult patient as Marilyn to him, and acknowledged the enormous emotional and psychological burden the therapy involved, she also said she was satisfied that she had made the right decision: Dr Greenson was the only psychotherapist she knew of with the right balance of humanity and wisdom to treat her. 'I have the feeling that even if the pills would not have taken effect so rapidly and she could have been saved this time, another impulse towards self-destruction was bound to come, and bound to succeed eventually,' she wrote.[10]

97

The battle over Marilyn's memoir

It didn't take long for there to be a revival of interest in Marilyn's memoir, which had been gathering dust since the fall-out with ghostwriter Ben Hecht. A few weeks after her death, the US publishing company Doubleday once again registered its interest. On 23 September 1962, Hecht's wife Rose wrote to lawyer friend Gregson Bautzer and asked him to look at some old contracts that she could study before agreeing to a new Doubleday deal. But nothing came of the proposed book and the Hechts tried to forget the debacle; Ben, before his death in 1964, described the saga as 'the longest series of log jams I've ever run into'.[1]

Things then went quiet on the memoir front until July 1973 when Norman Mailer's 'biography' hit the shelves. Light on research, Mailer questioned the authenticity of the 1954 *Empire News* series, labelling the articles a 'prodigiously factoidal enterprise ... Hecht was never a writer to tell the truth when a concoction could put life in his prose.'[2] The controversy generated by Mailer's book revived interest in Marilyn's memoir. Rose Hecht received a letter from a New York law firm asking her to sign a quitclaim, renouncing all rights to the Marilyn book. William Fitelson, one of the partners, informed her that his client Milton H. Greene owned the rights, a statement Rose dismissed with the words scrawled on the letter, 'BIG LIE'. The lawyer outlined how, in return for signing the quitclaim, Milton Greene would not use the name Ben Hecht in connection with the book; next to this, Rose wrote, 'WHY would I – For what consideration.'

Fitelson wrote another legal letter in January 1974, which she ignored.[3]

On 8 April 1974, Sol Stein, president of the publisher Stein & Day, held a press conference at the Beverly Hills Hotel – one of the locations where Marilyn had sat down with Ben Hecht to relate the details of her life – to announce the publication of Marilyn's 'new-found' memoir, *My Story*. He described the news as 'the book story of the year, maybe the decade'. But when, five days later, the *Los Angeles Times* revealed to him that the memoir he had bought from Milton Greene for $25,000 contained almost exactly the same material as the extracts that had run in the *Empire News* back in 1954, he appeared shocked. 'This could be very serious,' said Stein. 'I have 50,000 copies of this book being published . . . Perhaps the only omission might be an "as told to" credit, if, in fact, anyone can prove that Ben Hecht was involving in the writing . . . How would I know to look in a defunct . . . newspaper? . . . If Ben Hecht were alive I would call him up and ask him if he wrote it.'[4]

The ghost may have been dead, but his widow was very much alive – and still full of fighting spirit. In June 1974, following the publication of *My Story*, Rose Hecht invited a *New York Post* journalist into her Central Park West duplex with the intention of setting the record straight. Although Sol Stein may have believed that the book was 'an original manuscript', the truth, according to Rose, was that 'Benny sweated and toiled for months working on that autobiography . . . But he never got a penny of the money.' She did not believe the claim put forward by Milton Greene that Marilyn had simply given him copyright of the material as a gift at the beginning of their three-year business partnership. 'Here, this is for you,' she is supposed to have said. 'I know you'll do the right thing with it.' Greene claimed he then kept the manuscript in a safe until he realised the time was right for publication. 'There is no power on earth that can make me believe Marilyn Monroe would give something like this away for nothing,' said Rose. 'She was squeezing Ben for every penny she could get out of the publishing rights we had sold. Moreover, she did not have a copy of the manuscript to give away. I have all of Benny's copies right here.'

Rose Hecht was sailing close to the wind. When Stein was contacted by the *Post*, he issued a statement threatening to sue to the tune of $2 million anybody who called into question the authenticity of the book. Rose, who was then seventy-six, said she did not have the resources – or the energy – to engage in a lengthy legal battle.[5] The *Post* followed up the story with an interview with Frank Delaney, the lawyer who, in 1955, had helped set up Marilyn Monroe Productions, the joint venture owned by the actress and Milton Greene. Delaney stated that the co-owners of the production company wanted the memoir to be 'a property of their corporation rather than something owned individually by Marilyn', so as to reduce her tax burden.[6] Yet Rose recognised a great deal of the material in *My Story*, although she believed that it was 'interlaced with a lot of pish-tosh'.[7] She went through a typescript, scribbling a series of barbed comments in the margins. For instance, in the first chapter, when Marilyn relates how her mother found her husband making love to another woman, the text reads, 'There was a big row, and her husband banged out of the flat.' Rose circled the phrases 'big row' and 'banged out', by which she added the handwritten annotation, '(this phrase suggests some English re-writer)'.[8] Although comments such as these have given rise to the claims that *My Story* is a work of fiction masquerading as memoir, documents from the archive of Ben Hecht lodged with the Newberry Library, Chicago, show that the book is a genuine transcript of Marilyn's narrated story.

There are occasions, however, when it's necessary to question the authorship of certain brief passages. One entry in particular stands out: in the 1954 newspaper serial, Marilyn relates how she was disappointed to learn that a producer who she thought was interested in her acting career only wanted to sleep with her. 'I walked through the door and out of the office where movie stars were made,' she writes. '"Maybe he's watching me," I thought. I mustn't let him see me upset.' However, in the published book there's additional material tagged onto the end of this that reads, 'I drove to my room in my car. Yes, there was something special about me, and I knew what it was. I was the kind of girl they found dead in a hall bedroom with an empty bottle of sleeping pills in her hand.'[9]

98

The mystery of Marilyn's possessions

The day after Marilyn's funeral, Inez Melson, her business manager, started to sort through the star's belongings at Fifth Helena Drive. Berniece Miracle, Marilyn's half-sister, recalled watching Melson burn papers in the fireplace, a task that took three days. 'We don't want the press to get hold of Marilyn's personal stuff,' said Inez. 'Some were important and had legal implications, and Inez sorted those out and kept them.'[1] Among the cache of papers, Melson discovered all the letters that Arthur Miller had sent Marilyn, letters which she said she did not read and which she duly returned to the playwright.

The public's desire to possess something – anything – that had once belonged to the star began soon after her death. A report filed with the probate court stated that there 'were mobs of curiosity seekers who came to the house, many of whom sought to buy or remove curios and memorabilia'.[2]

Under the terms of Marilyn's will, which she had made on 14 January 1961, the actress left her half-sister $10,000; she gave $5,000 to Hedda and Norman Rosten for the education of their daughter; she bequeathed the widow of her former acting coach, Michael Chekhov, $2,500 a year; she set aside $5,000 a year (from a $100,000 trust fund) for the care of her mother Gladys Baker, who was still a patient at Rockhaven Sanitarium in Glendale, California, and who would live until 1984; she left $10,000 to former secretary May Reis, plus an additional 25 per cent of the balance (an amount not to exceed $40,000); and to Dr Marianne

Kris she gave another 25 per cent of the balance to be used for the benefit of a psychiatric institution of her choice (this is the bequest that eventually went to the Anna Freud Centre in London). However, the bulk of the estate – 50 per cent – Marilyn left to Lee Strasberg, plus her 'personal effects and clothing ... [to be distributed] among my friends, colleagues and those to whom I am devoted'.

The will was admitted to probate on 30 October 1962, with an estate valued at a reported $1 million. Inez Melson must have been thoughtful that Marilyn – whom she had served loyally since 1951 – did not leave her a cent. Indeed, Melson wrote in a letter to Joe DiMaggio that she was 'very suspicious of that will'.[3] Mrs Melson, who served as a special administrator, tried to bring a legal challenge, alleging that Marilyn had been under the influence of either Lee Strasberg or Marianne Kris, or perhaps both of them, when she wrote the will. But the objection was thrown out.

Perhaps this is what inspired the behaviour that came later. In 1963, at the sale of some of Marilyn's belongings, Melson bought one of her two filing cabinets, both of which were still filled with the star's personal papers. But instead of using her own name, Melson registered for the sale under the name of her nephew, Walter Davis. Later, she also acquired the second filing cabinet, a brown one. These – together with some of Marilyn's other belongings such as dresses, hats, furs, jewellery, handbags, even a bronze Rodin sculpture – remained in Mrs Melson's possession until her death in July 1985. She had returned a few items to the Monroe estate, such as dresses designed by Jean Louis and the Rodin statue, but kept the filing cabinets and their contents.

After Melson's death, the full filing cabinets passed first to her sister-in-law Ruth Conroy, and then to her son Millington 'Mill' Conroy. The 'perfume and cosmetics salesman' wasn't quite sure what to do with the stash of treasures from Marilyn's filing cabinets, but he knew they were valuable.[4] He also believed he had a legal right to dispose of them, because he assumed that Mrs Melson had been the rightful owner of the archive. In May 1994, he organised for a sale of over sixty lots of Marilyn's possessions with the California-based Odyssey Auctions. However, on 12 May, the auction house was served with a legal action that resulted in the withdrawal from sale of all the items.

At the heart of the resulting legal battle was the issue of ownership. The Monroe estate was now controlled not by Lee Strasberg, who had died in February 1982, but by his widow, the Venezuelan actress Anna Mizrahi, whom he had married in 1967, the year after the death of Paula. Since her husband's death, Anna, who was thirty-eight years younger than Lee, had built up the Monroe estate into a highly profitable business: she launched a licensing company in 1982 and, with the help of a Los Angeles lawyer, she went on to open a Marilyn Monroe boutique at Bloomingdale's in New York, introduce a range of Marilyn dolls, coffee mugs and T-shirts, and broker print and television advertising tie-ins with big brands such as Revlon and Absolut Vodka. 'Anna thinks about and handles Ms. Monroe's image from the moment she wakes up,' said one of her attorneys.[5]

So it wasn't surprising that Anna Strasberg was determined to come down hard on the Odyssey Auctions sale. She knew the importance and value of the documents from the filing cabinets. 'This archive represents the ultimate offering of Marilyn Monroe material ever to be offered anywhere, at any time,' boasted the sale catalogue. 'The collection, which belonged to a close Monroe associate [Inez Melson], has been stored away for over thirty years and never before viewed by the public.'[6] Anna also believed that as Lee Strasberg's widow – under the terms of Marilyn's will – she was the rightful owner of everything on sale. After the auction house withdrew the Marilyn lots, years of legal wrangling followed.

In 1989, annual revenue from the Monroe estate was $1.1

million, a figure that had increased to $17 million by 2014. In January 2011, Anna sold her 75 per cent stake in the estate to the Authentic Brands Group for an estimated $20 million to $30 million (the company also owns the likeness rights to Elvis Presley and Muhammad Ali). Some of the products bearing Marilyn's image were in questionable taste: there was a Napa Valley red wine branded a 'Marilyn Merlot'; there were lottery cards featuring her dress from *The Seven Year Itch* (a scratch of the panels would reveal the prizes); and a Marilyn novelty telephone in the form of a likeness of the star – when the phone rang her skirt flew above her head. Today it's even possible to buy a Marilyn Monroe vibrator – 'Womanizer honors the icon Marilyn Monroe with an elegant, joyful tribute – an indulgent clitoral stimulator for the free-spirited'.[7]

Although Lee Strasberg had been sentimental about the possessions he inherited from Marilyn, it seems Anna did not feel the same. Over two days in October 1999, she organised an epic sale of the star's personal property at Christie's in New York, an auction that netted $13.4 million. Here you could pick up the platinum and diamond eternity band that Joe DiMaggio bought Marilyn, which had an estimate of between $30,000 and $50,000 (final price: $772,500). Or the star's hand-knitted cardigan that she wore for her famous last sitting with photographer George Barris in the summer of 1962 (estimate: $30,000–$50,000; final price: $167,500). There were annotated scripts, poems, books, tableware, glasses, furniture, shoes, hats, jewellery, furs, bikinis, make-up; as well as the star items such as the dress she wore to sing 'Happy Birthday' to President Kennedy, and the white piano from her childhood. The opportunity to buy a slice of Marilyn delighted many fans. 'There are many people who admire Marilyn and love her,' said Anna Strasberg before her death in January 2024 at the age of eighty-four. 'Whatever their reasons, all they want is to feel close to her with whichever memento they possess.'[8] Yet some fans and commentators were saddened that this extraordinary collection was being broken up. Marilyn, in her will, stipulated that Lee Strasberg could distribute her possessions among her friends, but the auction meant that, as fan James Haspiel said, the objects she loved were bought by 'anyone with the right money'.[9]

There were others, too, who had their own particular grievances. 'Marilyn Monroe, who was not so unreasonably paranoid about strangers, now belonged to them,' Susan Strasberg, who received nothing in her father's will, told a journalist in 2003.[10] Her brother John was equally damning. 'I find it fundamentally sad that people who never knew Marilyn continue to want to profit from her, and in the lowest form possible.'[11]

99

FAKE OR FORTUNE?

In September 1997, news spread that a huge story was about to break. Pulitzer Prize-winning investigative journalist Seymour Hersh had what appeared to be the scoop of the century on his hands: documentary proof that John F. Kennedy and Marilyn Monroe had had an affair. The 'evidence', uncovered for Hersh's new book *The Dark Side of Camelot*, included a contract drawn up between the president and the actress to pay Marilyn's mother $600,000 in exchange for Marilyn's silence about their affair, and another document that proved JFK's secret ties to mob boss Sam Giancana.

However, just as Hersh – who was known for his exposé of the My Lai massacre in Vietnam as well as investigations about the CIA, Henry Kissinger and Richard Nixon – was checking the book before it went to press, he discovered that the stash of documents he had in his possession were forgeries. The ABC programme *20/20* was also set to air an exclusive about the revelations. The documents had been forged – in a blatant exercise to make a huge amount of money – by the grandly named Lawrence X. Cusack III, known as Lex, whose father Lawrence X. Cusack had been a well-known New York lawyer, and had once represented the Monroe estate.

The seed of the fraudulent enterprise had its roots back in 1986, when a woman approached Lex Cusack claiming to be the long-lost daughter of Marilyn Monroe. He dismissed her allegations as nonsense, but was intrigued enough to examine the files kept by his father. By 1993, Lex, who had trained as an artist and draftsman but worked as a paralegal, claimed to have uncovered nearly 350 documents supposedly written by JFK which he then sold – via a middleman, Tom Cloud – to a group of investors for between $6 million and $7 million. In 1994, Seymour Hersh, researching his new book on the Kennedys, heard a rumour about the documents and contacted Lex Cusack. 'The Marilyn contracts are obvious dynamite,' Hersh wrote to Lex on 14 April 1995, but the journalist refused to pay for information. 'We must be holier than the Pope,' he said. In order to gain access to the documents, Hersh argued that if he were able to place the documents within their appropriate historical context then the archive would shoot up in value. 'I'm a newspaperman,' said Hersh during the case. 'You go after stories. That's a great story.'[1]

But just as Hersh's book was going through production, and as *20/20* was about to air, forensic expert Jerry Richards declared Cusack's documents to be fake. There were some tell-tale signs: for instance, one document that was supposed to have been written in 1961 bore a ZIP code, but these were not introduced until two years later. Instead of cancelling the *20/20* special, the ABC executives turned the story on its head and made it about the forgery rather than the JFK–Marilyn revelations.

In May 1999, Lex Cusack was found guilty of thirteen counts of forgery at a court in Manhattan. George Spencer, foreman of the jury, concluded, 'It was the dollar signs – period. Obviously people wanted to believe this stuff. It was the cash cow.' The court heard evidence from the prosecution that proved beyond doubt the fraudulent nature of the archive: one of the documents that was 'signed' by Marilyn Monroe and JFK at the Carlyle Hotel in 1960 also bore the signature of Janet Des Rosiers, one of Kennedy's secretaries – but she testified that she had never seen it. Another piece of paper carried the words – in JFK's handwriting – 'Secretary of Education' but this department had not been created at the time.

Although Hersh was criticised by some for gullibility, he maintained that he had been repeatedly assured that JFK's handwriting was genuine – he had had independent handwriting experts carry out detailed analysis. Most importantly, he argued, none of the faked papers were used in his book. 'I got excited by it,' he said. 'I checked it out, found out it wasn't good and went on. That's what I do for a living.'[2]

Perhaps it was Hersh's bad experience with the fake Monroe–JFK documents that made him reluctant to get involved when Millington Conroy – the man who had inherited 'his' Marilyn possessions (including the two filing cabinets) from his mother – approached him to write a foreword to a proposed book, with accompanying images taken by photographer Mark Anderson. Hersh met Conroy and Anderson, but told them he was busy. In 2006, Anderson, still looking for someone to write the foreword, approached Anthony Summers, who had interviewed both Inez Melson and Ruth Conroy in the 1980s. Anderson then put Summers in touch with Millington Conroy, who told the biographer, 'The truth is my mother only showed you one of the two filing cabinets.' Summers was informed that the contents of Marilyn's secret filing cabinets included six letters from the Kennedy brothers, a note from Sam Giancana, one hundred sealed envelopes, Marilyn's doodles, as well as letters from Joe DiMaggio and T. S. Eliot.

'I knew Inez Melson had worked for Monroe, I knew she'd kept at least one filing cabinet, and I knew it had contained some interesting material,' remembered Summers, whose book on Marilyn had been published years before. 'So I thought to myself, "It looks like I'm going to have to get myself out to LA, then, doesn't it?"' Although he'd been lured to California with the promise of the JFK letters, after flying on 29 July 2006 he was told that the documents had gone missing. Not only that but the letters supposedly written by T. S. Eliot turned out to be ones penned by Marilyn's friend, the poet Norman Rosten (who signed notes to Marilyn with the name 'T. S. Eliot' in a spirit of ironic jest).[3]

Summers withdrew from the project, so Conroy and Anderson turned to academic and Marilyn Monroe researcher Lois Banner. 'I knew I wanted to be involved,' said Banner. 'What I saw in them [the photographs of her possessions] was a kind of aesthetic beauty that could help put Marilyn into a realm where she would be honored and respected.' Banner was amazed by the extent of the collection from the two filing cabinets – there were thousands of items in the private archive – and the way it reflected the myriad aspects of Marilyn's complex personality. 'This shows us Marilyn Monroe living her life, one day at a time,' she said. 'It shows us different sides of Marilyn that are not in the biographies. It adds depth and understanding of who she was as a private person.'

Yet the more Anderson got involved, the more he became suspicious of Millington Conroy, who had told him that he had won the 1994 case brought by Anna Strasberg. On 4 September 2007, Anderson took a trip to the Los Angeles Superior Court Archives & Records Center, where he discovered that Conroy had lost the 1994 case. 'I felt like going over there and just doing something bad to him,' said Anderson. 'I know martial arts, I hold several belts.' Anderson was so furious with Conroy that he wrote an anonymous letter to David Strasberg, Anna's son, telling him what had happened. He also informed Lois Banner of his suspicions, and she made contact with the Strasbergs.

'David Strasberg went around to Mill's house with two lawyers,' recalled Anderson, 'and apparently Mill was upset and kept saying, "I don't know why Mark and Lois did this to me. I'd never sell! Why would I do that?" It was really funny, because there was a little note in his handwriting on the back of a white envelope that said, "Sell to [autograph dealer] Todd Mueller for 3 million."'[4] On 25 October 2007, the Monroe estate sued Conroy, seeking the return of objects in his possession. A few days later, it was reported that 'a significant collection' of the star's personal property had been moved to a secure location and it was said both parties were confident they could come to a settlement.[5]

The proposed book about Marilyn's private archive, so long in the making, was finally published in 2011. In the preface to *MM – Personal*, Lois Banner reported how Anna Strasberg had told her that one day she would like the Marilyn collection to be placed in a proper museum. In her last interview with Richard Meryman for *Life* magazine in the summer of 1962, Marilyn had said, 'There aren't really any kind of monuments or museums [in Hollywood] ... Nobody left anything behind.'[6] Over the next decade, items from the collection came up for sale again. As a result, the things Marilyn held so dear are now scattered all around the world in private collections.

100

A CONSTANT HAUNTING

If there's a place that would have made the perfect home for Marilyn's personal belongings, it is the Academy Museum of Motion Pictures in Los Angeles. Opened in 2021, and housed in a building designed by Renzo Piano, it holds more than thirteen million objects relating to the film industry. Here you can see Judy Garland's ruby slippers from *The Wizard of Oz*; a cape worn by Bela Lugosi in *Dracula* from 1931; and the typewriter used to write the screenplay of *Psycho*.

The Academy Museum is the sister organisation of the Margaret Herrick Library, only five minutes' drive away, which holds the archives of many of the directors who worked with Marilyn: John Huston, George Cukor, Jean Negulesco and Billy Wilder. It would have been the best place for her papers, which are now dispersed. However, the library houses hundreds of taped interviews with Marilyn's friends, lovers and colleagues, carried out by biographers Donald Spoto and Anthony Summers. There are also some recordings of Marilyn talking. One of these is particularly poignant, the interview she gave to Richard Meryman for *Life* magazine, which hit the newsstands the weekend of her death.

The subject of the interview was fame, which Marilyn compared to caviar; it was lovely to have, she said, but not every damned day. 'It might be a kind of relief to be finished,' she reflected. 'You have to start all over again. But I believe you're always as good as your potential. I now live in my work and in a few relationships with the few people I can really count on. Fame will go by, and, so long,

I've had you fame. If it goes by, I've always known it was fickle. So at least it's something I experienced, but that's not where I live.'[1]

Yet with each passing year, Marilyn's fame seems to grow. Her image continues to haunt our culture. The life story of 'the Love Goddess of the Nuclear Age', as she was dubbed by Clare Boothe Luce in 1964, is told and retold.[2] She is on the airwaves and on streaming services: Elton John singing goodbye to Norma Jeane in 'Candle in the Wind'; The Kinks in 'Celluloid Heroes' warning sightseers to the Hollywood Walk of Fame not to step on Marilyn's hand and feet prints; Madonna dropping her name in 'Vogue'.

She is around us, reproduced, reinterpreted, reborn. She is there in the hundreds of thousands of images that were taken of her by the most famous photographers of her day. 'The first day a photographer took a picture of her, she was a genius,' said Billy Wilder.[3] More than sixty years on from her death, celebrities still reference her in shoots for magazines, music videos, television shows: from Christina Aguilera to Gwen Stefani, Drew Barrymore to Beyoncé, Miley Cyrus to Nicole Kidman, Lindsay Lohan and Kylie Minogue. She is featured in films, fashion spreads, advertising, novels, poetry, opera, video games and plays.

Artists such as Willem de Kooning, Douglas Gordon, Barbara Kruger, Peter Blake, Christo, Audrey Flack, Richard Hamilton, Allen Jones, Cindy Sherman, Claes Oldenburg and Richard Serra have all used Marilyn's image in their works. At Tate Britain, you can see her in Pauline Boty's 1963 *The Only Blonde in the World*, which shows Marilyn wearing a white dress from *Some Like It Hot*, running down a colourless street or a studio lot, imprisoned in what looks like a strip of film that is sandwiched by the vibrant green of the rest of the canvas. In Andy Warhol's silkscreen portraits, she is there in repeated form, her make-up garish, her blonde hair exaggerated – his 1964 *Shot Sage Blue Marilyn* sold for $195 million in 2022. Salvador Dalí, at his personal museum in Figueres, Spain, reconstructed Marilyn's individual features – her red lips, her blonde hair, her sultry eyes – into a three-dimensional room, its femininity so excessive it approaches the hyper-real realm of the drag queen. At the V&A's 'Diva' exhibition (London, 2023–24) Marilyn's form – wearing the dress from *The Seven Year Itch* – watched over the show like a colossus. In Palm Springs, there is *Forever Marilyn*, a highly controversial, 26-foot-tall statue; here she is again wearing the same iconic dress, but the sculpture taps into lower instincts – spectators are invited to walk under her skirts and look upwards.

Marilyn's movies play on a constant loop, in cinemas, on television, inside our heads. She is still, many years after her death, the 'supernova of American postwar celebrities against which all others are measured'.[4]

Marilyn is forever sashaying through the Grunion Detective Agency, with Groucho Marx raising his eyes to the sky, mouthing, 'Some men are following me,' in *Love Happy*.

She is standing in Margo Channing's (Bette Davis) home in *All About Eve*, looking across the room at an ugly male producer with whom she has to flirt in order to further her career – 'Why do they always look like unhappy rabbits?' she asks.

She's pulling her tongue out in defiance at her bad-tempered boss in *As Young as You Feel*.

She's sitting behind a desk as secretary Lois Laurel in *Monkey Business* telling scientist Dr Fulton, played by Cary Grant, that her boss 'has been complaining about my punctuation, so I'm careful to get here before nine'.

She is the psychologically disturbed Nell Forbes in *Don't Bother to Knock*, catatonic as she walks through the hotel lobby, stopping by a razor blade stand as she contemplates ending her life.

She's walking towards the bell tower in *Niagara*, swinging her hips, a brief smile of triumph on her face.

Dressed in a fuchsia-pink gown and gloves nearly up to her shoulders, she sings about diamonds being a girl's best friend in *Gentlemen Prefer Blondes*.

She is the extremely short-sighted and vain Pola Debevoise in *How to Marry a Millionaire* who would rather walk into a wall than wear her glasses.

She is forever 'The Girl', wearing a white halter dress, looking almost like a swan, standing over the subway grille, wind blowing her skirts up around her in *The Seven Year Itch*.

She is Cherie in *Bus Stop*, wearing make-up as white as a performer in Kabuki theatre, talking about love and what she wants from a man: 'Maybe I don't know what love is. I want a guy I can look up to and admire. But I don't want him to browbeat me. I want a guy who'll be sweet with me. But I don't want him to baby me either! I just gotta feel that whoever I marry has some real regard for me – aside from all that lovin' stuff. You know what I mean?'

She will be forever known as Sugar Kane in *Some Like It Hot* – strumming her ukulele, singing 'I Wanna Be Loved By You', and saying lines like, 'I'm tired of getting the fuzzy end of the lollipop.'

She is there in *The Misfits* – surrounded by the expanse of an empty desert – screaming into the wind, venting her fury against the men responsible for the sick world in which she lives. 'Murderers! You're liars! All of you, liars! You're only happy when you can see something die!'

And she is there in the ghostly fragments of her final, and unreleased, film *Something's Got to Give*, in which she plays a woman who comes back from the dead. Her character, Ellen, a photographer, has been lost at sea in the Pacific for five years, but unknown to her family has just been rescued. When she returns home she sees her two children, who don't recognise her. 'I used to come here a long time ago,' she explains to them, looking longingly at the children. Later, at night, she takes her clothes off and swims naked in the family's pool. Her laugh is high-pitched, and as she swims to the side, the light glistening on the water, she says, 'Come on in – the water's so refreshing.'

It's easy to imagine Marilyn still swimming in her own kidney-shaped pool at Fifth Helena Drive, her laugh dancing off the water. Or perhaps she's there inside the house, lounging on the bed, talking on the telephone, whispering into the receiver.

For some, it's not such an outlandish idea. 'I believe that she was very close to us,' said Ana de Armas, who portrayed Marilyn in *Blonde*, the 2022 Netflix movie that used Marilyn's Brentwood home as a filming location. 'She was with us ... Being in the same places that she was, filming in her house, it was a very strong sensation. There was something in the air.' The actress told a press conference at the Venice Film Festival that when the spirit of Marilyn was unhappy with one of the sequences being shot she would manifest herself in spirit form and make something fly off the wall.[5]

It's no surprise that because Marilyn's life was cut short, we will always want to imagine the possibilities for the time she had left, dream up the movies she might have made, muse over the loves she might have experienced. She inspires, she arouses, she transfixes, she mesmerises, she brings us together, she divides us: aspects of her biography fuel heated debates. Above all, she continues to make us feel.

Towards the end of his life, director John Huston was asked about Marilyn's continuing appeal. Why did interest in her endure? What did this mean, both for him and for the public? He paused and then replied, 'Well, simply that she's still *alive*.'[6]

Notes

AS: Anthony Summers
MHL: Lois Banner collection on Marilyn Monroe, Margaret Herrick Library, Academy of Motion Picture Arts and Sciences, Los Angeles
HRC: Harry Ransom Center, The University of Texas at Austin

Introduction

1. Interview with Jane Russell, AS, MHL.
2. Interview with Marion Marshall, AS, MHL.
3. Interview with William Travilla, AS, MHL.
4. *Marilyn Monroe: The Biography*, Donald Spoto, Chatto & Windus, London, 1993, p. 674.
5. *Marilyn Monroe*, Maurice Zolotow, updated and expanded edition, Perennial Library, Harper & Row, New York, 1990, p.9, first edition published 1960 by Harcourt, Brace & Company.
6. *Conversations with Marilyn*, W. J. Weatherby, Mason/Charter, New York, 1976, p. 55.
7. *Orlando, A Biography*, Virginia Woolf, Harcourt, Brace & Company, New York, 1928, p. 309.
8. *Conversations with Marilyn*, p. 228.

Chapter 1

1. *Marilyn Monroe: The Biography*, p. 356.
2. Interview with Joan Greenson, AS, MHL.
3. *Nobody's Perfect: Billy Wilder, A Personal Biography*, Charlotte Chandler, Simon & Schuster, New York, 2002, p. 10.
4. Interview notes with Billy Wilder, AS archive, MHL.

Chapter 2

1 *Conversations with Wilder*, Cameron Crowe, Alfred A. Knopf, New York, 1999, p. 165.
2 Marilyn's interview with Georges Belmont, originally published in French in *Marie Claire*, 1960, included in *Marilyn Monroe and the Camera*, Schirmer Art Books, Schirmer/Mosel Verlag GmbH, Munich, 1989, p. 10.
3 *The Unabridged Marilyn*, Randall Riese and Neal Hitchens, Corgi Books, London, 1988, p. 197, originally published 1987.
4 *The Unabridged Marilyn*, p. 487.
5 *Before Marilyn: The Blue Book Modelling Years*, Astrid Franse and Michelle Morgan, The History Press, Stroud, 2015, p. 86.
6 *The Marilyn Encyclopedia*, Adam Victor, Overlook Press, Woodstock, New York, 1999, p. 135.
7 'George Masters, Hair Stylist, Makeup Expert to the Stars', *Los Angeles Times*, Myrna Oliver, 21 April 1998.
8 *The Unabridged Marilyn*, p. 197.
9 'The Things She Left Behind', *Vanity Fair*, Sam Kashner, October 2008.
10 *The Legend of Marilyn Monroe*, documentary directed by Terry Sanders, 1966.
11 'The 1951 Model Blonde', *Collier's*, Robert Cahn, 8 September 1951.

Chapter 3

1 *The Many Loves of Marilyn Monroe*, E! True Hollywood Story, 2001.
2 'Marilyn Monroe: My Story – Uncensored', *Empire News*, 9 May 1954.
3 *Marilyn Monroe*, Zolotow, 1960, p. 26.
4 *The Legend of Marilyn Monroe*.
5 *Marilyn: An Untold Story*, Norman Rosten, New American Library, New York, 1973, p 22.
6 Interview with Christopher Isherwood, AS, MHL.
7 *Conversations with Marilyn*, p. 146.

Chapter 4

1. *Timebends: A Life*, Arthur Miller, Methuen, London, 1987, p. 415.

Chapter 5

1. Georges Belmont interview, Marilyn Monroe and the Camera, p. 9.
2. *The Legend of Marilyn Monroe*.
3. *Norma Jean: The Life of Marilyn Monroe*, Fred Lawrence Guiles, McGraw-Hill, New York, 1969, p. 25.
4. *Dream Girl: The Making of Marilyn Monroe*, directed by Ian Ayres, 2022.
5. 'To Aristophanes & Back', *Time*, Brad Darrach, 14 May 1956.
6. *Marilyn: Her Life in Her Own Words*, George Barris, Headline, London, 1995, p. 13.
7. *My Sister Marilyn: A Memoir of Marilyn Monroe*, Berniece Baker Miracle and Mona Rae Miracle, Algonquin Books, Chapel Hill, 1994, p. 12.
8. 'Marilyn Monroe: My Story – Uncensored'.
9. *My Sister Marilyn*, p. 16.

Chapter 6

1. Cursum Perficio: http://www.cursumperficio.net/G8Updated2023.eng.html
2. Georges Belmont interview, *Marilyn Monroe and the Camera*, p. 10.
3. 'Rewriting History: Marilyn Monroe and Stanley Gifford', *All Things Marilyn* podcast, 23 November 2022.
4. *My Sister Marilyn*, p. 177.
5. *My Story*, Marilyn Monroe, Stein and Day, New York, 1974, p. 12. Copyright Milton H. Greene.
6. Norma Jeane Dougherty, Letter to Grace Goddard, 14 September 1942, Bonhams, Los Angeles, Manuscripts from the Estate of Charles Williamson & Tucker Fleming, 20 April 2011, lot 521.
7. *Icon: The Life, Times, and Films of Marilyn Monroe: Volume 1, 1926 to 1956*, Gary Vitacco-Robles, BearManor Media, Albany, Kindle edition: https://read.amazon.co.uk/kp/kshare?asin=B00WPVT4G8&id=leo5sbtc6vhthoatokulpsfefm

8 *My Years With Marilyn Monroe*, Natasha Lytess, as told to Jane Wilkie, p. 9, Maurice Zolotow Collection, Harry Ransom Center, The University of Texas at Austin.
9 *My Years with Marlyn Monroe*, p. 10.
10 Letter from Ralph Roberts to Anthony Summers, summer 1984, AS archive.
11 'Star Solves Mystery of Marilyn Monroe's Missing Father', *The Star*, 24 November 1987, Anthony Summers.
12 'Marilyn Monroe's Hair and "Falsies" Are Being Auctioned By Former Funeral Home Employee', *artnet*, Amah-Rose Abrams, 15 August 2015, https://news.artnet.com/art-world/marilyn-monroes-hair-falsies-auctioned-former-funeral-home-employee-322754
13 'Marilyn Monroe could still be alive if she hadn't been rejected by her dad, niece says', *Daily Mirror*, Graeme Culliford, 6 August 2022.
14 Interview with Henry Rosenfeld, AS, MHL.
15 Letter from Dr Ralph Greenson to Dr Marianne Kris, 20 August 1962, AS archive.

Chapter 7

1 *Marilyn: Her Life in Her Own Words*, pp. 4–5.
2 *Marilyn Monroe*, Zolotow, 1960, p. 8.
3 'Marilyn Monroe: My Story – Uncensored'.

Chapter 8

1 *Marilyn Monroe*, Zolotow, 1960, p. 11.
2 *Marilyn: Her Life in Her Own Words*, p. 11.
3 'The 1951 Model Blonde'.
4 *Fragments: Poems, Intimate Notes, Letters*, Marilyn Monroe, ed. Stanley Buchthal and Bernard Comment, HarperCollins, London, 2010, pp. 52–3.
5 *Fragments*, p. 101.

Chapter 9

1. 'Marilyn Monroe: My Story – Uncensored'.
2. *Marilyn Monroe: Private and Undisclosed*, Michelle Morgan, Carroll & Graf, New York, 2007, p. 17.
3. *Marilyn Monroe: Private and Undisclosed*, p. 19.
4. 'To Aristophanes & Back'.
5. *Marilyn Monroe: Private and Undisclosed*, p. 18.
6. 'The New Marilyn Monroe', *Saturday Evening Post*, Pete Martin, 5 May 1956.
7. *Marilyn: Her Life in Her Own Words*, p. 25.
8. *Marilyn Monroe: Private and Undisclosed*, p. 19.
9. 'Marilyn Monroe: My Story – Uncensored'.
10. Letter from Harry Charles Wilson to Berniece Miracle, 15 August 1962, quoted in *MM – Personal: From the Private Archive of Marilyn Monroe*, Abrams, New York, 2011, p. 174.

Chapter 10

1. *The Secret Life of Marilyn Monroe*, J. Randy Taraborrelli, Grand Central Publishing, New York, p. 18.
2. *Marilyn Monroe: The Biography*, p. 4.
3. *No Magic Bullet: A Social History of Venereal Disease in the United States Since 1880*, Allan M. Brandt, Oxford University Press, New York, 1985, p. 9.
4. Email from Professor Khalil Ghanem to Andrew Wilson, 23 February 2024.
5. *Conversations with Marilyn*, p. 147.

Chapter 11

1. 'An Album of Film Stars', John Player & Sons, 1935, Margaret Herrick Library, Academy of Motion Picture Arts and Sciences, Core Collection Books.
2. *Marilyn Monroe: The Biography*, pp. 41–2.
3. *Marilyn Monroe*, Zolotow, 1960, p. 8.
4. *Body and Soul: Harlow and Monroe*, Alexander Walker, in *Marilyn*

Monroe: A Composite View, ed. Edward Wagenknecht, Chilton Book Co., Philadelphia, 1969, p. 150.
5 *The Marilyn Encyclopedia*, p. 136.
6 *Marilyn Monroe: The Biography*, p. 333.
7 'Ben Lyon, 78, Silent-Screen Star Who "Discovered" Marilyn Monroe', *New York Times*, 26 March 1979.
8 'My Wife Marilyn', *Life*, Arthur Miller, 22 December 1958.
9 Interview with Darrell Rooney, *All Things Marilyn* podcast, 10 October 2022.

Chapter 12

1 *My Story*, p. 13.
2 'This Is My Story', *Australian Women's Weekly*, Marilyn Monroe, 12 January 1955.
3 *My Story*, p. 14.
4 'The Alchemy of an Icon: Marilyn Monroe at Auction; The Piano She Took Everywhere Is No Longer So Humble', *New York Times*, Mitchell Owen, 26 September 1999.
5 The Personal Property of Marilyn Monroe, Christie's, New York, 1999, p 39.
6 *The Meaning of Mariah Carey*, Mariah Carey with Michaela Angela Davis, Kindle edition, 2020, p. 49.
7 'The Wit and Wisdom of Mariah Carey', *Observer*, Aaron Hicklin, 26 April 2014.
8 *The Meaning of Mariah Carey*, p. 49.
9 'Mariah Carey: Who are you calling a diva?', *Observer*, Elizabeth Day, 17 January 2010.
10 *Marilyn and Me*, p. 10.
11 Anthony Summers, Notes on Steffi Skolsky, 18 August 1983, AS archive.
12 *Marilyn Monroe*, Zolotow, 1960, p. 14.

Chapter 13

1 *Marilyn: Her Life in Her Own Words*, p. 15.
2 Letter from Grace McKee Goddard to Mrs Dewey, 4 December 1935,

Julien's Auctions: https://bid.juliensauctions.com/lot-details/index/catalog/316/lot/124046/MARILYN-MONROE-CHILDHOOD-ORPHANAGE-DOCUMENTS

3 Letter from Mrs Dewey to Grace McKee Goddard, 6 December 1935, Julien's Auctions: https://www.julienslive.com/lot-details/index/catalog/316/lot/124046?url=%2Fauctions%2Fcatalog%2Fid%2F316%3Fpage%3D4

CHAPTER 14

1 *My Story*, p. 21.
2 *The Last Days of Marilyn Monroe*, Donald Wolfe, Morrow, New York, 1998, p. 120.
3 'Marilyn Monroe – Why Won't They Let Her Rest in Peace?', *Parade, Dallas Times Herald*, Lloyd Shearer, 5 August 1973.
4 *Marilyn: A Biography*, Norman Mailer, Grosset & Dunlap, p. 41.
5 *Marilyn: A Biography*, p. 15.
6 *Marilyn: Her Life in Her Own Words*, pp. 23–4.
7 Interview with Peggy Feury, AS, MHL.
8 'To Aristophanes & Back'.
9 'My Romance with Marilyn Monroe', *People Weekly Magazine*, Brad Darrach, 2 July 1984.
10 *Marilyn: The Passion and the Paradox*, Lois Banner, Bloomsbury, London, 2012, p. 50.
11 *Marilyn: Her Life in Her Own Words*, p. 24.
12 'To Aristophanes & Back'.
13 'Star Secrets', *New Society*, Pamala Klein and Zsuzsanna Adler, 7 February 1986.
14 Letter from Dr Ralph Greenson to Anna Freud, 20 August 1962, Box 37, Folder 10, Anna Freud Papers, Library of Congress.

CHAPTER 15

1 Interview with Amy Greene, AS, MHL.
2 *Nobody's Perfect*, p. 219.
3 'I Was an Orphan', *Modern Screen*, Marilyn Monroe, February 1951.
4 *Marilyn Monroe: Private and Undisclosed*, p. 27.

5 *Dream Girl: The Making of Marilyn Monroe*.
6 *Googie's – Hollywood's Favorite Coffee Shop*, Steve Hayes, Sixgold Books, Kindle edition, 2012.
7 *Marilyn Monroe: The Biography*, p. 74.
8 'Taking It on Blonde Faith', *Los Angeles Times*, Robert W. Welkos, 23 March 2006.
9 *The Secret Happiness of Marilyn Monroe*, James Dougherty, Playboy Press, Chicago, 1976, p. 9.

Chapter 16

1 *Marilyn Monroe Confidential*, pp. 85–7.
2 *Marilyn: The Passion and the Paradox*, p. 9.
3 Interview with Lena Pepitone, AS, MHL.
4 *Marilyn: The Ultimate Look at the Legend*, James Haspiel, Henry Holt, New York, 1991, pp. 71–2.
5 Interview with Sheila Stewart Renour, AS, MHL.

Chapter 17

1 *Marilyn: Her Life in Her Own Words*, p. 16.
2 'To Aristophanes & Back'.
3 Interview with Kay Little, AS, MHL.
4 *The Secret Happiness of Marilyn Monroe*, p. 59.
5 *Marilyn: Her Life in Her Own Words*, p. 26.

Chapter 18

1 'Marilyn Monroe Was My Wife', *Photoplay*, James Dougherty, March 1953.
2 *The Secret Happiness of Marilyn Monroe*, p. 19.
3 *The Secret Happiness of Marilyn Monroe*, p. 21.
4 *The Secret Happiness of Marilyn Monroe*, p. 26.
5 *The Secret Happiness of Marilyn Monroe*, p. 30.
6 *The Secret Happiness of Marilyn Monroe*, p. 35.
7 *The Secret Happiness of Marilyn Monroe*, p. 37.
8 *Hollywood Greats: Marilyn Monroe*, BBC, 1979.

9 *The Secret Happiness of Marilyn Monroe*, pp. 51–2.
10 'At Sixteen I was a Frightened Bride', *Empire News*, Marilyn Monroe, 16 May 1954.
11 Ibid.
12 'To Aristophanes & Back'.
13 Letter from Norma Jeane to Grace Goddard, 15 June 1944, quoted in *Marilyn: The Ultimate Look at the Legend*, p. 12.
14 *The Secret Happiness of Marilyn Monroe*, p. 74.

Chapter 19

1 *Finding Marilyn: A Romance*, David Conover, Grosset & Dunlap, New York, 1981, p. 7.
2 Letter from Norma Jeane Dougherty to Grace Goddard, 4 June 1945, reproduced in *Marilyn: The Ultimate Look at the Legend*, pp. 14–5.
3 'Marilyn Monroe's Night of Love in the Sand with JFK', *Star*, David Conover, 1 September 1981.
4 Notes on David Conover, Anthony Summers, AS archive.
5 *Finding Marilyn: A Romance*, p. 12.

Chapter 20

1 *Before Marilyn*, p. 53.
2 *Before Marilyn*, pp. 54–6.
3 *Before Marilyn*, p. 58.
4 *Holding a Good Thought for Marilyn: 1926–1954 The Hollywood Years*, Stacy Eubank, 2015, p. 67.
5 Ibid.
6 Interview with Marion Marshall, AS, MHL.

Chapter 21

1 *Marilyn, Mon Amour: the private album of André de Dienes*, André de Dienes, Sidgwick & Jackson, London, 1985, p. 16.
2 *Marilyn, Mon Amour*, p. 27.
3 *Marilyn, Mon Amour*, p. 17.
4 *Marilyn, Mon Amour*, p. 51.

5 *Marilyn, Mon Amour*, p. 65.
6 *Marilyn, Mon Amour*, p. 67.
7 *Marilyn, Mon Amour*, p. 69.
8 *Marilyn, Mon Amour*, p. 68.
9 *Marilyn, Mon Amour*, p. 70.
10 Letter from André de Dienes to Anthony Summers, 9 September 1984, AS archive.
11 Letter from Grace Goddard to Norma Jeane Dougherty, 14 June 1946, Bonhams: https://www.bonhams.com/auction/24838/lot/312/a-marilyn-monroe-letter-from-her-guardian-grace-goddard/
12 Letter from Ana Lower to Norma Jeane Dougherty, 5 July 1946, Bonhams: https://www.bonhams.com/auction/24838/lot/308/a-marilyn-monroe-pair-of-letters-from-ana-lower/
13 Letter from André de Dienes to Anthony Summers, 9 September 1984, AS archive.
14 *Marilyn, Mon Amour*, p. 78.
15 *Marilyn, Mon Amour*, p.147.
16 *Marilyn, Mon Amour*, p. 83.
17 Letter from André de Dienes to Marilyn Monroe, 29 March 1960, Stars and Letters: https://starsandletters.blogspot.com/2015/04/dear-turkey-foot.html
18 Telegram from André de Dienes to Marilyn Monroe, 11 February 1961, Inez Melson file, AS archive.
19 *Marilyn, Mon Amour*, p. 154.
20 Ibid.
21 *Marilyn, Mon Amour*, p. 155.

Chapter 22

1 *Marilyn Monroe: Ten Years On*, BBC, 1972.
2 *The Marilyn Scandal*, Sandra Shevey, Arrow, London, 1990, p. 104.
3 'Mighty Marilyn', *Screen Guide*, December 1951, quoted in *Holding a Good Thought for Marilyn*, p. 90.
4 *Marilyn Monroe*, Zolotow, 1960, p. 51.

Chapter 23

1. Interview with Sheila Graham, AS, MHL.
2. *The Zanucks of Hollywood: The Dark Legacy of an American Dynasty*, Marlys J. Harris, Crown, New York, 1989, pp. 47–8.
3. *Goddess: The Secret Lives of Marilyn Monroe*, Anthony Summers, Victor Gollancz Ltd, London, 1985, p. 37.
4. *Remembering Marilyn Monroe*, Larry King Live, CNN, 1 June 2001.
5. *Conversations with Marilyn*, p. 186.
6. 'Hollywood's Casting Couch & How I Lost My Part As Cleopatra', *Daily Mail*, Joan Collins, 14 October 2017.
7. *Marilyn Monroe*, Zolotow, 1960, p. 101.
8. *The Secret Life of Marilyn Monroe*, p. 178.
9. *The Many Loves of Marilyn Monroe*.
10. Interview with Nico Minardos, AS, MHL.
11. 'Hollywood's Casting Couch & How I Lost My Part As Cleopatra', *Daily Mail*, Joan Collins, 14 October 2017.
12. Georges Belmont interview, *Marilyn Monroe and the Camera*, p. 13.
13. *Don't Say Yes Until I Finish Talking: A Biography of Darryl F. Zanuck*, Mel Gussow, Doubleday, London, p. 173.
14. 'Wolves I Have Known, Marilyn Monroe as told to Florabel Muir', *Motion Picture and Television*, January 1953.
15. *Marilyn: The Passion and the Paradox*, p. 148.
16. Interview with John Huston, AS, MHL.
17. In Defense of Marilyn, typescript, p. 14, Box 41, Folder 1, Earl Wilson Papers, Lawrence and Lee Theatre Research Institute of The Ohio State University Libraries.
18. Interview with Jane Russell, AS, MHL.

Chapter 24

1. *The Many Loves of Marilyn Monroe*.
2. *Marilyn: Her Life in Her Own Words*, p. 84.
3. 'Hugh Hefner Talks About His Memories Of Marilyn Monroe', CBS, 3 August 2012: https://www.cbsnews.com/losangeles/news/hugh-hefner-talks-about-his-memories-of-marilyn-monroe/

Chapter 25

1 *Timebends*, p. 371.

Chapter 26

1 *The Marilyn Encyclopedia*, p. 261.
2 Interview with Marion Marshall, AS, MHL.
3 *Marilyn: The Passion and the Paradox*, p. 143.
4 *My Years With Marilyn Monroe*, Natasha Lytess, p. 12.
5 *My Story*, p. 77.
6 *My Years With Marilyn Monroe*, p. 6.
7 'The Men Who Made Marilyn', *Untold Secrets*, M. David Levin, October 1961.
8 Ibid.
9 'The Mystery of Marilyn Monroe's Plastic Surgery', *Allure*, Joan Kron, 9 October 2013.
10 Reminiscences of Nunnally Johnson, Oral History Transcript, Center for Oral History Research, UCLA Library Special Collections.
11 *The Many Loves of Marilyn Monroe*.
12 *Norma Jean: The Life of Marilyn Monroe*, p. 158.
13 *My Years With Marilyn Monroe*, p. 13.
14 Reminiscences of Nunnally Johnson, Oral History Transcript, Center for Oral History Research, UCLA Library Special Collections.
15 *Norma Jean: The Life of Marilyn Monroe*, p.182.
16 *My Years with Marilyn Monroe*, p. 14.

Chapter 27

1 'Actress Treated For Overdose of Sleeping Pills', *Los Angeles Times*, 25 February 1943.
2 *My Years With Marilyn Monroe*, p. 1.
3 *My Years With Marilyn Monroe*, p. 5.
4 Ibid.
5 *My Years With Marilyn Monroe*, p. 1.
6 Interview with Jane Russell, AS, MHL.
7 *My Years With Marilyn Monroe*, pp. 25–6.

8 *My Years With Marilyn Monroe*, p. 22.
9 *Marilyn Monroe Confidential*, p. 217.
10 Interview with Henry Rosenfeld, AS, MHL.
11 Interview with Jim Haspiel, 17 January 2023, Andrew Wilson.

Chapter 28

1 *Marilyn: The Passion and the Paradox*, p. 159.
2 *Don't Get Me Wrong – I Love Hollywood*, Sidney Skolsky, G. P. Putnam's Sons, New York, 1975, p. 231.
3 *Initiales B.B.: mémoires*, Brigitte Bardot, Grasset, Paris, 1996, p. 172.
4 *Legend: The Life and Death of Marilyn Monroe*, Frederick Guiles, Stein and Day, New York, 1984, p. 200.
5 *My Story*, p. 111.
6 *My Story*, p. 112.
7 *Legend*, Guiles, p. 200.
8 *Joan Crawford: Hollywood Martyr*, David Bret, Robson, London, 2006, pp. 197–8.
9 'Florabel Muir Reporting', Los Angeles Mirror, 10 February 1953.
10 'Joan Crawford Tells Marilyn To Be a Lady', *The Times*, San Mateo, 2 March 1953.
11 *The Marilyn Encyclopedia*, p. 65.
12 'New Chapter in the Mystery of Marilyn: Her Own Words?', *Los Angeles Times*, Robert W. Welkos, 5 August 2005.
13 'Marilyn Tapes Mere Vaporous Stuff', Letter from Anthony Summers, *Irish Independent*, 14 August 2005.
14 'New Chapter in the Mystery of Marilyn: Her Own Words?'.
15 'Marilyn Tapes Mere Vaporous Stuff', Letter from Anthony Summers, *Irish Independent*, 14 August 2005.

Chapter 29

1 *Shelley: Also Known as Shirley*, Shelley Winters, Morrow, New York, 1980, pp. 307–8.
2 *Marilyn Monroe: Beyond the Legend*, 1987, directed by Gene Feldman, Suzette Winter.
3 *Late Night With David Letterman*, 8 September 1989.

4   *The Full Wax*, BBC, 6 May 1993.
5   *Insignificance*, Terry Johnson, Methuen, London, 1982, p. 11.

CHAPTER 30

1   *Shelley II: The Middle of My Century*, Shelley Winters, Simon & Schuster, New York, 1989, p. 34.
2   *Goddess*, p. 29.
3   *Icon: Volume 1, 1926–1956*, Kindle edition, Chapter 19.
4   *The Marilyn Encyclopaedia*, p. 40.
5   *Elia Kazan: A Life*, Elia Kazan, Knopf, New York, 1997, p. 403.
6   *Elia Kazan*, p. 404.
7   *Elia Kazan*, p. 408.
8   *The Selected Letters of Elia Kazan*, ed. Albert J. Devlin with Marlene J. Devlin, Editor's note, Knopf, New York, 2014, p. 327.
9   Letter from Elia Kazan to Molly Day Thacher, 29 November 1955, *The Selected Letters of Elia Kazan*, p. 325.
10 Letter from Elia Kazan to MM, 1951, reproduced in *Holding a Good Thought for Marilyn*, pp. 196–7.
11 *Marilyn Monroe, Private and Undisclosed*, p. 90.
12 'Marilyn Monroe: The Image and Her Photographers', *Popular Photography*, January 1966, Ralph Hattersley, reproduced in *Marilyn Monroe: A Composite View*, p. 63.
13 *Timebends*, p. 241.
14 *Holding a Good Thought for Marilyn*, p. 306.
15 *Timebends*, p. 532.
16 *Marilyn Monroe: A Composite View*, p. 99.
17 *Fragments*, p. 17.
18 Letter from Eve Arnold to Richard Brown, 20 July 1993, reproduced in 'Marilyn Monroe Reading Ulysses: Goddess or Post-Cultural Cyborg', Richard Brown, in *Joyce and Popular Culture*, ed. R. B. Kershner, University Press of Florida, Gainesville, 1996, p. 174.
19 *Goddess*, p. 140.

Chapter 31

1. 'Pete Rose Says He Gave Joe DiMaggio A Shower Then Praises His Penis', *Huffington Post*, Ron Dicker, 6 June 2019.
2. *Marilyn: The Passion and the Paradox*, p. 210.
3. Interview with Amy Greene, AS, MHL.
4. *Dinner With DiMaggio: Memories of an American Hero*, Rock G. Positano, Simon & Schuster, New York, 2017, p. 176.
5. Georges Belmont interview, *Marilyn Monroe and the Camera*, p. 15.
6. *My Story*, p. 127.
7. 'I was There When Marilyn Posed', *Movie Stars Parade*, Natalie Kelley Grasco, July 1953.
8. 'Nude calendar beauty at last is identified: Marilyn Monroe', UPI, Aline Mosby, 13 May 1952.
9. *My Story*, p. 39.
10. *My Story*, p. 59.
11. 'Iconomania: Sex, Death, Photography, and the Myth of Marilyn Monroe', Richard B. Woodward, in *All the Available Light: A Marilyn Monroe Reader*, ed. Yona Zeldis McDonough, Touchstone, New York, 2002, p. 23.
12. 'The New Marilyn Monroe', *Saturday Evening Post*, Pete Martin, 5 May 1956.
13. 'Posed In Nude when Hungry, Marilyn Says', *Cincinnati Enquirer*, Milton Shulman, 23 May 1956.
14. *The Many Loves of Marilyn Monroe*.
15. 'Hollywood By Louella Parsons', *Bangor Daily News*, 20 March 1952.
16. Marilyn Monroe Studio bio, 7 February 1951, Harry Brand, *The Unabridged Marilyn*, p. 49.
17. 'Marilyn Monroe Confesses Mother Alive, Living Here', *Los Angeles Daily News*, Erskine Johnson, 3 May 1952.
18. *Marilyn Monroe: The Biography*, pp. 240–1.
19. *Elia Kazan*, p. 455.
20. Letter from Joe DiMaggio to MM, postmarked 15 July 1952, sold at auction on 18 December 2012: https://historical.ha.com/itm/miscellaneous/dimaggio-joseph-autograph-letter-signed-joe-on-the-

madison-hotel-letterhead-stationery-3-pages-10-x-8-1-2-in-276-x/a/997004-1272.s?ic4=GalleryView-ShortDescription-071515-new

21 Interview with William Travilla, AS, MHL.

Chapter 32

1. *Finding Nico*, directed by Owen Prell, 2010.
2. Interview with Nico Minardos, AS, MHL.
3. *Finding Nico*.
4. Interview with Nico Minardos, AS, MHL.
5. *Finding Nico*.
6. Ibid.
7. *Goddess*, p. 70.
8. *Holding a Good Thought for Marilyn*, p. 339.

Chapter 33

1. *The Unabridged Marilyn*, p. 541.
2. 'The New Marilyn Monroe', *Saturday Evening Post*, Pete Martin, 5 May 1956.
3. *Marilyn Monroe*, Zolotow, 1960, p. 148.
4. 'Marilyn Monroe: The Image and her Photographers', *Popular Photography*, Ralph Hattersley, January 1966, reproduced in *Marilyn Monroe: A Composite View*, p. 63.
5. *Marilyn Monroe: A Composite View*, p. 143.
6. *Goddess*, p. 44.
7. 'The New Marilyn Monroe'.
8. 'Marilyn: Studio Couldn't Change Monroe's U-N-I-Q-U-E Walk', *Sacramento Union*, Kendis Rochlen and Charles Park, 7 March 1954, *The Unabridged Marilyn*, p. 541.
9. *The Thinking Body*, Mabel Elsworth Todd, Princeton Book Company, 1968 edition, p. 198.
10. *Timebends*, p. 303.
11. *Mimosa: Memories of Marilyn & the Making of 'The Misfits'*, Ralph L. Roberts, with Chris Jacobs and Hap Roberts, Roadhouse Books, Salisbury, North Carolina, 2021, Kindle edition, p. 45.

12 Ibid.
13 Interview with Ralph Roberts, *20/20*, ABC, 28 August 1985.
14 Interview with Joan Greenson, AS, MHL.
15 *Holding a Good Thought for Marilyn*, p. 238.
16 *Margot Fonteyn: Autobiography*, Margot Fonteyn, Knopf, New York, 1976, p. 154.

Chapter 34

1 *Taken Care Of: The Autobiography of Edith Sitwell*, Edith Sitwell, Atheneum, New York, p. 222.
2 Edith Sitwell, Notebook 72, Box 38.5, Harry Ransom Center, The University of Texas at Austin.
3 *Taken Care Of*, p. 222.
4 *Taken Care Of*, p. 223.
5 *Edith Sitwell, A Unicorn Among Lions*, Victoria Glendinning, Knopf, New York, 1981, p. 15.
6 Edith Sitwell talking to John Freeman, *Face to Face*, BBC, 1959: https://www.bbc.co.uk/programmes/p04qh1gk
7 *Conversations with Marilyn*, p. 186.
8 Letter from Edith Sitwell to Stanley Kauffmann, 16 April 1955, *The Selected Letters of Edith Sitwell*, ed. Richard Greene, Virago, London, 1997, pp. 361–2.
9 *Face to Face*.
10 'Marilyn and the Literati', Jeffrey Meyers, *Michigan Quarterly Review*, Winter 2008.
11 Letter from Isak Dinesen to Fleur Cowles Meye, 21 February 1961, quoted in *Fragments*, p. 234.

Chapter 35

1 Ben Hecht Papers, Newberry Library, Chicago.
2 *Holding a Good Thought for Marilyn*, p. 413.
3 *My Years With Marilyn Monroe*, pp. 19–20.
4 Interview with Amy Greene, AS, MHL.
5 *Parade*, Lloyd Shearer, 28 February 1954.
6 'To Aristophanes & Back'.

7 *Holding a Good Thought for Marilyn*, p. 444.
8 Ibid.
9 *The Unabridged Marilyn*, p. 400.
10 *Holding a Good Thought for Marilyn*, p. 444.
11 *Holding a Good Thought for Marilyn*, p. 442.
12 Interview with Amy Greene, AS, MHL.
13 *Marilyn Monroe: The Private Life of a Public Icon*, Charles Casillo, St. Martin's, New York, 2018, p. 91.
14 *Marilyn Revealed: The Ambitious Life of an American Icon*, Ted Schwarz, Taylor Trade Publishing, Lanham, Maryland, 2009, p. 422.
15 Interview with Henry Rosenfeld, AS, MHL.
16 *Holding a Good Thought for Marilyn*, p. 476.
17 'Voice of Broadway, Marilyn Monroe Writes', *The Record-Argus*, 11 June 1954.

CHAPTER 36

1 *The Seven Year Itch*, dir. By Billy Wilder, Twentieth Century-Fox, 1955.
2 *Nobody's Perfect*, p. 179.
3 Ibid.
4 *Conversations with Wilder*, p. 85.
5 Interview with Amy Greene, AS, MHL.
6 Ibid.

CHAPTER 37

1 Letter from Marilyn Monroe to Joe DiMaggio, 28 February 1954, Hunt Auctions: https://www.huntauctions.com/liveimg27/866.jpg
2 *Dinner With DiMaggio*, p. 176.
3 Letter from Marilyn Monroe to Joe DiMaggio, undated (c. 1954), Christie's: https://www.christies.com/en/lot/lot-6296638
4 'Marilyn Back at Work Looking Bewildered', *Fort Worth Star-Telegram*, James Bacon, 7 October 1954.
5 Letter from Joe DiMaggio to Marilyn Monroe, 9 October 1954: https://bid.juliensauctions.com/lot-details/index/catalog/142/lot/57692/MARILYN-MONROE-LETTER-FROM-JOE-DiMAGGIO

6 'Marilyn Monroe Given Divorce From DiMaggio', *Los Angeles Times*, 28 October 1954.
7 *Marilyn Monroe*, Zolotow, 1960, p. 217.

CHAPTER 38

1 Interview with Hal Schaefer, AS, MHL.

CHAPTER 39

1 'Sinatra, DiMaggio Sued Over "Wrong-Door" Raid', *Los Angeles Times*, 1 June 1957.
2 'The Real Reason for Marilyn Monroe's Divorce', *Confidential*, September 1955.
3 Interview with Hal Schaefer, AS, MHL.
4 'Sinatra's Testimony On Raid Called "Lie"', *Los Angeles Times*, 28 February 1957.
5 Interview with Sheila Stewart Renour, AS, MHL.
6 Interview with Hal Schaefer, AS, MHL.

CHAPTER 40

1 'New Monroe Book From Old Memoirs', *Los Angeles Times*, Digby Diehl, 15 April 1974.
2 Letter from Ben Hecht to Ken McCormack, spring 1954: https://marilynmonroefanatic.tumblr.com/ben
3 Letter from Ben Hecht to Gregson Bautzer, 11 August 1954, Ben Hecht Papers, Newberry Library, Chicago.
4 Letter from Marilyn Monroe to Ben Hecht, 16 March 1954, Cursum Perficio: http://www.cursumperficio.net/CD/NJ/Pap/Oth/CBHecht1.jpg
5 Letter from Ben Hecht to Gregson Bautzer, 11 August 1954, Ben Hecht Papers, Newberry Library, Chicago.
6 Letter from Ben Hecht to Ken McCormack, undated: https://marilynmonroefanatic.tumblr.com/ben
7 Letter from Ben Hecht to Gregson Bautzer, 11 August 1954, Ben Hecht Papers, Newberry Library, Chicago.
8 Letter from Ben Hecht to Loyd Wright Jr, 19 May 1954, Ben Hecht Papers, Newberry Library, Chicago.

9 'Marilyn Monroe Confesses', *Empire News*, 2 May 1954.
10 Letter from Loyd Wright Jr to Ben Hecht and Jacques Chambrun, 1 June 1954, Cursum Perficio: https://www.cursumperficio.net/CD/Peop/Avo/Wright/Wright5.jpg
11 Letter from Mrs Hecht to Loyd Wright, 2 June 1954, Ben Hecht Papers, Newberry Library, Chicago.

CHAPTER 41

1 Letter from Ben Hecht to Jacques Chambrun, c. June 1954: https://marilynmonroefanatic.tumblr.com/ben
2 'Mavis Gallant's Double-Dealing Literary Agent', *New Yorker*, Jessica Weisberg, 11 July 2012.
3 Letter from Robert Slatzer to Anthony Summers, 7 January 1985, AS archive.
4 'Marilyn's "My Story" Was a Ben Hecht Script, *New York Post*, George Carpozi Jr, 21 June 1974.
5 *Holding a Good Thought for Marilyn*, p. 492.

CHAPTER 43

1 'Surgery Due for Marilyn', *LA Herald Examiner*, Louella P. Parsons, 4 November 1954.
2 'Marilyn Monroe Will Undergo Minor Surgery', *Los Angeles Times*, 6 November 1954.
3 Interview with Amy Greene, AS, MHL.
4 'Medical Issues on Marilyn Monroe's Life and Death: a retrospective', *International Medical Journal*, Sachi Sri Kantha, Yuri Matsui, April 2022, vol. 29, no. 2, pp. 132–6.
5 https://www.fredhutch.org/en/news/center-news/2018/07/endometriosis-linked-to-childhood-abuse.html, see also: 'Early life abuse and risk of endometriosis', *Human Reproduction*, vol. 33, issue 9, September 2018, pp.1657–68: https://doi.org/10.1093/humrep/dey248
6 'I Was Marilyn's Doctor', *Ladies' Home Journal*, Dr Richard Cottrell, January 1965.
7 Interview Notes with Dr Lee Siegel, AS archive.

Chapter 44

1 *Marilyn Monroe*, Barbara Leaming, Crown, New York, 1998, p. 115.
2 'Scott Feinberg Interviews Amy Greene', *Hollywood Reporter*, November 2012: https://www.hollywoodreporter.com/video/scott-feinberg-interviews-amy-greene-371176/
3 Interview with Amy Greene, AS, MHL.
4 Transcription of telephone call between Jack Gordean and Darryl Zanuck, Charles K. Feldman archive, Heritage Auctions: https://entertainment.ha.com/itm/movie-tv-memorabilia/marilyn-monroe-extensive-archive-of-her-agent-charles-k-feldman-s-files-of-150-typed-and-handwritten-letters-memos-clipp/a/997052-1088.s
5 Reminiscences of Nunnally Johnson, Oral History Transcript, Center for Oral History Research, UCLA Library Special Collections.
6 '"River of No Return" Has Strong Boxoffice Pull', *Hollywood Reporter*, Milton Luban, 23 April 1954.
7 *Marilyn in Manhattan – Her Year of Joy*, Elizabeth Winder, Flatiron Books, New York, 2017, p. 10.
8 *Marilyn in Manhattan*, p. 21.
9 *Marilyn in Manhattan*, p. 29.
10 Interview with Milton Greene, AS, MHL.
11 'Scott Feinberg Interviews Amy Greene', November 2012.
12 'Marilyn in the house', *Photoplay*, Helen Bolstad, September 1955.
13 *Marilyn in Manhattan*, p. 39.
14 'Marilyn in the house', *Photoplay*.

Chapter 45

1 *Marilyn and Me*, p. 118.
2 Interview with Amy Greene, AS, MHL.
3 *My Story*, p. 69.
4 Letter from Dr Ralph Greenson to Norman Rosten, 15 August 1962, AS archive.
5 *Marilyn Monroe*, Zolotow, 1960, p. 185.
6 *Marilyn Monroe*, Zolotow, 1960, pp. 183–4.
7 *Marilyn: The Passion and the Paradox*, p. 217.

8 *Goddess*, p. 84.
9 *The Marilyn Encyclopedia*, p. 90.
10 *Marilyn and Me*, p. 94.
11 *Goddess*, p. 85.
12 'There'll Always Be Another Encore', *McCall's*, January/February 1964.
13 *Marilyn Monroe: The Biography*, p. 366.
14 Interview with Milton Greene, AS, MHL.
15 Susan Strasberg, *Sally Jessy Raphael Show*, 15 April 1992.
16 *Marilyn and Me*, p. 94.
17 *Marilyn and Me*, p. 90.
18 *Marilyn and Me*, p. 91.

Chapter 46

1 'My Beauty Secrets By Marilyn Monroe', *Photoplay*, October 1953.
2 *The Marilyn Encyclopedia*, p. 98.
3 *Blonde*, p. 395.
4 The Personal Property of Marilyn Monroe, Christie's, Lot 310, 1999: https://www.christies.com/en/lot/lot-1646728
5 Notes on Interview with Sylvia Lane, Dr Litman's secretary, 28 October 1983, AS archive.
6 'Marilyn: A Rip-Off With Genius', *New York Times*, Pauline Kael, 22 July 1973.
7 Interview with William Travilla, AS, MHL.
8 In Defense of Marilyn, typescript, p. 12, Box 41, Folder 1, Earl Wilson Papers, Lawrence and Lee Theatre Research Institute of The Ohio State University Libraries.
9 'A Beautiful Child', *Portraits and Observations: The Essays of Truman Capote*, Truman Capote, Random House, New York, 2007, p. 480.

Chapter 47

1 'With Respect To Roseanne', *New Yorker*, James Wolcott, 18 February 1996, https://www.newyorker.com/magazine/1996/02/26/with-respect-to-roseanne
2 *Allure*, January 2000.

3 'How I Stay in Shape By Marilyn Monroe', *Pageant*, September 1952.
4 Marilyn Monroe Diet Plan, Lot 154, Julien's Auctions, 17 November 2016: https://www.julienslive.com/lot-details/index/catalog/180/lot/83039
5 'My Beauty Secrets By Marilyn Monroe', *Photoplay*, October 1953.
6 Hansard, Volume 574, Column 428, 24 July 1957.
7 'Marilyn Monroe's Two Secrets', *Slate*, Simon Doonan: https://slate.com/culture/2013/12/was-marilyn-monroe-fat-her-secrets-revealed.html

Chapter 48

1 'Marilyn Monroe's Dress', Met Gala 2022, *Vogue*, YouTube.
2 'Kim Kardashian Takes Marilyn Monroe's "Happy Birthday, Mr President" Dress Out For A Spin', *Vogue*, Chioma Nnadi, 3 May 2022.
3 'Bob Mackie says Kim Kardashian wearing Marilyn Monroe's gown to Met Gala was a "big mistake"', *Entertainment Weekly*, Maureen Lee Lenker, 16 May 2022.
4 'Historians Complain Kim Kardashian Endangered Marilyn Monroe's Iconic Dress: "Putting It at Risk"', *People*, Charmaine Patterson, Julie Farin, 3 May 2022.
5 'Marilyn Monroe Birthday Dress Designer Bob Mackie Calls Kim Kardashian Rewear a "Big Mistake"', *People*, Janine Henni, 17 May 2022.
6 'Ripley's Believe It Or Not! Assists In Making History With Kim Kardashian At Met Gala', 3 May 2022: https://www.ripleyentertainment.com/kim-kardashian-met-gala/
7 'They called it! Kim Kardashian really did damage that iconic Marilyn Monroe dress', *Los Angeles Times*, Nardine Saad, 14 June 2022.
8 Scott Fortner, Marilyn Monroe Collection: https://themarilynmonroecollection.com/marilyn-monroe-famous-jfk-dress-loaned-by-ripleys-is-permanently-damaged-after-kimk-met-gala-red-carpet-walk/

Chapter 49

1 'The Bluest Marilyn Monroe', *Penthouse*, October 1980.
2 'Penthouse Magazine Tells a Lie', *Hollywood Star Newspaper*, vol. 1, no. 11, 1980.

3   Notes on *The Apple Knockers and the Coke*, AS archive.
4   'Collector to sell Monroe's "secret porn film debut"', *Guardian*, Gary Abramson, 15 January 1997.
5   'Alleged Marilyn Monroe Porn Film Nets No Bidders at Auction', *Hollywood Reporter*, Agustin Mango, 8 August 2011.
6   'Marilyn Monroe Porno? The Widow's Peak Speaks', The Marilyn Monroe Collection, Scott Fortner, 23 July 2011: https://themarilynmonroecollection.com/marilyn-monroe-porno-the-widows-peak-speaks/
7   'Marilyn Monroe sex film to be kept from public', *Guardian*, 14 April 2008.
8   'Marilyn Monroe Sex Film Hoax', The Smoking Gun, 18 April 2008: http://www.thesmokinggun.com/documents/crime/marilyn-monroe-sex-film-hoax
9   MSNBC, 'FBI: NO Marilyn Monroe sex film', Jim Popkin, 1 May 2008.
10 'Hardcore Marilyn', *New York Post*, Hasani Gittens, 14 April 2008.
11 'Seized "Monroe threesome sex tape starring JFK and his brother Robert" will not be auctioned after owner settles $200,000 court debt', Daily Mail, 4 March 2014: https://www.dailymail.co.uk/news/article-2572826/Monroe-JFK-RFK-threeway-sex-tape-auction-cancelled.html
12 'Alleged Sex Tape With Kennedys Going to Auction', 28 February 2014, TMZ: https://www.tmz.com/2014/02/28/marilyn-monroe-sex-tape-john-kennedy-robert/
13 '"Blonde" Review: Exploiting Marilyn Monroe for Old Times' Sake', *New York Times*, Manohla Dargis, 28 September 2022.
14 'Andrew Dominik Blames "Blonde" Backlash on Americans Wanting Marilyn Monroe Portrayed as "Empowered Woman"', *Hollywood Reporter*, Alex Ritman, 4 December 2022.

Chapter 50

1   'Marilyn and Ella', *Guardian*, Michael Billington, 23 February 2008.
2   Interview with Hal Schaefer, AS, MHL.

3 'The True Story of Marilyn Monroe, Ella Fitzgerald and the Mocambo Club', *All Things Marilyn* podcast, 31 October 2022.
4 *Goddess*, p. 219.
5 *Conversations with Marilyn*, p. 104.
6 *Conversations with Marilyn*, p. 146.
7 *Fragments*, pp. 222–3.
8 *Conversations with Marilyn*, p. 132.
9 'A Rumbling of Things Unknown', *London Review of Books*, Jacqueline Rose, 26 April 2012.

Chapter 51

1 *Life Itself*, Elaine Dundy, Virago, London, 2002, p. 162.
2 Brownie McGhee, African American Museum & Library at Oakland: https://archive.org/details/caolaam_000055/caolaam_000055_t02_a_access.mp3

Chapter 52

1 'A Good Long Look At Myself', *Redbook*, Alan Levy, August 1962.
2 'Circus Opening Will Aid Arthritis Foundation', *New York Times*, 27 March 1955.
3 'Old-Time Circus Opens At Garden', *New York Times*, Edith Evans Asbury, 31 March 1955.
4 'Marilyn in the house', *Photoplay*, September 1955.
5 *Person to Person with Edward R. Murrow*, CBS Television, 8 April 1955.
6 'An Elephant, A Boy, and Marilyn Monroe', *All Things Marilyn* podcast, 22 December 2022.

Chapter 53

1 *A Beautiful Child*, p. 471.
2 *A Beautiful Child*, p. 472.
3 *A Beautiful Child*, p. 473.
4 *A Beautiful Child*, p. 474.
5 'Marilyn Monroe's Death Report Totally Unfounded', *Fort Worth Star-Telegram*, Dorothy Kilgallen, 10 July 1953.

6   *A Beautiful Child*, p. 476.
7   *A Beautiful Child*, p. 480.
8   *A Beautiful Child*, p. 482.

Chapter 54

1   *Marilyn and Me*, p. 5.
2   *Marilyn and Me*, p. 7.
3   *Marilyn and Me*, p. 11.
4   *Marilyn and Me*, p. 10.
5   *Marilyn and Me*, p. 30.
6   'To Aristophanes & Back'.
7   *Nobody's Perfect*, p. 182.
8   *Marilyn and Me*, p. 34.
9   Ibid.
10 *Marilyn and Me*, p. 35.
11 *The Good, the Bad, and Me: In My Anecdotage*, Eli Wallach, Harcout, New York, 2005, p. 210.
12 *Elia Kazan*, pp. 439–40.
13 'Marilyn Monroe's Marriage', *Redbook*, Robert J. Levin, February 1958.
14 Ibid.
15 *Marilyn and Me*, p. 100.
16 *The Hairy Ape, Anna Christie, The First Man*, Eugene O'Neill, Boni and Liveright, New York, 1922, pp. 114–5.
17 *Marilyn and Me*, p. 101.
18 'Marilyn Monroe's Marriage'.
19 *A Dream of Passion: The Development of the Method*, Lee Strasberg, Little, Brown, New York, 1987, p. 14.
20 *Elia Kazan*, p. 539.
21 *Elia Kazan*, p. 713.
22 *Nobody's Perfect*, p. 215.
23 Letter from Marilyn Monroe to Lee and Paula Strasberg, 1 June 1962, Julien's Auctions: https://www.julienslive.com/lot-details/index/catalog/212/lot/89146
24 *Bitter Sweet*, Susan Strasberg, G. P. Putnam's Sons, New York, 1980, p. 52.

Chapter 55

1. 'Marilyn and Her Monsters', *Vanity Fair*, Sam Kashner, November 2010.
2. *Fragments*, pp. 52–3.
3. *Fragments*, pp. 56–7.
4. *Fragments*, pp. 58–9.
5. Georges Belmont interview, *Marilyn Monroe and the Camera*, p. 15.
6. *Fragments*, pp. 76–7.

Chapter 56

1. *Timebends*, p. 369.
2. Letter from Arthur Miller to his parents, 9 May 1956, quoted by John Lahr, American Witness Talk, John Lahr and John Guare, Museum of Jewish Heritage, 22 February 2023.
3. 'Miller's Crossing', *Vanity Fair*, James Kaplan, November 1991.
4. *Timebends*, p. 307.
5. *Elia Kazan*, p. 413.
6. Letter from Arthur Miller to his parents, 9 May 1956, quoted by John Lahr, American Witness Talk, John Lahr and John Guare, Museum of Jewish Heritage, 22 February 2023.
7. *Arthur Miller: 1915–1962*, Christopher Bigsby, Weidenfeld & Nicolson, London, 2008, p. 499.
8. *Arthur Miller: 1915–1962*, p. 401.
9. *Elia Kazan*, p. 439.
10. *Arthur Miller: Writer*, HBO documentary (directed by Rebecca Miller), 2017.
11. 'The Dilemma of Marilyn Monroe', *American Weekly*, Elsa Maxwell, 12 May 1957.
12. *Omnibus: Arthur Miller*, BBC, 1987.
13. 'Marilyn Monroe's Marriage', *Redbook*, Robert J. Levin, February 1958.
14. *Arthur Miller: Writer*.
15. *Timebends*, p. 369.

Chapter 57

1. *Arthur Miller: 1915–1962*, p. 507.
2. *Timebends*, p. 387.
3. *Arthur Miller: 1915–1962*, p. 648.

Chapter 58

1. Undated letter but written in response to letter Miller wrote to her, dated 21 April 1956, Julien's Auctions: https://www.julienslive.com/lot-details/index/catalog/142/lot/57748
2. Letter from Arthur Miller to his parents, 9 May 1956, quoted by John Lahr, 'Along Came Marilyn', Air Mail, 22 October 2022; Talk between John Lahr and John Guare, American Witness, Museum of Jewish Heritage, 22 February 2023.
3. Letter from Arthur Miller to Marilyn Monroe, 17 May 1956, Heritage Auctions: https://entertainment.ha.com/itm/movie-tv-memorabilia/arthur-miller-passionate-love-letter-in-which-he-bears-his-soul-to-his-new-love-and-future-wife-marilyn-monroe/a/997027-2185.s

Chapter 59

1. 'Miller Admits Aiding Reds, Risks Contempt', *Daily News*, Gwen Gibson, 22 June 1956.
2. *Arthur Miller: 1915–1962*, p. 526.
3. 'Marilyn's 5-Year Love Secret Revealed', *Pittsburgh Press*, Jim Cook, 16 July 1956.
4. *Marilyn: An Untold Story*, p. 34.
5. Reminiscences of Joshua Logan, Oral History Archives at Columbia, Rare Book and Manuscript Library, Columbia University in the City of New York.

Chapter 60

1. *Marilyn Monroe*, Zolotow, 1960, p. 290.
2. Letter from William Styron to John Marquand, 4 July 1956, in *Selected*

Letters of William Styron, ed. Rose Styron with R. Blakeslee Gilpin, Random House, New York, 2012, pp. 219–20.
3. *Marilyn Monroe*, Zolotow, 1960, p. 291.
4. 'Writer Killed in Car Pursuing Marilyn's, *Daily News*, Robert Conway and Neal Patterson, 30 June 1956.
5. *Marilyn Monroe*, Zolotow, 1960, p. 291.
6. Marilyn Monroe and Arthur Miller Press Conference, 29 June 1956: https://youtu.be/av2iTWyVp5Q?si=l1qnmfpxjzFbY6Wm
7. 'Marilyn Monroe Enters A Jewish Family', *Modern Screen*, Susan Wender, November 1956.
8. *My Odyssey*, Stephane Groueff, Writers Advantage, iUniverse, Lincoln, 2003, p. 377.
9. *Timebends*, p. 522.

Chapter 61

1. 'Marilyn Monroe Enters A Jewish Family'.
2. Letter from Rabbi Robert Goldburg to Dr Jacob Marcus, 24 August 1962, Rabbi Goldburg Letters, SC-8325, American Jewish Archives, Cincinnati, Ohio.
3. Letter from Rabbi Robert Goldburg to Dr Jacob Rader Marcus, 6 August 1986, Rabbi Goldburg Letters.
4. Letter from Rabbi Robert Goldburg to Dr Jacob Rader Marcus, 24 August 1962, Rabbi Goldburg Letters.
5. 'Marilyn Monroe Enters A Jewish Family'.
6. *Marilyn: An Untold Story*, p. 38.
7. 'My Moments With Marilyn – P.S. Arthur Was There Too', *Esquire*, Morton Miller, June 1989.
8. *Marilyn: An Untold Story*, p. 38.
9. Letter from Arthur Miller to Christopher Bigsby, quoted in *Arthur Miller: 1915–1962*, p. 570.
10. *Marilyn Monroe*, Zolotow, 1960, p. 289.
11. *Marilyn Monroe*, Zolotow, 1960, p. 290.
12. 'Chicken soup, please: foodies discover a taste for Jewish fare', *Independent*, Steve Bloomfield, 4 April 2004.
13. *Marilyn and Me*, p. 112.

14 Letter from Arthur Miller to Christopher Bigsby, quoted in *Arthur Miller: 1915–1962*, p. 570.
15 *Marilyn and Me*, p. 112.
16 Ibid.

Chapter 62

1 *Timebends*, p. 413.
2 *Confessions of an Actor*, Laurence Olivier, Weidenfeld & Nicholson, London, 1982, p. 175.
3 *Timebends*, p. 428.
4 Ibid.
5 'To Aristophanes & Back'.
6 *Timebends*, p. 415.
7 *Timebends*, p. 413.

Chapter 63

1 *Confessions of an Actor*, p. 172.
2 Letter from Colin Clark to Peter Pitt-Millward, 26 November 1956, reproduced in *My Week with Marilyn*, Colin Clark, Weinstein Books, New York, 2011, p. 113.
3 *My Father Laurence Olivier*, Tarquin Olivier, Headline, London, 1992, p. 203.
4 *My Father Laurence Olivier*, p. 204.
5 *My Father Laurence Olivier*, p. 206.
6 *Confessions of an Actor*, p. 169.
7 *Legend*, Guiles, p. 313.
8 *Confessions of an Actor*, p. 225.
9 *Confessions of an Actor*, p. 226.
10 Interview with Elaine Schreyeck, 11 June 2021, Andrew Wilson.
11 Letter from Hugh Perceval to Cecil Tennant, 9 January 1957, Sir Laurence Olivier Archive, British Library, London, Add MS 80495.
12 *Timebends*, p. 418.
13 *Arthur Miller: 1915–1962*, p. 587.
14 *Legend*, Guiles, p. 320.
15 *Mimosa*, Kindle edition, p. 56.

16 *Marilyn and Me*, p. 122.
17 *Legend*, Guiles, p. 319.
18 *After the Fall*, Arthur Miller, Secker & Warburg, London, 1964, p. 123.
19 *Timebends*, p. 424.
20 *Legend*, Guiles, p. 320.
21 *Fragments*, pp. 114–15.

Chapter 64

1 *Olivier*, Anthony Holden, Weidenfeld & Nicolson, London, 1988, p. 308.
2 'Paper Says Marilyn May Be "Expecting"', *Los Angeles Times*, 5 September 1956.
3 'Marilyn's Woe: Baby Talk, Not Talk of a Baby', *Daily News*, 7 September 1956.
4 *Leicester Evening Mail*, 5 September 1956.
5 *My Week with Marilyn*, p. 97.
6 *My Week with Marilyn*, p. 101.
7 *My Week with Marilyn*, p. 235.
8 *My Week with Marilyn*, p. 244.
9 'The Fact, And Fiction, Of *My Week With Marilyn*', NPR, December 26, 2011.
10 *My Week with Marilyn*, p. 1.
11 *Marilyn Monroe: The Biography*, p. 414.

Chapter 65

1 *Timebends*, p. 425.
2 *Alltag bei Familie Freud: Die Erinnerungen der Paula Fichtl*, Detlef Berthelsen, Hoffman und Campe, Hamburg, 1987, pp. 152–3.
3 'Quarter of Monroe's Estate Must Go to London Child Centre, Judge Rules', *Guardian*, 13 March 1990.

Chapter 66

1 *Timebends*, p. 457.
2 *Please Don't Kill Anything, I Don't Need You Anymore*, Arthur Miller, Viking, New York, 1967, p. 74.

3   *Timebends*, p. 457.
4   *Marilyn and Me*, p. 163.
5   'The Lord Taketh Away', *Modern Screen*, N. Polsky, November 1957.
6   'Marilyn Fights to Save Baby', *LA Herald Examiner*, Louella Parsons, 2 August 1957.
7   'Marilyn Monroe Loses Baby; May Have More', *Los Angeles Times*, 3 August 1957.
8   'The Lord Taketh Away'.
9   Letter from Marilyn Monroe to Jane Miller, 9 August 1957, Julien's Auctions: https://www.juliensauctions.com/en/lots/111674/marilyn-monroe-letters-to-arthur-miller-s-daughter-jane
10 Letter from Marilyn Monroe to Bobby Miller, 9 August 1957, Julien's Auctions: https://bid.juliensauctions.com/lot-details/index/catalog/474/lot/215492/Marilyn-Monroe-Sent-Bobby-Miller-Letters#mz-expanded-view-775402019632
11 *Timebends*, p. 458.
12 *Marilyn and Me*, p. 163.
13 *Marilyn: An Untold Story*, p. 71.
14 Letter from Marilyn Monroe to Norman and Hedda Rosten, quoted in *Marilyn: An Untold Story*, p. 72.
15 *Marilyn and Me*, p. 134.
16 Interview with Marjorie Plecher, AS, MHL.
17 Telegram from Arthur Miller to Billy Wilder, 11 February 1959.
18 'Sleeping Beauty Marilyn Pouts At Chubby Remark', *LA Examiner*, Henry Sutherland, 9 July 1958.
19 Letter from Marilyn Monroe to Jane Miller, 16 July 1958, Julien's Auctions: https://www.juliensauctions.com/en/lots/111674/marilyn-monroe-letters-to-arthur-miller-s-daughter-jane
20 'Marilyn Monroe's Film Comeback', *Pittsburgh Press*, Hedda Hopper, 7 September 1958.
21 Letter from Arthur Miller to Marilyn Monroe, dated 12 September 1958, Bonhams: https://www.bonhams.com/auction/15284/lot/1013/a-marilyn-monroe-received-letter-from-arthur-miller-circa-1958/

Chapter 67

1 *Conversations with Wilder*, p. 159.
2 *Conversations with Wilder*, p. 160.
3 *Nobody's Perfect*, p. 212.
4 *Conversations with Wilder*, p. 86.
5 Dr Leon Krohn file, AS archive.
6 Ibid.
7 'Marilyn Monroe – Upsetting', *New York Herald Tribune*, Joe Hyams, 10 February 1959.
8 Telegram from Arthur Miller to Billy Wilder, 11 February 1958, RR Auction: https://www.rrauction.com/auctions/lot-detail/32891600407358-some-like-it-hot-arthur-miller-and-marilyn-monroe/?cat=0
9 Telegram from Billy Wilder to Arthur Miller, quoted in *Arthur Miller: 1915–1962*, pp. 610–11.
10 Telegram from Billy Wilder to Arthur Miller, quoted in *Marilyn Monroe*, Zolotow, p. 325.

Chapter 68

1 'The Empty Crib in the Nursery', *Photoplay*, Radie Harris, December 1958.
2 *Frank Lloyd Wright: Recollections by Those Who Knew Him*, Edgar Tafel, Dover Publications, Mineola, 2001, p. xiv.
3 *Timebends*, p. 468.
4 *Timebends*, p. 467.
5 'The Empty Crib in the Nursery'.

Chapter 69

1 'Marilyn Monroe – The Sex Symbol Versus the Good Wife, On Location with Jon Whitcomb', *Cosmopolitan*, December 1960.
2 Ibid.

Chapter 70

1. Letter from Dr Ralph Greenson to Dr Marianne Kris, 20 March 1960, AS archive.
2. *Arthur Miller: 1915–1962*, p. 603.
3. Letter from Dr Ralph Greenson to Dr Marianne Kris, 20 March 1960, AS archive.

Chapter 71

1. *You See, I Haven't Forgotten*, Yves Montand with Hervé Hamon and Patrick Rotman, translated from the French by Jeremy Leggatt, Chatto & Windus, London, 1992, p. 316.
2. *You See, I Haven't Forgotten*, p. 295.
3. *You See, I Haven't Forgotten*, p. 316.
4. *You See, I Haven't Forgotten*, p. 319.
5. *You See, I Haven't Forgotten*, p. 320.
6. *You See, I Haven't Forgotten*, p. 324.
7. Arthur Miller interview with Christopher Bigsby, quoted in *Arthur Miller: 1915–1962*, p. 613.
8. *You See, I Haven't Forgotten*, p. 326.
9. *Nostalgia Isn't What It Used to Be*, Simone Signoret, Harper & Row, New York, 1978, p. 298.
10. *Nostalgia Isn't What It Used to Be*, pp. 301–2.
11. *Mimosa*, Kindle edition, p. 73.
12. *You See, I Haven't Forgotten*, p. 326.
13. *You See, I Haven't Forgotten*, p. 329.
14. *Conversations with Marilyn*, p. 166.
15. *The Whole Truth and Nothing But*, Hedda Hopper and James Brough, Doubleday & Company, New York, 1962, p. 42.
16. 'Montand Denies Divorce Plan Over Marilyn Monroe', *Los Angeles Times*, Hedda Hopper, 2 September 1960.
17. Ibid.

Chapter 72

1. Interview with John Huston, AS, MHL.

2   *An Open Book*, John Huston, Knopf, New York, 1980, p. 288.
3   *The Making of The Misfits*, directed by Gail Stevens, 2001.
4   *Timebends*, p. 462.
5   *Timebends*, p. 466.
6   *Timebends*, p. 473.
7   *The Legend of Marilyn Monroe*.
8   *The Good, the Bad, and Me*, p. 217.
9   'Eli Wallach: The Gun Beneath the Bubbles', *Sight and Sound*, John Exshaw, January 2006.
10 *Marilyn and Me*, p. 210.
11 *Misfits*, Arthur Miller, Methuen, London, 2002, p. 46.
12 Arthur Miller, interview with Christopher Bigsby, *Arthur Miller: 1915–1962*, p. 628.
13 Anne Jackson, Unpublished Memoir, Anne Jackson and Eli Wallach Papers, Box 73.2, HRC.
14 *The Good, the Bad, and Me*, p. 223.
15 *Conversations with Marilyn*, p. 187.
16 *Timebends*, pp. 481–2.
17 *Timebends*, p. 483.
18 Ibid.
19 *People Will Talk*, John Kobal, Knopf, New York, 1985, p. 613.
20 *Arthur Miller: 1915–1962*, p. 632.
21 *An Open Book*, p. 288.
22 'Marilyn Monroe – The Sex Symbol Versus the Good Wife, On Location with Jon Whitcomb'.

CHAPTER 73

1   Interview with Angela Allen, 8 June 2021, Andrew Wilson.

CHAPTER 74

1   Interview with Curtice Taylor, 11 June 2021, Andrew Wilson.

CHAPTER 75

1   Letter from Dr Ralph Greenson to Dr Marianne Kris, 21 October 1960, AS archive.

2   Dr Litman's notes of interview with Dr Greenson, 13 August 1962, Suicide Prevention Team, AS archive.
3   Letter from Dr Ralph Greenson to Dr Marianne Kris, 21 October 1960, AS archive.
4   Letter from Dr Ralph Greenson to Dr Marianne Kris, 30 October 1960, AS archive.
5   *Mimosa*, Kindle edition, p. 100.
6   *Mimosa*, Kindle edition, p. 99.
7   'Marilyn Monroe's Life as a Divorcee', *Modern Screen*, Louella Parsons, October 1961.
8   'Gable and Monroe Star in Script by Miller', *New York Times*, Bosley Crowther, 2 February 1961.
9   Letter from Marilyn Monroe to Dr Greenson, 1, 2 March 1961, reproduced in *Fragments*, pp. 208–13.
10 Ibid.
11 *Mimosa*, Kindle edition, p. 111.
12 Interview with Gloria Romanoff, AS, MHL.
13 Letter from Marilyn Monroe to Paula and Lee Strasberg, 8 February 1961.
14 *Marilyn: An Untold Story*, p. 93.
15 Telegram from Rupert Allan to Marilyn Monroe, 10 February 1961, Julien's Auctions: https://www.julienslive.com/lot-details/index/catalog/314/lot/125493/MARILYN-MONROE-RECEIVED-TELEGRAM-FROM-RUPERT-ALLAN
16 'Marilyn Whisked from Hospital', *LA Examiner*, 6 March 1961.
17 'MM Closes 23-Day Hospital Run and "Feels Wonderful"', *New York Journal-American*, John Pascal, 6 March 1961.

Chapter 76

1   *Marilyn Monroe Confidential*, p. 221.
2   *Mimosa*, Kindle edition, p. 110.
3   Letter from Marilyn Monroe to Dr Greenson, 2 March 1961, *Fragments*, p. 213.
4   *Marilyn Monroe Confidential*, p. 222.
5   *My Life, My Loves*, Eddie Fisher, Harper & Row, New York, 1981, p. 193.

6 *The Secret Life of Marilyn Monroe*, p. 365.
7 Interview with Jeanne Martin, AS, MHL.
8 Letter from Dr Ralph Greenson to Dr Marianne Kris, 15 May 1961, AS archive.
9 *Marilyn Monroe Confidential*, p. 224.
10 'Dateline Hollywood', *Hollywood Reporter*, Radie Harris 12 September 1961.
11 *Marilyn Monroe Confidential*, p. 232.
12 *Marilyn Monroe Confidential*, p. 204.
13 *Marilyn Monroe Confidential*, p. 232.
14 *Marilyn Monroe Confidential*, p. 193.
15 Letter from Constance Hutchinson to Marilyn Monroe, 14 December 1961, Julien's Auctions: https://www.julienslive.com/lot-details/index/catalog/180/lot/83384/MARILYN-MONROE-INVOICE-FOR-BOARDING-MAF?uact=5&aid=180&lid=83384&current_page=0
16 *The Unabridged Marilyn*, p. 391.
17 Interview with Inez Melson, AS, MHL.
18 *The Life and Opinions of Maf the Dog, and of His Friend Marilyn Monroe*, Andrew O'Hagan, Faber & Faber, London, 2010, p. 62.
19 'Andrew O'Hagan on Maf the Dog', *Paris Review*, Kate Waldman, 24 January 2011.
20 *Marilyn: Her Life In Her Own Words*, p. 143.

Chapter 77

1 *Marilyn Monroe Confidential*, p. 206.
2 *Marilyn Monroe Confidential*, p. 297.
3 Letter from Dr Ralph Greenson to Dr Marianne Kris, 15 May 1961, AS archive.
4 'Marilyn Monroe's Psychiatrist Speaks Out in Her Defense', *Medical Tribune*, Ken Sandler, 24 October 1973.
5 Pat Newcomb interviewed by Robert Slatzer, 1972, AS archive, MHL.
6 Western Union Telegram, Marilyn Monroe to Dr Ralph Greenson, 1 June 1961, AS archive.
7 Interview with Danny Greenson, AS, MHL.

8   Letter from Dr Ralph Greenson to Anna Freud, 4 December 1961, Box 37, Folder 10, Anna Freud Papers, Library of Congress.
9   Letter from Dr Greenson to Dr Marianne Kris, 20 August 1962, AS archive.
10 Interview with Danny Greenson, AS, MHL.
11 'A Good Long Look at Myself'.

CHAPTER 78

1   *Icon: The Life, Times, and Films of Marilyn Monroe: Volume 2, 1956 to 1962 and Beyond*, Gary Vitacco-Robles, Kindle edition, Chapter 19.
2   Ibid.
3   'A Good Long Look at Myself'.
4   Ibid.
5   Letter from Dr Greenson to Dr Marianne Kris, 20 August 1962, AS archive.
6   Letter from Marilyn Monroe to Bobby Miller, 2 February 1962, Julien's Auctions: https://www.julienslive.com/lot-details/index/catalog/180/lot/82963/MARILYN-MONROE-LETTER-TO-BOBBY-MILLER-MENTIONING-ROBERT-KENNEDY
7   *Marilyn: Her Life in Her Own Words*, p. 143.

CHAPTER 79

1   *Marilyn Monroe Confidential*, p. 234.
2   'Marilyn Monroe in Mexico', *El Pais*, Micaela Varela, 15 October 2022.
3   *Marilyn Monroe Confidential*, pp. 234–5.
4   Letter from Frederick V. Field to Anthony Summers, 29 April 1986, AS archive.
5   *From Right to Left: An Autobiography*, Frederick V. Field, Lawrence Hill & Co., Westport, p. 220.
6   *Marilyn: The Last Months*, Eunice Murray and Rose Shade, Pyramid Books, New York, 1975, p. 62.
7   *Marilyn and Me*, pp. 238–9.

Chapter 80

1. Marilyn Monroe's annotated script, Something's Got to Give, Christie's: https://www.christies.com/en/lot/lot-1646513
2. Marilyn Monroe's annotated script, Something's Got to Give, Christie's: https://www.christies.com/en/lot/lot-4518528
3. Telegram from Joe DiMaggio to Marilyn Monroe, 1 June 1962, Julien's Auctions: https://www.julienslive.com/lot-details/index/catalog/316/lot/124143/MARILYN-MONROE-RECEIVED-BIRTHDAY-TELEGRAM-FROM-JOE
4. *Icon: Volume 2*, Chapter 26.
5. Pat Newcomb interviewed by Robert Slatzer, AS archive, MHL.
6. Interview with Danny Greenson, AS, MHL.
7. Marilyn Monroe, undated, Arthur P. Jacobs Collection, Coll. 023. Series 1: Publicist Files. Department of Archives and Special Collections, William H. Hannon Library, Loyola Marymount University.
8. Ibid.
9. 'Studio Scraps Film as Martin Quits', *Daily Journal*, 12 June 1962.
10. 'Hedda Hopper Says " ... Marilyn Monroe Has Had It"', *Detroit Free Press*, Hedda Hopper, 19 June 1962.
11. *On Cukor*, Gavin Lambert, ed. Robert Trachtenberg, Rizzoli, New York, 2000, p. 135.
12. *Marilyn Monroe: The Biography*, p. 589.
13. *Joe DiMaggio: The Hero's Life*, Richard Ben Cramer, Simon & Schuster, New York, p. 410.
14. 'Remembering Marilyn Monroe', *Larry King Live*, CNN, 1 June 2001.
15. Letter from Marilyn Monroe to Joe DiMaggio, undated but thought to be 1962, Bonhams: https://www.bonhams.com/auctions/16151/lot/1009/
16. *Marilyn and Me*, p. 94.

Chapter 81

1. Letter from Pat Newcomb to Marilyn Monroe, undated, from Marilyn Monroe's filing cabinets, Inez Melson file, AS archive.

2 'Remembrance of Marilyn', *Good Housekeeping*, Flora Rheta Schreiber, January 1963.
3 Letter from Dr Greenson to Norman Rosten, 15 August 1962, AS archive.
4 Interview with Eunice Murray, AS, MHL.
5 Letter from Dr Ralph Greenson to Norman Rosten, 15 August 1962, AS archive.
6 Letter from Dr Ralph Greenson to Dr Marianne Kris, 20 August 1962, AS archive.
7 Interview with Eunice Murray, AS, MHL.
8 'Seek Mexican in MM Mystery Call', *Daily News*, Florabel Muir, 8 August 1962.
9 Transcript of interview with Eunice Murray, *Say Goodbye to the President*, AS archive.
10 Interview with Eunice Murray, AS, MHL.
11 'Mystery Phone Call Received By Marilyn May Have Caused Her to Take Additional Dose of Sleep Pills', *Los Angeles Times*, Frank Laro and Bill Beebe, 7 August 1962.
12 Letter from Dr Ralph Greenson to Norman Rosten, 15 August 1962, AS archive.
13 Interview with Eunice Murray, AS, MHL.
14 Police Report, Sgt Byron, 10 August 1962, AS archive.
15 Transcript of interview with Eunice Murray, *Say Goodbye to the President*, AS archive.
16 Letter from Dr Ralph Greenson to Dr Marianne Kris, 20 August 1962, AS archive.

Chapter 82

1 Interview with Eunice Murray, AS, MHL.
2 Letter from Dr Greenson to Norman Rosten, 15 August 1962, AS archive.
3 Ibid.
4 Pat Newcomb interviewed by Robert Slatzer, AS archive, MHL.
5 Interview with Dr Hyman Engelberg by Alan Tomich, 27 September 1982: https://youtu.be/Fcg-oVZEgQw?si=G0PNfIj124lRRW3J

6 'Marilyn Monroe and the Prescription Drugs that Killed Her', Dr Howard Markel, 5 August 2016: https://www.pbs.org/newshour/health/marilyn-monroe-and-the-prescription-drugs-that-killed-her
7 Letter from Marilyn Monroe to Dr Greenson, 1/2 March 1961, reproduced in *Fragments*, pp. 208–13.
8 *Fragments*, p. ix.
9 *Conversations with Marilyn*, p. 189.
10 Letter from Dr Robert Litman to the LA County District Attorney's Office, 1982, AS archive.

Chapter 83

1 Pat Newcomb interviewed by Robert Slatzer, 1972, AS archive, MHL.
2 Ibid.
3 Interview with Pat Newcomb, AS, MHL.
4 Dr Ralph Greenson interviewed by Maurice Zolotow, 22 August 1973, AS archive.
5 *Legend*, Guiles, p. 290.
6 *Legend*, Guiles, p. 291.
7 *Goddess*, p. 154.
8 Interview with Rupert Allan, AS, MHL.
9 Letter from Dr Greenson to Marianne Kris, 20 August 1962, AS archive.
10 Ibid.
11 Notes on interview with Pat Newcomb, 6 February 1984, AS.
12 Dr Litman's notes of interview with Dr Greenson, 13 August 1962, Suicide Prevention Team, AS archive.
13 George Barris, Pat Newcomb folder, AS archive.
14 *The Richard Burton Diaries*, ed. Chris Williams, Yale University Press, New Haven, 2012, p. 198.
15 *Natural Blonde: A Memoir*, Liz Smith, Hyperion, New York, 2000, p. 298.
16 'The Press Rep and Marilyn', *Los Angeles Times*, Liz Smith, 10 March 1992.
17 'The Press Rep and Marilyn'.
18 Pat Newcomb interviewed by Robert Slatzer, AS archive, MHL.
19 'The Press Rep and Marilyn'.

Chapter 84

1. Interview with Natalie Jacobs, née Trundy, AS, MHL.
2. In Defense of Marilyn, typescript, Chapter 2, p. 6, Box 41, Folder 1, Earl Wilson Papers, Lawrence and Lee Theatre Research Institute of The Ohio State University Libraries.

Chapter 85

1. Fire and Police Research Association of Los Angeles Newsletter, February 1963.
2. Interview with Jim Dougherty, AS, MHL.
3. 'Accuser Regards Himself As A Patriot And Crusader', *Courier-Journal*, 28 February 1965.
4. *The Strange Death of Marilyn Monroe*, Frank A. Capell, The Herald of Freedom, 1964, p. 6.
5. *The Strange Death of Marilyn Monroe*, p. 68.
6. Letter from Frank Capell to Helen Clay, 3 September 1964, Will Fowler Papers, Special Collections & Archives, University Library, California State University, Northridge (CSUN).
7. 'Winchell . . . on Broadway', *Tribune*, 25 August 1964.
8. 'Walter Winchell in New York', *Ledger-Enquirer*, 5 June 1967.
9. Memo from J. Edgar Hoover to Robert Kennedy, 8 July 1964: https://www.archives.gov/files/research/jfk/releases/docid-32423593.pdf
10. Memo from R. W. Smith to W. C. Sullivan, 14 July 1964: https://www.archives.gov/files/research/jfk/releases/docid-32423593.pdf
11. *The Bureau: My Thirty Years in Hoover's FBI*, William C. Sullivan with Bill Brown, Norton, New York, 1979, p. 56.

Chapter 86

1. 'Accuser Regards Himself As A Patriot And Crusader', 28 February 1965.
2. '1973: A Selection Of Noteworthy Titles', *New York Times*, 2 December 1973.
3. *The Deer Park*, Norman Mailer, G. P. Putnam's Sons, New York, 1955, p. 90.

4 *Marilyn: A Biography*, Norman Mailer, Grosset & Dunlap, New York, 1973, p. 19.
5 'Two Myths Converge: NM Discovers MM', *Time*, 16 July 1973.
6 'Mailer Answers Plagiarism Charge', *News-Press*, Florida, 6 July 1973.
7 'Two Myths Converge'.
8 *Marilyn: A Biography*, p. 18.
9 Norman Mailer interviewed by Johnny Carson, *Tonight Show*, 22 May 1974.
10 'Marilyn Monroe – Why Won't They Let Her Rest in Peace?'

Chapter 87

1 'Platinum Pain', *New Yorker*, Daphne Merkin, 31 January 1999.
2 *The Life and Curious Death of Marilyn Monroe*, Robert F. Slatzer, W. H. Allen, London, 1975, p. 133.
3 Memo from Bob Slatzer to Will Fowler, 30 August 1972, Will Fowler Papers, CSUN.
4 Will Fowler notes, CSUN.
5 Agreement between Frank A. Capell, Will Fowler, Robert F. Slatzer, 16 February 1973, Classic Blondes: https://classicblondes.com/2018/06/13/who-wrote-the-life-and-curious-death-of-marilyn-monroe-part-1/
6 Will Fowler notes, CSUN.
7 Letter from Joseph Jasgur to Will Fowler, 28 October 1991, Will Fowler Papers, CSUN.
8 Letter from Will Fowler to Howard Rosenberg, 7 August 1991, Will Fowler Papers, CSUN.
9 *The Life and Curious Death of Marilyn Monroe*, p. 1.
10 'Marilyn Nails Her Murderer', *Globe*, Robert F. Slatzer, 24 August 1982.
11 Letter from Will Fowler to Howard Rosenberg, 7 August 1991, Will Fowler Papers, CSUN.
12 https://classicblondes.com/2018/04/10/robert-slatzer/

Chapter 88

1 'Marilyn "Cover-up To Protect JFK"', *Evening Standard*, 3 September 1975.

2. Investigation Re: Article in 'Oui' Magazine, 'Who Killed Marilyn Monroe?', LAPD Report, 22 October 1975, p. 10.
3. *Marilyn Monroe: Murder Cover-Up*, Milo Speriglio, Seville Publishing, Van Nuys, 1982, p. 115.
4. *Marilyn Monroe: Murder Cover-Up*, p. 127.
5. 'Actor Claims RFK Involved in Marilyn Death Mystery', *Examiner*, Alan Drake, 16 July 1985.
6. Letter from Robert Slatzer to Anthony Summers, undated, Ted Jordan File, AS archive.
7. 'The Enduring Mystery of Marilyn Monroe', UPI, Joan Goulding, 15 August 1982.
8. 'No Foul Play Uncovered in 1962 Death of Marilyn Monroe', *Los Angeles Times*, Ted Rohrlich, 29 December 1982.
9. Ibid.

Chapter 89

1. Will Fowler research notes, Will Fowler Papers, CSUN.
2. Transcript of interview with Eunice Murray, *Say Goodbye to the President*, AS archive.
3. 'Miner's Account of Monroe's Death', *Los Angeles Times*, John Miner, 4 August 2005.
4. *Marilyn: The Passion and the Paradox*, p. 420.
5. Ronald 'Mike' Carroll interview with Thomas Noguchi, 31 October 1985, *Icon, Volume 2*.

Chapter 90

1. *Goddess*, p. 324.
2. *Say Goodbye to the President*, 25 October 1985, BBC documentary: https://youtu.be/VZSJmEI_X60?si=6JZMlMqhcF2qTw1s
3. *Goddess*, p. 248.
4. *Say Goodbye to the President*.
5. Ibid.
6. Ibid.
7. *Goddess*, p. 347.
8. 'Marilyn Monroe Mystery Persists: 23 Years After Her Death,

Questions Continue to Generate Controversy', *Los Angeles Times*, Robert Welkos and Ted Rohrlich, 29 September 1985.

CHAPTER 91

1. *Fragments*, p, 221.
2. Dr Litman's notes of interview with Dr Greenson, 13 August 1962, Suicide Prevention Team, AS archive.
3. Notes of meeting with Dr Norman Tabachnick, 27 September 1983, Suicide Prevention Team, AS archive.
4. 'Remembrance of Marilyn', *Good Housekeeping*, Flora Rheta Schreiber, January 1963.
5. *Marilyn: The Ultimate Look at the Legend*, pp. 194–6.
6. Interview with Henry Rosenfeld, AS, MHL.
7. *Show Business Laid Bare*, Earl Wilson, G. P. Putnam's Sons, New York, 1974, p. 85.
8. Ibid.
9. *Mimosa*, Kindle edition, p. 192.
10. *Marilyn and Me*, p. 244.
11. *Marilyn and Me*, p. 246.
12. Interview with Natalie Jacobs, AS, MHL.

CHAPTER 92

1. Interview with Danny Greenson, AS, MHL.
2. Letter from Marilyn Monroe to Bobby Miller, 2 February 1962, Julien's Auctions: https://www.julienslive.com/lot-details/index/catalog/180/lot/82963/MARILYN-MONROE-LETTER-TO-BOBBY-MILLER-MENTIONING-ROBERT-KENNEDY
3. Letter from Marilyn Monroe to Isidore Miller, 2 February 1962, *MM – Personal*, p. 233.
4. Letter from Marilyn Monroe to Bobby Miller, 2 February 1962.
5. Telegram from Marilyn Monroe to Mr and Mrs Robert Kennedy, 13 June 1962, AS archive.
6. Letter from Jean Kennedy Smith to Marilyn Monroe, undated but the summer of 1962, Julien's Auctions: https://bid.juliensauctions.com/lot-details/index/catalog/180/lot/82964/

MARILYN-MONROE-RECEIVED-LETTER-FROM-JEAN-KENNEDY-SMITH

7 *Mimosa*, Kindle edition, p. 196.
8 Interview with Ralph Roberts, *20/20*, ABC, 28 August 1985.
9 Interview with Danny Greenson, AS, MHL.
10 Interview with Joan Greenson, AS, MHL.
11 *Say Goodbye to the President*.
12 Transcript of interview with Eunice Murray, *Say Goodbye to the President*, AS archive.

Chapter 93

1 *Goddess*, New American Library, 1986, p. 401.
2 *Say Goodbye to the President*.
3 Transcript of taped conversation between Billy Woodfield and Dr Ralph Greenson, 1964, Billy Woodfield file, AS archive.
4 *Marilyn and Me*, p. 250.
5 Letter from John Bates to Bruno Bernard, 8 October 1986, quoted in *Marilyn: Intimate Exposures*, Susan Bernard, Sterling Publishing, New York, 2011, p. 185.
6 'Rumors of Plot in Marilyn Monroe Death Abound, But Proof Lacking', UPI, Scott Vernon, 5 October 1985.
7 Patricia Newcomb interviewed by Bob Slatzer, AS archive, MHL.

Chapter 94

1 'Could this be Monroe's last lover?', *Miami Herald*, Beatriz Parga, 8 September 1992.
2 'Marilyn Had No Cause for Suicide', *Los Angeles Herald-Examiner*, Alfred Robbins, 16 August 1962.
3 'The Last Romance of Marilyn Monroe', *Gallery*, Bill Stadiem, May 1980.
4 AS interview notes with José Bolaños, AS archive.
5 Letter from Dr Robert Litman to the LA County District Attorney's Office, 1982, AS archive.
6 Ibid.
7 'Bolanos Says Last Good-by With Flowers', *Daily News*, 18 August 1962.

8 'Seek Mexican in MM Mystery Call', *Daily News*, Florabel Muir, 8 August 1962.

Chapter 95

1 'Marilyn Lauded, World's Press "Regrets"', UPI, *Los Angeles Herald-Examiner*, 6 August 1962.
2 'Marilyn Monroe', *Vogue*, September 1962.
3 Letter from Truman Capote to Newton Arvin, 8 August 1962, in *Too Brief a Treat: The Letters of Truman Capote*, ed. Gerald Clarke, Random House, New York, 2004, p. 359.
4 'Marilyn was "Pitchforked" Into World She Didn't Know', *Columbus Ledger*, Raymond E. Palmer, 6 August 1962.
5 'Did Hollywood Kill Marilyn Monroe?', Tara Hanks: https://tarahanks.com/2011/08/04/did-hollywood-kill-marilyn-monroe/
6 'Contagious Death?', *Valley News*, Paul Taylor, 14 March 1984.
7 'Marilyn's Mayfair Friend Found Dead', *Evening Standard*, 7 August 1962.
8 'Typist Was Found Dead In Flat, Had Talked Of Star's Death', *Liverpool Echo*, 28 August 1962.
9 'The "Love Goddess" Who Never Found Any Love', *Life*, Clare Boothe Luce, 7 August 1964.

Chapter 96

1 Services for Marilyn Monroe, Statement of Berniece Miracle, Inez Melson, Joe DiMaggio, 8 August 1962.
2 'Joe to Marilyn at Rites: "I Love You"', *Daily News*, Florabel Muir, 9 August 1962.
3 *Timebends*, p. 531.
4 Marilyn Monroe inscription, Tiffany money clip, Julien's Auctions: https://www.julienslive.com/lot-details/index/catalog/68/lot/25775/MARILYN-MONROE-GIFTED-MONEY-CLIP
5 Lee Strasberg, Eulogy, 9 August 1962, *Fragments*, p. 231.
6 'Her Final and Irrevocable Role', *San Francisco Examiner*, Bob Considine, 9 August 1962.

7   'Joe to Marilyn at Rites: "I Love You"', *Daily News*, Florabel Muir, 9 August 1962.
8   Letter from Norman Rosten to Dr Greenson, undated, AS archive.
9   Letter from Dr Greenson to Norman Rosten, 15 August 1962, AS archive.
10 Letter from Dr Marianne Kris to Dr Greenson, 6 August 1962, AS archive.

Chapter 97

1   *Ben Hecht: Fighting Words, Moving Pictures*, Adina Hoffman, Yale University Press, New Haven, 2019, p. 198.
2   *Marilyn: A Biography*, p. 18.
3   Annotations by Rose Hecht, Letter from H. William Fitelson to Rose Hecht, 17 December 1973, Ben Hecht Papers, Newberry Library, Chicago.
4   'New Monroe Book From Old Memoirs', *Los Angeles Times*, Digby Diehl, 15 April 1974.
5   'Marilyn's "My Story" Was a Ben Hecht Script', *New York Post*, George Carpozi Jr, 21 June 1974.
6   'Hecht's Script, Greene Knew', *New York Post*, George Carpozi Jr, 22 June 1974.
7   Rose Hecht, handwritten comment on *Newsweek* story, 22 April 1974, Ben Hecht Papers, Newberry Library, Chicago.
8   Rose Hecht annotations to typescript of Chapter 1 of *My Story*, Ben Hecht Papers, Newberry Library, Chicago.
9   *My Story*, p. 66.

Chapter 98

1   *My Sister Marilyn*, p. 224.
2   Strasberg v Odyssey Group Inc (1996), Court of Appeal, Second District, Division 7, California: https://caselaw.findlaw.com/court/ca-court-of-appeal/1847294.html
3   Letter from Inez Melson to Joe DiMaggio, 6 September 1962, Inez Melson file, AS archive.
4   'The Things She Left Behind'.

5   'Blonde Ambitions: A Battle Erupts Over the Right To Market Marilyn', *Wall Street Journal*, Nathan Koppel, 10 April 2006.
6   The Marilyn Monroe Collection, Auction Catalogue, Odyssey Auctions, May 1994.
7   Classic 2 Marilyn Monroe™ Edition, Womanizer: https://www.womanizer.com/uk/marilyn-monroe-special-edition
8   Interview with Anna Strasberg by Scott Fortner, Marilyn Monroe Collection: https://themarilynmonroecollection.com/finding-marilyn-monroe-a-fans-journey-of-discovery-with-anna-strasberg-part-2/
9   'Blonde Ambitions: A Battle Erupts Over the Right To Market Marilyn'.
10 'The Mentor and the Movie Star', *Vanity Fair*, Patricia Bosworth, June 2003.
11 'Blonde Ambitions: A Battle Erupts Over the Right To Market Marilyn'.

Chapter 99

1   'Reporter Chasing Fraudulent Source Finds Methods Under Scrutiny', *New York Times*, Benjamin Weiser, 3 May 1999.
2   'JFK-Monroe "Affair" Papers Faked', ABC Reports, *Los Angeles Times*, Eleanor Randolph, 26 September 1997.
3   'The Things She Left Behind'.
4   Ibid.
5   'Agreement on Monroe Stuff Draws Closer', *Hollywood Reporter*, Leslie Simmons, 1 November 2007.
6   *MM – Personal*, p. 23.

Chapter 100

1   'Marilyn Monroe Lets Her Hair Down About Being Famous', *Life*, Richard Meryman, 3 August 1962.
2   'The "Love Goddess" Who Never Found Any Love', *Life*, Clare Boothe Luce, 7 August 1964.
3   *All the Available Light*, p. 29.
4   *All the Available Light*, p. 12.

5 'Marilyn's ghost got physical in filming of *Blonde*, star says', Reuters, Crispian Balmer, 8 September 2022.
6 '*Saints and Stinkers*: Director John Huston', *Rolling Stone*, Peter S. Greenberg, 19 February 1981, reproduced in *John Huston: Interviews*, ed. Robert Emmet Long, University Press of Mississippi, Jackson, 2001, p. 111.

Acknowledgements

My first – and biggest acknowledgement – goes to Anthony Summers, author of *Goddess*, first published in 1985. He gave me unrestricted access to his enormous Marilyn archive and allowed me to reproduce extracts from his unpublished audio tapes, which remain his copyright.

Anthony Summers also gave me special permission to remotely access copies of these tapes held at Margaret Herrick Library, Academy of Motion Picture Arts and Sciences, in Los Angeles. I must thank Warren Sherk, director of Special Collections at the Margaret Herrick Library, and also Genevieve Maxwell and Louise Hilton, who went out of their way to deal with numerous queries and for granting me access to their brilliant digital collections of historical material and e-resources.

Many other libraries gave me access to their wonderful special collections, where I found a wealth of mostly unpublished archival material. Thank you to:

The African American Museum and Library, Oakland for providing access to the oral testimony of Brownie McGhee.

Joe Weber at the American Jewish Archives, Cincinnati, Ohio for providing access to the Rabbi Goldburg Letters.

Zoe Stansell and the staff at the Manuscripts Reading Room, British Library, London for providing access to The Sir Laurence Olivier Archive. Also to the staff at Humanities 1, for providing access to the *Empire News* archive and numerous out-of-print books.

David Sigler, Special Collections & Archives, University

Library, California State University, Northridge for providing access to the Will Fowler Papers.

Oral History Archives at Columbia, Rare Book and Manuscript Library, Columbia University in the City of New York for providing access to the Reminiscences of Joshua Logan.

Cathy Henderson at the Harry Ransom Center, The University of Texas at Austin for providing access to the archives of Norman Mailer, Arthur Miller, Maurice Zolotow (including Natasha Lytess's unpublished memoir), Edith Sitwell, Eli Wallach and Anne Jackson. Thank you to Peter Wallach for copyright permission to quote from the unpublished writings of his mother, Anna Jackson.

Cynthia Becht and Jessica Guardado, Department of Archives and Special Collections, William H. Hannon Library, Loyola Marymount University for providing access to the Arthur P. Jacobs Collection.

Kerrie Cotten Williams, Library of Congress, Washington for providing access to the Anna Freud Papers.

Catherine Grandgeorge at the Newberry Library, Chicago for providing access to the Ben Hecht Papers.

Rebecca Jewett at Lawrence and Lee Theatre Research Institute of The Ohio State University Libraries for providing access to the Earl Wilson papers.

Simon Elliott at Center for Oral History Research, UCLA Library Special Collections for providing access to the Reminiscences of Nunnally Johnson.

Wellcome Library, London.

Thank you to all the interviewees featured in this book: Rupert Allan, James 'Jim' Dougherty, Peggy Feury, Sheila Graham, Amy Greene, Milton Greene, Danny Greenson, Joan Greenson, John Huston, Christopher Isherwood, Natalie Jacobs, Kay Little, Marion Marshall, Jeanne Martin, Inez Melson, Nico Minardos, Eunice Murray, Pat Newcomb, Lena Pepitone, Marjorie Plecher,

Gloria Romanoff, Henry Rosenfeld, Jane Russell, Hal Schaefer, Sheila Stewart Renour, William Travilla and Billy Wilder.

I must acknowledge many of the authors who have written about Marilyn and from whose work I have drawn: Lois Banner, George Barris, Georges Belmont, Susan Bernard, Clare Boothe Luce, Stanley Buchthal and Bernard Comment, Truman Capote, Charles Casillo, Sarah Churchwell, André de Dienes, James Dougherty, Stacy Eubank, Astrid Franse, Fred Lawrence Guiles, Jim Haspiel, Ben Hecht, Barbara Leaming, Norman Mailer, Richard Meryman, Arthur Miller, Berniece Baker Miracle and Mona Rae Miracle, Michelle Morgan, Eunice Murray and Rose Shade, Joyce Carol Oates, Lena Pepitone, Ralph Roberts, Randall Riese and Neal Hitchens, Carl Rollyson, Norman Rosten, Ted Schwarz, Sandra Shevey, Robert F. Slatzer, Milo Speriglio, Donald Spoto, Bill Stadiem, Susan Strasberg, Anthony Summers, J. Randy Taraborrelli, Adam Victor, Gary Vitacco-Robles, Edward Wagenknecht, Alexander Walker, W. J. Weatherby, Elizabeth Winder, Donald Wolfe and Maurice Zolotow.

In addition, there are a number of other authors whose books, essays or talks I've quoted from, including: Brigitte Bardot, Detlef Berthelsen, Christopher Bigsby, David Bret, Richard Burton, Frank Capell, Charlotte Chandler, Colin Clark, Richard Ben Cramer, Cameron Crowe, Elaine Dundy, Eddie Fisher, Margot Fonteyn, Stephane Groueff, Adina Hoffman, Anthony Holden, Hedda Hopper (and James Brough), John Huston, Terry Johnson, Elia Kazan, John Kobal, John Lahr, Gavin Lambert, Jeffrey Meyers, Yves Montand (with Hervé Hamon and Patrick Rotman), Andrew O'Hagan, Laurence Olivier, Tarquin Olivier, Rock G. Positano, Sidney Skolsky, Simone Signoret, Edith Sitwell, Milo Speriglio, Liz Smith, Lee Strasberg, William Styron, William C. Sullivan (with Bill Brown), Edgar Tafel, Eli Wallach, Earl Wilson, Shelley Winters and Richard B. Woodward.

Thank you too to the people I spoke to while researching this book. Some gave me leads, others granted in-depth interviews: Angela Allen, Julie Burchill, Marie Corvino, Gail Crowther, Scott Fortner, Professor Khalil Ghanem, Laraine Goldberg, Joshua Greene, Dean and James Haspiel, Carrie Kania, Suzie Kennedy, Jay Kanter, Sanford 'Sandy' Lieberson, Elaine Schreyeck, Curtice Taylor, Roy Turner and Chris Williams.

I also drew on a number of important film and television sources. In addition to Marilyn's movies these include: *The Tonight Show starring Johnny Carson*; *Dream Girl: The Making of Marilyn Monroe*; *Finding Nico*; *The Full Wax*, BBC; *Hollywood Greats: Marilyn Monroe*, BBC; *Late Night With David Letterman*; *The Legend of Marilyn Monroe*; *Marilyn Monroe: Ten Years On*, BBC; *Marilyn Monroe: Beyond the Legend*; *The Many Loves of Marilyn Monroe, E! A True Hollywood Story*; *Omnibus: Arthur Miller*, BBC; *The Mystery of Marilyn Monroe: The Unheard Tapes*, Netflix; *Person to Person with Edward R. Murrow*, CBS; *Arthur Miller: Writer*, HBO; *Remembering Marilyn Monroe, Larry King Live*, CNN; *The Sally Jessy Raphael Show*; *Say Goodbye to the President*, BBC.

Newspapers, magazines and journals proved vital too: *Allure, American Weekly, Australian Women's Weekly, Bangor Daily News, Cincinnati Enquirer, Columbus Ledger, Confidential, Collier's, Cosmopolitan, Courier-Journal, Daily Journal, Daily Mail, Daily Mirror, Daily News, Dallas Times Herald, Detroit Free Press, El Pais, Empire News, Entertainment Weekly, Esquire, Evening Standard,* Florida News-Press*, Fort Worth Star-Telegram, Gallery, Globe, Good Housekeeping, Guardian, Hansard, Hollywood Reporter, Hollywood Star, Huffington Post, Human Reproduction, Independent, International Medical Journal, Irish Independent, Los Angeles Herald Examiner, Ladies' Home Journal, Ledger-Enquirer, Leicester Evening Mail, Life, Liverpool Echo, London Review of Books, New Society, New York Herald Tribune, New York Journal-American, New Yorker, New York Post, McCall's, Medical Tribune, Miami Herald, Modern Screen, Motion Picture and Television, Movie Stars Parade, Observer, Pageant, Paris Review, Penthouse, People*

Weekly, Photoplay, Pittsburgh Press, Popular Photography, Record-Argus, Redbook, Reuters, Rolling Stone, Sacramento Union, San Francisco Examiner, San Mateo Times, Saturday Evening Post, Screen Guide, Slate, The Star, New York Times, Los Angeles Times, Time, UPI, Valley News, Vanity Fair, Vogue and *Wall St Journal.*

Auction houses I must thank include: Bonham's, Christie's, Heritage Auctions, Hunt, Julien's and RR Auction.

Websites and podcasts were also incredibly helpful: ClassicBlondes.com; cursumperficio.net; themarilynmonroecollection.com; marilynmonroefanatic.tumblr.com; TaraHanks.com; StarsandLetters.blogspot.com; TMZ.com; YouTube.com; *All Things Marilyn* podcast; *Marilyn: Behind the Icon* podcast; *The Rest is History* podcast.

At Aitken Alexander Associates I'm lucky to have the most fabulous team, headed by my super-agent and good friend Clare Alexander. Thanks too to Lesley Thorne, Alice De Abaitua, Matilda Southern-Wilkins and the rest of the staff at the agency.

I'd like to thank Suzanne Baboneau who commissioned this book for Simon & Schuster in the UK and Colin Dickerman who commissioned it for Grand Central Publishing, Hachette, in the US. At S&S I'd also like to thank Perminder Mann, Holly Harris, Sophia Akhtar, Florence Garnett, the fabulous copy editor Tamsin Shelton, proofreader Clare Wallis, designer India Minter, indexer Ben Murphy, and freelance editor Mike Jones. At Grand Central I'd like to thank Ian Dorset and the fabulous team in America.

For the reproduction of images of Marilyn I'd like to thank various picture agencies: Alamy, Getty, Photofest and Shutterstock.

Finally, I'd like to thank my friends and family for their support while I've been working on this book, but particularly Marcus Field.

INDEX

MM indicates Marilyn Monroe.

Abbott, Allan 24–5
Abbott, Kathy 25
Academy of Motion Picture Arts and
    Sciences 3, 4
  Academy Museum of Motion
    Pictures, Los Angeles 421
  Awards (Oscars) 60, 84, 113, 281,
    282, 283, 307
Actors Studio, New York 7, 185, 215–
    21, 289, 332
Adler, Zsuzsanna 52–3
Aguirre, Elsa 323
'An Album of Film Stars', John Player
    & Sons 38
Aldeburgh Festival 135
All About Eve (film) 10, 96, 111, 423
All About Marilyn (podcast) 4
All Things Marilyn (podcast) 204
Allan, Rupert 3, 171, 306–7, 347
Allen, Angela 295
Amagansett, Long Island 260–61
Ambassador Hotel, Los Angeles 72
American Communist Group in
    Mexico 324
Anderson, Mark 418, 419
Anna Freud Centre for the
    Psychoanalytic Study and
    Treatment of Children, London
    258–9, 420
Anna Freud Foundation 258
Any Number Can Play (film) 364
Apple Knockers and the Coke, The
    (film) 198
Arens, Richard 236
Armas, Ana de 85, 201, 425

Arnold, Eve 115, 116, 210, 296
Arthur P. Jacobs 328–9, 333, 351
As Young as You Feel (film) 10, 111–12,
    114, 129, 231, 423
Asphalt Jungle, The (film) 10, 96, 185
Astor Theatre, New York 218
Atkinson, George 31–2, 33, 49, 57
Atkinson, Maude 31–2, 33, 57
Atkinson, Nellie 31
Authentic Brands Group (ABG)
    199, 414
Avedon, Richard 40, 171, 183

Bacall, Lauren 177
Baker, Jasper Newton 18–19, 21, 65
Banner, Lois 58, 419–20
  MM – Personal 102, 375, 420
Bardot, Brigitte 102–3, 400
Barnhart, Sylvia 9–10
Barnum and Bailey 208
Barr, Roseanne 186
Barris, George 32, 46–7, 51, 315, 322,
    326, 349, 414
Barsa, Mikel 198–9
Bates, John 392–3
Bates, Nancy 392–3
Bautzer, Gregson 158, 407
Beaton, Cecil 401
Becker, Marion Rombauer: *The New
    Joy of Cooking* 273–4
Bello, Jean 41
Bellow, Saul 135
Belmont, Georges 21
Bergman, Ingrid 75
Bern, Paul 39

Bernard, Bruno 393
Berry, Simon: *The Dame and the Showgirl* 134
Berthelsen, Detlef: *Alltag bei Familie Freud: Die Erinnerungen der Paula Fichtl* 257
Bigsby, Christopher 226–7, 255
Blixen, Karen 135–6
Blonde (Netflix film) 85, 201–2, 425
Blue Book Modeling Agency 9–10, 72–3, 76, 186, 188
Bogart, Humphrey 165, 177
Bolaños, José 323–5, 327, 396–8
Bolender family (foster parents of MM) 16–18, 28–30, 31, 32, 46, 47, 50, 65, 223, 313
Bolender, Ida 16, 17, 28, 29, 30, 47, 50, 223
Bolender, Lester 28
Bolender, Nancy 17, 31
Bolender, Wayne 17, 28, 29
Boty, Pauline: *The Only Blonde in the World* 422
Brando, Marlon 216–18, 220, 326, 327, 401
Bret, David 104
British Library 4, 251
Britten, Benjamin 135
Broccoli, Albert 'Cubby' 93
Burnside, Bill 110–11
Burton, Richard 349
Bus Stop (film) 11, 123, 220, 233, 245, 346, 424

Calcar, Jan Steven van 131
Calvert, Gerry 402
Capell, Frank 354–5
   The Strange Death of Marilyn Monroe 355–9, 364–5, 373, 390–91, 393–4
Capote, Truman 185, 206, 401
   A Beautiful Child 211–14
Carey, Mariah 43–4
Carlyle Hotel, New York 381–2, 417
Carmen, Jeanne 3
Carroll, Ronald 'Mike' 371–2, 375–6
Castleberry, William 201
Cat on a Hot Tin Roof (play) 206–7

Cavanagh, June 402
Chambrun, Jacques 157, 158, 161–4
Chaplin, Charlie 11, 108, 110, 112, 280
Chaplin Jr, Charlie 55, 130
Chaplin, Sydney 55
Chekhov, Michael 115, 131, 132, 411
Chissell, Noble 'Kid' 365
chloral hydrate 302, 331–2, 337, 342–3, 374–5, 397
Christie's, New York, sale of MM's personal property (1999) 43, 115, 183–4, 186, 189–90, 191, 273, 314, 414
Churchwell, Sarah: *The Many Lives of Marilyn Monroe* 255
CIA 361, 366, 371, 416
civil rights 318, 385, 386
Clark, Colin 248, 254
   My Week with Marilyn 254–5
Clash by Night (film) 118–19
classicblondes.com 204
Clay, Helen 356–7
Clemmons, Jack 333, 339, 340, 354–6, 374
Cleopatra (film) 84, 328–9
Clift, Montgomery 205, 257, 287, 303–4, 312, 347
Cloud, Tom 417
Cohn, Harry 88–9
Collier, Constance 211–12
Collier's magazine 11, 159, 163
Collins, Joan 86, 87, 173
Columbia Pictures 32, 88–9, 93
Columbia-Presbyterian Medical Center, New York 306, 307, 309, 313
Confidential magazine 153, 154
Conover, David 68–71, 72, 78
   Finding Marilyn: A Romance 68–71
Conroy, Millington 'Mill' 412–13, 418–19
Conroy, Ruth 412, 418
Consolidated Film Industries 20
Corday, Elliot 187
Cottrell, Richard 169
Coward, Noël: *Conversation Piece* 270
Cramer, Richard Ben 331

Crawford, Joan 38, 103–5, 219
Crosby, Bing 70, 131, 383
Cukor, George 280, 330, 421
Curtis, Tony 54, 86, 265–6
Cusack, Lawrence X 416–17
Cusack III, Lawrence X. 'Lex' 416–17

Dagens Nyheter 400
Daily Mirror 25, 399
Daily Sketch 231, 253, 399
Dalí, Salvador 422
Dargis, Manohla 202
Darrach, Brad 51
De Young, Justine 193–4
Deir, Francine Gifford 25
Delaney, Frank 174, 409
Denny, Reginald 68
DeWitt, Addison 96
DiCicco, Pat 113
Didion, Joan 400
Die Welt 400
Dienes, André de: *Marilyn, mon Amour* 75–81
Dietrich, Marlene 102
DiMaggio, Joe 3, 61, 72, 100, 167, 170, 179, 364, 414, 418
   divorce from MM 147–51, 208
   domestic violence, MM endures bouts of during marriage to 144–5, 147, 164, 179, 331
   first meets MM 117–18, 121–3, 126–7
   friendship with MM after divorce 208, 306, 309, 319, 320, 326, 331, 398
   funeral of MM and 403, 405
   gold medal inscribed with quotation from Saint-Exupéry, MM gives to 116
   marriage to MM (14 January 1954) 138–9
   Miller on 228
   'My Dad', MM's letters to 146–9
   My Story, reaction to 157, 163
   'Pa', signs letters to MM 25–6
   Schaefer and 150–52, 154–6
   sex life with MM 117, 146–7, 214, 279
   toxic relationship with MM, highly charged 137–49, 164, 179, 331
   will of MM and 412
   wrong door raid and 153–6
DiMaggio Jr, Joe 336
DiMaggio, Marie 138–9
Dominik, Andrew 201, 202
Don't Bother to Knock (film) 10, 17, 86–7, 89, 123, 305, 423
Doonan, Simon 189–90
Doubleday 158, 159, 163, 407
Dougherty, Jim 23, 42, 49, 64–7, 78, 82, 94, 114, 313, 354, 363
   The Secret Happiness of Marilyn Monroe 56, 63
'Dream Show', New York (1955) 208–10
Dundy, Elaine: *Life Itself* 206

East of Eden (film) 218
Ebbins, Milton 333, 337, 338, 394
Egyptian, The (film) 173
Einstein, Albert 107–10, 241–2
El Rodeo School, Beverly Hills 7
Eliot, T. S. 418–19
Elton John: 'Candle in the Wind' 422
Empire News 160–62, 163, 407
Engelberg, Hyman 37, 331, 333, 341–3, 356, 394
Esquire 260

Famous Artists 173
Fay, Paul B. 393
FBI 200, 201, 324, 357, 358, 361, 371
Feldman, Charles 111, 112, 173–4
Feury, Peggy 51
FIB aktuellt 196
Fichtl, Paula 257
Field, Frederick Vanderbilt 324
Field, Nieves 324
Fields, Leila 27, 39
Fields, W. C. 271
Finkelhor, David 52
Fire and Police Research Association of Los Angeles 354
First Motion Picture Unit 68
Fisher, Eddie 310
Fitzgerald, Ella 203–4

Flynn, Errol 212
Fonda, Jane 185
Fonteyn, Margot 132
Forever Marilyn (statue) 423
Fortner, Scott 22, 189, 194, 199
Fowler, Will 364–7, 373
Franco, Amy 171–2
Frank and Joseph's Beauty Salon 9–10
Frankfurter Abendpost 399
Fredenhall, Bill 55
Freud, Anna 53, 256–9, 319, 406, 412
Freud, Sigmund 26, 53, 111, 222
   The Interpretation of Dreams 257
Frosch, Aaron 258

Gable, Clark 20, 38, 40, 107, 287, 291, 295–9, 303, 329–30
Garbo, Greta 4, 38, 212, 218, 380
Garland, Judy 179, 204, 309, 421
Gentlemen Prefer Blondes (film) 1, 44, 100, 111, 139, 150, 172, 222, 404, 423
Ghanem, Professor Khalil 37
Giancana, Sam 366, 416, 418
Giesler, Jerry 147
Gifford, Charles Stanley 20–25, 27, 94
Gifford, Lillian 20
Girl in Pink Tights, The (film) 173
Girl in the Red Swing, The (film) 174
Goddard, Eleanor 'Bebe' 55–6, 64
Goddard, Erwin 'Doc' 46, 55–6, 64, 78
Goddard, Grace (née McKee) 23, 27, 32, 33, 39, 46–7, 57–60, 62, 64–5, 67, 69, 78, 137–8
Goldburg, Rabbi Robert 241–4
Golden Age of Hollywood 1
Goldwyn Studios 88
Googie's 55
Gottesman, Abraham 222
Gould, Deborah 377–9
Goulden, Mark 360
Graham, Sheila 85, 127, 132
Grainger, Charles 18
Grandison, Lionel 371–3
Graves, Lyle Arthur 18
Green, Bernard 259
Greene, Amy 40, 54, 57, 59, 60, 86, 87, 96, 117, 138, 140–41, 144, 167–8, 169, 176, 180, 209
Greene, Milton 60, 98, 171–2, 174, 175, 180, 208–9, 222, 239, 407–9
Greenson, Danny 317, 318, 319, 327, 328, 385, 387
Greenson, Hildi 3–4, 317
Greenson, Joan 7, 8, 131–2, 205, 317–20, 327, 342, 387–8, 404, 405
Greenson, Ralph
   adolescent girl, compares MM to 311
   'borderline paranoid addict', describes MM as 319
   bruised nose of MM and 330
   case notes 3–4, 275
   death of MM and 53, 333, 335–6, 338–50, 352–3, 374, 380, 390–91, 394, 397, 405–6
   family of, MM encouraged to socialise with 317–18
   Fifth Helena Drive home of MM and 321, 322
   hospitalisation of MM and 302–6
   'Jesus', MM calls her 316
   lecture given by, MM attends 7–8
   'Marilyn tapes' and 105, 106
   personal appearance of MM, on 184
   professional-patient relationship with MM 316
   Sinatra and 309–10
   sleeping pills, on MM's habit of taking 177
   Something's Got to Give, firing of MM from and 327–9
   surrogate parent, casts himself in role of 26
   therapy with, MM begins 275–9
Grosset & Dunlap 360
Grunion Detective Agency 423
Guastafeste, Al 140
Guccione, Bob 370
Gurdin, Maria 313
Gurdin, Michael 95, 330–31

Hall, Bobby 55
Halsman, Philippe 113–14, 129

'Happy Birthday', MM sings to JFK, Madison Square Garden (1962) 40, 189, 191, 192, 195, 328, 381, 397, 414
Hard Copy (television show) 349–50
Harlow, Jean 10, 38–41, 72, 84, 211, 327
Harris, Holly 168–9
Harris, Marlys 85
Harris, Radie 270, 312
Haspiel, James 60, 101, 331, 382, 415
Hayes, Steve 55
Hecht, Ben 157–9, 161–2, 163, 407–9
Hecht, Rose 162, 164, 407–9
Hefner, Hugh 90–91, 121–2
Hell's Angels (film) 38, 40
Herald of Freedom 355
Herbuveaux, Nanette 157
Hersh, Seymour: *The Dark Side of Camelot* 416–18
Hoffa, Jimmy 366, 369
Hogan, Tilford Marion (great-grandfather of MM) 33
Hohenberg, Margaret 222, 224, 256–7
Hoja del Lunes 400
Hollywood Blue (compilation of 'stag films') 198
Hollywood Reporter 174, 312
Hollywood Star Newspaper 197
Hoover, J. Edgar 200, 357–8
Hopper, Hedda 88, 264, 284–5, 329–30
Hornblow Jr. Arthur 94
House Un-American Activities Committee 235, 318–19, 385
How to Be Very, Very Popular (film) 174
How to Marry a Millionaire (film) 139, 177, 246, 424
Howells, Chester 65
Hueth, Potter 72
Human Reproduction 168–9
Hunter, Arline 198
Hurley, Elizabeth 186–8
Huston, John 89, 96, 107, 257–8, 276, 286–9, 292, 294, 295–9, 421, 425
Hyams, Joe 267, 390
Hyde, Johnny 93–7, 100, 111–12, 125, 156
Hyde, Mozelle 95, 96

I Love Lucy (television show) 165–7
'I Wanna Be Loved By You' (song) 13, 424
Il Tempo 400
Insignificance (play and film) 108–9
International Church of the Foursquare Gospel 29
Irvin, Philip 153, 154

Jackson, Alison 380
Jackson, Anne 289–91
Jacobs, Arthur P. 329, 333, 335, 347, 351–3, 384
Jacobs, Natalie 351–3, 384
Jasgur, Joseph 365
Jean Harlow Story, The (script) 41
Jessel, George 89
Johnson, Erskine 121–2
Johnson, Nunnally 95–6, 173, 177
Johnson, Terry 108
Jones, Harmon 129
Jordan, Ted 370
  Norma Jean: A Hollywood Love Story 370
Josefa (chihuahua) 93, 313
Joyce, James: *Ulysses* 115–16
Julien's Auctions, Los Angeles 22, 95, 191–2, 343

Kael, Pauline 17, 185
Kamber, Bernie 127
Kardashian, Kim 191–5, 196
Karger, Anne 94
Karger, Fred 93–4, 112, 156
Karger, Mary 94
Kazan, Elia 111–14, 122–3, 207, 217–18, 220, 227–9
Kazan, Molly 112
Kelley, Natalie 90, 118–19
Kelley, Tom 90, 118, 119, 120
Kelly, Gene 87, 172

Kennedy, Ethel 385
Kennedy, John F.
  assassination 192, 333, 349, 379
  death of MM and 333, 334, 345, 349–50, 353, 354–8, 364, 368, 377, 378, 379, 380
  'Happy Birthday', MM sings to, Madison Square Garden, New York (1962) 40, 189, 191, 192, 195, 328, 381, 414
  inaugural address 303
  Palm Springs, spends time with MM at Bing Crosby's home in 70, 131, 343
  sex tape allegedly starring MM and 200
  sexual relationship with MM 70, 333–4, 345, 349–50, 353–8, 364, 368, 377, 378, 379, 380–84, 416–18
Kennedy, Joe 386–7
Kennedy, Robert
  assassination 72, 192, 334, 379
  baby with MM, rumours of 70
  death of MM and 333, 334, 345, 349–50, 353, 354–8, 362–3, 364, 366, 368–9, 377, 378–9, 388–9, 390–95
  sex tape allegedly starring MM and 201
  sexual relationship with MM 70, 333, 334, 345, 349–50, 353, 354–8, 362–3, 364, 366, 368–9, 377, 378–9, 385–95
The Enemy Within 357, 392
Kilgallen, Dorothy 213, 282, 363
Kimmel, Mr 48–9
Kinks, The 'Celluloid Heroes' 422
Kinnell, Murray 49
Kiss Me, Stupid (film) 327
Klein, Pamala 52–3
Kotz, Florence 153
Krim, Arthur 381–2, 384
Krim, Mathilde 381–2, 384
Kris, Dr Marianne 258–9, 275, 279, 294, 302–4, 306, 311, 316, 319, 336, 347–9, 406–7, 411–12
Kris, Ernst 258

Krohn, Dr Leon 122, 167, 168, 169, 187–8, 266–7, 309
Kuchel, Thomas 355

Laderman, Ezra 115
Ladies of the Chorus (film) 88, 99
Lambert, Gavin 129
Lawford, Peter 192, 326, 333, 337, 338, 368–9, 377–9, 385, 386, 387, 390, 394, 403
Lawford, Patricia Kennedy 326, 333, 385–7, 403
Lawrence Guiles, Fred 17
  Legend: The Life and Death of Marilyn Monroe 103
Legion of Decency 299
Lemmon, Jack 265–6, 326
Let's Make It Legal (film) 10
Let's Make Love (film) 275–7, 279, 280
Levathes, Peter 329
Life magazine 40, 89, 113–14, 120, 133, 329, 334–5, 402, 420, 421
Linden, Donald 24
Lipton, Harry 13
Litman, Robert 397–8
Little, Kay 63
Lloyd Wright, Frank 270–72
Logan, Joshua 11, 236, 245, 346
Look magazine 3, 171, 174, 347
Los Angeles
  Board of Supervisors 370–71
  District Attorney's Office 342, 371
  Fifth Helena Drive, MM home on 314–15, 321–2, 327, 333–7, 350–52, 361–2, 368, 374, 384, 387, 388, 390, 392, 394, 396, 411, 425
  Police Department (LAPD) 333, 354, 368–9
Los Angeles Times 338, 349, 374–5
Louis, Jean 191, 412
Love Happy (film) 111, 423
Love Nest (film) 10
Lower, 'Aunt' Ana (foster mother of MM) 45, 62, 92
Luce, Clare Boothe 402, 422
Lyon, Ben 40, 82–3, 86

Lytess, Natasha 11, 23–4, 105, 107, 113, 364
  My Years With Marilyn 93, 94, 96–101, 138

Mackie, Bob 193
MacLaine, Shirley 335
Madison Square Garden, New York
  'Dream Show' (1955) 208–10
  JFK birthday celebration (1962) 40, 189, 191, 192, 195, 328, 381, 397, 414
Madonna: 'Vogue' 422
Maf (dog Sinatra gives to MM) 313–15
Mailer, Norman: *Marilyn: A Biography* 50, 52, 345, 346, 359–62, 363, 394, 407
Manchester Guardian 4–5
Mankiewicz, Joseph L. 96, 111
Mansfield, Jayne 131
March, Fredric 42
Margaret Herrick Library, Beverly Hills 3, 4, 58, 421
Marilyn (opera) 115
Marilyn and Ella (musical play) 203
Marilyn and Me (television movie) 366–7
Marilyn: Behind the Icon (podcast) 4
'Marilyn Monroe – The Legend and The Truth' (exhibition) 360
Marilyn Monroe boutique, Bloomingdale's, New York 413
Marilyn Monroe Productions 98, 171–5, 245, 409
'Marilyn tapes' 1–4, 105–6
Markel, Howard 343
Marlowe, Patricia 402
Marshall, Marion 1, 74, 93
Martin, Dean 310, 327, 329, 335
Martin, Ida 30, 223
Martin, Jeanne 311
Masters, George 10
MCA 249, 392
McCullers, Carson 135, 206
McGhee, Brownie 207
McGuire, Dorothy 75
McPherson, Aimee Semple 30

Melson, Inez 314, 403, 405, 411–13, 418
Meryman, Richard 334–5, 420–21
Met Gala (2022) 191, 194, 195
Miller, Arthur 42, 314–15, 359, 381
  After the Fall 251–2, 301
  bike of MM, stores in garage 232
  childhood of MM and 16
  children, MM's love for 262, 322, 385–6
  cycling with MM 231, 232
  divorce from first wife 233–4
  divorce from MM 303, 306, 330
  dreams, MM appears in 15
  dreams, MM's and 224
  fame of MM and 15, 237–40
  first meets MM 111, 114, 226–30, 324
  footprints of MM, on 130
  Frank Lloyd Wright plans house for MM and 270–72
  grievances held against, MM's lists 275
  Harlow, on MM's identification with 40
  House Un-American Activities Committee, called before 235–6
  Inge Morath, relationship with 303–4
  Let's Make Love and 280, 281
  letters between MM and returned following MM's death 411
  letters between MM and, MM keeps 232
  list of ideal lovers, MM's and 107
  Mara Scherbatoff death and 237–40
  Montand and 281, 283–4
  Please Don't Kill Anything 260
  pregnancies and miscarriages of MM and 253–5, 260, 261–3, 264, 266–9
  reading of MM and 114
  Some Like It Hot, writes to Wilder on treatment of wife during filming of 267–8
  The Misfits and 260, 276, 281–2, 286–9, 291–4, 298–300, 301, 303

Arthur Miller – *continued*
  The Prince and the Showgirl and 102, 245–6, 247, 248–54, 256
  Timebends 15, 226, 252
  wedding to MM/MM conversion to Judaism and 241–4, 404
Miller, Augusta 234, 243
Miller, Isidore 243, 334, 381, 382, 386
Miller, Jane 227, 233, 262, 264, 322
Miller, Joan 270
Miller, Morton 237–8
Miller, Robert 'Bobby' 262, 322, 385–6
Millette, Dorothy 39
Minardos, Nico 87, 124–7
Miner, John W. 105–6, 374–5
Misfits, The (film) 108
  filming 5, 205, 232, 285, 286–94, 295, 296, 302, 303, 307, 329–30, 424
  lost footage 298–301
  origins 260, 276, 282
Mocambo nightclub, Los Angeles 203–4
Modern Screen 54, 261
Monkey Business 10, 124, 157, 423
Monroe, Berniece (half-sister of MM) 18–19, 22, 32, 36, 45, 49, 403, 411
Monroe, Della (maternal grandmother of MM) 15–17, 18, 35–7, 65
Monroe, Gladys (mother of MM) 17–23, 27–8, 31–46, 49–52, 59–60, 65, 77, 94, 108, 121–2, 320, 409, 411, 416
Monroe, Ida Mae (cousin of MM) 51
Monroe, Marion (uncle of MM) 37
Monroe, Marilyn
  abortions, rumours around possibility of 59, 70, 169
  Actors Studio and *see* Actors Studio
  addiction to medication 176–81, 276–7, 285–94, 296–7, 331–2
  afterlife/legacy 421–5
  ageing, fear of 185
  alcohol and 182, 266, 277, 310–11
  anaemia 188

animals, special bond with 313–15
appendectomy 60, 61, 122, 168
Backgrounds of Literature course, UCLA, enrols on 113
baptised 29
beauty secrets 182–5
bipolar disorder, possibility of 37
blonde hair 5, 7, 9–11, 12, 38, 39, 40, 73, 91, 160, 197, 216, 226, 247, 293
book collection 115
borderline paranoid addict, Greenson diagnoses as 319
borderline personality disorder, possibility of 37, 319
bust 62–3, 73, 186–8, 290
casting couch and 85–9, 124–5
childhood 9, 12, 13, 16–53, 54, 55, 56, 60–61, 117, 121–2, 157, 160–61, 168–9, 181, 199, 226, 251, 256, 258, 259, 276, 296, 336, 344, 414
childlike nature/'beautiful child' 54, 65, 74, 76, 211, 212, 229, 285, 311, 317, 342, 405
children, ambition to have 60, 66, 109, 168, 242, 254–5, 260–63, 267, 268, 270, 315, 321
children, bond with 290–91
children, rumours of secret 57–61
chin implant 95
cinema, love of 38–9
Collier coaches 211–12
cooking 273–4
crowds and 15
cycling 231–2
death 2, 3, 16, 22, 41, 53, 70, 92, 105, 106, 199, 211, 212, 220, 258–9, 267, 331–425
  autopsy 3, 24–5, 105, 342, 355–6, 373, 375, 376
  Bolaños and 396–8
  diary, 'missing' and 366, 368–72
  discolouration of colon 373–4
  funeral 94, 213, 398, 403–6, 411
  Gould and 377–9
  last night 333–40
  timelines of 333–53

Kennedys and 354–8, 380–95, 416–20
Mailer and 359–62
memoir and 407–10
Monroe estate/possessions and 22, 108, 199, 258–9, 300, 411–15, 416, 419
Newcomb and 345–50
public reaction to 399–402
Slatzer and 363–7
suicide note 379
Trundy and 333, 351–53
Westwood Village Memorial Park Cemetery 91, 92, 373, 403
will 258–9, 411–12, 413, 415
divorces 78, 147–9, 208, 232, 243, 285, 303, 306, 331, 334, 357, 363, 385–6
dogs 28, 93, 313–15
domestic violence victim 144–7, 164, 179, 330–31
'dumb blonde' 5, 11, 226, 247
eating habits/dieting 187–9, 317
endometriosis 22, 167–9, 176, 187, 261
enemas 106, 187, 374–6, 377
England, films *The Prince and the Showgirl* in 245–54
English accent 32, 73
equal rights/civil rights, passionate about 204–5, 243, 318, 385, 386
estate, Monroe 22, 108, 199, 258–9, 300, 412–15, 416, 419
exercise 186–8, 344
fame 12–13, 39, 40, 63, 80, 81, 125, 139–40, 160, 164–6, 178, 237, 245–6, 421–2
family and *see individual family member name*
family, search for 316–20
father figure, absence of a 25–6, 108
figures who inspired 380
filing cabinets 22, 58, 412–13, 418–19
fired from *Something's Got to Give* 328–9
Fifth Helena Drive home, Los Angeles 314–15, 321–2, 327, 333–7, 350–52, 361–2, 368, 374, 384, 387, 388, 390, 392, 394, 396, 411, 425
flirtatious 62–3
gall bladder operation 169, 180, 311, 312, 317, 327
'Happy Birthday', sings to President John F. Kennedy, Madison Square Garden (1962) 40, 189, 191, 192, 195, 328, 381, 397, 414
Harlow and 38–41
Henrietta Award for World Film Favorite, Golden Globe Awards (1961) 139, 325
homosexuality and 102, 205, 347–9
hospitalised, Columbia-Presbyterian Medical Center 306–7
hospitalised, Payne Whitney Clinic 80, 304–8, 309
hospitalised, Westside Hospital 285
I Love Lucy and 165–6, 167
image manipulation, talent for 118–22
insatiable 12–13, 111
Judaism, conversion to 241–4, 404
Kennedys and *see* Kennedy, John F. *and* Kennedy, Robert
Korea, entertains American troops in 140
lesbianism and 101–6, 155, 349
Lloyd Wright designs house for 270–72
lock of hair 24–5
lovers *see individual lover name*
Mara Scherbatoff death and 237–40
'Marilyn tapes' 105–6
marriages *see individual husband name*
men who made 93–7
mental health crises 277–8, 302, 306
modelling 9–10, 69, 72–3, 76, 186, 188
miscarriages 169, 253–5, 260–71, 290, 314–15, 384
My Story 48, 138, 157–64, 407–10
name 74, 82

Marilyn Monroe – *continued*
  newspaper column 141–2
  nose injury 330–31
  notebooks 2, 30, 133, 223–5
  nude calendar (1949) 3, 90–91, 111, 118–21, 134, 160, 246
  nude scene, *Misfits* 298, 299
  nude scenes/photographs, *Something's Got to Give* 326, 334, 360, 390
  nude, sleeps in 39, 187
  orphan, as a 46–7, 48, 52, 55, 62, 64, 66, 112, 121, 161, 213, 276, 279
  orphanage 46–7, 48, 52, 55, 62, 64, 66, 161, 213
  overdoses 97, 98, 262, 337, 343–4, 350, 352, 356, 370, 371
  paternity 21–6
  piano, baby grand 42–5, 108, 112, 414
  Playboy and 90–91, 334, 360
  poetry 115, 252, 370
  possessions, mystery of after death 411–15
  poverty and 63
  pregnancies 59, 60, 61, 66, 70, 169, 253–5, 256, 260–68, 270, 276, 290, 384
  private archive 419–20
  professional shot, first 69–71
  psychoanalysis 3–4, 26, 53, 222–5, 256–8, 275–9, 294, 316, 317, 385, 406. *See also* Greenson, Ralph
  psychological autopsy 381, 397
  Radioplane, position at 68–9
  rape, possibility of during childhood 49, 50, 51, 58–61
  rejection and 23, 24, 46, 65, 257, 279, 297, 348, 397, 404–5
  religion and 29–30, 241–4, 404
  school 29, 54, 62–4, 110
  screen tests 84, 86, 87–8, 89, 95
  self-improvement, quest for 110–16
  sex tapes, rumoured 196–202
  sexual abuse of 48–53, 56, 65–6, 168–9, 177
  sexual appeal of/sex symbol 50–51, 73, 84, 87, 121, 128–9, 165, 172, 174, 183, 203, 215, 229, 245, 247, 248, 250, 290, 293, 295, 301, 307–8, 371
  sexuality/sex life 30, 50, 65–6, 101–7, 117–18, 126, 155–6, 214, 223, 232, 257, 323, 346, 347–9
  shape 62, 187–90, 248, 302, 305, 311
  shyness 9, 89, 216, 241, 291, 404–5
  sleeping pills and 97, 98, 176–7, 179–81, 251, 263, 278, 311, 332, 334, 336, 337–8, 342, 344, 346, 348, 374, 410
  sleeping problems 79–81, 135, 179–81, 187, 188, 267, 275, 276, 278, 328, 335, 344, 345, 346
  stammer 48, 51–2, 63, 68
  storyteller 54–6
  syphilis and 36–7
  telephone, love of 13–14, 112, 334, 339, 414
  'The Empty Crib in the Nursery' (magazine interview) 270
  Twentieth Century-Fox, acting career and *see* Twentieth Century-Fox
  'two-panty shot', *The Seven Year Itch* 143–5
  underdog, instincts always with 205, 318–19
  underwear, eschews 39, 104, 139–40, 297
  uniqueness 4, 131, 269
  'veiled woman' 100
  walk 128–32, 140, 290, 359, 383–4
  weddings 65, 241–3, 252, 364–6
  weight 187–90, 264, 286, 295, 312, 317, 374
  'Wolves I Have Known' (article for *Motion Picture and Television* magazine) 87
  woman who made 98–101
  'wrong door raid' and 153–6, 167, 309
  X-rays auctioned 95, 169–70
Monroe, Otis (grandfather of MM) 17, 18, 35–7

Monroe, Robert (nicknamed Jackie) (half-brother of MM) 18–19, 32–3
Montand, Yves 107, 279–85, 296, 330
Morath, Inge 303–4
Moriarty, Evelyn 326
Morrison, Charlie 203
Mortensen, Martin Edward 21
Mosby, Aline 119
Motion Picture Alliance for the Preservation of American Ideals 354–5
Mr President (musical) 383
Muir, Florabel 105, 404
Murray, Conrad 343
Murray, Eunice 321, 323, 325–7, 333, 334–40, 341, 343–4, 350, 352–3, 362, 374, 388–9, 394
Murray, John 321
My Week with Marilyn (film) 255
Mystery of Marilyn Monroe: The Unheard Tapes, The (documentary) 2

Nabokov, Vladimir 135
National Enquirer 60
NBC 201, 309
Negulesco, Jean 178, 421
Nelson, Elyda 42
Nembutal 180, 332, 336, 337, 342–4, 346, 371, 374, 375, 397, 402
New York Arthritis and Rheumatism Foundation 208
New York Herald Tribune 267, 390
New York Journal-American 307–8
New York Mirror 399
New York Post 164, 274, 371, 408
New York Times 17, 43, 202, 209, 304, 362, 399
Newberry Library, Chicago 4, 409
Newcomb, Patricia 307, 318, 323, 326–7
  death of MM and 333–5, 342, 343–4, 345–52, 381, 394–7
Niagara (film) 105, 128–30, 137, 139, 293, 363, 367, 423
Noguchi, Thomas 355–6, 368–9, 373, 376
Norell, Norman 311–12
Novak, Kim 327, 385

O'Doul, Lefty 139
O'Hagan, Andrew: *The Life and Opinions of Maf the Dog, and of His Friend Marilyn Monroe* 314
O'Neill, Eugene: *Anna Christie* 218–19
Oates, Joyce Carol: *Blonde* 85, 183
Odets, Clifford 107, 114
Odyssey Auctions 413
Olivier, Laurence 107, 245, 247–51, 253, 256
Olivier, Tarquin 248
Oui 368, 369

P. J. Clarke's, New York 213
Pangman, Dr John 95
Paris Ball, Waldorf-Astoria, New York (1957) 381
Paris Match magazine 237
Parsons, Louella 121, 162, 167, 261, 303
Pascal, John 307–8
Penthouse 196–7, 370
Pepitone, Lena: *Marilyn Monroe Confidential* 57–60, 101, 309–13, 316, 323, 397
Perceval, Hugh 249, 250
Phillips, David 401
Photoplay 175, 182–3, 264, 270
  awards (1953) 104–5
Pitt-Millward, Peter 248
Playboy 90, 91, 334, 360
Plecher, Marjorie 263
Porterfield, Pearl 10–11
Positano, Rock G. 117, 147
Prince and the Showgirl, The (film) 102, 135, 180, 231, 235, 241, 245–55, 256, 260
Prowse, Juliet 312

R., Dr 276
Rabwin, Dr Marcus 122
Radioplane 68–9, 76
Rain (film) 219–20, 309
Rasmussen, Gladys 10
Rattigan, Terence 132
  The Sleeping Prince 245
Rauh Jr, Joseph L. 235
Raymond, Janet 60
Reagan, Ronald 68, 126

Reis, May 411
Renour, Sheila Stewart 61, 154–5
Richards, Jerry 417
Rie, Oskar 258
Ries, Maurice 354, 355
Ringling Brothers 208
Ripley's Believe It or Not 192, 194–5
River of No Return (film) 138, 173–4
RKO 20, 27
Roberts, Ralph 24, 131, 251, 283, 303, 305, 309, 335–6, 382–4, 387, 392
Robinson Jr, Edward G. 178–9
Roeg, Nicolas 108
Romanoff, Gloria 305–6, 311–12
Romanoff, Mike 305–6, 311–12
Rombauer, Irma: *The New Fannie Farmer Boston Cooking-School Cook Book* 273
Roosevelt, Eleanor 380
Roosevelt, Franklin D. 31, 40
Rose, Jacqueline 205
Rose, Pete 117
Roselli, Johnny 366
Rosenfeld, Henry 26, 101, 141, 382–3
Rosiers, Janet Des 417
Roskin, Sheldon 294
Rosten, Hedda 236, 242, 256, 263, 356, 405–6, 411
Rosten, Norman 13, 115, 177, 242, 256, 263, 306, 335, 341, 356, 411, 419
Royal Command Performance (1956) 102–3
Rudin, Mickey 24, 333, 350, 394
Rudin, Milton 333, 337–8
Ruditsky, Barney 152, 153
Russell, Jane 1, 89, 100, 111, 172, 222

Saint-Exupéry, Antoine de: *The Little Prince* 116
Sandburg, Carl 115, 228, 380
Sands Hotel and casino, Las Vegas 310
Say Goodbye to the President (documentary) 374, 377, 378, 388, 391, 393
Scaduto, Anthony (pen-name Tony Sciacca): 'Who Killed Marilyn Monroe?' 368–9
Schaefer, Hal 146, 150–52, 154–6, 204
Schagrin, Bob 191
Schenck, Joseph M. 93–4, 103, 157, 313
Scherbatoff, Princess Mara 237–40
Schiller, Lawrence 334, 360, 362, 390
Schreyeck, Elaine 249
Schwab's drugstore, Sunset Boulevard 55, 78, 178–9
Schwab, Jack 179
Scott, Marvin 209–10
Seven Year Itch, The (film) 99, 143–4, 217, 232, 414, 423, 424
Shade, Rose: *Marilyn: The Last Months* 387–8
Shamroy, Leon 84, 86
Shearer, Lloyd 50, 362
Shields, Paul 214
Siegel, Lee 169, 179, 187, 276, 343
Signoret, Simone 280, 281–2, 283, 296
Silk, George 133
Sinatra, Frank 43, 153, 154, 156, 204, 249, 309–13, 315, 335, 383, 403
Sitwell, Edith 133–5, 401
60 Minutes 360
Skolsky, Sidney 23, 41, 44, 118, 138, 141, 178–9, 205, 228; *Don't Get Me Wrong – I Love Hollywood* 102
Skolsky, Steffi 44, 179
Skouras, Spyros 124–5
Slade, Ira 237, 238
Slade, Paul 237
Slattery, Mary 227, 233–4, 243
Slatzer, Robert
  Jordan and 370
  marriage to MM, claims 3, 363–7
  The Life and Curious Death of Marilyn Monroe 345, 350, 363–9, 372, 373, 394
  The Marilyn Files 367
  'The Toad' 367
Smith, Betty: *Tree Grows in Brooklyn, A* 335
Smith, Jean Kennedy 386–7

Smith, Liz 349–50
  Natural Blonde 349
Smith, Matthew: *Victim: The Secret Tapes of Marilyn Monroe* 106
Smith Jr, Delos V. 332
Smoking Gun, The 200
Snively, Emmeline 9, 72–3, 130
Snyder, Allan 'Whitey' 122, 263, 404
Soldan, A. J. 404
Some Like It Hot (film) 8, 9, 12, 13, 54, 173, 264, 265–9, 270, 313–14, 422, 424, 427n
Something's Got to Give (film) 10, 125, 198, 220, 326–32, 334, 335, 360, 386, 390, 392, 424
Song of Bernadette, The (film) 174
Soule, Claire 113
Spencer, George 417
Speriglio, Milo: *Marilyn Monroe: Murder Cover-Up* 369–71
Spiegel, Sam 89
Spindel, Bernard 369
Spoto, Donald 3, 55–6, 171, 179–80, 255, 351, 374, 421
Springer, John 307
St. Regis Hotel, New York 145, 147, 206
Stanislavski, Konstantin 130
Stanley, Kim 216, 219
Stapleton, Maureen 218
Stein & Day 408
Stein, Sol 408, 409
Steiner, Rudolph 133
Stern 390
Stern, Bert 400
Strange Death of Marilyn Monroe, The (pamphlet) 355–7, 390
Strasberg, Anna 22, 259, 413–14, 419, 420
Strasberg, John 216, 415
Strasberg, Lee 7, 44, 248, 356
  Actors Studio, MM studies in New York with 180, 181, 215–21, 222, 224
  estate of MM and 22, 108, 259, 412–15
  funeral of MM and 404–5
  list of ideal lovers, MM's and 107
  production company, MM plans to form with Marlon Brando and 220–21, 327
  The Misfits and 291–2
  The Prince and the Showgirl and 248, 251, 252
Strasberg, Paula 44, 98, 306, 356
  acting coach for MM 220, 221, 247–9, 287, 292, 295
  death 413
  first meets MM 215, 217
  The Misfits and 287, 292, 295
  The Prince and the Showgirl and 247–9
Strasberg, Susan
  estate of MM and 415
  first meets MM 215–17, 219–21
  Golden Globe Awards (1961), witnesses MM's entrance 325
  insatiable nature of MM, remembers 12
  JFK relationship with MM, confirms 382, 384
  'Marilyn Monroe' persona, remembers 7
  piano, on MM's embellished story of 44
  pill-taking, remembers MM's 176, 180–81
  pregnancies of MM, on reaction to news of 260, 262–3
  The Misfits, visits set of 289
  The Prince and the Showgirl, parents relay stories from set of 251
Styne, Jule 335
Styron, William 237
Suicide Prevention Team 349, 398
Summers, Anthony
  archive 1–4
  Goddess: The Secret Lives of Marilyn Monroe 2, 8, 44, 58–9, 70, 106, 126, 172, 178, 197–8, 323, 338–40, 349, 351, 377–9, 384, 388, 397, 418–19, 421
Swan, Robbyn 2, 3
Swanson, Gloria 84, 219
syphilis 36–7

Tabachnick, Norman 381
Talese, Gay 401
Tate Britain 422
Taylor, Curtice 298–301
Taylor, Elizabeth 213, 310–11, 329, 349, 400
Taylor, Frank 298, 304
Taylor, Paul 296
Temple, Shirley 75
Tennant, Cecil 249
There's No Business Like Show Business (film) 84, 100, 150, 179, 180, 215
Thomas, Dylan 110–11, 135
Ticket to Tomahawk, A (film) 1
Tiffany Club, Los Angeles 204
Time magazine 51, 139, 245, 246, 360
Tippy (childhood dog of MM) 28, 313
Todd, Mabel Elsworth: *The Thinking Body* 130
Todd, Michael 208
Tomich, Alan 342
Travilla, William (Billy) 1, 104, 123, 185, 189
Traube, Lenny 357
Twentieth Century-Fox 1, 41, 118, 121, 124, 140, 150, 151, 176, 178, 189, 215, 216, 263, 363, 367, 370, 392
  contract, MM's 87, 96, 172–4, 208, 326
  doctors/medical staff 169, 179, 187, 276, 343
  fires MM from *Something's Got to Give* 328–9
  signs MM 74, 82–4, 89
  suspends MM and threatens with legal action (1954) 173
  war of attrition with, MM's 172–4
  Zanuck relations with MM 84, 85–9, 173, 174, 209
20/20 (television programme) 416, 417

United Artists 287
United Press International 119, 307, 371, 394

Victoria and Albert Museum (V&A)
  'Diva' exhibition, London (2023–24) 423
Vanity Fair 106
Vesalius, Andreas: *De Humani Corporis Fabrica Libri Septem (On the Fabric of the Human Body)* 131–2
VeVea, April 204
Vogue 192, 400–401

W. H. Allen 360
Wallace, Mike 361–2
Wallach, Eli 107, 108, 115, 217, 287–91
Walter, Francis 235
Warhol, Andy: *Shot Sage Blue Marilyn* 422
Warren, Maria 197
We're Not Married (film) 10
Weatherby, W. J.: *Love in the Shadows* 4–5, 86, 205, 291, 344
We Were Strangers (film) 89
Wexler, Milton 328
Wharton, John F. 258
What a Way to Go! (film) 335
What Price Glory (film) 174
Whitten, Gladys 144–5
Wigan, Gareth 349
Wilde, Oscar: *Portrait of Dorian Gray* 212
Wilder, Billy 8, 9, 12, 120, 144, 173, 220, 265–9, 312, 327, 335, 421, 422
Wilkie, Jane 98
William Morris Agency 94
Williams, Edwina 206
Williams, Tennessee: *Cat on a Hot Tin Roof* 206–7
Wilson, Earl 89, 118, 119, 311, 352
Wilson, Harry Charles 33–4
Winchell, Walter 144, 357
Winters, Shelley 11, 107, 108, 110, 216
Wolfe, Donald: *The Last Days of Marilyn Monroe* 49
Wolfe, Thomas 111
  Look Homeward, Angel 363

Woodburn, Arthur 189
Woodfield, Billy 390–91
Woodward, Richard B. 120
Woolf, Virginia 5, 145
Wright Jr., Loyd 158, 159, 161–2

You Were Meant for Me (film) 177

Zanuck, Darryl F. 84, 85–9, 173, 174, 209
Zolotow, Maurice: *Marilyn Monroe* 3, 4, 12–13, 45, 80, 86, 149, 157, 176–8, 237, 239, 346, 360
Zweig, Martin 191–2